Research Methodology in Management

Research Methodology in Management

Dr. V.P. Michael

M.A. (Econ.), M.A. (Socio.), M.B.A., CNIPM, F.I.B.M. (Ind.), Ph.D. Mgt. (U.S.A.), Ph.D. Eco. (Bombay), D.D., F.B.I.M. (London)

Director

Institute for Entrepreneurship & Management

Management & HRD Consultant, Trainer and Renowned Author, Kolhapur-3

Himalaya Publishing House

MUMBAI • NEW DELHI • NAGPUR • BENGALURU • HYDERABAD • CHENNAI • PUNE
LUCKNOW • AHMEDABAD • ERNAKULAM • BHUBANESWAR • INDORE • KOLKATA • GUWAHATI

First Edition	: 1985	Reprint : 2003, 2004
Second Revised Edition	: 1990	Reprint : 2007, 2008
Third Edition	: 1995	Reprint : 2009
Second Revised Edition	: 1996	Reprint : 2010
Fifth Revised & Enlarged Edition (Millennium Year)	: 2000	Reprint : 2012
		Reprint : 2013

Published by : Mrs. Meena Pandey
for **HIMALAYA PUBLISHING HOUSE PVT. LTD.,**
"Ramdoot", Dr. Bhalerao Marg, Girgaon, **Mumbai - 400 004.**
Phones: 2386 01 70/2386 38 63, Fax: 022-2387 71 78
Email: himpub@vsnl.com
Website: www.himpub.com

Branch Offices:

New Delhi : "Pooja Apartments", 4-B, Murari Lal Street, Ansari Road, Darya Ganj, **New Delhi - 110 002.** Phone: 23270392, 23278631 Fax: 011-23256286

Nagpur : Kundanlal Chandak Industrial Estate, Ghat Road, **Nagpur - 440 018.** Phone: 2738731, 3296733 Telefax : 0712-2721215

Bengaluru : No. 16/1 (Old 12/1), 1st Floor, Next to Hotel Highlands, Madhava Nagar, Race Course Road, **Bengaluru - 560 001.** Phone : 22281541, 22385461, Telefax: 080-22286611

Hyderabad : No. 3-4-184, Lingampally, Besides Raghavendra Swamy Matham, Kachiguda, **Hyderabad - 500 027.** Phone: 040-27560041, 27550139, Mobile: 09848130433 Telfax: 040-27560041

Chennai : No. 8/2, Madley 2nd Street, Ground Floor, T. Nagar, **Chennai - 600 017.** Mobile: 09345345055.

Pune : No. 527, "Laksha" Apartment, First Floor, Mehunpura, Shaniwarpeth, (Near Prabhat Theatre), **Pune - 411 030.** Phone: 020-24496323/24496333/32326733

Lucknow : House No. 731, Sehkhupura Colony, Near B.D. Convent School, **Lucknow - 226 024.** Mobile : 09307501549

Ahmedabad : No. 114, "SHAIL", 1st Floor, Opp. Madhu Sudan House, C.G.Road, Navrang Pura, **Ahmedabad – 380 009.** Phone: 079-26560126, Mobiles: 09327324149,09314679413

Ernakulam : No. 39/104 A, Lakshmi Apartment, Karikkamuri Cross Road., Ernakulam, **Cochin – 682011**, Kerala. Phone: 0484-2378012, 2378016, Mob.: 09344199799

Bhubaneswar : 5 Station Square, **Bhubaneswar (Orissa) - 751 001.** Mobile: 9861046007, E-mail:- orissa@himpub.com

Indore : Kesardeep Avenue Extension, 73, Narayan Bagh, Flat No. 302, IIIrd Floor, Near Humpty Dumpty School, Narayan Bagh, **Indore (M.P.) - 452 007** Mobile: 09301386468

Kolkata : 108/4, Beliaghata, Main Road, Near ID Hospital, Opp. SBI Bank, **Kolkata - 700 010.** Mobile: 09910440956, E-mail:- nkmitra@himpub.com

Guwahati : House No. 15, Behind Prajjyotish College, Near Sharma Printing Press, P.O. Bharalumukh, **Guwahati - 781009** (Assam) Mobile: 07439040301; 07439040302

Printed by : Shri Krishna Offset Press, Delhi

PREFACE TO THE FIFTH EDITION

Research Methodology in Management has now become an important area of study for students, teachers and practitioners in management. This is particularly so because of the changes which take place in the management concept itself. In place of the traditional principles of management, a strategic management philosophy is emerging fast, in which managerial analysis has an integral part. Thus, managerial analysis and managerial research receive widespread attention of all those who are interested in management.

This is, perhaps, the reason why our book "Research Methodology in Management" has received extensive appreciation, and has gone in for the next edition. On the basis of the suggestions of the various sections of the readers, the book has undergone revisions and enlargements. It has undergone a thorough revision. The needs and views of my readers have been the main force before me in incorporating various additions and deletions in this edition. In the context of the emerging globalisation of business, the next millennium has great things in store for thinkers and practitioners in Management. Managerial research has a great role to play in this respect.

I am, therefore, confident that the needs of a large number of my readers are properly met by the revision incorporated in this book, and hence it has become more utility-oriented. While placing it before my readers, it is my sincere desire that it should serve the needs of my esteemed readers and students in the days to come.

Kolhapur **Dr. V.P. MICHAEL**

PREFACE TO THE FIRST EDITION

Many business organisations in India have become increasingly research-minded, recent trends in business throw light on the fact that managerial research occupies a prominent position in the optimum use of the scarce resources. Evidently, many organisations have a research budget, as well as Research and Development Department In this context, a systematic approach to research methodology is the prime need of the hour.

Though there are many publications on research methodology in social sciences, this area in business management has been sadly neglected. This book, therefore, deals with the research aspect in management in the simplest and the most systematic way.

The stimulus to my desire to make a modest contribution to research writing came mainly from the student community and teachers of management science, as well as from executives. I, therefore, express my deep gratitude to a vast community of management students and managers. My sincere thanks also go to Dr. D.T. Lakdawala, Dr. P. R. Panchamukhi, Dr. P. R. Brahmananda of the University of Bombay. I am also thankful to the business organisations for having provided the necessary background material for the case studies and examples used in this book.

Kolhapur **Dr. V.P. MICHAEL**

SOME OF THE MOST PROMINENT WORKS OF THE SAME AUTHOR

1. Perspective Management
2. Globalisation, Lliberalisation and Strategic Management
3. Human Resources Management and Human Relations
4. Management for Managers
5. Research Methodology in Management
6. Business Policy and Environment
7. Communication and Research for Management
8. O. B. and Managerial Effectiveness
9. The Successful Manager
10. Spirit of God and the Second Advent
11. Sales Management in India
12. Financing a City Government
13. A Study of Wage & Salary Administration
14. Management of Organisational Behaviour
15. Management of Balanced Distribution System
16. Determinants of Consumer Behaviour
17. A Study of Textile Workers' Management
18. Management of Human Resources
19. Industrial Relations in India and Workers' Involvement in Management

CONTENTS

Chapter 1

Research in Management: An Introductory Approach

Research is a part and parcel of any systematic knowledge. It has occupied the realm of human understanding in some form or the other from times immemorial. The human urge for new areas of knowledge has developed a faculty for search and re-search in him. The scanty way of search in the past has achieved an evolution to the more judgemental areas of operations research, through analytical and scientific methods of investigation. Research has now become an integral part, not only of academic pursuits, but also of all the areas of human activity. Sociologists, economists, physical scientists, natural scientists and nuclear scientists — all would advocate an extensive use of research for the sake of their academic advancement, while practitioners like industrial engineers, physicians, surgeons, managers and businessmen emphasise the great utility of research in their day-to-day decision-making. Even in agricultural and religious pursuits, research plays a very vital role. To be precise, no academic body of knowledge nor functional area of activity would progress without adequate advancement in terms of research.

It would be proper to assert here that the 20th century has witnessed a rapid growth in the size and complexity of human organisations. Industrial and economic activities in India in the latter half of the 20th century have achieved unprecedented dimensions. The size of modern business indicates that managerial and administrative decisions can affect vast quantities of capital and large number of people. Mistakes can be tremendously costly, and a single wrong decision may require years for rectification. Moreover, decisions are needed to be quicker than ever before. Both postponement of decisions would be costly, which can give an added advantage to the competitors. Trial-and-error methods can no longer be appreciated. Decisions must be accurate and timely, and should be based on facts and realities. It is in this context that business decisions are now tremendously influenced by research and research findings.

There was a time when widespread feeling existed that substantial oil resources would not be available in India. But as a result of the extensive research carried out by the ONGC, India is now considered to be an oil-rich country, and she is going to be self-sufficient in oil in the years to come. This is nothing but the achievement of research. In a nutshell, it may be observed that research is a catalyst of any organised activity or knowledge.

Decisions, Meaning and Nature

Research is the process of systematic and in-depth study or search for any particular topic, subject or area of investigation, backed by collection, compilation, presentation and interpretation of relevant details or data. It is a careful search or inquiry into any subject or subject matter, which is an endeavour to discover or find out valuable facts which would be useful for further application or utilisation. Research may involve a scientific study or experimentation, and result in discovery or invention, which would aid either scientific development or decision-making. It may be concerned with general, abstract, or concrete subjects. There cannot be any research which does not increase knowledge or improve scientific knowledge. A research that involves scientific analysis would result in the formulation of new theories, discovery of new ideas or techniques, modification of old concepts or knocking-off of an existing theory, concept or technique. It may develop hypothesis and test it. It may also establish relationships between variables and identify the ways and means for problem-solving.

Research, being a fact finding process, profoundly influences business decisions. The business manager is interested in choosing that course of action which is most effective in attaining the goals of the organisation. Research not only provides facts and figures in support of such business decisions, but also enables one to choose a measuring rod to judge the effectiveness of each decision. This may be the reason why executives and business professionals consider research and research findings a boon in their problem-solving process.

Model building has become an integral part of report writing now-a-days, which makes executive decisions more effective. The decision-maker wants the simplest model that predicts outcomes reasonably well which is consistent with effective action on his part. Research has a tremendous potentiality to assist him in this respect substantially. In management, it can, therefore, be defined as the process of systematic investigation of any management problem.

Considerable number of business problems are now given quantitative treatment with some degree of success with the help of operations research. One cannot simply hold the view that a quantitative treatment of business problem is associated with operations research alone. In fact, the quantitative treatment is much older than even the term *operations research.* For example, financial problems were dealt with quantitatively even in the distant past. However, quantitative analysis has now been extended to many other areas of business. Of course, business decisions are now quantitatively dealt with more than ever before, irrespective of the functional distinctions. There may not, however, be any reason now to believe that business is more dependent on research than ever before since research and development played important role in the past too.

Research and analysis of management problems would result in certain conclusions by means of logical analysis which the decision-maker may use for his action or solution. If the logic in deriving the conclusions from abstracted variables is correct, and if the relevant variables are aptly abstracted, then the solution to the problems arrived at by research findings would be helpful in solving identical problems. For example, if an observation highlights that an interest rate of 10 per cent increases the annual opportunity cost of money for a firm, then it can make decision on the construction of the building by computing the present value of the cash flows. It may not be necessary for the firm to take into account the alternative investment opportunities in detail, if the opportunity cost of the building project is within the given range; of course, if the *ceteris paribus* (other things being the same) principle applies. The premise that the interest rate represents an opportunity cost may be valid. But the conclusion that the use of this discount rate applies to all investments is an error. On such occasions, a detailed research that takes into account all the relevant variables such as the time, value of money, the risk elements, alternative investment opportunities, etc. alone would enable the decision maker to arrive at an appropriate decision. Research, therefore, is the very core of managing a business economically.

Research in management is broadly a systematic activity directed towards investigating managerial or business problems, which may result in invention or discovery of management tools for problem-solving and decision-making. It can be a detailed investigation of the existing problems, practices or processes.

Scope and Objects of Research

Any social or economic research may have two objectives — academic objectives and utilitarian objectives. An urge for knowledge is the basic ingredient of academic research, while research for the sake of research too has found favour with some academicians. There was a time when academic research was very well regarded. But the trend has achieved a tremendous change, and research is now expected to be more utility-oriented than merely academic purpose oriented. This trend is evident in many recent reports of researchers, which are directly linked with policy formulation. Of course, in many cases, it has become a fashion to engage in research, even when it does not serve any practical purpose. The scope of any such research is very limited, for it has limited potential for the achievement of organisational objectives. A research which does not serve a practical purpose is largely pointless as far as a manager is concerned. Research in management is basically meant for a specific purpose; and that is why management researchers are, by and large, result-oriented.

Research provides an analytical framework for the subject matter of investigation. It establishes the relationship between the different variables, especially the relationship of the dependent variables with the independent variables. The cause-effect relationship between different variables can also be identified, leading to valuable observations, generalisations, and conclusions. Inductions and deductions are also possible in a systematic research. *Induction* is the process of inferring a general law from particular instances, *i.e.,* a generalisation is arrived at on the basis of the observation or result of particular instances. *Deduction,* on the other hand, is a way of making a particular inference from a generalisation. In the deductive method, specific conclusions are derived from generalisations, while a generalisation is made from particular situations in the inductive method.

Empirical studies have a great potential, for they lead to inductions and deductions. Thus, research enables one to develop theories and principles, on the one hand, and to arrive at generalisations, on the other. Both are aids to problem-solving. As research is based on observations and empirical evidences, it improves knowledge and understanding, as well as decision-making skill and ability. Gathering primary data for analytical purposes or using secondary data for first-hand investigation should be involved in research. It stimulates the process of understanding, on the one hand and deepens the insight, on the other. Obviously, managerial efficiency increases. Moreover, a systematic research involves various formalities and procedures, and hence the decision-maker gets sufficient time for postponing decisions if he desires to do so in certain circumstances. On such occasions, research can be a blessing in disguise.

To generalise, managerial research can have the following general objectives:

(a) Decision-making objective;

(b) Project objective;

(c) Policy objective;

(d) Controlling objective;

(e) Economic and business environmental objective;

(f) Market objective;

(g) Product development objective;

(h) Innovation objective;

(i) Customer satisfaction objective;

(j) Profit objective;

(k) Promotional objective; and

(l) Corporate image objective.

Obviously, managerial research has unlimited scope in a business organisation. It has already been pointed out that decision-making is considerably influenced by research in the relevant area, while the project objective stands for the role played by research in project identification, feasibility and project implementation. There is a corporate policy for any organisation, which is linked with the corporate objectives and organisational philosophy, culture, and climate. As research findings influence corporate policy, research has a conspicuous role in shaping organisational philosophy, culture and climate. Managerial research, as a matter of fact, cannot be separated from managerial decisions and business policy. Moreover, research is bound to throw some light on risk and uncertainty, which is turn underscore the role of research in policy formulation and decision-making. The element of personal Judgement plays a less critical role until the executive is able to rely almost completely on a standard formula or set of rules when arriving at routine decisions.

Research helps the formulation of a standard formula, enabling the executives to rely moderately on personal judgement, especially at the middle and lower levels. Decision-making calls for alternative courses of action; and in identifying alternatives managerial research plays an important role. Every manager is expected to be a controller, and every management function has an element of controlling function in it. Though controlling is not separated as a function in many cases, there was a time when controlling was the main function of the manager.

But giving due weightage to McGregorian and Maslowian approaches, one should consider controlling as an effect and not as a cause. Instead of controlling, motivation should be provided for self-control, while controlling should be the result of motivation. However, one cannot deny the important role played by the controlling function in the modern age of "too few resources chasing too much demand" and of indiscriminate, irrational and illegitimate trade union practices. A manager has not only to control manpower, but other resources as well. Controlling would be effective only if the controller has a comprehensive knowledge of man, money, machine and material. It is here that managerial research comes to picture. Planning and controlling are twins, and obviously planning can be effective only when it is based on the facts and figures supplied by research.

Economic use of resources is one of the most important managerial functions. Optimum resource utilisation has to take into account at least five major areas, *viz.,*

(i) Investment problems;

(b) Pricing problems;

(c) Allocation problems;

(d) Queueing and inventory problems; and

(e) Human resources problems.

Optimisation decisions are necessarily to be based on adequate investigation and analysis of all the foregoing areas. Similarly, any economic decision must take into account what is called the company's own environment, because the environmental forces influence business a great deal. For example, it may not be possible for the sales manager to meet the sales budget, if the Reserve Bank of India introduces a credit squeeze. This is exactly what has been happening in India in the early 1980s. Government intervention in wage negotiations and bonus decisions. MRTP or even fiscal instruments such as national budgetary policies, Government control (LIC-Escrorts controversy), even nationalisation (nationalisation of textile mills), changes in tastes and preferences or fashions, social change or policies of the governments abroad affecting India's export — all these may be treated as environmental forces which require a systematic investigation prior to any managerial or economic decision.

The market objective of managerial research may be defined as a research objective for the sake of a comfortable positioning in the market. It may include market share, penetration, profit margin, sales volume, business growth, etc. Market research or marketing research may come under this category. In connection with product development too, extensive researches are carried out; both for new product development and existing product modification. Similarly, for the purpose of innovation, extensive researches are carried out. The constraints that generally affect new product development are shortage of important new product ideas, fragmented market, social and governmental restrictions, and shorter life span of successful products. Research has a great role to play in order to minimise the magnitude of these problems. Researches which are conducted with the sole objective of customer satisfaction are also not rare. The product selling approach has already given way to customer satisfaction approach of marketing. Actual needs of the customers or consumers are first ascertained, and the product is produced accordingly. This is why Peter Drucker observes that what is sold now is satisfaction against goods and services sold in the past. The reinforcement principle, which is the central concept of learning theories, has been originated against this background. For example Thorndike observes in his Classic Law of Effect: "Of several responses made to the same situation, those which are accompanied or closely followed by satisfaction (reinforcement)... will be more likely to recur; those which are accompanied or closely followed by discomfort (punishment) will be less likely to occur." How can reinforcement be determined without appropriate research?[1]

For the sake of profit maximisation, many companies do conduct researches, while some engage consultants. At the same time, some marketing executives prefer to conduct surveys for the purpose of identifying variables in support of promotion. As a matter of fact, both profit maximisation and promotion are assisted by research findings, though they are not solely dependent on research.

Shaping of the corporate image is inextricably tied in with the company's relations with external groups. The manner and method it employs to attain its desired place in industry will have a profound effect on its employees, customers, competitors, and the general public. The business entity develops an institutional social philosophy which guides its actions in personnel relations, community relations, the relations with

1. Thorndike, Edward L. *Animal Intelligence,* MacMillan Co. New York, 1911, p. 244.

business associates and competitors, the government, the shareholders, etc. Research has a vital role to play in this respect. To sum up, research has a very vital role to play in the realm of management, and hence its scope is tremendous as far as a business executive is concerned.

Utility of Research

It has been observed that research is of extensive use for a manager in planning, forecasting, coordinating, motivating, controlling, decision-making, etc. This is examined in 12th chapter. While managerial research helps in managerial analysis, academic research helps in academic objectives. In a nutshell, managerial research acts as an aid to managerial decision-making, while academic research is of academic utility. Utility of social research includes social prediction, social enlightenment social welfare, social growth, social cohesion, social control, improving and perfecting the tools of social research, etc. On the other hand, managerial research has substantial relevance from the functional point of view of a manager.

Utility of managerial research can be summed up as:

(a) Research is an aid to decision-making;

(b) Research facilitates the process of thinking, analysis, evaluation, and interpretation of the business environment; and of the various business situations;

(c) Research provides a basis for innovation;

(d) Research and development helps to develop new products and to modify the existing products;

(e) Research identifies problem areas;

(f) Research establishes the relationship not only between variables in each functional area, but also between the various functional areas;

(g) Research is an aid to forecasting which is an effective tool in the hands of managers;

(h) Research helps all the managerial functions;

(i) Research helps in the economic utilisation of resources;

(j) Market and marketing analysis may be based on research;

(k) Research is an aid to management information systems; and

(l) Research is helpful in the formulation of policy and strategy.

However, despite its great utility, managerial research suffers from certain limitations also.

Limitations of Research

Any managerial decision or executive action is concerned with human beings in one way or the other. Managerial research is also relate to human beings who are not beyond changes. Hence, validity of data collected, conclusions, observations, and suugestions are bound to undergo changes. This is perhaps one of the most prominent limitations of managerial research.

Research results in theory, and theoretical treatment is a part of any research and analysis. There are many variables which are important from the point of view of theoretical treatment. But these variables need not be of much practical use in management decision-making. Moreover, management practitioners very seldom view such research or its reports as an important instrument for their own decision-making process though many relevant aspects are covered by the research.

Business decisions are always influenced by various internal and external factors. Unless such factors are systematically analysed decisions are bound to be biased. Under ordinary circumstances research has a limited scope, since it may not be able to consider all relevant factors and forces in a detailed manner. Obviously, its utility becomes very limited.

R & D department has become a common feature in many organisations nowadays. But decision-makers do not appear to be very keen on implementing the findings of their R & D departments. Many of the routine decisions are taken without much analytical background, while the decision-makers' own value judgements, guide many other decisions. In both the cases research is not taken seriously, where R & D department is maintained just as a fashion.

At the same time, small organisations, which form a major component of economic activity in India, cannot afford to have the luxury of R & D departments at all. Even engaging a consultant seems to be costly for them. Moreover, consultants' reports are very seldom applicable to the situations which exist in small organisations. Several organisations do employ consultants to assist them in their problem solving, while they hesitate to reveal many of the details. If a patient deliberately refuses to divulge the relevant facts regarding his ailment, the physician is bound to go wrong. Some companies, for example, never like to disclose their financial data.

Many people seriously feel that research does not have any useful purpose to serve in the management of their business. They largely depend on customs, traditions, routines, formalities, and practices. A routine way of decision-making is very common for them for which no research is necessary. Moreover, research is handicapped by many shortcomings, which impel the decision-makers not to rely on it.

Sample studies are very popular with researchers, though they suffer from many limitations. Such reports need not always be accurate and hence their utility, for situations which demand accurate decisions, becomes insignificant. On many occasions, research may be biased by the views of the researcher which cannot be depended upon for decision-making. Similarly, many researchers may not be properly exposed to the intricacies of the practical areas of business. Research findings of such researchers have very limited practical utility though they may use high-sounding business jargon.

In spite of all the limitations a business enterprise cannot avoid research in the interest of updating its attitudes, approaches, products, goals, methods, machinery and techniques in accordance with the rapidly changing environment in which it operates. Hence, research enjoys a considerable amount of prominence in the realm of Indian business.

Chapter 2

Types of Research

After having discussed the nature, scope, objectives and utility of research with special reference to management, it is not out of place here to briefly classify research for the sake of easily understanding the concept. On the basis of application, research may be classified under three general titles, *viz.*

(a) Policy Research;

(b) Applied Research; and

(c) Fundamental Research (pure or theoretical research).

Policy research is basically the research with policy implications. Researches which are conducted for the specific purpose of application, or researches with policy implications may be treated as policy researches. The results of such studies are used as indices for policy formulation and implementation. Many management researches are policy researches, because they are not merely of theoretical value. They are more of practical utility than of theoretical knowledge.

Applied researches are meant for testing the known theories and models of the population. The validity of the established theories may have to be tested under certain other conditions. For example, Samuelson's *Revealed Preference* theory may be tested in the market conditions in India. The research that is conducted for that purpose may be called applied research. A theory that is established with the help of research in a particular population, at a particular time or in a given environment, need not be valid in a different situation; and hence the need for testing it elsewhere.

Researches conducted for this purpose may be called applied research. First, they make it possible for us to make comparisons between different populations, communities or organisations. Second, a better generalisation becomes possible. Third, the validity of the theory increases. And fourth, it makes a greater contribution to knowledge within limited means.

Fundamental researches are original and investigative studies of a basic nature. The topic or area of investigation would be new, and fresh investigation would be carried out to originate a new theory, making additional contribution to knowledge. It may also throw additional light on the existing theory or body of knowledge. Its contribution, therefore, can be two-fold, developing a new theory and improving upon the existing theory. The Tata Institute of Fundamental Research conducts many such studies.

On the basis of the method of investigation, research may be classified under eight heads:

(a) Experimental research;

(b) Surveys research;

(c) Case studies;

(d) *Ex-post facto* research;

(e) Action research;

(f) Field investigation;

(g) Evaluation research; and

(h) Library research.

Experimental Research

This is based on experiments conducted in a laboratory. Hence, it is also known as laboratory research. Research in terms of laboratory experiments in physics, chemistry, biology, nuclear science, etc. are examples of laboratory research. Certain social science researchers feel that laboratory research is impossible or extremely difficult in social sciences and it may not serve a useful purpose. There is no ground for such scepticism. Laboratory research is highly useful, though a bit difficult, even in social sciences. The only problem is to set up a social research laboratory, and to create environmental conditions. Then it will produced excellent results. In management science also laboratory research can produces tremendous results. The Hawthorne experiments are of immense use in management, for example, even today.

While a team of researchers headed by Elton Mayo investigated the causes of a very high turnover in the mule spinning department of a

Philadephia (USA) textile mill in 1923 and 1924, the National Research Council sponsored an identical study at Hawthorne. Experiments were carried out in the latter study to determine the effect varying degrees of illumination had on the productivity of workers. The illumination experiments were carried out on female workers, who were divided into two groups. One group was placed in a test room where the intensity of illumination was varied. Another group worked in a control room with constant conditions. However, due to the complex human approach, production registered a substantial growth in both the rooms, which was baffling to the researchers. The illumination experiment failed; but it persuaded the researchers to start the Relay Room Experiments, leaving aside the serendipitous discovery.

In fact, the Relay Room Experiments, which were started in 1927, may be treated as the actual beginning of the Hawthorne studies, which have been represented by Elton Mayo (and his colleagues). They have tested thirteen variables, *viz.,* place of work, place and length of rest pause, length of working day, length of work week, method of payment, a free mid-morning lunch etc., in relation to productivity. Two female assemblers were selected for the experiment. The test room was segregated from the rest of the plant; and the two selected female assemblers were permitted to choose four others to join them in the test room. They were given opportunities to express themselves, while they were treated and recognised as individuals who had to make a substantial contribution to the organisation. Each test period yielded higher productivity than what was in the previous period. The productivity of those who were subjected to experiment had increased even in the normal environment. The relay room experiments did not yield the expected results. However, the researchers did not lose heart; they followed it up; and this resulted in a second relay room study.

The Second Relay Room Experiment and Mica Splitting Test Room Study were taken up.[1] The impact of wage incentives on output was investigated. Environments like supervision, general working conditions and the setting were basically kept the same as in normal conditions, The difference was that the assemblers in the second relay group were placed on a separate, small group, piece-rate incentive system that duplicated the third test period of the first relay room experiment. This experiment resulted in a 12 per cent increase in production by the experimental group. The segregated test room conditions of the original relay study were reproduced

---

1. Roethlisberger, F. J. and Dickson, W. J., *Management and the Worker,* Harward University Press, Cambridge, Massachusetts, 1939, p. 160.

in the Mica Splitting Study, while the mica splitting operators worked under their normal individual piece-rate plan instead of the small group incentive system implemented in the relay room experiment. Over a period of 14 months, the Mica Splitting Room showed an average production increase of 15 per cent. (In the original relay room, output increased by about 30 per cent.) The researchers did not succeed in providing their hypotheses. These hypotheses were:

(i) The continuous increase in output in the Relay Assembly Test Room during the first two years may be attributed to the wage incentive factor alone; and

(ii) The efficacy of a wage incentive was so dependent on its relation to other factors that it was impossible to consider it as a thing in itself having an independent effect on the individuals.

The next stage in the Hawthorne experiment was the mass interviewing programme. During the period from 1928 to 1930, 20,000 interviews were conducted with a view to improving the supervisory training programme. Though stereotype answers were the outcome of the first part of the survey, the second part of it yielded encouraging results because of the non-directive interview method. The Bank Wiring Room study was the final phase of the research programme, which was conducted from November 1931 to May 1932. The primary objective of the Bank Wiring Study was to make an observational analysis of the informal work group. The informants consisted of 14 male operators, 9 wiremen, 3 soldermen and 2 inspectors. The bank wirers were placed in a separate test room, though they were not segregated. Unlike the relay room experiments, the bank wiring study involved no experimental changes. Objective data were collected with the help of an observer and an interviewer. In course of time, the observer was recognised as a regular member of the group, while the inteviewer remained an outsider, who had obtained the data on the workers' attitudes, thoughts, and feelings. Conditions of the bank wiring department were duplicated in the study room; and the regular supervisors maintained order and control of the experiment room. The results in the bank wiring room were not equivalent to those in the relay room; there was no substantial increase in productivity. It was observed that the output-was actually restricted by the bank wirers. The observations included:

(i) All the men stopped work before quitting time;

(ii) The workers were able to turn out more work, according to their own contention; and

(iii) Tests of dexterity and intelligence indicated no relationship between capacity to perform and actual performance.

Such factors as fear of unemployment, fear of raising the standard, protection of the slower workers, satisfaction on the part of the management, etc., have really affected production in the bank wiring room experiment, and not in the relay room experiment.

Though the study did not achieve any spectacular results, it paved the way for further researches in management, as Landsberger[2] puts it. "A most spectacular academic battle has raged since then — or perhaps it would be more accurate to say that a limited number of gunners has kept upon a steady barrage, reusing the same ammunition.... The beleaguered Mayo garrison, however, has continued its existence behind the solid protection of factory walls." There has been a marked difference in the results of the relay room experiment compared to the bank wiring room experiment. This was so because of some factors — a small group (cohesive group), the type of supervision available, earnings, the novelty of the situation, interest in the experiment, and attention received in the test room. Some are of the opinion that it was the *Hawthorne effect* that enabled the relay room to produce better. Mayo, however, was of the opinion that it was because of effective supervision that the output in the relay room registered an increase. In spite of the differences of opinion, the fact remains that the Hawthorne studies have proved that experimental research can play a vital role in management research. Yet it cannot be denied that the social situations cannot be fully confined to an artificial laboratory, as we have already seen in the Hawthorne experiment; and such studies may not necessarily be perfect.

Survey Research

This kind of research finds favour with almost all the social science researchers. It is one of the most popular methods of investigation, because a study of the attributes and variables in relation to the population (the entire group of people, inhabitants, items, etc,, under study) is easier, and is more accurate. It suffers from a negligible magnitude of error. Nowadays, sample survey has become an effective method for research. This is possible with the help of personal interviews which are backed by questionnaires, a mailed questionnaire, direct oral observation, indirect oral investigation, etc. Management researchers extensively make use of the survey research method for the purpose of evaluating various functional areas of management. For example, Dr. Michael's survey of "Worker's Participation in Management" in the textile mills of Mumbai has made valuable findings in respect of the workers' attitudes and approaches to participation. "The

---

2. Landsberger, Henry A., *Hawthorne, Revised,* Cornell University, Ithaca, New York, 1958, p. 1-2,

workers aspire for a mechanism through which they can express themselves before the management. They do not want to share the authority. But they wish to hear and to be heard."[3] Thus survey research has a considerable potential for making substantial contribution to the organised body of knowledge, though it has its limitatios too.

One of the most important criticisms levelled against this type of research is that the information usually collected by such surveys is only the periphery level information. In-depth conclusions may not, therefore, be possible. Similarly, survey researches are generally sample surveys, and hence there is a possibility of ambiguity and a greater magnitude of error or bias. Moreover, personal inhibitions, indifference, ignorance or bias may affect the result. As the survey is time-consuming, there is a possibility that the result may not conform to the existing reality. However, in spite of all the drawbacks, survey research is the most popular method of research even in management.

Survey research has been widely accepted, mainly because of its acknowledged merits, *viz.*,

(a) It has a greater amount of objectivity;

(b) As the researcher comes in direct contact with the informant, he is able to understand the situation better. Hence, the study has a greater reality in its findings and conclusions;

(c) Though there is a possibility of some amount of error, which would be negligible, the survey method is the most scientific method for obtaining reliable data and dependable results;

(d) It is possible during the course of the survey, to throw light on many actual important problems, which would otherwise have been hidden. The survey is extensively used in all the areas of investigation, especially because of its obvious merits.

(e) Direct observation of the population is possible resulting in accurate or near accurate results.

Case Study

This is a method of exploring and analysing life situations. It is a compact and intensive study of the actuality of a business situation, on which the researcher brings to bear all his skills and ingenuity, or it is a systematic gathering of adequate information about a business situation so that others understand the various realities of how it functions. Case discussion is usually like an autopsy. It is a form of qualitative and

3. Micheal V. P. Dr., *Industrial Relations in India and Workers' Involvement in Management,* Himalaya Publishing House, Bombay, second edition, 1984, p. 258.

quantitative analysis of a careful and complete observation of a business situation, a problem, a person or an institution. Obviously, it is an in-depth and detailed study of the real situation as a whole.

However, a case study, in spite of all its declared realistic nature, cannot be all-inclusive or unique. On the contrary, it portrays the picture of a business problem, which has some applicability in identical situations.

Some are of the opinion that a case study is merely a qualitative expression, and one has to rely more upon one's power of observation and sense of logic. In fact, quantitative data, analytical framework, and overall evaluation and interpretation are essential ingredients of case studies, because they are expected to provide very valuable lessons of practical implication. As far as the students of management are concerned, case studies are very valuable exercises. Hence a little detailed discussion is called for.

Case Studies in Management

A case describes the actual working of a company or business situation at the time it was conducted. It can be an eye-witness narrative of a real life business situation, covering all the aspects of managerial decision and executive action against the background of the environment and the industry situation within which it operates. The working results and financial statements of the company are examined to assess the effectiveness of managerial decisions. Almost always, a case contains some information about the industry and its competitive conditions, some historical background of the company itself, information about the company's products, production facilities, marketing and general organisation plan, and the background of its top management and organisational culture, as well as the company's organisational climate.

The data for the preparation of a case may be gathered either from the company sources (internal) or from published material (external). Company sources may be tapped by gaining access to its records, discussion with executives (both managerial and functional), and by observing the key areas of its operations. The case writer may be provided with such documents as the company's memorandum of association, its long-range plans, annual budgets, accounting policies, procedures and systems, organisation chart, management information systems, etc. More over, he can gather valuable information on management philosophy, managerial skills, views and opinions of the key executives involved in decisions and actions, and so on.

Published materials generally include the company's annual reports, stock exchange reports, press information, industry association's publications, etc. The success of the case writer depends more on a systematic presentation of the data in a proper sequential form rather than on the presentation of a variety of information. It is, however, obvious that certain minimum data are required to make a case meaningful.

Cases may be written on various functional areas to highlight certain problems, or they may be general management cases which underscore policy decision and their implications in a certain environmental setting. Sometimes, it is essential to use ficitious names of companies and executives, and conceal their geographical locations. In no case, however, can all the information on the industry and the environmental factors, its products, markets, the consumer profile, the governmental regulations, etc. be disguised.

Why a Case Study?

A case is, thus, a report containing facts, opinions and views of people within the company in the broad framework of a certain environmental situation. It serves a dual purpose:

(a) It introduces the participants to the influence of varied environmental factors on business enterprises; and

(b) It exposes them to various problem areas, and the effectiveness of managerial decisions, under given circumstances.

Cases are not generally designed to bring out a correct or incorrect handling of business matters, but to acclimatise the participants to management situations. They do not specifically state problems; not do they suggest solutions. That task is left to participants themselves.

Cases, thus, provide the raw material for the participant's use who, in the course of analysis, discover problems and work out practical plans for dealing with them. In the process, the participants assume the role of executives in the actual business situation; scan the available alternative courses of action; work out the impact of each of them and select the best suited alternatives under the given environmental setting. In other words, it provides the participants with the skills for dealing with such business situations, and also the thrills of a real life business executive, who is required to take decisions.

Experience is, perhaps, the best teacher. A participant can learn from the experience of other managers. In real life, a manager is not expected to resort to trial-and-error methods for the impact of a decision taken by him is long-lasting. If it is good, well if not, he will be liable for the losses. A case provides a description of the decisions taken in a particular situation, at a particular period of time and its impact on the enterprise, which acts as an eye-opener for the participants. A thorough analysis of the causes of what and where things went wrong, why, and what could have been a better alternative, would enable one to avoid such decisions in one's real business life.

It should, however, be remembered that no two business situations are exactly alike. There is always a change in the environmental trends, and this change makes one situation different from the other. A decision, which may be good in one situation, may be wrong in another. The participants should, therefore, be cautious while dealing with such situations.

Again, the cases are not examples and should not be treated as such Companies are not selected because they are "the best" or "the worst" in their industry, nor because they are "average" or "typical". Some companies are well managed, some others not so well; some are in a very good condition, others in a critical situation. In each case, the persons responsible for a particular venture have to recognise and deal with the problems as they arise and as they are. The problems in a business policy case may be desperate emergencies calling for drastic action; they may be basic policy decisions of long-range significance; or they may be somewhat less drastic, but nevertheless important, and problems of routine administration.

By using cases, the instructor and the participants can together create "ways of thinking, feeling and doing," which accelerates both intellectual growth and emotional development. Discussions of the cases may be identical to the kind of discussion that the officers concerned face in their office or committee room. Case discussions do create insights, intellectual power, judgement, a sense of leadership, responsibility and self-confidence.

A case study provides feedback to the company. First, it enables it to have all the data about it systematically collected and tabulated, which help the management to look back to the past, to understand its strong and weak points, identify the wrong decisions and assess their impact on the concern. Second, it makes it possible for the top management to feel the pulse of the lower level and functional level executives. An interview by the case writer with these executives will reveal some of the inherent interpersonal and managerial problems of the organisation. Third, the case writer will generally provide feedback to the management upon areas requiring, improvement or modification. All are helpful in initiating corrective measures, wherever required. A case study is, therefore, a sort of free consultancy service for the organisation.

How to Analyse a Case

There is no particular formula for analysing cases. Each situation must be handled in a new and unique way, and the approach should be changed to deal with each new situation. Each case is a new situation; there is no basic pattern that can be passed on. However, the following general steps may be followed while analysing any case situation.

(a) First, go through the case carefully to get a general impression of what it is about, how it comes about and what kinds of information it contains. Once a good grasp of the problem involved is acquired, the participant may mull over it, both consciously and subconsciously.

(b) For the second reading, take time to proceed slowly and carefully, studying the tables and exhibits and making some notes of your own. Make specific summaries of those aspects of the case that your consider are important.

(c) Try to answer such questions as: "Does this company seem generally to be doing well or not doing well"? "Is it making or losing money?" "Is its current financial position strong or weak?" "Does it seem to be faring better or worse than its competitors?" "On what basis must any company compete with the others in this particular industry?" "In what kinds of things does it have to be especially competent in order to succeed?" "How is the whole industry doing?" And so on.

(d) Try to identify the strategy of the company, its objectives, its personal value systems and achievements.

(e) Identify the strengths, weaknesses, opportunities and threats to the company.

(f) What was the environmental setting within the company? Were the strategies consistent with the environmental trends?

(g) Try to identify the inconsistency, if any, in the implementation of the strategy. What were the forces leading to such executive action? What was its impact on the enterprise?

(h) Try to identify the problems involved, and the possible solutions.

(i) Apply the appropriate management tools for the solution of the problems. What were the alternatives available, and which was the best?

(j) Assess what would have been the company's position had it implemented the best alternative.

It will be beneficial for the participants to discuss the cases with one another while preparing them for case discussion. "Two heads are better than one." Business executives often discuss their problems with other key people. The exchange of ideas with knowledgeable people always enlarges vision and understanding.

The role of the instructor in the class room during case discussion is one of co-ordination and moderation. He assists the participants in grapsing important points by a proper direction of the discussion. Case discussion often leads to the creation of excitement among participants, which may generate arguments. The participants should be very careful to ensure that they keep cool when they address the instructor as well as their fellow participants, in order to avoid unnecessary annoyance or ill feeling.

A few minutes are generally spent by the instructor at the end of the session on summing up the case. All the participants are generally encouraged to actively take part in the discussion; but non-participation or wrong statements on the part of a participant during the discussion does not indicate that he has not adequately understood the problems involved. The main purpose of the case discussion is to educate the participants in the salient characteristics of various decision areas; and this is done by sharing and exchange of ideas, rather than by testing the level of knowledge of the participants.

Role Play

Role play is an advanced form of case discussion and is used to improve the decision-making ability of the participants. In a case the background information provided to the participants includes the historical framework, the management philosophy, policies and procedures, the environmental setting, the relevant industry data and the competitive situation. In addition, the long-term objectives of the company — both financial and social — are given, together with the expected standard of achievements, the anticipated direction that the enterprise should take, the financial capabilities or limitations of the enterprise, the different alternatives available to the company for the achievement of its long-term objectives, the criteria governing the evaluation of these alternatives, etc.

The task of the participants involves a critical evaluation of all the given alternatives in the light of the above criteria and the various decision techniques that they may have learnt to decide upon the best course of action.

For the role play to be effective, it is essential that the participants are arranged in groups — each advocating one of the alternative courses of action — which will be given enough time to work out and discuss it among their members. Each group prepares its arguments and counter-arguments, and the group leader presents them in the class, substantiating them with figures, if available. Each group is allotted a specified period of time for presentation.

The instructor's role here is one of a moderator. He does not take sides, nor does he provide any clue to any group. At the end, he indicates which one is the better alternative; and deals with any points which had not been touched by any group.

Here again, the participants should be temperamentally and emotionally cool. The final decision does not have much bearing on the level of the knowledge and understanding of any group member, but is purely based on the superiority of the particular alternative over the others. The method of presentation, the logic behind the arguments, the ability to persuade and the analytical skills of the participants will be exposed. This helps the participants to learn, in a particular way, the application of the various decision techniques, and the method of evaluating the various alternatives.

Business Game

A business game is a more improved version of the role play technique. Here, instead of one decision at a particular point of time, the participants are required to take a series of decisions at different time periods. For example, they are divided into groups, each group representing an independent firm in the same industry.

A game is played in different situations, each situation covering a particular operating and a strategic decision. The "O" period situation provides all the basic information, as in the role play, and also the economic forecast for the next period. Other situations throw up the capabilities and limitations of the company and set of alternatives courses of action. The participants evaluate all the available alternatives, take appropriate decisions and cast proforma financial statements for the next year, wherever necessary. The instructor works out the performance of the enterprise in accordance with the decisions, which form part of the information for the next period in which a new set of alternatives are provided for the participants to select from.

At the end of all the situations, the group that shows the best performance is adjudged the best decision-maker. Generally, during the course of the game, the participants are exposed to a number of strategic and operational decisions, covering all the functional areas.

In a business game, the discussions are confined to the members of each group, and no presentation is made in the class room. The need to evaluate the likely performance as a result of the decision provides the additional exercise for participants. Second, the participants can get a feel of the continuity of the effects of their decisions upon the enterprise in the long-run. They can watch the progress of the enterprise over a period of years, assess the direction which it takes, and initiate corrective measures with their counter-decisions, allowances for which are provided in subsequent situations.

The case method creates immense excitement as well as a sense of competition as in the practical business life among the participants. It offers the participants enough scope to acquaint themselves with the problems and intricacies involved in the real business world. The benefits of participative learning and group discussion on business situations enlarge their vision and improve their decision-making ability. Actually, it is one of the most prominent methods of management education.

Ex-Post Facto Research

This is the type of research which is based on an analytical and scientific examination of the relationship between independent and dependent variables. This is an empirical research; and the researcher does not have any control over independent variables because they have already been manifested. Independent variables already exist, and their relationship with the dependent variables is established in this type of empirical research. For example, advertising expenditure is an independent variable, while the sales volume or turnover may be treated as a dependent one on advertising expenditure. An increase in advertising expenditure results in a proportionate growth in the sales revenue. The *ex-post facto* research has its own weaknesses. For example, the testing of a hypothesis is likely to make spurious relationship between independent and dependent variables. Independent variables are not subjected to much control, and there is a possibility of some sort of biased interpretation. However, this method is extensively used when such statistical methods as the coefficient of correlation or regression are used.

Action Research

This is a recent classification. This type of research is conducted through direct action. The actual study may consist of a number of phases, say, base-line survey, systematic action, periodical assessment, etc. A good example of action research is a study of test marketing. A base-line survey is initially conducted and the informat is identified; and this is followed by the distribution of the product under study, and then an assessment or survey is conducted. It is a very useful method in consumer products. Even in the case of industrial products, machinery and consumer durables, the action research method is used when instead of distributing the product, demonstration is made as a part of action research.

Field Investigation

This method is used not only in social science research, but more extensively in managerial research. Many studies are field investigations. Laboratory experiments are conducted under controlled conditions, while field experiments are conducted in actual situations. Since the study is conducted in real life situations, the results are obviously more realistic. One should, however, take care of accuracy in the selection of population. It is admittedly a difficult task to ensure control over variables, informants and the forces that operate in the field. This is, perhaps, the most important handicap of field investigation.

Evaluation Research

This is the type of study which is made use for the purpose of evaluating a project which has already been implemented, or a work that has already been carried out. Performance evaluation, job evaluation, programme evaluation and review technique (PERT), etc. are examples of this research method. Evaluation research includes periodic evaluation, terminal evaluation and concurrent evaluation. This is a very useful method for the evaluation of actual operational efficiency.

Library Research

This is the type of research which is based on the books, periodicals, journals, documentation, secondary data, etc. which are available in the library. The researcher depends, and has to depends, only on the materials which can be collected from library sources. Many social science researchers nowadays make use of this method, mainly because of its convenience. Moreover, individual researchers find it suitable from the point of view of economy of time, resources and manpower. However, for want of adequate primary data and access to actual life situations, the observations and conclusions often turn out to be biased. There is also a danger of deterioration in the standard of the report to the level of hotchpotch compilation. However, the library research method is widely used, especially in social sciences. Many such compilation of works, however, can very seldom be called research; and a sort of confusion exists regarding the process of research in the minds of many. This may, perhaps, be the reason why some practitioners are under the false impression that research is nothing, but a useless mental exercise, by which academic and literary materials from various publications are compiled. On the contrary, even the library research is pregnant with scope to make original and meaningful contribution if systematic investigation and interpretation can be made.

In a nutshell, it can be concluded that research fulfils a meaningful purpose when it is carried out systematically for the achievement of predetermined and meaningful objectives.

Chapter 3
Research Design

We have examined the nature and objectives of managerial research in the first chapter. The very managerial job of managing is based on managerial analysis which takes care of the organisational objectives. Hence, an appropriate design, focusing on the objectives for which a research is planned, must be made in advance.

What is Research Design?

Research design is a purposeful scheme of action proposed to be carried out in a sequence during the process of research focusing on the management problem to be tackled. It must be a scheme of problem solving through proper analysis, for which systematic arrangement of managerial efforts to investigate the problem is necessary. It defines the task of a researcher from identifying a managerial problem and problem area to report writing with the help of collection, tabulation analysis and interpretation of data. Though not exhaustive, Claire Selltiz's definition of research design reveals some important aspects of a research design. "A research design is the arrangement of conditions for collection and analysis of data in a manner that aims to combine relevance to the research purpose with economy in procedure.[1]"

Though collection and analysis of data make an important aspect of research and hence of the research design, these are not the only aspects of research design as Claire Selltiz has put it. As a matter of fact, research

1. Claire Selltiz and associates, *Research Methods in Social Sciences,* 1962, p. 50.

design must include all the aspects of a research project including formulation of scheme for testing of hypothesis and drawing logical conclusions. Goode and Hatt have, however, emphasised about drawing logical conclusions; "a basic aspect of research design, therefore, is setting up the research so as to allow logical conclusions to be drawn."[2]

Decisions on the method of investigation and the formulation of hypothesis form a substantial part of the research design in which the steps, methods and techniques of research are crystallised. A research design indicates the observations to be made, how to make them and how to make a quantitative analysis of such observations, which hypotheses should be tested, how should the study be carried out, what type of data should be collected and from which source; how to make an analysis, how to interpret and present, how much money to spend, and within how much time the project should be completed. The various aspects of research, especially the process of research, are discussed in Chapter 4.

A research design is a plan of action to be carried out in connection with a research project. It is, however, not an unbreakable rule, nor a hard-and-fast strategy. On the contrary, it is only a guideline for the researcher to enable him to keep tract of his actions and to know whether he was moving in the right direction in order to achieve his goal. The design may be a logical presentation of the various steps in the process of research. These steps include the selection of a research problem, the presentation of the problem, the formulation of the hypothesis, conceptual clarity, methodology, data collection, survey of literature and documentation, the testing of the hypothesis, interpretation, bibliography, presentation and report writing. All these stages have been discussed in detail in the fourth, fifth, sixth and seventh chapters. It is the chief function of the research design to specify and state the sequence of these steps in an orderly manner.

Identification and presentation of an appropriate research problem is perhaps one of the most important needs of any research design. An academic researcher is at liberty to take up any research problem of academic interest. But this is not exactly the practice as far as a management researcher or a managerial analyst is concerned. Specifically speaking, a managerial research problem is not merely a research problem of academic interest; it is rather a restatement of a management problem that requires a detailed analysis. Such analytical interpretations have great policy implications and managerial applications.

---

2 Goode and Hatt, *Methods in Social Research,* McGraw Hill, 1952, p. 74.

Steps in Research Design

The very purpose of a research design is, therefore, to set up a research project which must result in logical conclusions. For this purpose, a research design may adopt the following steps:

(i) Identifying and stating the management problem and the problem area;

(ii) Restating the management problems as the research problem;

(iii) Recognising and reconciling with the organisational goals and objectives;

(iv) Planning the project in such a way that the observation (particularly controlled observation) empirically demonstrates the probability or non-probability of the relationships between phenomena;

(v) Formulating a hypothesis (or a couple of them), identifying the variables, and skeptically demonstrating the relation between variables (both dependent and independent variables);

(vi) Crystallising, the objectives, purposes, rationale, scope and expected limitations of the research;

(vii) Planning to formulate the research project identifying the resources including financial and human resources;

(viii) Specifying the time period within which the research should be completed;

(ix) Identifying the types of data to be collected and its sources;

(x) Specifying the method of data collection and analysis;

(xi) Estimating the expected result and comparing it with the company's expectations for problem-solving and decision-making; and

(xii) Finalising a systematic scheme for proceeding with the project including sampling, survey, analytical framework and report writing.

A brief examination of these aspects of research design may facilitate our further discussion.

Identifying the Management Problem

Identification of the management problem and making observation of the problem situation make the first step in designing a managerial research, because a managerial research problem is a management problem. Various types of problems like long-term problem, short-term problem, policy problem, operational problem, general management problem, functional area problem, and so on are generally to be tackled. These problems are always linked with the company's objectives and goals. These are problems of top priority and problems which can wait. Top priority problems need immediate attention while an unimportant problem can even be dropped. Routine problems can be tackled in a routine manner in the light of the past experience. Readily available management information, value judgement, observations, principles and procedures may help to solve routine problems. Past experience in similar situations and in similar type of problems may assist in value judgement and decision-making.

However, there are a host of other problems which are not of a routine nature. Such problems need special attention, managerial analysis and in-depth investigation. A subordinate executive, who has a behavioural problem due to an adverse remark of his boss may reveal a defence mechanism on a particular day, which is a common problem. The boss can effectively tackle it in the light of his past experience. But if all the workers and executives, enmasse, numbering about 2000 do not report for duty and declare an indefinite strike, an in-depth investigation and a detailed analysis are called for before arriving at a proper solution. It is the responsibility of a managerial analyst to identify the problem in its proper perspective and priority before he enters into a research exercise. Identifying and choosing the most appropriate problem for analysis goes a long way in maximising result, since every managerial research problem is expected to solve a management problem by facilitating proper decision-making.

Statement of a Research Problem: Re-statement of a Management Problem

Once a management problem is identified, a managerial researcher must restate it to be a managerial research problem, since a research problem for a managerial analyst is nothing but a management problem.

A proper statement of the research problem is the primary step in any research design. An academic research problem is generally based on academic considerations, while a managerial research problem is based on management practices, needs, objectives and goals, because a managerial research is designed to aid managerial decisions.

Managerial research recognises organisational goals, identifies operational and functional objectives and constraints, recognises relationships between relevant variables, makes use of the scientific method, and suggests solutions to the problems. In other words, a research problem in the realm of management is closely associated with organisational goals, operational and functional areas, corporate plan and strategy, and the company's strengths, weaknesses, opportunities and threats in the context of its interaction with its environment. It is a management problem that requires a managerial anlaysis; that is to say, management research and managerial analysis are closely linked with each other, if at all they are not synonymous terms.

Managerial analysis is "the systematic investigation, compilation, manipulation, and presentation of information to a decision-maker in order to aid in the decision-making process,"[3] according to Schellenberger, "It is basically a process rather than a specific tool or model." It may be accomplished by using specific analytical tools and models which have been used in its conduct, which is an aid to decision-making. The process of analysis recognises organisational goals because it exists to aid managerial decisions. Any managerial analyst is, therefore, expected to take into account the organisational goals, which presupposes the ability to empathise with the managerial viewpoint, attitudes, and approaches as well as with the organisational philosophy and culture. To be precise, managerial analysis identifies tools to aid decision-making, and the effectiveness of such tools can be tested with the help of managerial research. Managerial analysis and research are, therefore, inter linked; and hence the managerial research problem is, more or less, a restatement of the managerial problem itself. A brief case would clearly explain this point.

The performance of Hindustan Aluminium Corporation (Hindalco) was not very satisfactory in 1983. There had been a substantial growth in operations as compared with the previous year. Yet there was only a marginal growth in the sales revenue (9.55 per cent) from Rs. 186.98 crores in 1982 to Rs. 204.84 crores in 1983. The gross profit rose from Rs. 6.97 crores in 1982 to Rs. 9.68 crores in 1983, which does not really represent the actual earnings during the year. A lion's share of the profit was from non-manufacturing activities. In the manufacturing activity, there was a substantial loss because of unremunerative retention prices.

The company's efforts were substantial. The fourth turbo-generator of Renusagar was commissioned in April 1983; and all the four units of the company became operative. The plants had undergone considerable modernisation by the end of 1982. The expansion of the reduction plant to 1.20 lakh tonnes per annum was completed in 1982. The expansions of the alumina plant to a capacity of 3 lakh tonnes per annum was in progress, under an agreement with a company in Hungary, and is expected to be completed by the end of 1985. The company's application for

3. Robert E. Schellenberger, *Managerial Analysis,* Richard D. Irwin Inc., Illinosis, 1969, p. 8

expansion in farbication facilities is pending with the Government. Under the modernisation programme, capital goods clearance for the import of dry scrubbing system for the smelter and gas suspension calciner for the aluminium plant was obtained. The management strove to maintain cordial labour-management relations; and there was a remarkable market potential. Yet the aggregate performance in terms of aggregate profit was not very conspicuous.

Production registered a very marginal growth of only 3.46 per cent from 90,735 tonnes in 1982 to 93,883 tonnes in 1983. After provisions for depreciation (Rs. 488 crores), investment allowance (Rs. 1.25 crores), and taxation (Rs. 1.6 crores), the net profit worked out to only Rs. 1.95 crores as against Rs. 1.17 crores in 1982. Thus, despite systematic and sincere efforts on the part of the management, the performance of the company was not very satisfactory.

The unsatisfactory outcome has been associated with various factors. Owing to the teething troubles in the new units and heavy maintenance shutdowns in the two older units, production was retarded. Following the failure of the State Electricity Board to supply power in terms of the revised agreement, the installed capacity of 1.20 lakh tonnes could not be fully utilised. The revised retention prices from May 9, 1983, did not compensate for the full escalation in input prices. Unless the prices are automatically adjusted to take full account of the escalation on costs, the problem of pricing would not be solved. This is an industry problem which may be satisfactorily solved if realistic policies are pursued by the government. Evidently, environmental, functions and operational problems have given birth to management problems.

The areas of managerial analysis in the existing situation of the company include:

(a) A detailed analysis of the retention prices;

(b) A study of the impact of the modernisation programme on output;

(c) Probing the effect of expansion on net profit;

(d) A detailed analysis of the teething troubles of the new units;

(e) A study of the heavy maintenance shutdown problems;

(f) A quantitative analysis of the relationship between the power supply position and installed capacity utilisation; and

(g) A study of the magnitude of the relationship between the dependent variable "Rupees sales volume" or "net profit margin"

and the independent variables, *viz.,* public policy, cost escalation, pricing etc.

The manager is a decision-maker. He is expected to make decisions on many problems both routine and fundamental. His decision becomes effective when it is based on facts, interpretations and analytical exposures, which are the basic contributions of research and managerial analysis. Research can make substantial contribution in this respect only if the relevant areas and problems are investigated in the context of the problems areas of the individual manager in particular and the company as a whole in general. Then it obviously means that the managerial analyst has to probe into the existing and expected problems of the company. Hence a managerial research problem should be nothing but a management problem.

Financial decisions are among the most crucial decisions of a firm. These decisions must be supported by conceptual and analytical insights. Capital is generated and invested by the firm with the expectation of returns on investments. The finance function is seriously concerned with it. Raising of capital and paying the returns to the suppliers of funds also come under the finance function. Profit maximisation is perhaps another area of concern for the financial executive. The streams of benefits (profits) may possess different degrees of certainty and uncertainty. According to Ezra Solomon, net present worth maximisation provides an unambiguous measure of what financial management should seek to maximise in making investment and financing decisions. Management would however be more interested in increasing certainty and reducing risk and uncertainty for which all the financial decisions must be backed by analytical insights. It obviously means that a managerial researcher has various financial management problems to be taken up as research problems for his analysis purpose. For example, current asset management problems, financing problems, risk return trade-off problems, capital budgeting problems, dividend decision problems, etc. etc. are problems to be probed by the research executive in order to aid the financial manager's decisions.

Production decisions are also not of lesser importance as far as a business organisation is concerned. Production decisions are, on the one hand, concerned with the design of the production system and on the other, related to the operation and control of the system. These decisions are bound to take care of the factors like cost, quality, delivery commitments, etc. Similarly, long-term decisions which affect the company's operations for a long time and short term decisions which are of a routine nature are to be taken by the management. Selection of equipment and process, location of the system, production design of items processed, facility of layout, job designs, etc. are long-term decisions related to the design of the production system.

Decisions regarding the selection of equipment and process should be taken only after mature thoughts, analysis and investigation. Alternative equipment and processes may be available for any production need. But a proper analysis alone will throw light on which process and equipment the company can invest its money in the most economic way possible. Every such decision would involve huge capital of the company and hence the management cannot afford to make decisions without proper investigation. Similarly, various issues related to the production design are problems of research because producing any in appropriate product or products which fail to fully satisfy the existing or expected needs of the buyers would lock up the scarce investment in unwanted inventories resulting in the sickness of the company. The story of Royal Enfield is a very relevant example in this context. The company which was a monopoly for 350 cc motor cycles (Bullets) in India had to carry an inventory of Rs. 2.5 crores on account of the unsuccessful scooter and three-wheeler projects, ultimately turning the company into a sick unit (to the extent of closure)[4].

Optimally designed job designs and the problems of location and layout are also to be subjected to an in-depth investigation which would enable the management to take appropriate decisions.

Decisions related to the design of operation and control may include decisions on inventory and production control, maintenance and reliability of the system, quality control, labour control, cost control and improvement, etc. Though the relative importance of these problems may vary on the basis of the nature of the individual production system, organisational philosophy, culture, climate, and the technological advancement, all these problems need proper analysis and investigation. Evidently, all the problems related to production management are research problems for the managerial analyst.

HRM function also needs investigation of many problem areas. Management becomes effective only when they are able to get the best results with people. All managers, except those who perform everything themselves, are expected to secure the co-operation of others, especially their subordinates. Hence there is an element of personnel function in the responsibilities of every manager. This may, perhaps, be the reason why

---

4. Dr. Michael V.P., *Business Policy and Environments,* S. Chand, New Delhi, pp. 179-185.

Pigors and Myers have remarked: "The responsibility for personnel administration, therefore, is clearly not something that can be assigned to a minor functionary in the organisation — a glorified office boy and backslapper who will 'handle personnel problems', keep the employees happy, and 'manage the men' while other more important executives manage machines, materials, and money."[5] It is evident that HRM function is not an unimportant staff function. In fact, the success of any organisation depends on the successful management of its people.

Human resource management is not just a function identical to the management of machinery. On the contrary, it is carrying out a vital job of effectively managing individuals, human beings and persons. Hence personnel management not only helps the people at work to perform better, but also helps the top management to formulate clear and constructive HR policies on a host of areas which come under HR function. Problems related to manpower planning, selection, training, placement, compensation, job evaluation, promotion, industrial relations, industrial disputes and their settlement, wages, strikes, lockouts, workers' participation, labour welfare, collective approaches of the trade unions, etc. are expected to be investigated in detail for the effective management of men, on the one hand, and for providing substantial assistance to the top management or general management, on the other. All such problems and a host of many other personnel problems are necessarily research problems as far as a managerial researcher is concerned.

Marketing problems too are among the most important managerial problems which require detailed investigation. As any firm is organised to profitably serve its market, the policy and strategy of the firm should be market-oriented. Moreover, the modern business firm has already shifted from a seller's market to a buyer's market, and no marketing man can effectively survive without taking into account the actual needs of the buyers. There are many problems related to it. Market surveys, marketing researches, motivation researches, dealership surveys, etc. are very common in this connection.

As the marketing man is expected to analyse his marketing opportunities, many of the problems related to it must be analysed and evaluated. Moreover, many problems related to rapidly changing customer wants, loss of flexibility on account of increasing costs of production and distribution, cut-throat competition, growing difficulties of internal and external communication, increasing government intervention in marketing activities, rapid changes in technology and various environmental forces,

5. Pigors and Myers, *Personnel Administration,* McGraw Hill, New York, 1961, p. 2.

revolutionary changes in the tastes and preferences of the consumers and the consequent problems of market segmentation and positioning, marketing manager's responsibility to match the marketing strategy and policy with the top management policies in the changing environment, pricing decisions, physical distribution decisions, market share analysis and profitability, promotion decisions, channel decisions, etc. are required to be evaluated. These are marketing management problems for research.

The managerial analyst is expected to take up not only the problem of functional areas but also the areas of top management and general management policies. While policies are the guidelines for the firm to operate, a basic strategy is formulated for operation. Strategy is an action plan showing the pattern of decisions to be taken in the company revealing the objectives, purposes, goals, and missions of the company. It identifies the chief policies and plans for achieving these goals, and defines the business the company intends to be in. As a matter of fact, it highlights the nature of the economic and non-economic contributions it intends to make with the help of the various functional areas. There are many problems to be analysed in connection with the top management policies and corporate strategies. Corporate planning is also based on extensive studies. In this context, it can be remarked that all management problems are research problems; and the statement of a research problem is nothing but the restatement of a management problem for a managerial researcher.

Managerial research problem, and the problem for managerial analyst can be one and the same; or may be identical problems, While the managerial analyst makes use of the data for evaluating the alternatives and studies the strengths and weaknesses in the context of the options available for the solution of the problem involved, a researcher never limits his exercises to mere analysis. He goes further and draws interpretations, inductions, deductions, conclusions, generalisations and suggestions. He goes deeper and identifies areas for further investigations. Hence, while restating the management problem to be a research problem, a managerial researcher keeps his eliciting and probing skills sharper and designs his project to gain greater investigational insurability. In this context it is proper to distinguish between managerial research problem and management problem.

Distinctions between a Management Problem and Managerial Research Problem

Though management problems and managerial research problems can be one and the same or identical problems, a researcher can drawn certain distinctions on a close observation of both.

Management Problem	*Managerial Research Problem*
1. Directly taken from the problem area for solution.	1. Adopted and re-stated for translating it into a research problem.
2. It is a problem in itself.	2. It is a subject matter for in-depth investigation
3. It can be a direct observation for managerial analysis for problem solving and decision-making.	3. It need not be directly observed, and its result need not always be used as aid for decision-making and problem solving.
4. A management problem analyst need not employ a hypothesis.	4. A research problem generally identifies a hypothesis for testing.
5. A management problem analyst need not always use scientific method.	5. A research problem must use scientific method.
6. Time element is most vital in managerial analysis and problem solving.	6. Very often it is difficult to maintain time limit due to various constraints.
7. Management problem analyst generally uses intuitions, past experiences natural laws.	7. Not merely intuitions past experiences, but well defined research methods are essential.
8. Management problem is definite.	8. Research problem, particularly hypothesis, is skeptical.
9. It is just an observation of a problem in the actual management practice.	9. Statement of a research problem thows light on variables and hypotheses which would be instrumental in invrestigation.
10. Management problem motivates a managerial analyst or practitioner to find solution.	10. Research interest is more active in a research problem.

These distinguishing features are, however, not very convincing, since a managerial research problem originates from a management problem itself. Both have, therefore, the same general characteristics. The following are the general characteristics of both managerial research problems and management problems.

Some General Characteristics of a Managerial Research Problem

A managerial research problem may have the following general characteristics.

(i) A managerial research problem is bound to be a management problem.

(ii) The statement of research problem, may be the restatement of a management problem.

(iii) A managerial research problem and a problem for a managerial analyst may be the same or identifical problems.

(iv) Managerial research problem statement should throw light on variables and hypotheses which should be instrumental in managerial problem solving.

(v) Managerial research problem statement should recognise and reconcile with the organisational objectives and goals.

(vi) A managerial research problem should motivate the managerial analyst to evaluate the alternatives so as to arrive at effective decisions.

(vii) Statement of a management problem or research problem need not be a tool for decision-making, but it helps to identify tools for problem solving and decision-making.

(viii) A properly stated research problem provides insight into the managerial research.

In this context it is relevant to examine a management problem of Daulat Electronics.

Daulat Electronics was incorporated in 1987. It was jointly promoted by Dureja Brothers, and the U.P. Hill Electronics Corporation (HILtron). The first phase of the project started commercial production at Kashipur (U.P.) in July 1989. It produces Video Housing (V.Os), and has an installed capacity of two million numbers per annum. During the first phase, the company invested Rs. 2.98 crores which was financed by equity capital from private promoters, term loans, and central subsidy. V.Os have good scope in India and abroad.

The company has already received several export enquiries. A memorandum of understanding has already been signed with a leading European importer for export of 10 million V.Os within a period of three years. In view of its export expectations the company is planning to double its capacity from 20 million to 40 million per annum with an additional investment of Rs. 70 lakhs.

The second phase of the project is to come up shortly. The company is planning to set up a plant for the manufacture of video magnetic tapes with an installed capacity of 900 million running metres per annum, equivalent to 35 lakhs video cassettes, each of 180 minutes duration. The investment in the second phase is Rs. 8.07 crores. The company entered the capital market in February 1990 with an issue of 18 lakh equity shares of Rs. 10 each. Public issue shares worth Rs. 30 lakhs are earmarked for the State Bank of India, mutual fund. Mr. A.K. Dureja Managing Director of the company indicated that the trial run of the second phase commenced by the end of February 1990, and commercial production would commence soon thereafter. The problem areas for detailed studies are:

(i) A detailed evaluation of performance in the first phase;

(ii) Viability of the expansion programme of the video housing from 20 million to 40 million deserves to be examined;

(iii) An in depth study of the export potential with special reference to the agreement with the European importer is due;

(iv) A market potential-cum-forecasting study of video magnetic tapes is necessary at this juncture;

(v) A financial viability study is essential for the purpose of estimating ROI (return on investment) before investment is made in the second phase; and

(vi) A detailed technical and technological study may be initiated on a long-term basis for further innovation and new product development.

These research problems are management problems which have been restated. Identifying the management problem and re-stating it as the research problem is a primary step in managerial research. It is, perhaps, the first and one of the most important steps in the managerial research design also. In this context one can identify a few steps involved in translating a management problem into a research problem.

Steps in Translating a Management Problem into a Research Problem

On the basis of the discussion, particularly of the case involving Daulat Electronics, we can notice some steps in translating a management problem into a research problem. These steps are:

(i) Identify the management problem including the problem area and the related factors;

(ii) Identify the important issues in the management problem and the cause-effect relationships involved in it;

(iii) Bifurcate the whole problem into sub-problems on the basis of the issues involved.

(iv) List the sub-problems on a priority basis; *i.e.,* the issues requiring immediate attention must be given first;

(v) Identify important factors involved in important issues and hypothesise their relationship;

(vi) Formulate relevant hypothesis relating to each important issue; to be taken up for detailed study;

(vii) Combine related issues together to make comprehensive research problems so that the research and investigation efforts will be exhaustive and economical;

(viii) Formulate specific research problems based on important issues, clubbing the related issues together and formulating and incorporating hypothesis if any;

(ix) Make statement of specific research problem or problems.

Thus, a management problem may have one or more than one research problems involved in it. However, certain management problems, rather many management problems, never require a research analysis at all, since solutions are found without a detailed analysis or research. Past experiences, intuitions, etc., help one to find out solutions without a detailed investigation of the matter. Very often a primary enquiry provides sufficient insight of the problem and problem situation. Any how there are many management problems which warrant managerial research and analysis. In such cases management problems are converted into research problems before the researcher really starts research and investigation.

Recognising and Reconciling with Organisational Objectives and Goals

Every managerial research is supposed to focus its attention on achieving the objectives and goals of the organisation, because every investment made and expenditure incurred by a business organisation must be consistent with the organisational purpose. No organisation can afford to utilise its scarce resources without an expectation of adequate returns. This is relevant even in respect of investment on research.

Objective is the standard of effectiveness sought to be achieved in the use of the resources of an organisation. Objectives define the standards desirable in maintaining the capacity of the resources for their continued and effective operation. Hence, objectives are essential to ensure that the specialised resources are not left impoverished in the course of operations over a period of time. In fact proper direction is necessary for the achievement of the goals and objectives of the enterprise which is possible only if the objectives are well defined, particularly in accordance with the opportunities and resources available.

Objective is concerned with predetermined results, on which all the activities must focus. Goal is the ultimate purpose of every activity which contributes toward the accomplishment of objectives. Investment on research is also expected to make its best contribution for the accomplishment of objectives and goals, and hence the researcher must recognise the organisational objectives and goals and reconcile the research activities with them, so that the best result can be achieved in conformity with the objectives and goals of the organisation. Thus, a research project is designed in such a way that it helps the orgnisation to achieve its objectives and goals.

Planning the Project

The researcher must ensure project planning as a part of research design since it is planning which takes him through proper path to accomplish the goals. Incorporating the project planning with the research design which facilitates the researcher's observation, data collection, analytical skill, formation of hypothesis, induction and deduction skills and final conclusions. In fact it streamlines the whole research process, and the researcher is enabled to foresee the result of the project. It enables the researcher to make observation which empirically demonstrates the probability of the relationship between phenomena.

Formulation of Hypothesis

Hypothesis forms an integral part of research design, since it is hypothesis that provides direction for a research. Though it is a skepitcal proposition which needs to be tested, it sharpens the observation and increases skill for analysis. Hence, the hypothesis is properly positioned in a research design. We have examined hypothesis in detail in 6th chapter.

Crystallising Objectives, Scope, etc.

Objectives of research, scope of research, purpose of the study, rationale and limitations must be identified when the research is designed. Objectives of research depend on problem identification, while scope of the study is based on its utility. Rationale portrays the reasoning of the study, *i.e.,* why should the study be undertaken. Limitations which may stand on the way of the study may also be foreseen it the designing stage itself, so that the researcher will be able to effectively tackle weaknesses and threats, and make the full use of the opportunities and strengths. Research design should include all these factors.

Identifying the Resources

Resources required to carry out the research project, including monetary and human resources, must be identified once the project is crystallised. This would enable the researcher to economise the resources and maximise the result. This is the next step in research design.

Specifying the Time Period

It is essential for the research design to stipulate a time period within which the research project will be completed. It is essential because every management problem has a time element in it.

The data and information pertaining to a given time period would be invalid for problem solving after a long interval. Hence, the research must be planned in such a way that it completes itself within the given period of time. We have examined time and money as determinants of research design later in this chapter.

Types of Data and its Sources

Data collection is the most essential aspect of any research because the whole result of research depends on the data and information. How much primary and secondary data must be collected, and which is the source; these and many related aspects must be decided well in advance. Hence, these aspects are covered in research design.

Method of Data Collection

Methodology of data collection, analysis and testing of hypothesis must also form a part of research design. Census method or sampling method, or even what type of sampling must be used, all such aspects must be covered so that the researcher will have a clear-cut idea about the data collection method. Sample size with confidence limit from specific population, how when and from where to collect the data, and how much sampling error can be tolerated and so on can be foreseen in research design. Which are the methods to be used for analysis and testing of hypothesis. Statistical methods, mathematical methods, econometric methods, etc., can be used for analysis while one-tailed test or two-tailed test can be used to test the null-hypothesis. These aspects are covered in research design so that the researcher will have a proper perspective of his research.

Expected Results in Comparison with the Company's Requirement

Expected result must be foreseen, and it should be determined whether the results will conform with the organisational needs, objectives and goals. Only when the researcher has expectations to produce a result in accordance with the expectations of the organisation he may proceed further because no company can use its resources without adequate result. This aspect must be of prime concern in the mind of every managerial researcher, and hence it has important place in the research design. The researcher must not forget that his observations and conclusions must aid managerial problem solving and decision-making.

Finalising a Systematic Scheme

The most important task of a researcher prior to plunging into active research is to finalise a systematic scheme of research which enables the researcher to move in a systematic manner to complete the project. It includes the sequence of steps including conducting survey, analysing the data and report writing and the planning for people time and money involved in it. A complete scheme of research is prepared at this point.

We have examined the steps in research design in the preceding paragraphs. In this context a researcher must not forget that there are many factors which affect the choice of a research design. These factors can be briefly explained here.

Factors Affecting Choice of Research Design

Important factors which influence the research design are:

1. Expectation about the potentiality of the research to aid, problem solving, decision-making and policy-making;
2. Hypothesis, particularly experimental and non-experimental hypotheses;
3. Variables, especially dependent, independent and extraneous variables;
4. Availability of data, particularly primary data;
5. Confounded relationship;
6. Possibility of exposure to the actual sources of data;
7. Top management's attitudes and approaches to research and its results;
8. Experimental and control groups;
9. Availability of time, money and manpower;
10. Treatments;
11. Control;
12. Ability, skill, knowledge and technical background of the researcher;

13. Experimentation and it facility;
14. Experimental units; and
15. Urgency and importance of the management problem to be tackled in the research project.

The potentially of the research project to aid problem solving, decision-making and policy-making is, perhaps, the first determinant factor for the choice of research design for a managerial research. Any amount of research or investigation would be futile if it fails to aid managerial decision-making or problem solving. Similarly, research hypothesis also exert influence on research design. There are researches which test either experimental hypothesis or non-experimental hypothesis. Experimental hypothesis-testing researches are the researches in which the independent variable is manipulated. In a non-experimental hypothesis-testing research, an independent variable is not manipulated. Choice of research design generally depends on these two types of hypothesis-testing.

Effectiveness of any hypothesis depends primarily on dependent variables and independent variables. On many occasions, extraneous variables also influence the choice of research design. A factor that can take on different quantitative values can be called a variable. The known variables are called the independent variables, and the variables which are to be predicted are called dependent variables. On the other hand qualitative phenomena can be called attributes. Phenomena which quantitatively can take on different values can be called continuous variables. Those which can be expressed only as integer values are discrete variables. If one variable exists or happens to exist as a consequence of another variable it is considered to be a dependent variable. The relation between dependent and independent variables in the process substantially determines the choice of research design.

Extraneous variables also influence the choice of the research design. Independent variables which are not related to the objective of the study, yet they affect the dependent variable are known as extraneous variables. There are occasions, when extraneous variables substantially affect the hypothesis and the study itself. In such cases research design depends on such extraneous variables also.

Availability, of data, particularly primary data is another influencial factor, while confounded relationship is also an important aspect. The relationship between the dependent variable and independent variable is said to be confounded by an extraneous variable, when the dependent variable is not free from the influence of extraneous variables.

Actual sources of data also influence the choice of research design. Descriptive and diagnostic research design is generally accepted if descriptive data and information are available in plenty. Similarly, experim-ental research design is popular when the research depend on experimental data.

Top management's attitudes and approaches toward research also play a vital role in the choice of research design. Some top bosses get the research work done. But they seldom take cognisance of the research findings in their decision-making process. In such cases the researcher does not have the incentive to make sincere efforts in research. Obviously research design also suffers from bias. On the contrary, when the researcher is convinced that his research findings would substantially influence the decision-making of the top management, his research process and research design would receive greater attention.

Experimental and control groups influence research design tremendously. When the group accepts certain novel or special condition, it becomes experimental group. On the other hand when the group is subject to usual general conditions in an experimental hypothesis testing, such a group is called control group. Both experimental and control groups considerably determine research design.

Availability of Time, Money and Manpower

Factors like time, money, and manpower are determinant factors too in the choice of research design. Every manager is time conscious and every management problem requires to be solved within a particular time frame. The researcher should make it a point to complete his project and to produce his report within the stipulated time. As time management is of prime importance in decision-making, time is a very important determinant in researcher design.

Some problems call for immediate attention, and some require on the spot decisions, while other decisions may be postponed or dropped. In every case, the managerial decision should be based on specific managerial analysis to be completed within the time frame. Project design, therefore, depends on the time available to the decision-maker. Each type of decision is supported by a corresponding type of managerial analysis, and the project is designed accordingly. Decisions on the outbreak of a fire in the factory or a fatal accident to a worker at work have to be quick, while decisions on modernisation or expansion costing billions of rupees must be well thought-out long-term decisions. Each of these decisions is influenced by the time element. An analytical framework behind each decision should, therefore, be planned with reference to the time element.

Any research design should broadly specify three aspects *viz.*, problem identification, statistical or factual analysis, interpretation and suggestion for solution. The time element plays a very vital role in all these phases, though problem identification places a greater degree of reliance on time. There are two stages in problem identification. A recognition that a potential problem exists in the first step. This is usually accomplished by comparing some quantitative or qualitative measure of performance with the actual performance. This search for a standard leads to the identification of the deficiency, if any. The deficiency may be merely an intuitive feeling that there is a problem or a potential problem.

The mechanism of identifying the problem involves considerable time. So does its solutions, especially for analytical purposes. However, it should be ensured that the true problem that faces the organisation is identified, so that the researcher may not grope in the dark. When an abnormal level of inventory of finished goods is noticed, and when there is a very low sales volume, the research executive may identify the problem and design the project which enables him to economise on time. The second step in problem identification is the identification of a standard, and a comparison of the performance with the standard. The research executive may then compare the sales performance in a specific period in the past with the sales decline for the purpose of identifying the problem.

A research design is also determined by the availability of resources, particularly money and manpower because of the attainment of goals largely depends on the money spent on research. The larger the amount of money invested in research, the greater the accuracy of the result. However, the optimum utility of the resources invested in research should be obtained. Money influences the size and magnitude of the selected problem, data collection, choice of sample, the quality and quantity of manpower, efficiency and expertise. The selection of a research problem, therefore, depends on the availability of financial resources and the time available for the completion of the project. These factors, therefore, influence the research design as well.

Another important element which influences the research and research design is manpower, i.e., capable people to execute the research plan. People with research bent of mind and managerial acumen are required to conduct managerial research. Moreover, there are many issues which need technical skill, for which research people with technical background are required. Statisticians, investigators, electronic data processing people, and computer people are required for managerial research. Hence, a research design must make provision for adequate manpower also.

The term "treatments" represents the different conditions or situations under which experimental and control groups are placed. Control, on the other hand, represents minimisation of the influence of extraneous variables. A researcher must be able to design his project in such a way that the influence of extraneous factors is minimised. Treatments and control influence research design.

Ability, knowledge, skill and technical background of the researcher himself determine the choice of research design. The more capable the researcher is, the greater would be the efficiency of research. In such cases greater details of research design may not be required. However, as long as the researcher is not fully aware of the various details, it is proper to have detailed research design.

Experiment and experimental units are also determinants of research design. Experiment is the examination or testing of hypothesis in controlled situations. There can be absolute experiments or comparative experiments. Experimental units are predetermined blocks or units where different treatments are used. Both the elements are influential in designing a research.

Urgency and importance of the management problem to be tackled also considerably influence the research design, data collection and the very research itself. A problem which needs in-depth analysis and a problem needing periphery level probe would have different type of research designs. Thus, various factors determine the type of research designs which the researcher chooses to adopt. In this context an examination of the various types of research design is relevant.

Types of Research Design

Various types of research designs are generally used by researchers. On the basis of the nature of research, research design can be classified as: *(a)* Census survey design or overall design, *(b)* Sampling design, *(c)* Statistical design, *(d)* Observational design, and *(e)* Operational design. A suitable design can be chosen consistent with the type of research.

On the basis of the methodology, research design can be classified under three titles *viz.*:

(i) Experimental Research Design;

(ii) Research Design for Exploratory Research Studies; and

(iii) Research Design for Diagnostic or Descriptive Research Studies.

Let us examine these three types of research designs briefly before we conclude this chapter.

Experimental Research Design

Experimental research designs, which can otherwise be called hypothesis-testing research designs, were originally made by R.A. Fisher in agricultural research in England. Experimental designs are generally used in experimental studies where hypotheses are tested. Experimental designs are now used in almost all the areas of scientific studies. These principles of experimental designs which Fisher prescribed are, viz.: *(a)* the principle of replication, *(b)* principle of randomisation, and *(c)* the principle of local control.

The principle of replication suggests that the experiment must be repeated also that the treatment is applied in many experimental units. This increases the statistical accuracy of the experiments. Randomisation indicating that the variations resulted by extraneous factors can be brought under "chance". Principle of local control indicates that the extraneous factor is allowed to vary deliberately over a wide range so that the variability it causes can be measured and eliminated from the experimental error.

Experimental designs can either be informal experimental designs or formal experimental designs. Informal experimental designs generally use less sophisticated form of analysis based on differences in magnitudes. Formal experimental designs provide relatively greater control and use statistical procedures for analysis. Informal experimental designs include: *(a)* Before-and-after without control design, *(b)* After-only with control design, and *(c)* Before-and-after with control design. Formal experimental designs include: *(i)* Completely Randomised Design (CRD), *(ii)* Randomised Block Design (RBD), *(iii)* Latin Square Design (LSD), and *(iv)* Factorial designs.

A single test group or area is selected and the dependent variable is measured before the introduction of the treatment in the "Before-and-after without control design" The dependent variable is again measured after the treatment. In the "After-only with control design" two groups or areas (test area and control area) are selected and the treatment is introduced into the test area only. The dependent variable is then measured in both the areas at the same time.

In the "Before-and-after with control design," two areas are selected in which the dependent variable is measured for an identical time period, before the treatment. Then the treatment is applied into the test area so that the dependent variable can be measured in both for an identical period of time after the treatment.

Completely Randomised Design (CRD) is a simple research design. Subjects are assinged at random for experimental treatment. Principle of replication and principle of randomisation of experimental designs are involved in this type of design. Subjects are assigned at random in CR designs. Two group simple randomised design and random replications design are the two forms of CR design. In the former a sample is selected at random from a defined population. In the latter a number of repetitive treatments are given in each case minimising the effect of differences.

Randomised block design (RB design) makes use of the principle of local control. Subjects are first divided into groups (blocks). Subjects are relatively homogeneous in regard to selected variables in the RB design. Latin squares dosing (L.S. design) is an experimental design. When two extraneous factors are applicable. Latin square design is effective, while items are placed in a square. Out of the many items; say for example, five items are placed in five places each in the square but used only once in each raw/column. The two blocking factors on two sides of the square (vertical and horizontal) are words. It is generally used in agriculture.

When a large number of factors affect a particular problem, factorial designs are used. There can be simple factorial designs and complex factorial designs. Generally two factors are involved in the former, and many factors (multi-factors) in the latter. The imdenpendent variable to be manipulated is called experimental variable, and the extraneous variable to be controlled by homogeneity is called control variable.

Research Design for Exploratory Research Studies

In this type of research designs, a specific problem is formulated for precise investigation or a specific hypothesis is formulated from an operational observation. Such studies are, therefore, known as formulative studies also. Generally flexible research designs are popular for exploratory studies because discovery of ideas and new insights are emphasised. Analysing relevant examples and cases to stimulate insight, literature survey, and evaluating the past experiences, etc., are generally associated with such designs. In many managerial studies, this type of design is commonly used.

Diagnostic Research Design

Diagostic research studies are generally descriptive and hence such studies are called descriptive studies. Cause-effect relationships are described in such studies. Diagnosis is made in which frequency of effect in the event of the occurrence of a cause is determined. These rigid designs generally concentrate on the aspects like setting objectives, defining and stating the problem under study, designing the method of data collection, including sampling and survey, analysis and interpretation of data, report writing, arriving at inductions, deductions and conclusions, etc. In managerial problem solving diagnostic studies are common, while in case analysis exploratory research designs are popular.

Selection of the Problem

Selection of the problem is one of the very important steps in research design, though the research problem is a management problem in itself. There is no dearth of problems in management; therefore, there cannot be any dearth of research problems. At the same time, there is no ready-made problem for investigation. "Open your eyes, and see, you are surrounded by problems." In point of fact, the selection of a problem demonstrates the interaction between goals and resources within a given period of time when they are recognised as constraints.

If the objective of research is of an academic nature, academic readings and observations would unveil the problems for investigation. If the research is of utilitarian interest, exposure to business environment, and observation of business activities would unveil the problems for investigation. As far as the business is concerned, academic research is considered to be a big tree, rich in its leaves, but bearing hardly any fruit. Such researches are of little value in business. Managerial research, however, whether it is small or big, has a direct relation with application in policy formualtion and decision-making. Only result-oriented research are useful for a business executive. The potential for results should, therefore, be the criterion for the selection of a research problem, though academic problems cannot be totally ignored.

There are many sources of research problems, *viz.,* (1) exposure to the business, (2) past researches, (3) day-to-day practical experience, (4) technological changes, (5) discussions with executives, (6) case studies, and (7) company news, (8) problems of competitor, etc. Problems should be specifically presented, together with the hypotheses, if any, before the research design is finalised. The definition of the concepts and variables, as well as the selection of an appropriate methodology for data collection and analysis, should also be included in the research design.

Research in management aims at specific tasks of problem-solving, decision-making, and result maximisation. Expected utility of research findings motivates the researcher to design a utility-oriented research in management. It is here that the research design receives the attention of a managerial analyst or researcher. Hence, a managerial research design is made in advance chiefly because it provides insights to the researcher about the process of research. We examine the process of research in the next chapter.

Chapter 4

The Process of Research

The discussion in the second chapter has thrown light on the fact that a lot of misunderstanding exists regarding research. This, is perhaps, the reason why some practitioners tend to level scathing criticism against research, while others misunderstand its process as a mere compilation work. An attempt has, therefore, been made here to evaluate briefly the process of research, with special reference to research in management.

Research is a source which can be draw upon to make a substantial contribution to the body of knowledge. Research should be followed by some sort of original contribution. The researches of J.G. Brainerd and others, for example, have resulted in the emergence of electronic computer (1942), while television (TV) is the result of the research done by John Logie Baird (Scot.1926). C. V. Raman's researchers have resulted in the discovery of the Raman Effect, and Marshallian studies have propounded the theory of the Consumer's Surplus, while the research by Mayo has thrown light on the Hawthorne Effect and Michael's research has uncovered the fact that seasonality and harvestability are determinants of consumer behaviour in a rural-based market.[1] Research, in fact, is never a compilation; it is the very basis of original contribution. Let us bring out the various steps in the process of research.

1. Michael V. P., "Determinants of Consumer Behaviour in a Rural-based Urban Retail Market: An Empirical Study of Footwear Market in Kolhapur," *Decision*, Indian Institute of Management, Calcutta, April, 1979.

For the sake of a systematic presentation, the process of research may be classified under three stages, viz., primary stage, secondary stage, and the tertiary stage.

The primary stage includes:

(i) Observation;

(ii) Interest;

(iii) Crystallisation, identification and statement of a research problem;

(iv) Formulation of hypothesis;

(v) Primary synopsis;

(vi) Conceptual clarity;

(vii) Documentation;

(viii) Preparation of a bibliography; and

(ix) Research design.

The secondary stage includes:

(i) Project planning;

(ii) Project formulation;

(iii) Questionnaire preparation;

(iv) Investigation and data collection;

(v) Preparation of final synopsis;

(vi) Compilation of data;

(vii) Classification;

(viiii) Tabulation and presentation of data;

(ix) Experimentation;

(x) Analysis;

(xi) Testing of hypothesis; and

(xii) Interpretation.

The tertiary stage includes.

(i) Report writing;

(ii) Observation, suggestions and conclusions.

Research is always an original work starting with an observation and ending with a report.

Observation

Research starts with observation, which leads to curiosity to learn more about what has been observed. Observation can either be unaided visual observation or guided and controlled observation. Sometimes, a casual or associated observation leading to substantial research and a great invention. Deliberate and guided observation can also form the basis for research. While observation leads to research, research results in elaborate observations and conclusions; or even further research. Observations can either be subjective or objective. There are participant observations, non-participant observations, controlled observations and non-controlled observations.

Participant observation is the type of observation where the observer himself is a participant in the group under study. It enables him to stdudy the group in its natural behaviour, without the group knowing anything about it; and observation here is closer than non-participant observation. A participant observer can observe the group from all angles, without any extra effort on his part. As a part of the research to be conducted in the weaving department of a textile mill, a worker in the same department can be entrusted with the task of observing the group; and this is participant observation. There is the possibility that such observation may be biased, while the members of the group may develop some sort of reservation affecting the objective nature of the observation. The participant observer need not necessarily have the expertise to act as an observer in certain respects, and he need not enjoy the confidence of all the members of the group. Participant observation, therefore, has both merits and demerits.

When someone, who is not a member of the group under observation, observes that group, this is known as *non-participant observation.* For example, a professional researcher observes the behaviour pattern of the workers in a factory, who are members of a particular trade union. The merits of non-participant observation include: objectivity and scientific approach, impartiality, unbiased observation and unprejudiced information, expertise, and efficiency. Its demerits include difficulty for detailed observation, biased and doubtful behaviour on the part of those who are observed, and delicacy on the part of both to behave objectively on certain occasions.

Controlled observation is the type of observation which suffers from some restrictions. It may include control over behaviour, control over phenomena, control over environment and observation. The observation is made under controlled conditions. A laboratory experiment is an example of controlled observation. For the purpose of control, a number of devices are usually used. These are: mechanical devices, schedules, and questionnaires, sociometric scales, detailed observation plans, team observation, control groups, etc. The observations made in natural surroundings, without any control or influence by any external forces are non-controlled observations. Such observations are realistic, and pave the way for research. Field observation studies and group observations are also done to lay the foundation of a research study.

The observation technique, however, suffers from some limitations. Some of the occurrences may not be open to observation, while many occurrences open for observation cannot be conveniently studied. Not all occurrences lend themselves to a study by observational techniques, mainly because of faulty perception, the awareness on the part of the people who are observed, the personal bias of the observer, lack of a system of observation, etc.

However, the observation method is widely used, mainly because of its simplicity, usefulness in the framing of hypothesis, its accuracy, the possibility of getting convincing results, the possibility of the test of validity, etc. It may be pointed out here that observation is a common method in all the sciences, and that is why its applicability has been widely accepted. To be precise, observation tends to be the basis of any research.

Interest

The observation of certain occurrences creates an interest and inquisitiveness in the mind of the researcher to study it further. This is the basis of interest to study the subject matter of observation. The interest may be academic interest or policy-making interest. It may be self-interest or group (social), interest. The interest is the guiding force behind any research.

Crystallisation

Crystallisation is the process of designing the definite form of research to be undertaken for the purpose of studying the subject matter. It is the formulation of the research project, defining its objectives, rationale, scope, methodology, limitations, including financial commitments and sources. It is at this stage that the research project is given a concrete shape and structure, forming a basis of further investigation.

Formulation of Hypothesis

At this stage, the hypothesis is formed on the basis of observation. Hypothesis is a part of the scientific method, and has been dealt with in detail in the chapter on "Scientific Method and Hypothesis." (Chapter 6).

Primary Synopsis

Prior to entering into the actual study, the researcher is expected to make a summary of what is going to be done in connection with the research. This enables him as well as others to gather a definite idea of what would be written in the final report. Accordingly, he would be able to collect the data and make interpretations. This may also be called a tentative chapter scheme.

Conceptual Clarity

Any researcher should have an in-depth background knowledge of the topic of his study. He can gain such basic knowledge only by an extensive reading of text books, specialised books and publications on the topic in addition to articles and research papers published in journals and periodicals, reports of the past studies, etc. He can also gain knowledge by a detailed discussion with the people concerned and by his own observation. However, it is imperative for a researcher to gain a deep knowledge from any reliable source prior to actually plunging himself into the research, so that he may have clear knowledge of the concepts which would be of value to him in his task.

Documentation

The documentary source is an important source of information for a researcher. A document is anything in writing — a record, files or diaries, published or unpublished — which can be extracted and used in research. It is a very valuable source of information for a research either in management or in social sciences. It may comprise office files, business and legal papers, biographies, official and unofficial records, letters, proceedings of any courts, committees, societies, Assemblies, and Parliaments, enactments, constitutions, reports of surveys, or research of commissions, official statistics, newspaper editorials, special articles, company news, cases or company directors' reports, etc. Documentation is the process of collecting and extracting the documents which are relevant to research.

Documents may be classified into:

(i) Personal documents;

(ii) Company documents;

(iii) Consultants' reports and published materials; and

(iv) Public documents.

Personal documents are those that are written by or on behalf of invididuals. They may include autobiographies, biographies, diaries, memoirs, letters, observations and inscriptions, which are primarily written for the use and satisfaction of individuals, and which can be utilised for research purposes. Personal documents play a very vital role in research, when certain information is not available from any other sources. However, such documents are subject to the difficulties of availability, reliability and validity of inferences.

Company documents are the most essential types of documents in management research, annual reports, statements of income and expenditure and balance sheets, files and records, policy statements, resolutions, minutes of board of directors, general bodies and executive conferences, performance records and evaluation files, specific forecasting and evaluation reports, ditrectors' reports, etc. Many of these documents are reliable ones, though they are subject to the problems of availability and adequacy. Such documents can be published or unpublished.

Consultants' published materials consist of reports of proferssional consultants, records of commodity boards, chambers of commerce, FICCI., manufacturers' associations; industry associations like the Engineering Association, the Textile Mill Owners' Association, the Jute Mills Association, etc., documents available with trade unions, the All India Management Association, management training institutions, etc. Public documents are documents, both published and unpublished, of government organisations and documents of public interest. They include government records and files, draft outlines of five-year plans, consultative committee reports, finance commission reports, special enquiry commission reports, Company Law Board reports, MRTP Commission reports, reports and files of the Registrar of Companies, the Registrar of Firms, the Ministry of Commerce and Industry, etc., reports of population census, National Sample Survey and such other government research institutions. Such documents are valuable if they are reliable and suitable for a particular study — if they can be obtained. Documentation is one of the most important needs of any management researcher at the primary stage of his research.

Bibliography

At the end of any research report a biliography is generally added. This is the list of books, publications, periodicals, journals, reports, etc., which are used by the researcher in connection with the study. It is a description of books, their authorship, editions, publishers, year of publication, place of publication etc. In ordinary circumstances, a researcher reads, and makes notes from, many books and publications at the primary stage of research in order to gain conceptual clarity. He prepares a list of such publications and reports then and there, which helps him in the course of his research. Some mistakenly believe that a bibliography is merely a list of publications compiled at the end of a report writing, like an appendix. On the contrary, a bibliography contains, and is composed of, the details of publications that the researcher has used in connection with his study. This facilitates any further reference to the matter either by the researcher himself or anybody who goes through the research report. Usually, the details are written in the sequence of (after serial nuber): say,

1. Michael V.P., *Busines Policy and Environment,* S. Chand, New Delhi, 1987.

(1) Serial No.

(i) The name of the author;

(ii) The title of the book;

(iiii) The name of the publisher;

(iv) The place of publication;

(v) The year of publication; and

(vi) The page number in the book, if necessary.

It is a journal or periodical, the sequence is:

(i) Serial No.

(ii) The name of the author;

(iiii) The title of the article or research paper;

(iv) The name of the journal;

(v) The place of publication;

(vi) Volume number, issue date; and

(vii) Pages.

For example:

2. Michael V.P., "Determinants of Consumer Behaviour", *Decision,* Journal, Indian Institute of Management, Cal. Vol., 6, No. 2, April 1979, pp. 175-186.

Though the bibliography is usually prepared at the primary stage, additions can be made whenever necessary until the report writing is over, because the reading process continues until the report is finalised.

Project Planning

The secondary stage of research consists of all the aspects of actually carrying out the research project. It starts with project planning, which is the process of selecting future courses of action in carrying out a research project. Project planning is the first step in actually conducting and directing a research project. It is one of the most important tasks of a researcher. This includes formulation of the research objectives and goals and determining ways of achieving them. A project plan provides a rational approach to research, enabling one to decide in advance what to do, how to do it, when to do it, where to do, and who is to do it in investigating the concerned subject. It enables the researcher to effectively carry out the project within the given time, means and available manpower for the achievement of the objectives of the research in the best way possible.

Project Formulation

A project plan results in project formulation. Once the project is planned, the research executive or the researcher makes a practical approach to carry out the project. It consists of deciding upon the objective of the research, identifying the various factors that influence it, determining the courses of action open to him — from framing the questionnaire to interpretation and presentation, and so on. It consists, too, of setting up priorities and determining the strategy for the collection of the data, identifyng the variables and establishing their relations. It calls for a thorough understanding of the environment under which the survey is to be conducted, as well as the informants and the population from whom the data would be collected. It includes the guidelines for the effective conduct of the research project, putting everything down in black and white, and specifying the research methodology. In other words, project formulation is a way of systematically setting forth the total research project with a view to conducting a systematic study. It includes the selection of a topic for research, the formulation of hypotheses, the identification of the sources of data, the utilisation of funds, and so on. Data collection methods, too, have to be specified. Project formulation is one of the most important steps in the conduct of a research.

Questionnaire and Schedule

Project formulation is followed by data collection. In order to systematically collect the primary data, questionnaires and schedules are employed. A questionnaire is a schedule consisting of a number of coherent questions related to the various aspects of the topic under study. A schedule is a tabulated statement of details. It may be almost identical to a questionnaire, which is usually used for the collection of information directly by the investigator himself. A questionnaire is a form of formulated series of questions relating to a survey or a research study. It is mailed to informants for the purpose of the collection of data. When a questionnaire is mailed, it is known as a mailed questionnaire. However, there is no bar in making use of a questionnaire for the purpose of interview and collection of data directly. In fact, a questionnaire is widely used more as a direct method nowadays than as an indirect way of collecting the data. However, for the collection of data from an informant at a distance, mailed questionnaires are preferable.

Questionnaires can be classified into:

(i) Structured questionnaires;

(ii) Non-structured questionnaires;

(iii) Codified questionnaires; and

(iv) Uncodified questionnaires.

P. V. Young has defined a structured questionnaire as one which contains definite, concrete and pre-ordinated questions, with additional questions limited to those necessary to classify inadequate answers or to elicit a more detailed response. For the purpose of better understanding, a structured questionnaire may be defined as the type of questionnaire which is segmented and designed to elicit detailed and accurate information under the given titles and sub-titles. It helps to obtain accurate response and apt information according to the needs and scope of the research. It enables the researcher to save much time and energy in processing the data. This is especially useful when the questionnaire is of a complex nature. For example, if the study is related to consumer behaviour, the questionnaire may be structured under various titles, *viz.,*

(i) Personal data;

(ii) Consumption pattern;

(iii) Consumer products market;

(iv) Industrial products market; and

(v) General information.

Each title may be sub-titled for the purpose of eliciting detailed and specific information.

Non-structured questionnaires are simple questionnaires without any segmentation or sub-division. A few simple questions are put, one after another in a proper sequence. This is useful only for very simple types of studies. For example, in a simple study of trade union membership, the questionnaire may contain a few questions, *viz.,* the name, age, educational background, section or department, name of the trade union, years of membership, remarks, if any, etc. Codified questionnaires are those questionnaires in which the expected answers are given in code numbers.

Against each question, four or five expected answers are given, and each answer is given a code number, say, 1, 2, 3, etc. (See Annexure I at the end of this chapter). The informat is expected to mark (or circle) the selected number only. This questionnaire is easier for processing, especially with the help of a computer. It is convenient for the informant also, since he has to spend only very little effort and time on it, while it is easily understandable. Uncodified questionnaires are very simple ones without any condification. As in the non-structured questionnaire, questions are asked without any condification. Codification is made at the time of compilation, if necessary.

Characteristics of a Good Questionnaire

A questionnaire, to be effective, must have some essential features. These are:

(i) The size of the questionnaire should be as modest as possible but not at the cost of necessary information to be collected.

(ii) It should have an elegant appearance.

(iii) Questions should be as simple as possible.

(iv) Maximum clarity should be maintained.

(v) Leading questions should be avoided as far as possible.

(vi) The sequence of questions should be maintained.

(vii) It should attract the attention and generate interest of the informant.

(viii) The reliability of the questionnaire and validity of the questions asked should be maintained.

(ix) Definitions should be maintained.

(x) Sufficient scope should be given for the informant to express all the relevant facts, thoughts and information.

There are certain merits and demerits of the questionnaire method. The merits include large coverage, low cost, greater validity, repetitive information, and rapidity of obtaining information. The demerits include unreliability, limited scope, biased nature of answers, etc. Mailed questionnaires suffer from such difficulties as incomplete entries, subjective and biased answers, illegible entries, poor response, lack of personal contact and observation, impossibility of in-depth information, etc. The questionnaire method is widely accepted as an effective method for the collection of primary data, not only for research in the social sciences and humanities, but in management research as well.

A Schedule

The schedule is also used as a tool for the collection of data. While a schedule is designed to enable the investigator to fill up and collect the information, a questionnaire is framed to enable the informants to fill up and furnish the information asked for. However, in order to avoid complications, bias, and irrelevant answers, it is safer on the part of the investigator to fill up the questionnaire himself in accordance with the views of the informants. Of course, the schedule is ususally filled up by the investigator. The questions, therefore, need not be detailed and explicit. Investigators are expected to elaborate the questions for the informants and elicit the answers in detail. There are various types of schedules, *viz.,* interview schedules, observation schedules, document schedules and rating schedules. Interview schedules are used for the conduct of interviews with, and the collection of information from, the informants. An observation schedule is meant for observation, while a document schedule is an aid in documentation. The rating schedule is a tool for evaluating an attitude or an opinion, and for this purpose, different types of scales are developed. When putting questions, the investigator should bear in mind certain principles.

The following types of questions should be avoided:

(i) Very long questions,

(ii) Ambiguous questions,

(iii) Leading questions;

(iv) Complex questions,

(v) Personal questions,

(vi) Questions causing suspicion,

(vii) Embarrassing questions,

(viii) Questions for which answers can be evoked otherwise,

(ix) Questions which are likely to yield wrong replies; and

(x) Irrelevant questions.

The characteristics of a good questionnaire are relevant in respect of schedules, too. (A sample questionnaire is given at the end of this chapter).

The interview technique has a number of adavantages, which may be summed up as follows (it is always useful to use a schedule or a questionnaire for interview):

(i) The investigator is able to create an image and confidence in the minds of the informants so that unbiased information can be elicited;

(ii) A higher percentage of response may be expected;

(iii) The informant feels free to provide the necessary information since the burden of filling in the schedule is on the investigator;

(iv) Detailed information could be collected;

(v) The investigator himself is in a position to observe a lot of things, by himself, during the course of a personal interview.

However, the interview method is costly, especially when the respondents are widely scattered and the study is extensive. There is a possibility for some most of bias arising out of the influence of the investigator; though this is negligible. Yet the fact remains that the interview method is the best and the most prominent method of collecting primary data; and hence it is very popular with researchers. In order to identify and overcome difficulties in the main project, however, pilot studies and pre-tests are often conducted.

Pilot Studies and Pre-tests

Pilot studies are preliminary studies conducted on a limited scale before the actual studies are carried out in order to gain some primary information, on the basis of which the main project would be planned and formulated. Prior to the preparation of the questionnaire or schedule for the principal study, pilot studies are conducted. Such studies need not necessarily have a hypothesis, though a provisional hypothesis can be temporarily tested. Pilot studies enable the researcher to gain some systematic knowledge of the universe and its population, on which the main studies would be based. It plays a very vital role in identifying the various variables involved in the research and to gain some awareness of the nature of the problems and the nature of the respondents. The schedules or questionnaires prepared after such studies may become more realistic and meaningful; and the environment of research becomes clearer to the researcher.

However, in complex studies, for the researcher to gain greater exposure, it is better to examine the various aspects of the research once more with the help of the initial questionnaire or the schedule that has been prepared. It is for this purpose that the questionnaire or schedule is tested on some sample of universe, prior to the original study or before the questionnaire is finalised. Such tests of the questionnaire may be called pre-tests. On the basis of pre-tests of the modifications, if any, are effected in the questionnaire, sampling strata, population, hypotheses or even research objectives, if necessary.

Pre-tests throw light on the various handicaps or constraints which may crop up in the main study. These handicaps are: a large number of respondents refuse to be interviewed; a majority of the respondents are too ignorant to be interviewed; the variables identified have proved to be non-existent; the hypothesis is falsified; sampling, stratification or population seem to be inappropriate; informants give unexpectedly biased information; questions are inappropriate, etc. Accordingly, any necessary change can be effected; or the very scheme of research itself be dropped. Pre-tests can be conducted any number of times in order to perfect the entire scheme.

Data Collection

Data collection is one of the most important aspects of research. It is dealt with in detail in the next chapter.

Compilation of Data

The data collected, both from the primary and secondary sources, should be tabulated and presented in at systematic form prior to classification. This is necessary for appropriate classification and interpretation.

Classification and Tabulation

Classification is the way of arranging the data in different classes in order to give a definite form and a coherent structure to the data collected, facilitating their use in the most systematic and effective manner. It is the process of grouping the statistical data under various understandable homogeneous groups for the purpose of convenient interpretation. A uniformity of attributes is the basic criterion for classification; and the grouping of data is made according to similarity. Classification becomes necessary when there is a diversity in the data collected for meaningful presentation and analysis. However, in respect of homogeneous presentation of data, classification may be unnecessary.

Objectives of classification of data:

(i) To group heterogeneous data under the homogeneous groups of common characteristics;

(ii) To facilitate similarity of various groups;

(iii) To facilitate effective comparison;

(iv) To present complex, haphazard and scattered data in a concise, logical, homogeneous, and intelligible form;

(v) To maintain clarity and simplicity of complex data;

(vi) To identify independent and dependent variables and establish their relationship;

(vii) To establish a cohesive nature for the diverse data for effective and logical analysis;

(viii) To make logical and effective quantification.

A good classification should have the characteristics of clarity, homogeneity, equality of scale, purposefulness, accuracy, stability, flexibility, and unambiguity.

Classification is of two types, *viz.,* quantitative classification, which is on the basis of variables or quantity; and qualitative classification (classification according to attributes). The former is the way of grouping the variables, say quantifying the variables in cohesive groups, while the latter groups the data on the basis of attributes or qualities. Again, it may be multiple classification or dichotomous classification. The former is the way of making many (more than two) groups on the basis of some quality or attributes, while the latter is the classification into two groups on the basis of the presence or absence of a certain quality. Grouping the workers of a factory under various income (class intervals) groups comes under multiple classification; and making two groups into skilled workers and unskilled workers is dichotomous classification. The tabular form of such classification is known as statistical series, which may be inclusive or exclusive.

The classified data may be arranged in tabular forms (tables) in columns and rows. Tabulation is the simplest way of arranging the data, so that anybody can understand it in the easiest way. It is the most systematic way of presenting numerical data in an easily understandable form. It facilitates a clear and simple presentation of the data, a clear expression of the implications, and an easier and more convenient comparison. There can be simple or complex tables, and general purpose or summary tables. Classification and tabulation are interdependent events in a research.

Experimentation

Experimentation is a basic ingredient of the research process, which is popular in the physical sciences for a long time because of the possibility of laboratory experiments. An experiment is the process of critically studying the contrasting aspects of the relationships between independent and dependent variables in a controlled situation. It is a test, or a trial procedure for testing a hypothesis in a laboratory. As laboratory experiments were not possible in the social sciences or in management, the physical sciences had owned them in the past. But now the monopoly has been shifted, and experimental methods are utilised not only by social sciences like sociology, anthropology, and psychology, but also by management science. According to Greenwood, there are five types of experiments, *viz.,* the trial-and-error experiment, the controlled observational study, the natural experiment, the *ex-post facto* experiment and the laboratory experiment.

The researcher makes a number of trial tests of the hypothesis that he has formed in various situations, commits errors and faces failures; at last reaching within a measurable distance of success which, however, is not definite. This is known as the trial-and-error experiment. This is a naive method, which had been in practice for a long time. Controlled observational studies are those which are made under controlled conditions in ordinary situations. Natural experiments are known as field experiments, as well. The researcher may try to manipulate the variables in a natural experiment, while the phenomenon is observed in observational studies. The *ex-post facto* technique which studies the actual effect of the present relation between the variables in the future, establishes the varying influence of two identical factors. For example, suppose a researcher desires to test the hypothesis that the career growth potential of engineering graduates is double that of ordinary commerce graduates. He selects a given number of engineering and commerce graduates of the same age, years of post-education experience, environment, etc. The research will continue over a period of ten or fifteen years, and the respondents should be located every two or three years for the purpose of evaluating the career growth, which is a very difficult process. In order to tide over this difficulty, Chapin has suggested that the study may be made from the present to the past; but this suggestion has been widely criticised because it amounts to an effect-cause relationship study, instead of a cause-effect relationship investigation.

A laboratory experiment is an experiment which is carried out in a situation created with exact conditions and facilities for the study. Though the physical sciences extensively employ this method, both the social sciences and management science are not barred from making use of it. (This has already been explained elsewhere.) However, experimental studies face some difficulties in social and management sciences, *viz.,* difficulties arising out of the absence of a laboratory setting, lack of adequate co-operation, and difficulty of appropriate control. In spite of the difficulties, however, it has its own merits. The results are accurate and real. The determination of a cause-effect relationship is possible; so is a greater amount of accuracy. It has universal acceptance; and the testing of hypothesis is more realistic. However, human beings may react in different ways in controlled situations resulting in inaccurate results.

Testing of Hypothesis

Hypothesis is discussed in detail in the chapter on Scientific Methods (Chapter 6).

Analysis and Interpretation

Collection, compiltation, classification, tabulation, and presentation of data enable the researcher to make appropriate analysis and interpretation. Proper analysis, on the other hand, results in unambiguous observations, suggestions, conclusions, inductions, and deductions, which may perhaps be the actual aid of the manager in his decision-making process. Testing of hypothesis, and identifying relationships between variables may also become a part and parcel of research, analysis and interpretation. Diagrammatic presentation, graphs, charts, mathematical models, statistical tools, etc. make the analysis more effective and meaningful.

Designing a Questionnaire

As already observed the basic requisite of any research study is the appropriate data which can be collected with the help of a schedule or a questionnaire. A quetionnaire is generally self-explanatory, while the schedule is explained and interpreted to the informants by the investigator himself. Questionnaires are usually mailed to the respondents. Both questionnaire and schedule are identical, and the former can be used in place of the latter. It should, however, be emphasised that the researcher must bestow extreme attention and care in designing a questionnaire (or schedule).

Some important points to be taken care of in designing a questionnaire are listed below:

1. The purpose, objective, and scope of the questionnaire in particular and the study as a whole in general must be clearly identified and specified.
2. The questionnaire should fit in with these objectives without any ambiguity which should be clearly mentioned so that the informants may have a clear-cut idea of the project enabling him to give the information without any bias.
3. Personal details like names, sex, age, educational level, etc. which are closely related to the basic aspects of the study should

have a proper place in the questionnaire.

4. As far as possible, the questions must be easily understandable, clearly presented, and simple and brief in appearance.
5. Unambiguity must be the fundamental characteristic of any questionnaire.
6. Predetermined and well planned answers can be provided though leading questions should be avoided.

Every study is bound to be based on relevant data. Hence, data collection is one of the most important responsibilities of any researcher. In this connection, the questionnaire plays a very vital role. General format of a questionnaire is given below (Annexure I):

Annexure I

Institute of Business Management

(Address)

A Market Survey for Toilet Soaps with Special Reference to "X" Soap in Bombay

Questionnaire/Schedule for Consumers[1]

Note: As far as possible, the number/numbers of the choice by the respondent may be indicated by rounding it. The study is only for academic purposes, and the information will be confidential.

Part I — Personal Information

1. Name of the Respondent Male 1 Female 2
2. Address (if necessary)
3. Age Group

(i) below 20	1	*(iv)*	40-50	4
(ii) 20-30	2	*(v)*	50-60	5
(iii) 30-40	3	*vi.*	Above 50	6

4. Income Group (monthly)

	(i)	Below Rs. 500	1
	(ii)	Rs. 500-1,000	2
	(iii)	Rs. 1,000-2,000	3
	(iv)	Rs. 2,000-4,000	4
	(v)	above Rs. 4,000	5

5. Educational Background

	(i)	Matric and below	1
	(ii)	Graduate and below (above matric)	2
	(iii)	Post-graduate	3
	(iv)	Professional graduate/ Prof. Post-graduate	4

6. Professional/Vocational Background

	(i)	Blue collar work	1
	(ii)	White collar (non-executive)	2
	(iii)	Executive (Business & Govt.)	3
	(iv)	Own business (non-industry)	4
	(v)	-do- (Small industry)	5
	(vi)	-do- (Large industry)	6
	(vii)	Anything else (specify)	7

1. For students: Structured questions used with answers as preconceived and codified. (This is not an exhaustive or all-pervasive questionnaire, one may incorporate any number of questions as per requirement.)

Part II — General Observation of Toilet Soaps

1. Would you please mention the names of a few toilet soaps that you remember?

	Product	*Producer*	*Market*
(i)			
(ii)			
(iii)			
(iv)			
(v)			

2. Which qualities do you expect of a toilet soap?

(i)	Fragrance	1	*(viii)*	Good shape (specify)	8
(ii)	Freshness	2	*(ix)*	Good colour	9
(iii)	Germicidal effect	3	*(x)*	Packing (specify)	10
(iv)	Transparency	4	*(xi)*	Advertising & publicity	11
(v)	Contents	5	*(xii)*	Popularity	12
(vi)	Low price	6	*(xiii)*	Easy availability	13
(vii)	High price	7	*(xiv)*	Anything else (specify)	14

3. Which channel of distribution, you feel is convenient and effective for toilet soaps?

(i)	Department store	1	*(v)*	Retailer	5
(ii)	Super market	2	*(vi)*	Local pan shops, etc.	6
(iii)	Chain stores	3	*(vii)*	Anything else (specify)	7
(iv)	Door-to-door delivery	4			

4. Do you feel that advertising and publicity are essential of a tiolet soap?

Yes 1 No. 2 Not known 3 No opinion 4

5. If the answer to Question 4 is "yes", please specify the media:

(i)	National newspapers	1	*(v)*	Colour TV programmes	5
(ii)	Local newspapers	2	*(vi)*	Attractive posters	6
(iii)	Local language magazines	3	*(vii)*	Incentive schemes	7
(iv)	National magazines	4	*(viii)*	Any other (specify)	8

Part III — Brand Loyalty

1. Would you please specify the name/names of the soap/soaps that you have bought and used more than once?

(i) Max Factor	1	*(viii)* Chandrika	8
(ii) Lavender Dew	2	*(ix)* Lux	9
(iii) Pears	3	*(x)* Ria	10
(iv) Moti	4	*(xi)* Margo	11
(v) Cinthol	5	*(xii)* Dettol Soap	12
(vi) Supreme	6	*(xiii)* X soap	13
(vii) Liril	7	*(xiv)* Anything else 1...	14
		(specify) 2...	15

2. Would you specify four or five brands that you use most often?

Product	Number of times used
1.	Many times (cannot count)
2.	10-20 times
3.	5-10 times
4.	3-5 times
5.	twice.

3. Would you give the reason why you have used these brands a greater number of times?

   (Any of the qualities, including any number from those mentioned in Question 2 of Part II, that determine your demand for the given brand may be specified. Any number of qualities can be mentioned in the order of priority).

1.	4.
2.	5.
3.	6.

4. Have you got a special preference for a particular brand; or do you opt from among the various alternatives?

(i) Specific choice for a particular Product (specify)	1
brands	2
(ii) Choose from the specific alternative of two or three	
(iii) No specific choice	3

5. If you prefer one particular brand, would you please mention a few most important factors that lead to this particular choice?

1.	3
2.	4.

6. If that particular brand is not available, what would be your choice, and in the absence of even the second one, what would be your third choice?

   Choice Number 2 . . . . Choice Number 3 . . . .

7. General Remarks.

Part IV — A Reference to Product 'X'

1. Have you ever heard of Product 'X'?

   Yes 1 No 2

2. Source (please specify)

3. Have you ever used it?

   Yes 1 No 2

4. If you have used it at least once, would you mention your impressions about it?

Excellent	1
Very good	2
Moderate	3
Tolerable	4
Not acceptable	5

5. Would you specify reasons for your answer in Question 4?

   (i)
   (ii)
   (iii)
   (iv)
   (v)

6. If your answer to Question 4 is anything other than 'Excellent' (No. 1) what would be your suggestions to make the product excellent?

   (i)
   (ii)
   (iii)
   (iv)

7. If Product X is your present brand, what are the reasons for this brand loyalty?

   (i)

   (ii)

   (iii)

   (iv)

8. If Product X is your present first preference, what priority would you give it (Product X) in the order of merit if your first preference product is not available?

First	1
Second	2
Third	3
Fourth	4
Never	5

9. In order to make Product X your first preference product, what improvements would you suggest?

   (i)

   (ii)

   (iii)

   (iv)

10. If you have not yet used Product X, would you like to try it?

    Yes 1 No 2

11. If the answer is 'Yes' to Question 10 under what conditions?

(i) under any circumstances	1
(ii) if easily available	2
(iii) if the price reduced	3
(iv) if it is costly	4
(v) if it is available free of cost	5
(vi) anything else (specify)	6

12. If the answer is 'No' to Question 10, please specify the reason, if any:

13. General remarks of the informant.

14. General remarks of the investigator on the basis of his observation of the informant.

Chapter 5

Data Collection and Analysis

The discussion in previous chapters has been couched largely in terms of carrying out a systematic research in management as an aid to effective decision-making. It has been pointed out that the analysis of any management problem should be based on appropriate data and facts. We, therefore, propose to throw some light on the relevant aspects of data collection in managerial research.

Data in Managerial Analysis

Facts, information or premises, systematically collected and formally presented for the purpose of drawing inferences, may be called data. Statistical information collected, compiled and presented for the purpose of establishing relationships between variables can be included in the data which play a very vital role in the research and analysis of management problems, as they do in any other area of investigation. This is the rationale of data collection in research.

Both primary and secondary data may be used for the purpose of analysis. The first hand information bearing on any research, which has been collected by the researcher or his agent or assistant may be called primary data. These are original observations collected for the first time. Such data facilitate original investigations and observations, leading to useful and valuable results. The results, which are based on primary data, are bound to be empirical and of great utility value. The primary data, collected and compiled without any bias, are more reliable and dependable, and are accurate and apt for specified investigations. Once the primary data have been put to use, the original character of these data disappears, and they become secondary. The data which are primary at one point of time are, therefore, bound to become secondary at a later stage.

The secondary data, on the other hand, are based on second-hand information. The data which have already been collected, compiled and presented earlier by any agency may be used for the purpose of investigation. Such data may be called secondary data. Population census reports, national sample survey reports, economic and statistical reports, data banks of any professional association or trade organisation — these are examples of secondary data. There are many printed and published reports of various government and private agencies, say, the Reserve Bank of India, the All-India Management Association, etc. which can be obtained and made use of by any researcher.

SURVEY

Data collection is the process of obtaining valuable and reliable information for purposes of research. As the secondary data consist of data from secondary sources, they may be obtained either personally or by post and may be presented and interpreted. The actual task of the researcher is, therefore, to collect the primary data, either by census survey or by sample survey. The latter is the most popular method of collecting primary data.

Census Method

Census method is the systematic way of collecting data from the whole population or the universe. The term *population* refers to a set of data, not to the sources of the data, from the whole universe. For a study of the consumption pattern of the textile workers in Mumbai, information from all the textile workers in Mumbai may be consider to be the *population,* and not the textile workers themselves. The term *universe* includes the whole community of textile workers. Thus, the population consists of the whole set of data or information from the entire universe, which is considered to be the whole source of information. It means that the largest set of data may be called the population, and not the set of persons. The measures of the characteristics of population are known as parameters, *i.e.,* the mean of a population is a parameter. There may be a number of possible sample results, as large as the population itself. The statistical inference may consist of three different distributions, *viz.,* population, sample, and probability and sampling.

The distribution of all the values about which some inferential statement has to be made is the population, while a smaller set of values selected from the population is the sample. Sample distribution is the distribution of all the possible sample results which might flow from all the possible sample means. The population is a set of values that exist but are not completely known to the researcher. The sample is a set of values which exists and is known to the researcher. Both sets are the realised values. At the same time, the sampling distribution is a set of values, most of which may not be realised, and hence the probability becomes a certainty, *i.e.*, a certain sample result can occur.

Direct personal observation is one of the prominent methods of collecting data. In this type of data collection, the researcher observes the situation in person and collects the relevant data. If the observation is unbiased, the data collected by direct personal observation would be the most reliable information. For example, if the researcher wants to study the behavioural pattern of workers in a traditionally managed foundry and to compare it with that in a modern foundry, the result would be realistic if the researcher himself observes the behavioural pattern in person. He has to identify the sources and fields of investigation. However, there are certain occasions when direct personal observation is not possible; and when the whims and fancies of the observer may affect the accuracy of the result. In such cases, it would be better for the researcher to be satisfied with either the indirect oral examination method or the schedules and questionnaires method.

Instead of collecting information from the informants direct the researcher may collect information from people who are supposed to have a correct knowledge of the actual situation, or indirect sources are tapped and the relevant information collected, which is called indirect oral investigation. This method may not be very fruitful the informants are biased. The schedules and questionnaires when most commonly used for the collection of data. This has been discussed in detail in Chapter 4. Reports from local correspondents and other localised agencies are also used for the collection of relevant data.

The census method, however, is not very practical, for it is difficult mainly because of its "callous" nature. Because of the requirement of enormous time, money, and manpower, the census method becomes practical only for government agencies. It is impossible for individual researchers to carry out census surveys unless the universe is limited and small. This is, perhaps, the reason why the sampling method is very popular with individual researchers.

Sampling Method

A sample is a small specimen or a separated part of the whole population, representing its general qualities, as far as possible. It is a smaller set of values selected from the population, reflecting its characteristics. The sampling technique is a procedure for the selection of a sample from the given population. the term *sampling* refers to the investigation of a part of the whole population or universe, while sampling distribution is the distribution of all the possible sample results of the whole population. According to Calvin F. Schmidt, "a statistical population or universe may consist of attributes, qualities or behaviour of the people, the behaviour of inanimate objects such as dice or cities or city blocks, households or dwelling structures, the day's output of a factory, or the opinions of the electorate of an entire nation.

Advantages and Problems of Sampling

Sampling has certain definite advantages over the census method. It limits the requirements of time, money and manpower to a great extent, though it enables one to conduct a detailed study with a limited error. There is also a possibility for considerable accuracy of results. Administrative convenience is another advantage of a sample study, in which almost all the limitations of the census study are absent. Because of its merits, sample studies are very popular with independent researchers. However, it does not mean that the sampling method does not suffer from any drawbacks. As a matter of fact, sampling also suffers from drawback. These drawbacks are:

(i) Chances for bias;

(ii) Difficulty of accuracy;

(iii) Difficulty of obtaining a representative sample;

(iv) Lack of trained manpower;

(v) Non-availability of informants;

(vi) Possibility for error in sampling; and

(vii) Inadequacy of samples.

Even though the sample survey method is convenient, there is a possibility for bias, both on the part of the investigator and the informants. The investigator is able to influence the informants to contribute to his biased views; and the possibility cannot be ruled out for the based views of the respondents. Both would affect the accuracy of the result. Moreover, on many occasions, accuracy is wanting not only in sample selection, but in satisfying the data; and this results in biased results. The difficulty in obtaining a representative sample is another important drawback. This is particularly true of problems of a complex nature. If the sample ceases to be representative, the result ceases to be accurate. Trained manpower is an essential pre-requisite of any sampling to be appropriate. But, unfortunately, trained experts are very few and, fewer still act as research executives. Similarly, the respondents who are selected as samples at random may not be available, in which case the researchers have to choose substitutes. Consequently, there is the possibility that the effect of sampling will change substantially.

One of the most widely accepted criticisms against sampling is that there is a possibility for error, which would lead to wrong conclusions. There is a some element of truth in this criticism. But the error is usually marginal, and hence its effect is negligible. Even in the census survey, some percentage of error is bound to occur. When the population is large in size, the sample becomes inadequate, unless a proportionately large sample is chosen. The selection of large samples has the disadvantages of the census method, while the selection of a small sample is inadequate, and the result may be wrong. But despite all the limitations of the sampling method of survey, it is extensively used as the most reliable method of primary data collection, not only in managerial analysis, but in all the areas of systematic human activity.

Types of Sampling

The sampling technique is a universal method of data collection. "When the measures like mean, median, mode, and standard deviation describe the characteristics of a sample, they are called statistics. When they describe the characteristic of a population, they are called parameters. As statistic is a characteristic of a sample, and a parameter is a characteristic of a population." The selection of a sample from the population is an important task of any statistical worker, researcher or investigator.

Sample may be selected from the population by *random* or *probability* sampling method, or *non-random* or judgement sampling method. In probability sampling, every item in the population has a chance of being selected for the sample. But the possibility of being selected as a sample is judged on the basis of personal knowledge, opinion, interest, and so on, of the researcher or someone who is associated with the researcher in the judgement sampling.

In order to make a systematic approach to sampling, we may present the sampling method as:

SAMPLING

Random Sampling or Probability Sampling

1. Simple Random Sampling
2. Stratified Random Sampling
3. Systematic Sampling
4. Cluster Sampling (Sub-sampling)
5. Sequential Sampling
6. Multi-Stage Sampling
7. Sampling with Probability Proportional to Size

Non-random, Non-Probability, or Judgement Sampling

8. Quota Sampling
9. Convenience Sampling and
10. On-the-spot Sampling

Simple Random Sampling

Each unit of the population has an equal probability of being picked in simple random sampling. "Simple random sampling selects samples by methods that allow each possible sample to have an equal probability of being picked and each item in the entire population to have an equal chance of being included in the sample"[1] This is also known as probability sampling. Samples are drawn at random from the population in a simple way. The probability that each unit of the population will be selected is equal. Then the probability for selection of each unit is *1/N*, where *N* is the total population. Probability at the second draw, *i.e., 1/N-1,* the probability at the third draw, *1/N-2,* and probability at the fourth draw is *1/N-3,* and so on. There is simple random sampling without replacement, and simple random sampling with replacement. When there are no repetitions or duplications of the units in the sample, it is called sampling without replacement. Each unit is distinct and yields specific information.

Sampling with replacement permits repetitions. In such sampling, the selected unit is replaced in the population before the selection of subsequent units, which means that there is a likelihood of a unit being selected more than once.

Four methods are generally employed to draw simple random sampling. They are: the lottery method, Tippes numbers, selection from the sequential list, and the grid system.

The lottery method makes a selection from the universe by drawing chits, L.H.C. Tippetts has constructed a list of 10,400 four digits numbers

1. *Ibid.*, p. 27.

written at random at every stage. They have been constructed out of 4,16,000 digits taken from census reports by combing them in fours.

Suppose a sample of 10 items is to be drawn from a list of 500 persons: then we shall number each unit from 0 to 500. Then any page is opened from Tippetts numbers, and we select the first ten numbers which are below 500. According to the sequential list, the names are first arranged serially in some particular order (alphabetically). Then every 10th or any other relevant value may be taken up. The midpoint would be ideal to begin with. In order to select a sample, the area grid system is usually employed. A screen with squares is placed on the map of the area, and some of the squares are selected at random. The areas falling under the selected squares are then selected.

Simple random sampling ensures that the selection of samples by any method will permit each possible sample to have an equal chance of being selected and each item in the entire population to have an equal chance of being included in the sample. But some conditions have to be accepted for the effectiveness of the random sample. The population should be clearly defined and specified. The equality of the size of the various units of the population should be maintained and each unit should be independent, and accessibility to each unit must be provided for. If the random sampling ensures accuracy and is unbiased, it will have certain advantages.

Properly selected random sampling is bound to be mostly unbiased and representative in nature because the researcher's whims and fancies do not affect it. It is, at the same time, simple and dependable. Error would be reduced to the minimum, and if any error has crept in there is a possibility of checking and rectifying it.

Stratified Random Sampling

The population is systematically segmented under various strata prior to the selection of samples at random in stratified random sampling. The samples are selected from each stratum at a given rate for further studies. It is a combination of both random sampling and purposive sampling, a method which is most commonly employed in surveys. If the stratification is correctly made, sampling becomes effective. Maximum care, however, should be taken to make strata on the basis of common characteristics, so that the sampling may become most effective, on the one hand, and the strata become homogeneous, on the other. The stratum should be large enough to provide sufficient number of samples at random; and it is better to maintain the same ratio in selecting samples from all the strata. Of course, each stratum should be clear-cut and free from overlapping. Stratified random sampling can generally be classified under three heads; proportional stratified sample, disproportional stratified sample, and stratified weighted sampling. In respect of the first type, the number of items drawn from the stratum maintains the same proportion it has in the universe. In the second type, an equal number of cases are taken from all the strata without maintaining any such proportion. The third one includes the advantages of both. Averages are taken from each stratum, but they are given weights in proportion to the size of the stratum in the universe. The criteria for stratification may vary from problem to problem. For example, educational groups, economic groups, skilled and unskilled groups, income groups, etc., may be made separate strata, if the workers of a factory are to be studied.

Like random sampling, stratified sampling has its own advantages and disadvantages. It ensures greater control over the sample as well as the universe. It enables one to achieve a representative character; and easy replacement is possible. Concentration of units is also possible in the stratification according to common characteristics; and that saves time, and helps to achieve convenience and efficiency. However, it suffers from certain disadvantages as well. There is the possibility of bias and error in stratification, which would affect the sampling, on the one hand, and the entire result, on the other. Proportionality is a characteristic of sampling, which would possibly be disturbed by stratification. However, proportionality in homogeneous data promotes accuracy. Stratification leads to a greater amount of homogeneity of the data in the strata, and obviously leads to better accuracy. A proportional stratified sample would have a better impact in such a situation. Another disadvantage of disproportionate stratification is that it requires weighing. An undue weighing destroys the representative character of the sample. But a little care in weighing would solve this problem. But in spite of these difficulties, the stratified random sampling is universally employed as an effective method of data collection.

Systematic Sampling or Purposive Sampling

Systematic sampling never leaves matter to chance, for samples are drawn in a systematic way. The first unit is drawn at random from the selected class interval, and the remaining units are systematically and purposively drawn. Suppose the size of the population (N) is 500, and the size of sample (n) is 50; then the proportion of the sample would be (N/n = 10) 1:10. The first unit may be chosen at random from the first class interval, i.e., 1 - 10. Suppose the first unit (sample) drawn is 5, then the second unit would be 5 + 10 = 15 (5 + k) - k stands for N/n; the third sample would then be, 5 + k + k *i.e.,* 5 + 2k = 25; the third unit would be 35, the fourth 45, the fifth 55, etc. Every selection is purposive. In this connection, Adolph Jenson observes: "A purposive selection denotes the method of the selecting a number of groups of units in such a way that the selected groups together yield, as nearly as possible, the same averages or proportions as the totality with respect to those characteristics which are already a matter of statistical knowledge." Purposive selection aims at gaining the most representative sample that possesses the qualities of the entire universe.

Quota Sampling

Quota sampling is a special form of stratified sampling. The number to be selected from each stratum, which is known as quota, is selected in advance. The research workers are at liberty to select the quota from each stratum. If the skilled workers of 10 engineering units in Madras are to be studied, the units and the departments are fixed in advance and the field worker is entrusted with the responsibility of selecting the workers at random. The random sampling technique can be used in all the areas.

Multi-Stage Sampling

The process of selecting the sample is completed in several stages by this method, which is effective when the universe is very large. For example, suppose a sample survey of engineering workers is conducted in India. States are first selected, and this is followed by the selection of one or more industrial centres. Then, from the selected industrial centres, sample industrial units are selected, and from the selected units, sample workers are drawn. To generalise: First, the extensive universe is divided into homogeneous segments, leading to the selection of primary sample areas, and then to the selection of one block cluster (group) from each primary sample area. The ultimate samples are then selected from each block cluster, mostly at random, for the collection of the desired data. Thus multi-stage sampling stands for the process of sampling at various levels, stage by stage. Complete information must be available at each stage to make the multi-stage sampling effective; and there should be a listing procedure. In a complicated universe, the multi-stage sampling method is very effective.

Cluster Sampling

In cluster sampling, clusters or groups are selected as samples, instead of individuals. When the sampling unit is a cluster of elements, cluster sampling alone is effective. Suppose a sample survey is conducted on the group cohesiveness of the work life of workers in West Bengal, then Calcutta would be selected as a sample of industrial territory. In the same way, industrial units may be selected at random. Small work groups under supervisors or foremen may be selected for detailed investigation. Each such group may be considered as a cluster. In such group behavioural studies, cluster sampling yields good results.

Sampling with Probability Proportional to Size

Probability and sampling are interlinked. In sampling distribution, the element of probability is bound to be taken into account. In other words, probability statements may be made on the occurrence of certain sample results, if the validity of the probability can be preserved. The researcher must be careful to select his sample in such a way that the actual probabilities associated with the sampling distribution are not modified. Each sample should have the same probability of being selected. But samples with a probability proportional to size would yield unequal probabilities, for it is according to size that the probabilities of selection are allotted. Suppose, in a study of 10 industrial units, with the following work force, samples of workers are selected in a ratio 100:1 (workers: sample). The total sample would be 74 workers as given below (the sample is drawn proportional to size):

Table 1

Industrial Units	*Total Workers Employed*	*Total Samples Drawn*
	N	*n*
1	200	2
2	400	4
3	500	5
4	600	6
5	700	7
6	790	8
7	800	8
8	820	8
9	900	9
10	1,700	17
Total	7,410	74

Sampling with probability proportional to size ensures the size of the sample in proportion to the size of the population.

Convenience Sampling

When a sample is drawn according to one's own convenience without any systematic method, it is know as convenience sampling. Though this method is unscientific, sometimes none other than convenience sampling is possible. For example, when the universe is not clearly defined, or when the sampling unit is not clear, or a complete source list is not available, or when scientific methods cannot be effective because of the complexity of any of the factors, convenience sampling is the last resort. Though the result may not be accurate, it may throw light on some important aspects of the study. Pre-testing or pilot studies may employ this type of sampling because of its convenience because the units which are conveniently available are selected as samples.

Sequential Sampling

Inductive inference is closely associated with statistical methods. Sequential sampling is the process of selecting a small number of samples from a large population for the purpose of making inferences. The population itself is a set of large number of objects which can be the total number of conceivable observations of a particular kind that possesses certain given specified common characteristics. The whole abstract concept or the area of study that represents the population is universe. Sequential sampling is the selection of small samples on the basis of sequence from a large population for the sake of possible inferences. However, if the expected inference or decision becomes impossible on the basis of the selected small sample, more samples would become necessary for the meaningful inferences further. Sequential sampling is generally useful in the statistical quality control of finished products. In a pharmaceutical company, small samples are drawn from each batch (lot) of every drug in a sequential manner to test the quality, in which case sequential sampling is useful.

Quota Sampling

A specified number of samples which are predetermined to be selected from the given population (either stratified or simple) may be considered as a quota. Once the quota is fixed, the investigator is at liberty to collect data from any sample unit. The investigator, however, has no powers to change the quota.

On-the-spot Sampling

Sometimes some persons opt for their own inclusion or non-inclusion in the sample units. In such cases, the researcher may select such samples on-the-spot. Sometimes, again the samples duly selected may not be available. On-the-spot samples would then have to be substituted.

Generally speaking, sample selection is a skilful task which should take into account various aspects like accurate definition of the universe under the investigation (whether a definite universe, an indefinite universe or a real or hypothetical universe), a definite sampling unit, a relevant source list, the sample size, etc. The size of the sample is affected by the homogeneity or heterogeneity of the universe, the number of classes proposed, the magnitude of the population, the nature and scope of the study, practical considerations, the standard of accuracy, the type of sampling, the nature of the cases to be contacted, etc. The size of the sample and its representative nature considerably influence the result of the research. The greater the relative size of the sample, the greater the accuracy of the result. Similarly, the greater the representative nature of the sample, the greater would be the possibility of accuracy.

In fact, the greatest quality of any sample is its representative nature, which stipulates that the sample should possess the greatest degree of similarity with the universe under study. The smaller the degree of similarity, the lower its representative character. As a matter of fact, the representative nature of the sample is affected by such factors as the biased samples, the biased approach to the universe or to the population, the smallness of the size of the sample, unsystematic sample selection, inadequate and biased sampling list imperfect stratification, incomplete source list, inappropriate replacement of samples, undue emphasis on some particular aspect or situation, inappropriate selection of sample, convenience sampling or judgement sampling faulty random sampling, complexity of the universe, etc.

Once the sample is selected, it is the responsibility of the researcher to collect the data, for which schedules and questionnaires are used. We have already had a detailed discussion on schedules and questionnaires in the previous chapter. Of course, there are many factors which affect the choice of data collection which deserves some explanation here.

Factors Affecting the Choice of Data Collection Model

Managerial research and analysis do not become realistic without meaningful data. The collection of meaningful data, however, depends on the method of data collection, while the method is determined by the type of data required for analysis, which is based on the nature of the research problem. Data collection and the methods of collecting them are mainly determined by the nature of the research problem.

Usually, two types of data are used for managerial analysis. These are primary and secondary data, which have already been examined elsewhere in this chapter. Both internal and external sources facilitate data collection. The external sources of secondary data are published reports of various governmental, semi-governmental and private organisations, while the internal sources include annual reports, other published internal statistical reports, past study reports of executives, etc. The external sources of primary data are the customers, buyers, users, consumers, prospects, dealers, including stockists, wholesalers and retailers and the general public at large. The internal primary sources of data are executive value judgement, sales people, executives and managers, the work force, etc. The methods of primary data collection are different from those of secondary data collection. The secondary data may be obtained easily, either directly or indirectly, personally or by post. The primary data may be collected by the following methods:

(i) Direct personal observation;

(ii) Indirect oral investigations;

(iii) Schedules and questionnaires; and

(iv) Local reports.

These four methods have been explained elsewhere in this chapter. The selection of the method, however, depends on many factors.

Various factors which affect the choice of data collection methods are:

(i) Nature of the problem to be analysed;

(ii) Type of data and the depth of information to be collected;

(iii) Practical implications of the results of the study;

(iv) Nature of the population and the length and breadth of the universe;

(v) Background and willingness of the informants, data sources;

(vi) Complexity of the population and the universe;

(vii) Accessibility to the informants and to the population;

(viii) Availability of skilled and trained manpower;

(ix) Magnitude of the problem; approach to the informants;

(x) Attitudes and approaches of the management to research;

(xi) Rate of accuracy, impartiality and representative nature of the data to be collected.

These factors not only affect the method of data collection but also the actual process of organising the collection of data, as well as the ultimate data.

Organising Data Collection

Organising data collection is the process of systematically planning, formulating, and establishing a system of data collection; and it starts from project planning and formulation. The selection and placement of manpower, the arrangement of the sources of funds and a prudent utilisation of money — all these are included in the process of organising the collection of data. A selection of the types of data, according to the magnitude of the problem, the rationale of the study, objectives and scope of investigation, also be taken of in the process of organising the data collection activity. The preparation of the questionnaire, the probability analysis and sampling, the setting out of clear-cut objectives and the data collection — all these are organised as a part of organising data collection.

The Interview

Once the project is designed and planned, the sample is selected and the questionnaire is prepared, the next step is to collect data. Interviewing the informants is the basic function. The interview may be regarded as the "systematic method by which a person enters more or less imaginatively into the life of a comparative stranger." It elicits information, arouses feelings, determines the attitudes and reactions of the people to a particular event or object in a planned manner. The interviewer tries to unveil the various areas of the subject of investigation by imaginatively motivating the respondent to speak out, without substantial bias, in the process of interview. In a way, it is a type of probing conversation, which is a very powerful instrument for obtaining information. The interviewer is expected to show a considerable amount of skill and imagination in conducting the interview, and he should be able to motivate and encourage the interviewee, so that accuracy of information he elicits may be maximised. The most effective interview is the one that creates a positive interest in the mind of the respondent to reveal all the possible areas of investigation objectively and without prejudice.

Interviews are usually classified as:

(i) Structured interveiws;

(ii) Unstructured interviews;

(iii) Focused interviews;

(iv) Repetitive interviews;

(v) Formal interviews;

(vi) Informal interviews;

(vii) Standardised interviews; and

(viii) Open interviews.

In the structured interviews, the given questions are designed, for which the answers are obtained. It means that the answers to the questions are preconceived and classified into possible groups. In codified questionnaires, possible answers ar prestructured and codified (see section on "Questionnaire" in Chapter 4).

Unstructured interviews do not put any control on the respondents, They may be in the form of free discussions. This method is usually employed in pilot studies. When the information sought for is a detailed appreciation, interpretation, or an expression of emotion, unstructured interviews are appropriate. For example, if the details of an industrial accident are evaluated, the respondents will be asked to narrate the incident in response to a few open-ended questions

A focused interview focuses the attention of the informant on a particular aspect and gets his reaction, If the impact of an incentive scheme is to be studied, the one who is subjected to that incentive scheme would be asked to explain his reactions on it; his experiences, attitudes, emotional response, etc., would be elicited by the individuals concerned.

An interview is repetitive in nature when it is desired to note the gradual influence of some social, psychological or economic process. Such interviews are conducted at regular intervals to mark the gradual effect repetitively. In order to study the impact of advertising for an industrial machinery, a repetitive study is necessary to investigate the gradual effect, say the informative effect, the educative effect, and the persuasive effect. Just an advertisement or an interview may not produce a substantial impact in such cases. A repetitive interview is, however, not very easy, and is costly and time-consuming, though it may become essential in respect of certain specific studies.

There are formal and informal interviews. In connection with making an observation, informal interviews are conducted. It may be in the form of a casual conversation or a discussion. But the researcher collects the necessary information from such informal interviews.

Formal interviews are conducted formally, with the help of formal questionnaires, at the appointed time and place. The samples are also selected systematically in the formal interviews. In other words, a formal interview is systematically planned and formally conducted.

Standardised interviews are usually conducted with the help of highly structured schedules or questionnaires. The polling interview is an apt example for this type of interviews. All the respondents are asked questions, in the same form, in the same order, and without any deviation. Though a comparative analysis is possible in such interviews, deep studies are usually not possible with such stereo-typed interviews.

In open interviews, informants are given sufficient opportunity to talk freely on the subject matter, and the researcher collects the necessary data from such open discussions. In pilot studies and observations, such interviews are very useful.

In many types of interviews, an interview guide is used. It is a brief written document that gives an outline of the various aspects of the topic of investigation. It gives a general plan for the interview. It helps in securing comparable data in the different interviews, while it enables one to collect the same range of items from various informants. Undue dependence on memory is avoided, while it acts as a tool for effective interview, especially in the early stages.

It is better for the interviewer to bear in mind certain principles to conduct an effective interview. The researcher should be skilful enough to establish contact with the respondents. A prior appointment would avoid much inconvenience. The interviewer should be polite and straightforward; he should be in a position to create an interest in the minds of the respondents. Securing rapport and recall is also the responsibility of the interviewer; and he should be able to give encouragement and guidance. The informants should not be placed in a puzzling or embarrassing position. Probing or leading questions should be avoided as far as possible, while self-confidence and respect should be created so that the interviewee is made to feel that he is the most appropriate person to provide the required information. The interviewer should be skilful enough to record the information without creating any element of doubt in the mind of the informant, and to conclude the interview well.

Scope and Limitations of Interview

The interview has been developed as one of the most prominent sources of information as far as a researcher is concerned. Not only in social sciences, but also in the management science, the interview technique plays a very vital role in data collection. Management scientists now depend on the interview for the collection of data in support of their managerial analysis. This is especially true, because of the emphasis on the human factor of the enterprise. In the areas of industrial dispute, motivation, workers' participation, labour welfare, etc., the interview method is the most effective tool for the collection of data. Similarly, in respect of the social aspect of business, consumer behaviour, market segmentation, product and pricing policies, the interview is the best method of collecting the primary data. In respect of the functional area of marketing, the societal approach to marketing impels the marketing man to determine what is most suited for the maximisation of social welfare. Interviewing the people concerned is the only source of data in this respect. Instead of selling what is produced, efforts are now made to determine what is actually required to be produced. The intrerview technique has, therefore, attained prominence in the management science.

It not only provides information according to the questionnaire; but the investigator himself gets as opportunity to personally observe the informants and the situations. It enables him to study even the events which are not open to observation. In order to study the abstract and intangible personal qualities and traits like attitude, feeling, reaction, etc., the interview method has great advantages. It enables the interviewer to obtain valuable information from a person. There is, moreover, an opportunity for estimating bias or ambiguity.

However, there is some percentage of possibility for ambiguity to creep in. The possibility of bias, too, is not ruled out. Many informants may be reluctant to provide adequate information, while some may not be amenable to the interview itself. The interviewer should take into account the behavioural aspect of the interviewee if his interview is to be successful. But many investigators lack this skill, which affects the reliability of data. Again, the interview method is very subjective — a fact which often leads to bias. At the same time, the verficiation of the information is also difficult. Thus there are merits and demerits. Yet the prominence of the interview method has never been falsified by any of these problems.

Eliciting Response

An interview may be considered to be successful only if the interviewer is able to elicit information from the informants with the minimum of bias and ambiguity. Establishing rapport between the interviewer and the respondent is a very essential aspect of eliciting response. It is a state of friendliness to the extent that the respondent is willing and capable of presenting the necessary details to the interviewer. When such a rapport is etablished, the latter can be confident of the former's co-operation in providing the necessary information. This may be the reason why Goode and Hatt have remarked: "The interview is not simply a conversation. It is, rather, a pseudo-conversation. In order to be successful, it must have all the warmth and personality exchange of a conversation, with the clarity and guidelines of scientific searching. Consequently, the interviewer cannot merely lose himself in being friendly. He must introduce himself as though beginning a conversation; but from the beginning the additional element of respect, of professional competence, should be maintained."[1]

---

1. Goode, William J. and Hatt, Paul K., *Methods in Social Research,* McGraw Hill Kogakusha, Ltd., 1952, p. 38.

Thus, the technique of eliciting response consists of establishing a rapport between the interviewer and the interviewee, gaining his confidence, maintaining a mutual regard and recognition, creating a warmth and friendliness between them, mutual identification, and obtaining the necessary information without much bias or ambiguity. The skill and insight of the investigator have a long way to go in this respect. The interviewer should be able to motivate the respondent to narrate the various aspects of the subject matter objectively, without fear or favour; while opportunity should be limited for the former to interrupt. However, the interviewer's scope for encouraging and guiding the informant to make a free and fair approach to the interview should not be limited, though leading questions should be avoided. Even if the latter beats about the bush, the former should patiently reveal his inclination towards what he talks, and gradually the discussion should be brought back to the track. The interviewer should always be a patient listener, though some sort of brief guiding remarks cannot be ruled out. The principle of "customer is king." should always be adopted by the investigator;and his approach should be straightforward and frank. He should be able to convince the informant that his views and approaches are highly regarded; and no argument or qurarrel should be developed. The former should make it a point to eliminate his bias; if any, so that it should not in any way influence the views of the informants. In a nutshell, mutual regard, respect, recognition, and objectivity are the basic ingredients of any successful interview; and by eliciting appropriate responses, the interviewer is able to carry the interview forward skilfully, until adequate information has been collected. Probing questions would, sometimes, become necessary, though leading questions are not desirable.

Probing Questions

On many occasions, it would become necessary for the interviewer to put questions directed toward deeper and difficult issues. For this purpose, the interview should not be highly structured, for that would narrow the range of possibilities. On certain occasions, the respondents may not understand the question while some may be indifferent about certain questions. Again, some informants may not be willing to give a certain type of information, while others would be biased against either the question or the answer containing the information. On all such occasions, the interviewer is expected to put more detailed and probing questions. This is, perhaps, the reason why, in addition to questions of "yes" and "no" answers, a number of questions calling for detailed answers are included in the questionnaires and schedules.

The interviewer cannot be satisfied with some formal answer to the questions. On the contrary, he should be convinced that the answer is comprehensive and inclusive of all the necessary pieces of information, and is relevant. It should also be ensured that the response received is adequate enough. Very often, this may require further questioning. Again, a deeper probe would become necessary when the interviewee is not able to answer the quesion. However, when the respondent deliberately avoids giving certain information, it is no use probing. In order to avoid any embarrassing situation, certain people would tend to give a "don't know" answer. It is here that a skilful appoach on the part of the interviewer becomes inevitable to elicit a more useful response, sometimes indirectly. It may be an "antagonistic probe," The rapport and the personal relations of the interviewer with the interviewee usually act as a vital tool for obtaining appropriate information. However, such good relations are not an end in themselves. If the situation demands antagonism it must be used, but only as a last resort, and only when all the other techniques fail. The interviewer should be tactful enough to use probing questions to obtain indepth information. In the absence of a skilful approach, there may be misunderstanding in the mind of the informant, leading to the failure of the interview itself. The interviewer should, therefore, take the greatest care not only to obtain the information he needs but to record it properly and systematically.

Recording and Closing

Conducting an interview and eliciting a reponse would be meaningless if the interviewer is not able to record adequately the results of the interview. The interviewer's ability to hear, comprehend, grasp, and record becomes essential if the interview is to be successful. Even for a highly structured questionnaire, some amount of skill is necessary not only to write the answers like yes, no, etc., but to record a certain degree of appreciation, comment and remark. During the course of the conversation, the interviewer should be able to make the answers without any extra effort or fuss. Nowadays management research or social research has increasingly become group research, and the interviewer is not the one who analyses the tabulated data. In such cases, accurate recording is obviously inevitable, because the actual interaction between the interviewer and the interviewee cannot be known to the analyst unless the information is properly included in the interview protocol. Even if the interviewer himself is the analyst, it may not be possible for any single individual to remember all that has been discussed with a large number of informants during the course of interview. The interviewer should, therefore, ensure that the information revealed by the informant is adequately recorded in the interview schedule.

It is necessary for the interviewer to record certain qualifying facts that assist in the interpretation of certain answers. When the respondents gives a series of consistent answers consecutively and takes leave of the interviewer immediately, the interviewer should have the necessary skill to check that all the necessary facts and figures have been recorded. When the interview is of an intensive, qualitative nature, with many structured probe questions, the problem of recording becomes difficult. It is here that a careful approach on the part of the interviewer can ease the situation. In certain cases there is the danger of omitting certain points in a hurry; or some answers are unheard in the speed of the conversation. The interviewer can, then, politely interrupt by asking, 'Would you mind repeating it?' The investigator should be skilful enough to make a recording.

The closing of an interview is equally decisive, especially in pilot surveys and pre-tests. In many cases, closing is more difficult than the opening. It should keep alive sweet memories of a cordial discussion.; and it should retain the beautiful web of friendliness that the interviewer has spun. The latter would dispel the illusion of great cordiality and friendliness, if he brusquely snatches away the papers and mumbles a good-bye. It is always good to prepare the ground before ending the interview — prepare the ground for it in the final stage of the conversation. This would set the stage for the final closing. To be precise, the interviewer should bear in mind that the final leave-taking should be dramatic so that a considerable impact may be left on the minds of the informants. A situation should not be created by the interviewer to make the experience a drudgery for the informants.

Analysis

An analysis of the data is equally important. A careful planning of the analytical framework should, therefore, be envisaged by the researcher. The basic ingredient of any analysis is the scientific method and the testing of hypotheses. However, in case studies, hypothesis may sometimes be absent. In normal circumstances, the statement of a hypothesis and an elaboration of the experimental design would provide for a rational analysis of the data.

An analysis should be preceded by tabulation and presentation of data in the most intelligible, attractive, appropriate, and comprehensible form. It would enable the researcher to identify relationship and to make inductions and deductions, wherever necessary. On the basis of statistical tables, it is possible to present the facts in the form of diagrams, graphs, pictograms, and statistical and mathematical models. Representation and analysis would become easier with the help of these tools. The analysis of data would throw light on the various problems areas, enabling the researcher to identify ways and means of arriving at a solution. "The problems raised by the analysis of data are directly related to the complexity of the hypothesis or hypotheses." Sometimes, the analysis would lead to rejection of the hypothesis, though most of the times it would enable the researcher to test and prove the validity of the hypothesis in the given situation. Research is often based on observation, while the analysis enables him to arrive at final observations and conclusions.

Analysis would be easier if all the relevant factors are known. But the appearance of an anomalous empirical regularity or the absence of an expected regularity would often be possible. Such aspects require the analysis. Similarly, the data gathered for some purpose are usually used for certain other purposes. In such cases, too, an anomalous empirical regularity may occur, when secondary analysis is not capable of being stated in terms of probability. However, this is very common in managerial analysis.

Statistical and mathematical representations have attained prominence in research analysis in recent times. Frequently distribution, tabulation, coefficient of correlation, regression, standard deviation, econometric models and various other mathematical techniques are usually employed in research and managerial analyses (some of these methods have been briefly dealt with in Chapters 10 to 15.) Percentages, ratios and proportions are also of very common use which simplify the process of comparison. The percentage is always useful in putting qualitative characteristics in a numerical form, making it possible for the researcher to compare the various quantitative and qualitative aspects in the observation. It reduces frequency distributions to a common base making comparison easier. However, there is the danger that some researchers tend to entertain the idea that mere comparison in terms of percentages is the sole purpose of analysis. "While percentages are a great aid to communication through simplification, they are also susceptible to misuse by obscuring signficant facts." In spite of many of its limitations, a statistical analysis of data enables the researcher to make a logical ordering which is the prerequisite of logical conclusions, preceded by interpretation, explanation, and specification, as Kendall and Lazarsfeld have put it.

In order to make a logical generalisation, one may observe that there are three phases in the the process of managerial analysis. These are:

(i) Establishing the objectives of the organisation, the purpose of the analysis, and a general understanding of the environment;

(ii) Developing relationships between variables (both dependent and independent), model-building, and identification of solutions; and

(iii) Evaluation and implementation considerations.

The first phase lays the foundation for the actual analysis, while the second phase is the action phase leading to a definite interpretation. The final phase is the evaluation phase, which investigates the validity of the recommended course of action.

An analysis of data for managerial research starts with an overall observation of the organisational climate and philosophy on the basis of the organisational objectives. Objectives are set in measurable terms; and the hierarchy of objectives is identified. The first stage involves investigating the business environment, identifying the problems areas, and determining the general nature of the business environment. It also includes the background preparation for the identification and understanding of the major determinants and environment forces. It is here that the analyst establishes an exact statement of the purpose, objective, scope, and methodology of the analysis. The decision involves an abstraction of the real life situations; and hence any managerial study starts with an analysis of these situations. In other words, an analysis of the whole system of the business and its sub-systems is a part of the first stage of any managerial analysis. An investigation of the environment and an identification of the objectives are followed by the establishment of the specific criteria to be used to measure the extent to which the objectives are to be achieved. The objectives are also to be compared, and priorities to be set in relation to the direct operating cost. Thus, the introductory part of the analysis ensures an overall analysis of the organisation and the environment in which it operates.

The analysis further depicts the system it deals with and identifies the possible course of action. "All the tools, methodologies, or techniques which are applicable in managerial analysis depict the environment as a model." A model is a physical or symbolic representation of the relevant aspects of the reality or system with which one is concerned. A series of connected and identifiable relationships that essentially demonstrate the various cause-effect or action-result links are represented by such models. Quantitative analysis and systems analysis are utilised for this purpose. A recommended course of action is chosen at this juncture. Obviously, a statement of assumptions is one of the baisc characteristics of the research analysis. At the final stage the validity of the recommended solution is evaluated in order to arrive at the degree of confidence. This involves a determination of the validity of the data inputs which are the bases for the determination of the relationships between the variables. Of course, the validity of the analysis and the relationships of the variables depend on the accuracy of the data.

Variables

It is evident that a determination of the relationship between the variables is a part and parcel of any analysis. It is, therefore, appropriate to make a reference to this concept. Mathematical and algebraic treatments are common in the process of analysis, as already mentioned. "The first and the most obvious distinction between algebra and analysis, on the one hand, and arithmetic, on the other, lies in use of 'variable' numbers, denoted by symbolic letters instead of particular numbers."

"A variable number is any number, an unspecified number, from a certain given set of real numbers, and it is always symbolised by a letter such as x, y or t." The variables usually stand for given values, and the whole set of possible values makes up the range of the variables. A range of variation, say, a set of numbers from which the values of the variables can be selected at will, is implied by a variable. Many variables have a range, including all real numbers, while no explicit reference need be made. Certain other variables have more restricted ranges, the range of positive numbers, of numbers between zero and unity or of integers only. Here, the range should be clearly indicated in the definition of the variables. In common terms, variables may be defined as the common letters like x, y, or z used to denote the common factors or characteristics of certain situations represented by the tabulated data in terms of a given set of real numbes.

In case a variable x represents the values of all real numbers of a particular case (say, income distribution of workers): and if the numbers lie between two given numbers a and b, then its range is called the interval (a, b). A variable is continuous if its range is either the whole set of real numbers or any interval of the set. The values of a continuous variable can be ordered so that they are indefinitely dense and without gaps. It takes values successively in the increasing order of magnitude, and we describe this by saying that "the variable increases continuously in value over such and such an interval." The values of the variables make up a range of variation which must be considered as a whole, and any change in the value of a variable is essentially timeless. A discontinuous variable, on the other hand, has a range which is neither the whole set of real numbers nor any interval of the set. The values of such variables cannot be arranged in the order of magnitude without gaps.

There are dependent and independent variables also. An independent variable is the one that exists independently, while a dependent variable depends on an independent variable for its occurrence. When advertising expenditure determines the sales revenue, advertising expenditure is independent, and the sales revenue is dependent on the independent variable, the advertising expenditure.

It is easier to study the relations of two variables, one of which is taken as a function of the other. There are also relations involving many variables; and by applying such relations to the interpretation of scientific phenomena, it is possible to analyse situations concerned with large numbers of linter-related variables. Suppose the dependent variable sales revenue (*s*) is a function of the independent variables, advertising expenditure (*a*), per capita income of the people (*p*), and the sales force motivation in terms of salary (*i*). Then, is general, we write:

$$s = f(a, p, i),$$

i.e., *s* is the function of *a, p* and *i.*

If there are $x_1, x_2, x_3 \ldots. x_n$ independent variables for the dependent variable m, then the function can be written as follows:

$$m = f(x_1, x_2, x_3 \ldots. x_n)$$

Many properties of scientific phenomena can be described by measurable quantities. However, there are certain other properties which are capable of order without the additive character necessary for direct measurement. Such variables can be described by ordered but non-measurable variables.

We have examined the methods of data collection in this chapter. Sample survey is a very popular method of data collection as we have noticed. However, when the universe is small and manageable it is always better to choose census survey. When the population is large, sample survey is bound to be the most convenient form of data collection. As a primary step of sample survey, therefore, an experienced researcher would make a sample design.

Sampling Design

A sampling design is a well formulated scheme of the researcher to obtain definite sample from a specific population. It includes the methods, techniques and procedures adopted by the researcher to fix a sample size, select sample informants, and fix the sampling procedure, so that appropriate sample data can be obtained from the universe under study. A good sampling design may satisfy certain characteristics viz : *(a)* A good sampling design implies truly representative samples, *(b)* Sample must be selected without bias, *(c)* Sampling error must be as minimum as possible; *(d)* Sample selected must be economical, *(e)* The result of the sample study must be capable to be applied in the whole universe with a reasonable level of confidence, and *(f)* Sample must be adequate enough to produce a result without substantial deviation.

Sampling design may adopt probability sampling or non-probability sampling as mentioned earlier in this chapter. The former provides every item in the universe having equal chance for being included in the sample. Non-probability sampling, on the other hand, does not provide equal chance for all items. It means that items in the non-probability sampling are deliberately selected by the researcher with a specific purpose. Hence, it is otherwise known as deliberate sampling or purposive sampling.

Some general steps can be suggested in formulating a sampling design. These steps are:

(i) *Proper Definition of the Universe:* The whole source of data or all the people from whom the information must be collected form the universe. (Population represents the whole set of data). Proper definition of the universe necessitates the researcher to specify the total number of people from whom samples can be selected. (Specify finite or inflinite universe).

(ii) *Specifying the Sample Size:* Once the universe is identified, total number of samples must be specified which should be adequate enough to properly represent the universe.

(iii) Adopting a proper sample frame or preparing a source list: *i.e.*, list of people who can be used as informants.

(iv) *Identifying the Sampling Unit:* Which represents the specific unit from where the sample is to be drawn. It can be a state, distirct, an area, an institution, or an industry.

(v) *Specifying the Population Parameters:* Determinant factors or homogeneous characteristtics of the population, must be specified.

(vi) *Fixing the Sampling Procedure:* The way or method how to go ahead in conducting the sample survey.

(vii) *Resource Planning (Budgeting):* Planning the monetary resources to be used in sampling so as to economise the whole process.

Certain precautions must be taken care of by every researcher in designing a good sample. Minimising the sampling error is, perhaps, the most required aspect of sampling; *i.e.*, the least minimum variation from the population parameters must be ensured. Other important features include checking of defective measuring devices, minimising bias, avoiding inappropriate sampling frame, avoiding indeterminancy of the informants (certain informants under observation behave much differently) avoiding in iappropriate sample size, maintaining the time limit, etc.

To conclude it can be remarked that data collection is the most pivotal task of a researcher. Data make the most important raw material for a good final output, or a good result. Survey is the best method for data collection, particularly sample survey when the universe is large. Sampling design attains importance in this context. Most often, however, a reseacher's data collection efforts are facilitated by an appropriate hypothesis and the scientific method. Next chapter deals with scientific method and hypothesis.

Chapter 6

Scientific Method and Hypothesis

Research plays an important role in managerial functions, not only in general management but also in functional areas. Managerial research is of great utility value if the method used is scientific, while hypothesis is an inseparable element of the scientific method. An attempt has, therefore, been made here to throw some light on the scientific method, and the role of hypothesis in it.

Scientific Method

The term "science" refers to the body of systematic and organised knowledge which makes use of the scientific method to advance knowledge in a particular field of enquiry. It refers to clear concepts, theory, and other accumulated knowledge developed by scientific methods and by a test of hypotheses. It may be treated as "method of approach to the entire empirical world." The scientific method is a method of systematic analysis leading to observations, propositions, and testing of hypotheses, and contributes to the organised body of knowledge. Science portrays a basic relationship between theory and fact; the scientific method deals with both theory and fact. A *fact* is an empirically verifiable observation, while *theory* deals with the established relationships between facts. The scientific method does not, therefore, refer to a mere collection of facts, but to interpretation, observation and theoretical treatment as well. Facts and theory are the two sides of the same coin, which is the scientific method. A consistent interaction between these two elements results in scientific knowledge. The collection of data (facts) and their theoretical treatment are the tools of the scientific method.

Theory provides the basis for the scientific method. Theory-based studies are strong in conceptual framework and classification of facts, enabling the researcher to crystallise the problem and choose the data relevant to it. Theoretical treatment facilitates the process of summarising while theory predicts facts. The possibility for extrapolation from the known to the unknown is the result of a strong theoretical base. For example, the growth of trade unionism and its impact on the decline of production and output can be theorised. Similarly, a strong theoretical base enables one to appreciate the facts that are necessary for a scientific enquiry, and underscores the gap, if any, in knowledge.

Theory is initiated by fact, while the latter is uncovered by the former. Both are in constant interaction with each other. Facts form the basis of theory, which is reformulated, redefined, and clarified, wherever necessary, by facts. Sometimes, new theoretical problems are presented by facts. Sometimes, a fact would falsify the existing theories and become the basis of a new theory. It is, therefore, evident that a theory should be adjusted to the facts. In certain cases, new and additional facts may redefine the theory. Induction and deduction from facts assist one to formulate and reformulate any theory. Theory is general and fact is particular; and the latter provides stimulus for the former. Values make a considerable impact on theoretical expression. To sum up, it may be asserted that the scientific method consists of theoretical treatment, factual expression and value judgement.

An important characteristic of science is that a series of postulates is its foundation, while assumptions are its basic organs. Postulates are valid observations, while may not always be proved, though they are true. The scientific method may, therefore, accommodate the evaluation of assumptions and the proving of postulates, among such other things as the collection and analysis of facts, a theoretical treatment and testing of hypothesis, in addition to a rational and systematic value judgement of organisational goals and managerial effectiveness. As science is not an end in itself but a means to an end, the scientific method cannot be considered as anything but a method of attainment of the means. As far as a manager is concerned, this method is an aid to decision making and problem-solving. It also assists one in making correct value judgements and enlightens the decision-maker to make an appropriate evaluation of the situation. It offers alternative methods for cost reduction, on the one hand, and provides a means for predicting and forecasting, on the other.

A practical application of science makes the scientific method more meaningful, as far as a managerial analyst is concerned. In this context, it is relevant to distinguish between pure science and applied science. Pure science stems basically from scientific experiments and studies of theoretical interest, while applied science is of practical value. But the scientific method cannot merely be limited to a particular practical problem or its solution. It goes much beyond it The solution of a simple practical problem is possible on the basis of common sense; but a scientific method of solution involves controlled experimentation. While broader generalisations and interpretations are associated with scientific solutions, scientific experimentation is made against the existing body of generalisations. Applied research puts theory to the test, and contributes to new facts. Conceptual clarification, too, is facilitated by applied research and assists in the integration of existing theories. Scientific research should assist in the application of theoretical knowledge to specific problem areas. Pure and applied areas of research cannot, therefore, be competitive; they are complementary. "For, ultimately, the great power of science appears to lie in the development of general principles which are applicable to many concrete problems."[1]

Science deals with conceptual systems and phenomena, which are investigated. Concepts are logical expressions created by sense impressions, percepts, or even by fairly complex experiences. They are the foundation of human communication and thought which symbolise empirical relationships and phenomena. Both concepts and facts are abstractions; but it is facts which express both concepts and phenomena. A logical construct of concepts or phenomena may, therefore, be called a fact. Concepts, on the other hand, consist of logical abstracts and generalisations of the sense of impressions, while phenomena stand for the factual expression of the concepts perceived.

The scientific method makes use of all these elements, and hypothesis has a central position in it. The hypothesis, therefore, deserves an elaborate treatment.

Scientific Method in Managerial Research

The scientific method is a systematic method of investigation, evaluation, experimentation, interpretation and theorising. It is characterised by critical discrimination generality and system, and empirical verification, according to Wolfe. Generally speaking, the scientific method is characterised by a systematic study, based on theory and facts, universality or generality, objectivity of observation, predictability of results, and verifiability of the

1. Goode & Hatt, *Methods in Social Research,* McGraw-Hill Kogakusha, p. 38.

phenomenon. It consists of a number of formalities and procedures, which are time consuming. Time management is the basic requirement for the success of managerial decisions. Many management problems require timely solutions and decisions. In such situations, the management may not have adequate time at its disposal to make use of scientific studies before arriving at decisions. Laboratory experiments occupy a prominent place in the scientific method, which may not be useful in many situations of managerial decision-making.

Physical science phenomena may be subjected to laboratory tests and physical control. Most of the managerial policies and decisions, however, affect human beings. An individual's behaviour differs substantially from that of another from time to time, place to place and environment to environment and it cannot be placed under absolute control, for it is very difficult to employ the scientific method in the pratice of management. Despite the development of dynamic methods of management information systems, many decision areas, such as those of labour productivity, materials handling, product planning and consumer behaviour, require complex data to be analysed as a part of the scientific method which may not be appropriate in quick managerial decisions. The greater the complexity of the data, the lesser is the possibility of accurancy and the lesser is its utility in the management process.

Consumer behaviour, a trade union's behaviour, workers' behaviour, the tastes, temperaments and fashions of the population at large, the demonstration effect in the market, technological development, political change, social change, geographic change, and such other forces influence business policy a great deal. Many of these forces, especially the human factor, are unpredictable. Despite a thorough scanning of the environment, a perfect prediction, on the basis of these variables, is just not possible, as it is in the physical sciences. The scientific method of research, therefore, has a limited applicability in such managerial decision areas.

The scientific method is effective in the physical sciences, because physical phenomena can be verified and evaluated by the senses; but many managerial factors, like the behavioural aspects in organisation, cannot be absolutely tested or verified physically. As a result, the scope of the scientific method in management is profoundly affected. Many management problems cannot be empirically tested, in spite of the extensive use of quantitative techniques in the latter half of this century. Though quantitative techniques are available for certain areas — inventory control, transportation problems, servicing, decision-making, marketing and promotional effectiveness, production planning — the complexity of these techniques makes them unpopular with many practitioners. At the same time, the scientific method does not find favour with many organisations and functional executives because of the heavy demand it makes on their time, exposure, resources and manpower. Even in the sciences where quantitative, empirical and scientific methods are extensively employed, the qualitative approach is made simultaneously, thus limiting the importance of scientific method.

The performance evaluation of the sales force is usually made by combining both quantitative and qualitative performance, though there is a possibility of making a quantitative analysis. The experimental method is seldom used in managerial analysis, unlike in the physical sciences, while the cause-effect relationship cannot be established beyond doubt in many cases. For example, there is a relationship between the sales revenue and the advertising budget; but it is not easy to establish which is the actual cause or effect because both are interlinked. The exact magnitude of the effect of each on the other cannot be easily determined, for various other factors — economic variables, market forces, changes in fashion, tastes, temperaments, and the competitors' policies — make a substantial impact on the sales volume. Similarly, business policies, marketing opportunities and product specifications attain dynamic dimensions in a dynamic economic, social and business environment. Evidently research, scientific methods and their results have very little policy implications in such situations; and that is why the resoures invested on research do not yield any considerable returns. However, the scientific method that empirically tests a hypothesis has a far-reaching utility value, not only for theoretical purposes, but also for practical applications and policy decisions.

Hypothesis

It has already been pointed out that the testing of a hypothesis is an important characteristic of the scientific method. It is a prerequisite of any successful research, for it enables us to get rid of vague approaches and meaningless interpretations. It establishes the relationship of concept with theory, and specifies the test to be applied especially in the context of a meaningful value judgement. The hypothesis, therefore, plays a very pivotal role in the scientific research method.

A hypothesis is a sceptical proposition, formulated to be tested in a certain given situation as a part of research, which states what the researcher is looking for. It is a tentative generalisation, according to Lundberg. Its validity can be determined only when it is tested. A close relationship, however, exists between theory and hypothesis; and the latter can be tested with the help of analysis of the data and facts. The hypothesis is, therefore, closely linked wlith both theory and facts, though it is neither. However, the testing and proving of a hypothesis leads to theory, though all hypotheses do not necessarily result in theory formation. Specific assum-ptions are generally involved in hypotheses relating to the level of abstraction.

Nature of Hypothesis

Thus, a hypothesis is skeptical, thought it is based on an observation, until it is tested. It can take the shape of a proposition which may involve assumptions in the given situation or context. It always looks forwad, since the skeptical proposition based on some observation or assumption need not be proved valid by being tested. This is the reason why no hypothesis is proved without empirical test. Goode and Hatt are therefore, right when they assert, "A hypothesis looks forward. It is a proposition which can be put to a test to determine its validity. It may seem contrary to or in accord with, common sense. It may prove to be correct or incorrect. In any event, however, it leads to an empirical test. Whatever the outcome, the hypothesis is a question put in such a way that an answer of some kind can be forthcoming. It is an example of the organised skepticism of science, the refusal to accept any statement without empirical verification."[2]

When the answer to the question put forward in a hypothesis is found, and when the hypothesis is tested and proved, the relation between variables in the hypothesis is confirmed and the proposition established, leading to the formulation of a theory. Hypothesis is, therefore, closely linked with both theory and facts though it is neither.

However, testing and proving of hypothesis may lead to theory although all hypotheses may not necessarily result in theory. Similarly, a hypothesis makes use of variables, and the relationship between variables can be established in proving the hypothesis, though it need not always result in formulation of theory. Actually speaking, it is the scientific method, which is closely linked with the hypothesis, that makes the basis for theory. The theory rests on empirical studies, value judgements and factual expressions, for which formulation and testing of hypothesis may become necessary.

While testing of a hypothesis may prove or disprove a theory, a theory, facilitates formulation of further hypotheses. On the other hand, testing of hypothesis will result in substantial contribution to existing theory or in generation of a new theory. Goode and Hatt have made a very relevant observation in this respect. "Every worthwhile theory, then, permits the formulation of additional hypothesis. These, when tested, are either

2. Goode & Hatt, *Methods in Social Research,* McGraw-Hill. Kogakusha, p. 56.

proved or disproved and in turn constitute further tests of the original theory. In either case, they may be of use to existing theory and may make possible the formulation of still other hypotheses. Such a simple outline, unfortunately, fails to indicate that the formulation of useful hypothesis is one of the most difficult steps in scientific method"[3]

Scope of Hypothesis

It is evident that hypothesis skeptically deals with the variables relating to the real life situation which provides the propositions and assumptions. If, by being tested, they help the formulation of theory. While scientific method helps to formulate theory, hypothesis is at the centre of scientific method. Science, on the other hand, integrates concepts, theory and accumulated knowledge developed from hypothesis, analytical framework and experimentation.

Thus, hypothesis is part of every organised knowledge, basis for analysis and inspiration for investigation. As scientific method involves determination of facts through observation, investigation and establishment of causal relationships between variables, hypothesis, which is part of scientific method, helps in all these activities. Thus, hypothesis has tremendous scope in science and scientific method.

As mentioned earlier, testing of hypothesis establishes relationship between variables which predicts the same relationships in identical situations giving birth to principles. Thus, hypothesis leads to principles which are the basis for every human activity. To sum up, both theory and principle which act as the foundation of practice on hypotheses. The scope of hypothesis is, therefore, extensive, and hence it has various sources.

Sources of Hypothesis

A researcher gets hypothesis from many sources, though his own thoughts, observation, investigation and value judgement can be the greatest source of hypothesis. The researcher's own observation helps him to formulate a hypothesis leading to investigation resulting in induction, deduction, invention or discovery which helps in the formulation of theory. A managerial researcher may generally identify his hypotheses from the following sources:

(i) Observation in the day-to-day-practice;

(ii) Suggestions from functional executives;

(iii) Suggestions from the shop floor;

---

3. Michael V.P. *Communication and Research for Management,* Himalaya Publlishing House, 1992, p. 261.

(iv) Scientific theory;

(v) Analogies (similarity between two phenomena);

(vi) Experiences or observations of the competitors;

(vii) Observations of the past studies; and

(viii) Findings of the Research and Development Department.

Observations in the Day-to-day Pratice

Very often, managerial analysts identify the hypothesis from the day-to-day practices. Research problem for the managerial researcher is generally a management problem itself. Every management problem may bring with it relevant hypothesis, since cause-effect relation may be involved in it. Such cause-effect relation is generally observed during the course of day-to-day practice.

Hypothesis generally determines the relationship between variables, say: independent variables are related to dependent variables. If the productivity doubles in a company which paid 25 per cent bonus as against 12.5 per cent bonus paid by all other companies in the same industry or the same locality, one can formulate a hypothesis correlating the two variables payment of bonus (independent variable) and increase in productivity (dependent variable). This relationship, *viz.,* double the bonus double the productivity, can be observed in the day-to-day practice on the basis of which the researcher can formulate his hypothesis for being tested.

Suggestions from Functional Executives

Managerial analysis is designed to aid managerial decisions. These decisions may be pertaining to *(a)* organisational goals and objectives at the top management or general management level, *(b)* operational management or strategic management, *(c)* developing plans for an effective operation for the accomplishment of objectives, *(d)* proper combination of human and physical resources for effective operational management, *(e)* identifyng solutions for the problems which affect the functional activities, and *(f)* monitoring the results to conform its contribution to the objectives.

In a nutshell, every managerial analysis is, one way or the other, connected to the accomplishment of objectives, while accomplishment of objectives depends on how the functional and operational departments succeed in operating successfully. Functional executives and managers are therefore, the best judges to identify the various forces which affect their operational efficiency. They are the people who may first notice the strengths, weaknesses, opportunities and threats which stand in the way of their operational effectiveness, and the variables which affect such factors. Such variables may be directly or indirectly related which are valuable elements in the hypothesis as far as the managerial researcher is concerned. Thus, functional executives are bound to be an important source of hypothesis.

Suggestions from the Shop-Floor

Shop-floor is another important source of hypothesis, since shop-floor is one of the most important problem areas for management and managerial analysis. Shop-floor is the area where most of the human, behavioural, operational, and industrial relation problems arise which deserve immediate attention of managerial analysts. Many of the problems and the determinant factors arise on the shop-floor itself. Hence, the shop-floor executives are competent enough to report a number of problems and the factors involved. Such factors and their correlation will make hypothesis.

Scientific Theory

Science, scientific methods and theories are good sources of hypotheses, not only for managerial analysts but for all researchers. Scientific method is examined in this chapter at considerable length. While hypotheses are important aspects of science and scientific method, they lead to the formation of further hypotheses. Scientific theory also facilitates derivation of mathematical models, OR models and even simulation models which help the managerial analysts to formulate hypotheses.

Science deals with conceptual systems and phenomena which are investigated with the help of hypothesis, while hypothesis symbolise empirical relationships and phenomena. Similarly, scientific method accommodates the evaluation of assumptions and proving of postulates, for which testing of hypothesis becomes necessary, while it provdes basis for further hypothesis. On the other hand, scientific experimentation is based on skeptical assumptions and propositions while experimentation helps to prove or disprove hypothesis and generate new hypothesis.

Analogies (Similarity between Phenomena)

Analogy is a similarity between phenomena which represents a process of reasoning. Analogy is generally drawn from similarity of phenomena. Phennomenon is a thing that is perceived by either the researcher himself or anybody else like an executive or a practitioner, or another researcher or R & D staff. Similarly in such phenomena noticed by a researcher gives birth to hypothesis very often.

Analogue models are also not scarce in the realm of research in management. Demand curves, flow charts in production control, frequency distribution curves in statistics, etc., examples of analogue models of the behaviour of events. Analogue are models represent dynamic situations, and "they are customarily used more than iconic models because of their vast capacity to depict the characteristics of the phenomenon or event under consideration," according to di Roccaferrera. In all such situations and in all the analogue models hypothesis is not absent.

Experiences or Observations of the Competitors

Managerial analysts and researcher derive factors, vairables, events, lessons or interrelations between variables from the experiences or observations of the competitors. Not very seldom, managerial researchers get research problems from the experiences of the competitors. In a competitive situation every company executive, particularly marketing executives formulate competition strategy not only on the basis of the opportunities and threats of the company but also on the strengths and weaknesses of its competitors. Hence, every company's marketing analysis includes the analysis of the marketing strategy of its competitors, say: market leaders, challengers, and nichers. Actually speaking, all functional departments take into account the moves and tactics of their competitors. Hence, management problems, research problems, the factors affecting their decisions, and hypotheses are generally taken from the competitors also.

Observations in Past Studies

Research problems and hypotheses are often taken by researchers from identical studies of the past. Hypothesis tested in one situation can be tested in another situation in order to conform its validity. Hence, one hypothesis can be used in different situations. Similarly, a study on one hypothesis or its testing in one situation may throw light on some other hypotheses giving birth to new hypotheses. On the basis of some past studies, therefore, a managerial researcher can formulate his hypothesis. In fact, previous studies provide sufficient light for new hypothesis and new research problems.

Findings of the Research and Development Department

Findings of the research and development department provide special light to managerial researchers. In recent times, particularly in the context of the globalisation of business, R & D has become an important organ of every progressive organisation In fact the very survival of a business of today depends on how the companies progress in their research and development activities. This is the reason why companies invest a considerable portion of their resources on R & D.

Research and Development department is involved in new product development, new technology and technique development, new process development, innovation, invention, etc. In the procress of their efforts in all these directions, they are bound to identify variables or factors and their relationships. Hypothetical observations and propositions identified in the R & D process provide hypothesis for managerial researchers.

Thus, managerial researchers rely on various sources not only for research problems but for hypotheses and factors involved in hypotheses. Formulation of hypothesis depends on the nature and magnitude of the problem and the factors influencing it.

Formulation of Hypothesis

As observed earlier, a hypothesis is a proposition or an assumption about a population parameter, which is skepitcally formulated being tested with the help of data collected and analysed. Identification of variables and their relationship can also be done in formulating a hypothesis. A case quoted by Richard I. Levin is relevant here.[4]

A roofing contract for a large sports complex has been awarded to a large architectural firm. Building specifications stipulate a movable roof covered by approximately 10,000 aluminium sheets of 0.04 inch thickness. This thickness must not increase substantially because the structure cannot support the additional weight; nor can the sheets be substantially thinner because of the problem of strength. The contracting firm is, therefore, very careful about the thickness restrictions, and it has selected 100 sheets as samples at random for quality check. The sample sheets have a mean thickness of 0.0408 inches. It is believed that these sheets come from a thickness population with a standard deviation of 0.004 inches. The characteristics of the samples (variables) can be used to test the hypothesis in this case, and find out whether the shipment of the sheet can be accepted by the company for the sports complex.

In case we assume (hypothesize) that the true mean thickness is .04 inches, and we are aware that the population standard deviation is .004 inches, how is it likely to get a sample mean of .0408 or more from that population? In other words, if the actual mean is 0.4 inches, and the standard deviation is .004 inches, what are the chances of getting a sample mean that differs from .04 inches by .0008 inches or more?

In order to determine whether the population *mean* is actually .04 inches, we must calculate the probability that a random sample with a mean of .0408 inches will be selected from a population with an assumed mean

4. Richard I. Levin, *Statistics for Management,* Prentice Hall, p. 359.

(μ) of .04 inches and a standard deviation (σ) of .004 inches. This probability will indicate whether it is reasonable to observe a sample like this, if the population mean is actually .04 inches. If this probability is far too low, it may be concluded that the aluminium company's statement is false, and that the mean thickness of the aluminium sheets is not .04 inches. The situation of probability, that $\overline{X}$ (actual average *i.e.,* mean) differs from hypothesized average (μ) i.e., .04 by 2 standard errors or more, is show in Fig. 1.

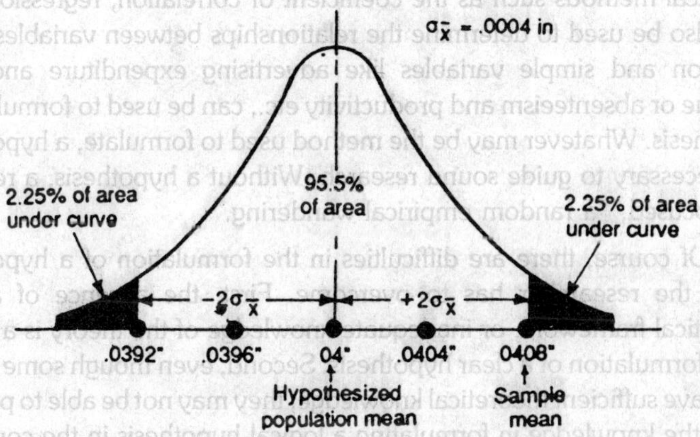

Fig. 1. Probability of $\overline{X}$ differing from hypothesized mean μ by 2 standard errors on both the sides of the continuum .04" is the hypothesized mean.

The hypothesized mean of the population is shown at the centre of the continuum (.04). Standard deviation is .004 inches. Then the chances of getting a sample mean may be either .0396 or .0392 on the negative side of the continuum. On the positive side the chances of getting samples are .0404 or .0408, which are shown in Fig.1. The sample .0408 (X) inches deviates by .0008 inches from the hypothesized population mean (.04), *i.e.,* the sample lies 2 standards errors to the right of the hypothesized population mean. In the present situation, it may be concluded that a population with a true mean of .04 inches may not be likely, and hence the hypothesis is rejected and the mean thickness claimed by the aluminium company should be rejected.

In order to find out the standard error of the mean:

$$\sigma \times \frac{\sigma}{n} = \frac{.004}{100} = \frac{004}{10} = .0004$$

Mean of the sample (.0408 inches) lies 2 standard errors to the right of the hypothesized population mean. (see the Fig.1)

$$\text{(No. of standard errors) } Z = \frac{X - \mu}{\sigma X} = \frac{.0408 - .04}{.0004} = 2 \text{ standard errors}$$

Here we have demonstrated a hypothesis, using the variables *viz* assumed average, standard deviation, and standard error (all statistical terms). The assumed average of the population parameter is compared with the true mean ($\overline{X}$) of the sample (100 aluminium sheets out of the universe of 10,000 sheets) in order to find out whether there is a substantial. Statistical methods such as the coefficient of correlation, regression, etc., may also be used to determine the relationships between variables. Even common and simple variables like advertising expenditure and sales revenue or absenteeism and productivity etc., can be used to formulate the hypothesis. Whatever may be the method used to formulate, a hypothesis, it is necessary to guide sound research. Without a hypothesis, a research is unfocused, "a random empirical wandering."

Of course, there are difficulties in the formulation of a hypothesis, which the researcher has to overcome. First, the absence of a clear theoretical framework, or inadequate knowledge of the theory is a barrier to the formulation of a clear hypothesis. Second, even though some people may have sufficient theoretical knowledge, they may not be able to properly utilise the knowledge in formulating a logical hypothesis in the context of the existing or expected situations. Third the inability to identify the relevant variables and establish proper relationship between these variables stand in the way of formulating a clear and sound hypothesis. Fourth, some researchers never care to get acquainted with research techniques and methods before they enter upon research. Fifth, many researchers lack actual exposure to the problem areas and hence they tend to formulate hypothesis which have no relation with the actual practical areas. This is perhaps the most impeding barrier for a managerial researcher; irrespective of the differences in the types of hypothesis.

Types of hypothesis

On the basis of the level of abstraction, hypothesis may be classified under three categories, *viz.*,

(i) Hypothesis that explain the existence of empirical uniformities;

(ii) Hypotheses that deal with the complex existence of logically-derived relationships between empirical uniformities; and

(iii) Hypotheses which are concerned with the relation of analytic variables.

The first type of hypotheses state some degree of uniformity among the empirical phenomena. For example, in an urban market like Bombay, the determinants of demand for TV sets are identical for all the prominent makes, say, Onida, BPL, Crown, Televista, etc. This is a common sense observation. The second type of hypotheses aim at testing the existence of logically-derived relationships between empirical uniformities. For example, we can compare, and then frame a sceptical proposition that there is some sort of relationship between the empirical uniformities:

(i) There exists a given magnitude of relationship between the percentage of colour TV programmes and the demand for colour TVs in Bombay;

(ii) The longer the time the TV viewers view the TV programmes, the greater the demand for TVs;

(iii) The more the entertainment programme is in colour, the more the time the viewers spend on watching the TV, etc.

The third type of hypotheses deal with a study of analytic variables between changes in one property and changes in another. The dependent variable "demand for TV" in Bombay, Madras and New Delhi and its relationship with the independent variables, *viz.,* the entertainment programmes, the economic standards of the city inhabitants, the demonstration effect, the promotional budget of the company concerned, etc., are related to one another. Hence the relationship between the magnitude of change in the demand for colour TVs in these three cities for various makes, models and ranges; and the change in the independent variables can be hypothesised and tested with the help of statistical methods the coefficient of correlation, regression models, etc.

A hypothesis provides the basis for investigation, and ensures the proper direction in which the study should proceed. It facilitate the collection of adequate facts, help one to arrive at appropriate conclusions, suggestions and observations. In order to draw inferences, certain methods are usually employed. These are: methods of agreement; the method of difference; joint methods; the method of residues; and the statistical method.

Characteristics of Hypothesis

There are certain characteristics of a hypothesis:

(i) It should be conceptually clear;

(ii) It should have empirical references;

(iii) It should be specific;

(iv) It should be related to available techniques;

(v) It should be related to the body of the theory;

(vi) It should be relevant to the existing environmental conditions for the purpose of testing; and

(vii) It should identify the specific variables and their relations.

A hypothesis that satisfies these characteristic makes a substantial contribution to the theory and the body of knowledge if it is tested. An empirical testing of the hypothesis is, therefore, as important as the formulation of the hypothesis.

Testing the Hypothesis

The specific relationship between phenomena or variables, which is sceptically formulated, should be empirically demonstrated by the hypothesis which is tested. This necessitates a systematic research and empirical investigation, which results in proving the hypothesis and facilitates theorising of the observation. In other words, the researcher decides, on the basis of the observed facts which he has collected, whether or not an assumption is valid. An example of the test of hypothesis in the realm of management science is its routine application in the area of statistical quality control. Tests have been reduced to standardised procedures that enable the management to discover variations in the quality of production or the quality of goods supplied by the suppliers. It facilitates the deter-mination of an acceptable quality level for all incoming lots. In order to test a hypothesis about a set of data, a sample selected at random is subjected to a detailed analysis, for it may not be possible to evaluate the universe as a whole. The result otained in the samples in then compared with what one would expect if the hypothesis had been true. The greater the disparity between the sample result and the expectation, the greater the doubt of the validity of the original hypothesis. At some level of doubt, the hypothesis may be rejected; and this level of doubt can be expressed as a probability. Thus, on the basis of probability theory, a hypothesis may be accepted or rejected after it has been tested. "The hypothesis is tested by making use of a predefined decision rule, which is applied to sample data and which guides the experimenter in deciding whether to accept or reject the hypothesis on the basis of the outcome of the sample or samples drawn. The rejection of a hypothesis presumably leads to one kind of consequence and the acceptance of hypothesis leads to another kind of consequence."[5]

Statistical methods, various mathematical methods, operations research and experimental methods, econometric methods, etc., are all

5. Croxton, Cowden and Botch, *Practical Business,* Prentice-Hall of India, 1974, p. 110.

useful tools in the testing of hypotheses. However, the hope that a common procedure will be followed for testing a hypothesis is a distant possibility. The technique to be adopted depends on convenience, the availability of data, exposure to various metods, etc. A general procedure consisting of a few steps in the form of a flow diagram may, however, be depicted here, as suggested by Chance.

The flow diagram may be explained with a simple example. Company X supplies automobile gear box castings to Company Y, which allows a maximum of 10 per cent rejection rate. When each consignment reaches the purchase department of Company Y, the hypothesis is that the rejection rate would not exceed 10 per cent. In order to ensure quality, Company Y quality control experts test this hypothesis. This is the first step in the statement of hypothesis according to the flow diagram. The hypothesis is that Company X's consignments of castings supplied to Company Y would not contain more than 10 per cent defectives.

A Flow Diagram

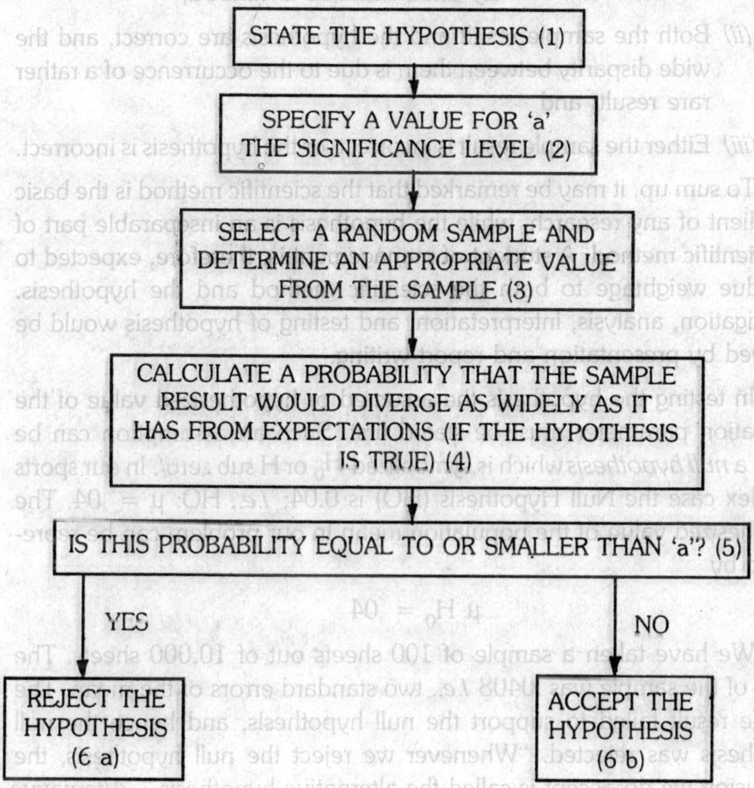

For the purpose of testing a hypothesis, the quality control experts of Company Y choose a given sample (10 per cent sample) from the total supply. If the total castings are 200 (N), the sample would be 20 castings (*n*); and the probability of defectives *(a)* would be 2 numbers of castings. The value of '*a*' should be determined, which is the next step. Then select the random sample items and determine the value of '*r*' (the number of defective items in the sample). The next step is to calculate the probability that the number of defective items in the sample is less than, or equal to, '*r*' if the hypothesis is true. If the probability is equal to or less than, '*a*', the hypothesis is accepted, and if the probability is more than '*a*', the hypothesis is rejected. The conclusion then is that the quality of the product is less than the probability rate of expectation, and that, therefore, the chances are greater for the consignment to be rejected. Three situations can be identified under which the hypothesis is falsified. They are:

(i) The sample is biased, and therefore, the probability calculated for this result actually understates its likelihood;

(ii) Both the sample result and the hypothesis are correct, and the wide disparity between them is due to the occurrence of a rather rare result; and

(iii) Either the sample result is incorrect, or the hypothesis is incorrect.

To sum up, it may be remarked that the scientific method is the basic ingredient of any research, while the hypothesis is an inseparable part of the scientific method. A student of management is, therefore, expected to give due weightage to both the scientific method and the hypothesis. Investigation, analysis, interpretation, and testing of hypothesis would be followed by presentation and report writing.

In testing the hypothesis the assumed or hypothesized value of the population parameter must be stated first. Such an assumption can be called a *null hypothesis* which is symbolized H_0 or H sub zero/. In our sports complex case the Null Hypothesis (HO) is 0.04; *i.e.,* HO: $\mu = .04$. The hypothesized value of the population mean in our problem can be represented by

$$\mu H_0 = .04$$

We have taken a sample of 100 sheets out of 10,000 sheets. The mean of the sample was .0408 *i.e.,* two standard errors of the mean. The sample result failed to support the null hypothesis, and hence the null hypothesis was rejected. "Whenever we reject the null hypothesis, the conclusion we do accept is called the alternative hypothesis." *Alternative hypothesis* is symbolized as H_1 (H sub-one).

$H_o : \mu = .04$ (The null hypothesis is that the population mean is equal to .04)

Then there may be three possible alternative hypotheses, *viz.,*

(i) The alternative hypothesis is that the population mean is not equal to .04 (H_1: μ = .04);

(ii) The alternative hypothesis is that the population mean is greater then .04 ($H_1 : \mu > .04$);

(iii) The alternative hypothesis is that the population mean is less than .04 ($H_1 : \mu < .04$)

We do not question the computed value of the sample by testing the hypothesis. What we do is to make a judgement about the differences between the value of the sample and a hypothesized population parameter. Hence, after stating the null hypothesis and the alternative hypothesis there should be some criterion for deciding whether to accept or reject the null hypothesis. In the above case a difference between the sample mean and the hypothesized population mean has been worked out as .045 (4.5 per cent), and hence the null hypothesis has been rejected. This difference between the sample means and the hypothesized population mean is statitsically known as the significance level. It means that a null hypothesis above 4 per cent significance level is bound to be rejected.

When the significance level indicates that the null hypothesis or the sample mean is within the given limits, the hypothesis is accepted. On the other hand, the confidence level indicates that the sample meant fell within the defined confidence limits. Figure 1, shows 25 per cent of the area on both sides of the curve (coloured parts) *i.e.,* a total of 4.5 per cent of the area indicates the significance level. Obviously, therefore, the hypothesis is rejected.

There can be two-tailed and one-tailed tests of a hypothesis. "A two-tailed test of hypothesis will reject the null hypothesis if the sample mean is significantly higher than or lower than the hypothesized population mean," *i.e.,* in two-tailed test, there are two rejection regions, as we have seen in the sports complex case (see page 100). If the aluminium sheets sample mean is either less than or more than the hypothesized population mean, the hypothesis is rejected (and the sheet is rejected). But in the second case, *i.e.,* the case of castings, if the defect rate is more than the assumed rate, *i.e.,* the right-tailed test, the hypothesized sample will be rejected. Left-tailed test is also called the one-tailed test which shows the negative side of the continuum. If the sample is proved less than the hypothesized population parameter, the hypothesis is rejected.

In any case, the probabilities for error must be small if the hypothesis is to be accepted. We must decide upon the significance level before we move ahead to test the hypothesis for this purpose. A good test must reject or accept the null hypothesis on the basis of the predetermined significance level.

Though there are various other situations where a hypothesis can be tested in statistical terms, we limit our discussion at this level because our objective in this book is to demonstrate the basic aspects of formulating and testing a hypothesis. A hypothesis is a part of the scientific method of research, which a researcher has to follow.

In testing a hypothesis, certain general steps can be followed *viz.*: *(a)* make a formal statement of the hypothesis (null hypothesis) as we have seen in the automobile gear box case earlier; *(b)* select a significance level which is generally influenced by the magnitude of the difference between sample means size of the samples, variability of measurements within samples, etc.; *(c)* decide the distribution to use; *(d)* compute an appropriate value on the basis of the samples drawn at random; *(e)* calculate the probability and *(f)* compare the probability. If the probability worked out is equal to or less than value in respect of one-tailed test or a/2 in respect of two-tailed test, the null hypothesis is rejected and an alternative hypothesis is accepted.

Statistical methods are in common use in testing a hypothesis. Statistical models are also appreciated which represent relationships to make a probability statement using notations or symbols. An assertion directly related to the purpose of investigation which is meant to be tested is formally called a hypothesis. Hence, hypothesis is a common element in a research design.

Chapter 7

Classification and Tabulation

Classification and tabulation are signficant for a reasearcher. We cannot ignore the importance of classification and tabulation, which are interrelated.

Classification

The voluminous data collected for the purpose of a study may be complex. In order to make use of such a large quantity of data in a convenient way, classification becomes necessary. If we study the trade union activities of the engineering workers in India, the relevant data may be enormous. For the determination of the relationships between various variables and factors, classification of the data under related factors or variables becomes necessary. Say: workers under each income group, income at each educational level, income under each range of experience, political affiliations and trade union memberships, to be grouped and classified. Management's approach and trade union membership — all these factors in each sector of the engineering industry, whether small-scale, medium-scale or large-scale, or the automobile industry, textile engineering, agricultural machinery etc. The data should be made intelligible under each relevant category by appropriate presentation, utilisation, and interpretation. Classification becomes essential in this respect.

Classification is the process of arranging data under homogeneous groups. "The process of arranging data in groups or classes according to resemblances and similarities is technically called classification." It is the process of arranging data either actually or notionally in groups or classes according to their common characteristics and affinities, giving expression to the unity of attributes that may subsist amongst a diversity of variables. As a matter of fact, classification precedes tabulation: that is, before tabulation, the heterogeneous data should be classified into homogeneous groups for easy presentation and interpretation. In this process, units with common characteristics are placed in one class and the data divided into a number of groups, facilitating the process of analysis and interpretation. Classification makes tabulation easier.

Classification has many objectives. These objectives are listed below:

Objectives of Classification

(a) To identity similarity in the data collected;

(b) To maintain homogeneity;

(c) To facilitate effective comparison;

(d) To present complex, haphazard and scattered data in a concise, logical and intelligible form;

(e) To maintain clarity;

(f) To identify independent and dependent variables and establish their relationships;

(g) To simplicity complex data;

(h) To specify diversity and unity of the data for the purpose of analysis;

(i) To achieve effective quantification; and

(j) To facilitate easy presentation and interpretation of data.

Irrespective of the differences in the objective, there are various determinants of classification.

Determinants of Classification

Classification may be determined by the common characteristics of different groups in the universe. The common characteristics may be qualitative or quantitative. The qualitative basis may be descriptive, while the quantitative factors may be numerical in nature. The job satisfaction of workers, their morale. self-actualisation, etc., may be described in qualitative terms. Wage increases, achievement of sales volume quota, bonus, over time compensation, etc., are examples of the numerical or quantitative basis for classification. Attributes are examined in qualitative or descriptive determinants. Class intervals are commonly used in numerical or quantitative factors.

Classification according to attributes may be simple classification, manifold classification, or arbitrary classification. When classification is made on the basis of attributes or qualities in a simple way, it may be considered *simple classification.* All the units or individuals with particular characteristics are grouped together, while all those which do not possess these common characteristics are placed separately in another group in simple classification. In simple classification, there can be two groups; *i. e.,* the groups with the given common characteristics, and the group which does not possess the given characteristics. This type of classification is also known as classification according to dichotomy. For example, when we classify toilet soap consumers of Pears soap we may classify them into two groups, *i. e.,* consumers with brand loyalty for Pears soap, and those who do not have any brand loyalty for Pears soap at all.

When more than one attribute is examined simultaneously, classification will have to be made into a number of groups. For example, income groups and consumer loyalty for Pears soap, educational level; and consumer loyalty for Pears soap, educational level of ladies and gentlemen, urban consumption patterns, rural consumption patterns, partial consumption of Pears soap, etc.. All these may be studied. When many such variables or attributes are simultaneously evaluated, we have *manifold classification.* Every class of data may be subject to further classification in accordance with the objective and scope of the study.

The arbitrary nature of classification becomes evident when the differences are not well defined in the various groups. If the universe is divided into two groups, say, low income group and high income group, the classification becomes arbitrary for want of an exact definition of the classes. The differences of the two groups are neither natural nor well-defined. Classification here becomes arbitrary, and the researcher himself arbitrarily gives definition according to his convenience. For the sale of Pears soap, a low income group may be defined as the people whose monthly income is below Rs. 2,000. Those whose monthly income is Rs. 2,000 and above may be defined as the high income group. This definition is arbitrary for any other purpose; one cannot draw a clear cut-line of demarcation in absolute terms, since it differs from situation to situation. Even for purpose of demand analysis for Pears soap, this classification often becomes arbitrary if we assume that the low-income group, does not prefer to buy Pears soap and that the high-income group goes in for it. Here, many factors have to be taken into account. For example, people without much financial burden or people who are advised by physicians would go in for Pears even if they are in the low-income group, while there may be many in the higher income group who would prefer to have some other cheaper products.

Classification according to class intervals is another type of classification; *i.e.,* classification is determined by class intervals. Wherever a quantitative measurement and presentation of data are possible, class intervals are used for convenient presentation and analysis. In these cases, classification is made on the basis of values or quantities For example, if we classify the income of 1,000 workers in a factory, the data may be classified under the following class intervals:

Income Group (Class Intervals)	*Number of Workers (Frequency)*
Rs.	
Below 250	30
250 - 500	100
500 - 750	350
750 - 1,000	340
1,000 - 1,250	150
1,250 and More	30
	Total 1,000

The limit in the class interval is called class limit, *i.e.,* in the class interval of 250-500, the lower limit is Rs. 250/- and the upper limit is Rs.500/-. The difference between two class limits is called the class magnitude or magnitude of the class interval (in this case, Rs. 250/-). the number of items which come under each class interval may be referred to as class frequency. Generally speaking, the basic consideration in classification according to class intervals are:

(i) Choice of class limits;

(ii) Number of classes and their magnitude;

(iii) Counting the number in each class; and

(iv) Relevance of the class interval to the situation.

On the basis of the total number of items in the series, classes are planned in a frequency distribution. The researcher should, however, be very cautious in making. the classes and the class interval; and the maximum accuracy, unambiguity, consistency, and relevance should be maintained. Moreover, the total distribution should not have such a large number of classes that it becomes unwieldy for the reader to understand; but the number of classes, should not also be very small (say, less than 5).

To generalise, it may be remarked that the frequency distribution ideally has 5 to 15 classes in it, though there is no hard and fast rule for the same. The range of the data, the expected accuracy, and the number of classes can be taken into account when making the magnitude of intervals. As far as possible, all the class intervals in a frequency distribution should be of equal magnitude. An important principle to be adhered to while choosing the class limits is that the midpoint of class interval and the actual average of items in that class interval should be as close to each other as possible with a view to avoiding obscurity in class limits.

The number of items coming under each class, which is otherwise known as frequency, may be determined with the help of tally sheets, punched cards and mechanical devices. Computers are of great value when the population is larger or the data to be analysed is extensive. In the context of the above discussion, certain characteristics may be generalised for effective classification, though no hard and fast rule can be laid down.

Characteristics of Effective Classification

Some characteristies of effective classification can be generalised as:

(i) Uniformity should be maintained;

(ii) Comparability should be ensured (always compare with the comparables);

(iii) Unambiguity should be ensured;

(iv) Classification should be flexible as far as possible;

(v) Consistency should be maintained in class intervals;

(vi) Stability should be secured;

(vii) Homogeneity is the backbone of classification;

(viii) Attributes should be appropriate and clear; and

(ix) Class intervals, limits, and magnitudes must be appropriate, accurate and consistent as far as possible.

Classification is synonymous with seriation. "If two variable quantities can be arranged side by side so that the measurable differences in the one correspond to the measurable differences in the other, the result is said so form a statistical series." Seriation is done statistically or quantitatively, while classification can be made both qualitatively and quantitatively. Series may, at the same time, be time spatial, sceptical series, and condition series. There are, again, discrete series and continuous series. Items which are capable of exact measurement form a discrete series, though various units are not capable of division because each unit of data is separate and complete. A statistical unit is capable of division and may be measured in fractions of any size in a *continuous series*.

There are *simple* and *cumulative* series also. Frequency against each class interval or value is shown separately and individually in the former, while frequencies are progressively cumulated to present the aggregates in the latter. The following examples of classification would be appropriate here.

Discrete and Continuous Series (Simple)

Data Pertaining to Low Income Workers in 100 Sample Small-scale Units at Thane

I-Direct Series		*II-Continuous Series*	
No. of Workers in Each	*No. of Factories*	*Monthly Income Group Rs.*	*No. of Workers*
5	12	100-150	120
10	25	151-200	140
15	40	201-250	800
20	15	251-300	250
25	8	301-350	100
Total	100		1,410

Discrete and Continuous Series (Cumulative Series)

Data Pertaining to Low Income Workers in 100 Selected Sample Small-scale Industrial Units at Thane

Discrete Series		*Continuous Series*	
No. of Workers	*No. of Factories*	*Monthly Income*	*No. of Workers*
up to 5	12	up to Rs. 150	120
up to 10	37	up to Rs. 200	260
up to 15	77	up to Rs. 250	1,060
up to 20	92	up to Rs. 300	1,310
up to 25	100	up to Rs. 350	1,410

Classification facilitates tabulation. It may be observed that the data collected for the purpose of any research must be tabulated for easy presentation and effective interpretation, for which classification becomes necessary. On the other hand, classification is followed by tabulation.

Tabulation

As already mentioned tabulation is an orderly arrangement of data in columns and rows (in tables). It is a systematic presentation of classified data on the basis of the nature of analysis and investigation. Tabulation is a proper arrangement of the data in accordance with classification in proper tabular form facilitating proper analysis. It enables the researcher to simplify the complex data so that comprehension becomes easier. Economy of time and space also become possible with the help of proper tabulation. So much so, the interpretation, induction, deduction, and conclusion become easier. Tabulation always depends on the nature, scope, objectives of the investigation.

The tabular form is one of the most commonly used methods of presenting complex data effectively and comprehensively. These are simple and complex tables. The more simple the table is, the more easily understandable it becomes. Following few factors may be taken into consideration when a table is prepared in order to make it meaningful and effective:

(i) A clear, brief and self-explanatory title is necessary for a table.

(ii) All the units used should be clearly indicated.

(iii) Stubs (row headings) and captions (column headings) should be clearly mentioned.

(iv) The body of the table must show all the relevant information according to description.

(v) As far as possible a brief form of the large figures should be used so that the reader may get a clear picture.

(vi) In order to specify certain aspects or to clear certain points or issues, an appropriate footnote may be used.

(vii) Headnotes are also necessary below the main title for giving any additional necessary information.

(viii) Data should be arranged systematically; that is chronologically, alphabetically and geographically; this will enable the readers to grasp the various relevant aspects easily.

(ix) Items which need special emphasis must be specifically marked.

(x) Adequate spacing should be given in between the columns and rows.

(xi) When stubs and captions are large in size, short forms can be used in the column and rows; but the full form of the same must be clearly mentioned in footnotes.

(xii) Always mention the sources of data at the foot of the table.

(xiii) Percentages, standard deviations, coefficients of correlation, etc., may be worked out and presented in the table whenever necessary.

(xiv) Important relationships between variables may be presented in the table itself, wherever necessary.

(xv) Border lines will make the table more attractive.

These are some of the points to be taken into account when a researcher makes a table out of the data available to him. However, no hard and fast rule can be laid down for his purpose. The success of tabulation depends on how effectively the data could be presented in the table. The following example is relevant in this context:

In XYZ Company, there were 1,700 workers in 1985, of whom, 1,200 were permanent. There were 200 ladies, of whom 150 were casual labourers (temporary). The number of permanent workers rose to 1,550 in 1986, of whom 1,280 were men. The number of temporary workers was 208, of whom 180 were men. There were 1,800 workers in 1987, of whom 1,600 were permanent. Out of 280 ladies, 8 were temporary in 1987. Let us present these data in a tabular form (statistical table).

Distribution of Workers in XYZ Company from 1985 to 1987 (Categorywise)

Year	*Number of Permanent Workers*			*Number of Temporary Workers*			*Total Number of Workers*		
	Male	*Female*	*Total*	*Male*	*Female*	*Total*	*Male*	*Female*	*Total*
1985	1,150	50	1,200	350	150	500	1,500	200	1,700
1986	1,280	270	1,550	180	28	208	1,460	2,981	758
1987	1,328	272	1,600	192	8	200	1,520	280	1,800

Source: Company files and records.

Let us work out another example. Crayon Textiles Ltd. had a sales revenue of Rs. 27.45 crores in 1980 from 4 brands *viz.,* A, B, C and D. The sales in the north zone amounted to Rs. 20 lakhs, 50 lakhs, 10 lakhs, and 10 lakhs respectively. In the south zone, these figures were 3.1 crores 1.2 crores, 1.1 crores, and 30 lakhs. In the east zone, products A and D were not distributed. Product C achieved a turnover of Rs. 20 lakhs out of a total turnover of Rs. 70 lakhs. The west zonal manager contributed Rs. 10.5 crores and the first three products contributed, equally, while the sales of the fourth product amounted to Rs. 1.5 crores. The total contribution of the central zone, where products C and D were not distributed, was Rs.7.35 crores and products. A contributed Rs. 2.85 crores. The company exported product C to the tune of Rs.2.30 crores. These figures may be presented in the following table (the data may be drawn from the files of the sales department).

Table Showing the Sales Revenue of Crayon Textiles Ltd., in 1980

(Rs. in Crores)

Zone	*Sales Revenue from Each Product*				*Total*
	A	*B*	*C*	*D*	
North	0.20	0.50	0.10	0.10	0.90
South	3.10	1.20	1.10	0.30	5.70
East	nil	0.50	0.20	nil	0.70
West	3.00	3.00	3.00	1.50	10.50
Central	2.85	4.50	nil	nil	7.35
Exports	nil	nil	2.30	nil	2.30
Total	9.15	9.70	6.70	1.90	24.75

Source: Files of the sales department of the company.

It may be observed that classification and tabulation form a substantial portion of research. Data may be presented, analysed and interpreted before writing the report. In fact, the clarity of the report depends on data presentation, analysis and interpretation.

Data Analysis and Interpretation

The data pertaining to Crayon Textiles can be briefly analysed and interpreted. On the basis of zonal analysis of data we can observe that west zone has made the largest contribution to the company's sales revenue which accounted for 38.25 per cent as against 26.78 per cent from the central zone and 20.77 per cent from the south zone. Product B has made the largest contribution (35.34 per cent), followed by Product A and then product C (33.33 per cent and 24.41 per cent respectively). An important indication is that export market contributed only one 8.38 per cent of the sales revenue which was the contribution of only one product, *i.e.,* product C, which has a great export potentiality. Out of the sales revenue from product C, 34.33 per cent comes from export. The company must, therefore explore possibilities to develop its export market not only in terms of product C but other products.

A product-wise analysis shows that product B has the highest potentiality in the central region, with over 61 per cent of the total sales, which made a contribution of over 16 per cent of the total sales of the company. At the same time, other than product B, only product. A could be sold in the central zone which made a contribution of 39 per cent. It means that adequate promotional programmes are needed for products C and D in the central zone while product B and A require further constant promotional efforts. Export market is fully the contribution of product C, which means that product C must be further promoted in the export market while the other 3 products need an entry into export market.

Though product C has shared about 25 per cent of the total market, it does not have any share in the central zone necessitating to launch a promotional effort in that zone, products A & B require a promotion campaign in all the zones since these two products have the largest market potentiality contributinր the largest share of the total sales revenue to the time of over 68 per cent. But in north and east zones these two products have not been widely accepted. Hence, a market survey for these two products must be conducted in these two zones. Though all the products have some presence in all the zones, the share of the above two zones is negligible. Hence, a constant promotional effort based on a market survey is required for product D in all the zones.

The analysis can be presented with the help of pie diagrams, bar diagrams or graphical representation. Statistical methods like coefficient of correlation can be used to determine the variables that affect the sales in various zones. These are various other statistical, mathematical and econometric models which can also be used for analysis and interpretation. Thus, classified and tabulated data must be presented, analysed and interpreted drawing inductions, deductions and observations. Conclusions and suggestions can also be drawn on the basis of the analysis of data. Every researcher must, on the other hand, be aware of the fact that data collection, classification, tabulation and presentation must be backed by proper analysis and interpretation of the data without which no research can bear adequate fruit. A simple analysis of Crayon Textile data is presented above as an example.

Classification and Tabulation: More Clarified

Analytical skill is an indispensable skill for a researcher which does not come in a day or two. One should build it up with a consta ıt effort. The more you analyse, the more capability you acquire. A lot oı skill for perception observation, co-relating interpretation, probing, pres ntation, etc., are required for making a proper analysis and interpretatic ı. Let us see a few examples in this connection.

Case I

Power consumption in X metropolitan area and its suburbs during the last 20 years is presented below: Present the data on a tabular form, workout the percentages and give your interpretation of the table.

Consumption is classified under four headings *viz.,* industrial use, commercial use, domestic use, and agricultural use respectively in million units.

Data Collected from State Electricity Board

	1970-71	*1980-81*	*1990-91*
Industrial use	30.50	46.00	138.00
Commercial use	20.00	40.00	120.00
Domestic use	9.25	19.25	38.50
Agricultural use	7.50	5.00	2.00

The above data can be presented rationally in the following table

Table Showing Power Consumption in X Metropolitan Area from 1970-71 to 1990-91 (in million units)

Sectors	*Year 1970-71*	*Year 1980-81*	*% Growth*	*Year 1990-91*	*Percentage Growth*
Industrial use	30.50	46.00	50.82	138.00	200
Commercial use	20.00	40.00	100.00	120.00	200
Domestic use	9.25	19.25	111.11	38.50	100
Agricultural use	7.50	5.00	-26.67	2.00	-60
Total	67.25	110.25	63.94	298.50	170.75

Source: State Elecricity Board

The table represents the data pertaining to power consumption in four economic sectors (*viz.,* industrial, commercial, domestic and agriculture) during the period from 1970-71 to 1990-91 in X metropolitan area and its suburbs. During the ten-year period from 1970-71 to 1980-81 there has been an average annual growth of 50 per cent in power consumption in industrial use. But during the period from 1980-81 to 1990-91 there has been 200 per cent growth marking an average annual rate of growth of 20 per cent. This represents a substantial industrial growth during the period. Increase in power consumption can be considered as a dependent variable, and industrial development as an independent variable. Growth of power consumption is an indicator of industrial development.

On the other hand, the table indicates that consumption of power in agriculture in the suburbs of X metropolitan area has substantially declined by 26.67 per cent during the first decade, and the decline has more than doubled to 60 per cent during the second decade under study. While industrialisation grew at an average of 20 per cent annually agriculture has declined by 6 per cent. This phenomena can be presented in the form of a hypothesis which can be tested on some other population.

During the first decade under study commercial consumption of power has marked a more than proportinate growth, *i.e.,* 100 per cent growth marking an average annual growth of 10 per cent as against 5 per cent growth of industrial use. It indicates that commercial activities grew more than proportionately (rather doubled the growth) compared to industrial growth during the first decade under study. During the second decade (1980-81 to 1990-91), however growth of both industrial and commercial activities have marked a proportional growth (200 per cent) at the rate of 20 per cent annually.

During the whole period of two decades domestic consumption has grown by an average annual consumption of over 10 per cent as against 15 per cent growth of commercial activities and 12.5 per cent of industrial growth. As urbanisation has also been growing in accordance with the growth of industrial and commercial activities, agricultural activities have declined, but less than proportionately. This reveals that there exists an inverse relationship between the growth of industrial and commercial activities and agricultural activities.

As against 30.5 million units of power used by industry in 1970-71, commercial sector has used 20 million units; *i.e.,* industrial sector has consumed 45.35 per cent of the total power consumed as against 29.74 per cent consumed by commercial sector and 13.75 per cent consumed by agriculture. This, being an urban area, has the lowest consumption of power in agriculture.

During 1980-81, consumption in industrial activities accounted for 46 million units as against 40 million units in commerce and 19.25 million in domestic consumption. It means that industrial sector has shared 41.72 per cent in 1980-81, as against 36.28 per cent in commerce and 17.46 per cent in domestic consumption. The same during 1990-91 accounted for 46.23 per cent, 40.2 per cent and 12.9 per cent respectively. It throws light on an interesting fact that in all the years industrial activities shared between 41.46 per cent of the total power consumed as against 36.40 per cent in commerce and 12.19 per cent in domestic consumption. Consumption in agriculture has declined from 7.5 million to 2 million. In the meanwhile industrial and commercial activities are growing tremendously.

Diagrammatic representation, graphical representation, statistical methods or mathematical methods can also be used extensively in analysis and interpretation of the data.

Case II

Study the following frequency distribution carefully, write a detailed analysis, and answer to the questions given at the end.

Distribution of 500 Selected Companies on the Basis of ROI

	Numbers of Companies				
Class Interval-ROI %	*1989*	*1990*	*1991*	*1992*	*1993*
No returns	36	68	48	33	21
Below 10	135	100	90	84	80
10-19.9	138	153	158	164	174
20 - 29.9	150	160	184	196	200
30 and above	41	19	20	23	25
Total Consumption	500	500	500	500	500

1. Which is the profitability range of the largest number of companies?
2. Analyse the Return on Investment of 500 companies and find out the year in which maximum profit could be made by these companies.
3. Which is the year with minimum profit?
4. Which is the class interval having greater number of companies taking into account all the years under study?

Analysis

The table represents frequency distribution of 500 companies on the basis of the return on investment placed in class intervals. The number of no return companies has been gradually declining from 68 in 1990 to 21 in 1993. Similarly, the number of highest return companies (30 per cent and above) has marked a minor growth from 19 companies in 1990 to 25 companies in 1993. The highest profitability group is 30 and above class interval which has been growing constantly from 1990 onwards. The largest number of companies are in the 4th category which grew from 150 to 200 within a period of five years. While number of companies below 10 per cent profitability has been steadily declining. All the other groups having ROI rate above 10 per cent has been constantly growing in all the years under study, revealing an important fact that profitability of about 92 per cent of the companies has been substantially growing in all the years under study. This is really a spectacular performance.

Largest number of companies are in the Return on Investment class interval of 20-29.9 percentage in all the years, and the number has been constantly growing in this category. The second highest ROI class interval is 10-19.9 per cent; and this group has also been constantly growing from 138 in 1989 to 174 in 1993. Except a little over 8 per cent of the companies (first category) ROI is good in all the companies, the lowest among which is below 10 per cent category.

Answers to the Questions

Question No.1

The profitability range of the largest number of companies in all the years has been 20-29.9 class interval. This number has been constantly growing in all the years, *i.e.,* from 150 in 1989 to 200 in 1993. Number of firms in this category has grown by over 33 per cent during the 5 years under study. The second largest number of companies come under the ROI class interval of 10-19.9 per cent which grew from 138 companies in 1989 to 174 companies in 1993.

Question No.2

In order to find out the year with the largest profit, we should find out the profitability of every year. ROI class intervals under four categories have been profit making companies. We work out total indicator at the mid-value of every class interval. Thus, total profitability indicator in every year can be worked out as follows:

1989 — 5 — 135 + 15 — 138 + 25 — 150 + 35 — 41 = 7,930

Indicator in 1990 — 5 — 100 + 15 — 153 + 25 — 160 + 35 — 19 = 7,460

Indicator for 1991 — 5 — 90 + 15 — 158 + 25 — 184 + 35 — 20 = 8,120

" for 1992 — 5 — 84 + 15 — 164 + 25 — 196 + 30 — 23 = 8,585

" for 1993 — 5 — 80 + 15 — 174 + 25 — 200 + 35 — 25 = 8,885

The year in which maximum profit was made was 1993

Question No. 3

1990 was the year with the minimum profit on the basis of the indicator worked out above.

Question No.4

The class interval 20-29.9 has the largest number of companies under it in all the years, with 150, 160, 184, 196 and 200 respectively from 1989 to 1993. The second largest number of companies are in the class interval of 10-19.9 per cent ROI. The third is the second class interval, while no profit companies are the 4th group. The last in the line is the highest profit (30 and above % group) group.

Chapter 8

Presentation of Data

We have examined the process of data collection, the role of survey in data collection and the need for classification and tabulation of data. Classified data may be presented in tabular form for the sake of effectiveness. Such processed data can be presented in graphic and diagra-mmatic forms also for attractive communication of the intricacies of the statistical data. We make an attempt to explain some important aspects of diagrams and graphs in the presentation of data pertaining to managerial analysis in this chapter.

There can be volumes of data to be analysed, interpreted, and presented in support of arguments or in respect of testing a hypothesis. It is the skill of a researcher or a statistician to attractively display and present the uninteresting and complex statistical data in an attractive way in support of managerial analysis and interpretation. Charts and diagrams play a vital role in this respect.

Role of Diagrams

Diagrammatic representation of the complex data enables the researcher to delineate an attractive and clear picture of the vast and complex data. It also facilitates an easy understanding of the diverse and complex data. Of course, diagrams must be carefully drawn to properly display the significance of the data. If the diagrams are skillfully constructed, they make the monotonous data memorable. It is quite possible that uninteresting data may easily slip away from the attention of both the researcher and the reader. But an attractive chart representing the same data may make a long-lasting impact on the minds of people.

Diagrammatic and graphic representations make comparison easy. It is a very difficult task to compare data convincingly. Diagrams and charts do this job without much difficulty. An enormous table that represents labour productivity and trade unionism in India may look very complicated because neither the researcher nor the reader would be able to easily understand it. Moreover, the executive of today is a busy person, who may not like to do a time-consuming and monotonous job of going through the information presented in the table and digesting it, and then comparing it with another identical table. Two simple graphs plotted between the X-axis and Y-axis would do the job of not only making it easier for him to understand the information but also facilitate comparison.

Diagrammatic and graphic presentation of data converts them into attractive and interesting pieces of information. Some readers develop interest when they observe attractive charts but they do not like to go through volumes of uninteresting figures and statistics. Diagrammatic representation also saves time and energy, not only of the readers, but also of the researcher. By mere observation of the diagram, one gets a vivid picture of the trends, effects, relations and prospects of the variables and factors involved in them. It gives a quick view of the data, facilitates perception, grasping them and relating them in memory. This may be the reason why diagrammatic and graphic presentation of data has become a popular tool in the hands of researchers and managerial analysts. Proper care should, however, be exercised in presenting data in graphs and diagrams. Some hints on this presentation would be pertinent at this stage.

Some Hints on Diagrammatic Presentation of Data

Diagrams and graphs are expected to simplify the complex data; they should therefore be as simple as possible. The report of the research is basically meant for the reader; and hence it would be effective only if the diagrams used are capable of making the reader comprehend and digest what is presented in the report. Obvisiouly, the diagrams must be in accordance with the readers' taste, understanding and comprehension level. Clarity and easy communication ability of the charts and diagrams must be maintained as far as posible. Some of the important points to be borne in mind when preparing diagrams can be generalised as follows:

(a) The diagram should be suitable for both the data and the report.

(b) Attractiveness, neatness, and proportionality must be maintained.

(c) A proper size in proportion to the paper, and in accordance with the tastes and preferences of the reader must be chosen.

(d) Diagrams must be geometrically accurate and proportionate.

(e) Convenience should be maintained. There are vertical and horizontal diagrams. But the choice of the diagram depends on its clarity and comparison ability. Vertical diagrams are generally preferred.

(f) Attractive colours should be chosen. Contrasting colours may be appropriate.

(g) A proper scale must be used to draw the diagrams.

(h) A good heading should be given to each diagram.

In brief, diagrams must be clearly, neatly, proportionately, and attractively drawn; and proper and attractive colours may be used for this purpose.

Graphs

Graphs are in common use in the presentation of data. Independent variables are generally marked on the horizontal axis and dependent variables on the vertical axis. Generally speaking, one or two curves are shown on one graph. In no circumstances should the graph be crowded with many curves. There are various types of graphs; scattergrams and functional graphs, time graphs, band charts and cartograms, semilogarithmic graphs, analytical graphs, etc.

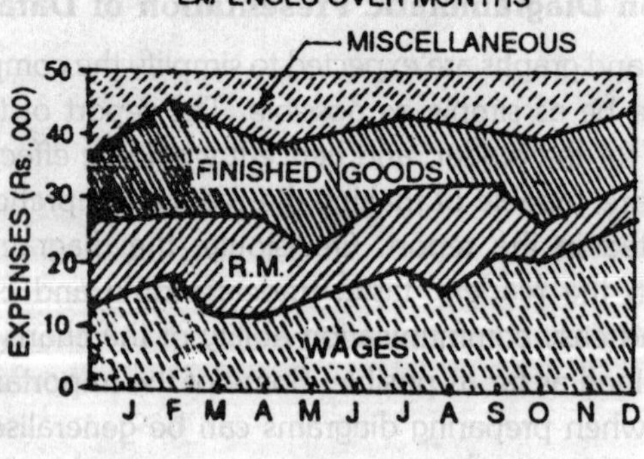

Fig. 1 A Band Chart.

Scatergrams represent the statistical relationship between two variables for both of which data can be recorded. Functional relationships between two variables can be plotted in the graph in scattergrams. *Time graphs,* on the other hand, show different values of one or more variables changing over time. *Band charts* represent several curves, each of which shows one stage in the build-up of a cumulative total. These curves take the form of bands running across the graphs. A percentage band chart portrays the variation of the relative proportions of the components with time.

Semilogarithmic or *ratio graph* has a logarithmic scale on the vertical axis and a normal scale (arithmetical scale) on the X-axis. Ratios are shown in their actual proportions. These graphs are useful in presenting relative changes and comparing series of widely different magnitudes. The slope of the curve indicates the rate at which the figures vary. The rate of change is constant in a straight-line graph. A semi-log graph can be drawn by using a semi-log graph paper, a slide rule, and taking logarithms of the values of the variables.

Analytical graphs perform analytical functions. Lorenz curves, scatter-grams, logarithmic graphs, etc., are analytical graphs. Most of the graphs perform an illustrative function. In fact, a considerable part of the statistical method deals with diagrams like frequency distribution charts, cumulative frequency curves, histograms, frequency polygons, etc.

Generally speaking, the most popular graphical representations are: time series graphical representation, and frequency series graphical representation. These deserve to be a examined in detail, for they are useful in charting values.

A straight line graph is shown below (Fig. 2), in which a demand problem has been worked out. The following demand schedule shows a series of alternative prices and the corresponding demand of X product in Y market.

Demand Schedule for X Computer (of various price ranges) in Y Market during a Given Period of Time

Price Per Unit of X Computer Rs. in Lakhs	*Number of Units Demanded*	*Symbols Representing Price Unit Combinations*
70	1	i
60	2	j
50	3	k
40	4	l
30	5	m
20	6	n
10	7	o

The above table shows that the demand for the computer increases when the price level goes down. A computer costing Rs. 70 lakhs has a demand for only 1 unit; but the brand costing Rs. 10 lakhs has a demand of 7 units. When the price decreases, the demand increaes, as shown in the Fig. 2.

Fig. 2 shows a demand curve which slopes downward to the right. This is a graphical presentation of the relationship between the price level and demand for X computer. The independent variable, the price level of the product, is measured on the X axis. The relationships between these two variables are plotted in the diagram (Fig. 2) *viz.,* i,j,k,l,m,n and o, which show that there is a demand level for every price level. Point j shows that for the price level 60 (Rs. 60 lakhs per unit of computer), the corresponding demand level is 2 computers on the X axis. Similarly, for the price level Rs. 30 lakhs, the demand level is 5 units. These figures show a straight line graph which registers a constant rate of change.

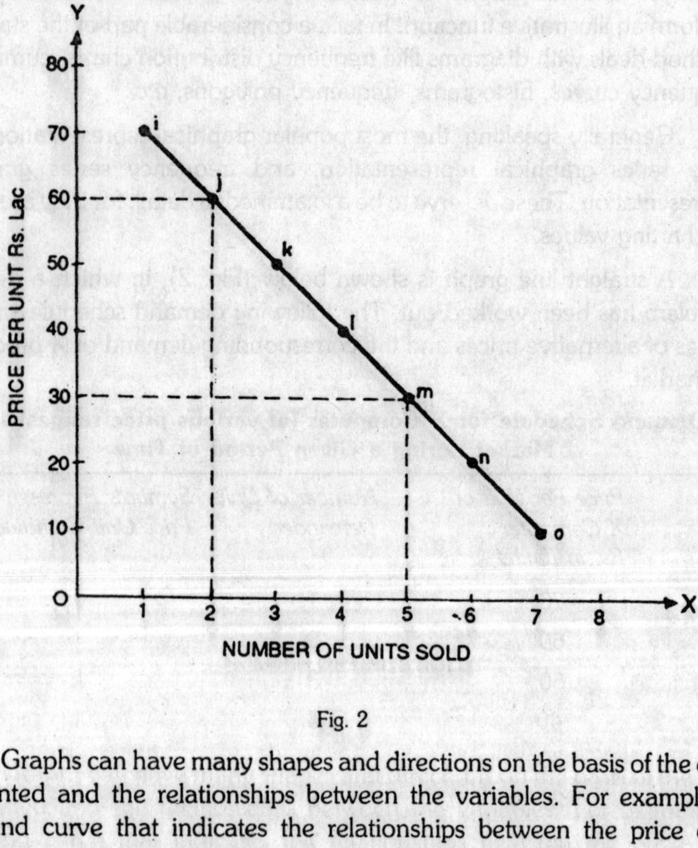

Fig. 2

Graphs can have many shapes and directions on the basis of the data presented and the relationships between the variables. For example, a demand curve that indicates the relationships between the price of a product and the demand for its substitute may show an upward shape from left to right. Similarly, the curve that shows the relationships between the price of a product and the demand for complementary goods may be almost a normal demand curve from left to right. (See Fig. 3)

Fig. 3,(a) is the curve that shows the relationships between two variables, the price of coffee and the demand for its substitute, tea. It shows that the demand for tea increases when the price of coffee increases. Fig. 3 (b) on the other hand shows that the demand for cars increases when the price of petrol decreases. It is obvious from these that a graph can be used to show any relationship between the dependent and independent variables. Independent variables are marked on the Y-axis.

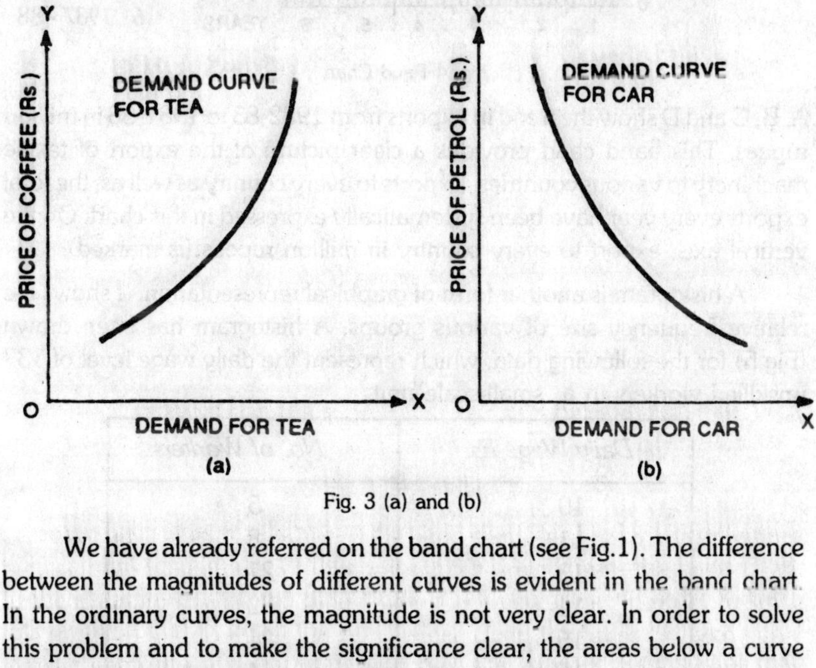

Fig. 3 (a) and (b)

We have already referred on the band chart (see Fig.1). The difference between the magnitudes of different curves is evident in the band chart. In the ordinary curves, the magnitude is not very clear. In order to solve this problem and to make the significance clear, the areas below a curve are shaded with some sort of designs (See Fig. 4). The shaded parts may look like many bands (if the curves do not overlap).

In Fig. 4, we present the data on the export of textile machinery (in million Rs.) for X machinery manufacturers to Pakistan, Afghanistan, Iraq, and Iran. The best way to present these data is to draw a band chart. The shaded portion in between the various curves look like bands, while the graph looks very attractive to the readers.

Fig. 4 shows the trends in the export of textile machinery by X machinery manufacturers to Pakistan, Afghanistan, Iraq, and Iran. Curves

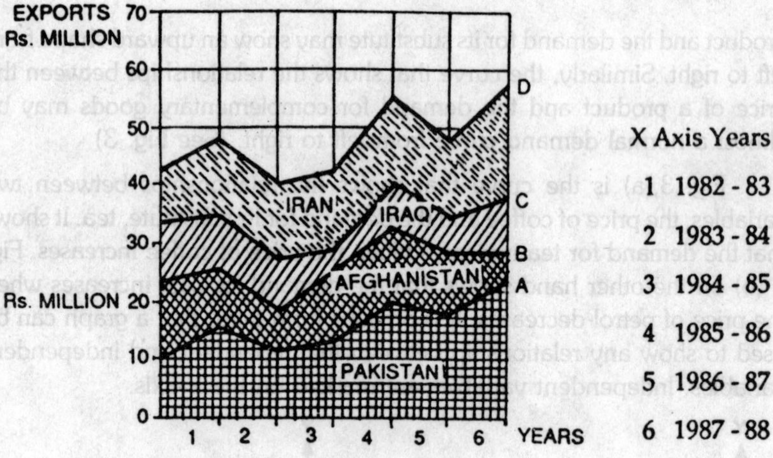

Fig. 4 Band Chart

A, B, C and D show the trend in exports from 1982-83 to 1987-88 in million rupees. This band chart provides a clear picture of the export of textile machinery to various countries. Exports to every country as well as, the total exports every year have been systematically expressed in this chart. On the vertical axis, export to every country in million rupees (is marked).

A histogram is another form of graphical representation. It shows the relative frequency size of various groups. A histogram has been drawn (Fig.5) for the following data, which represent the daily wage level of 137 unskilled workers in a small-scale unit.

Daily Wage Rs.	*No. of Workers*
10	5
11	8
13	27
14	32
15	24
16	14
17	6
18	4

(Every higher figure is the upper limit of the lower class interval *i.e.,* first class interval is Rs. 10-11 and the last class interval is Rs. 18-19).

On the X axis, the class interval of income level is marked and on the Y axis, the number of workers in each class interval is marked. This is an effective method of presenting the data in managerial analysis. A

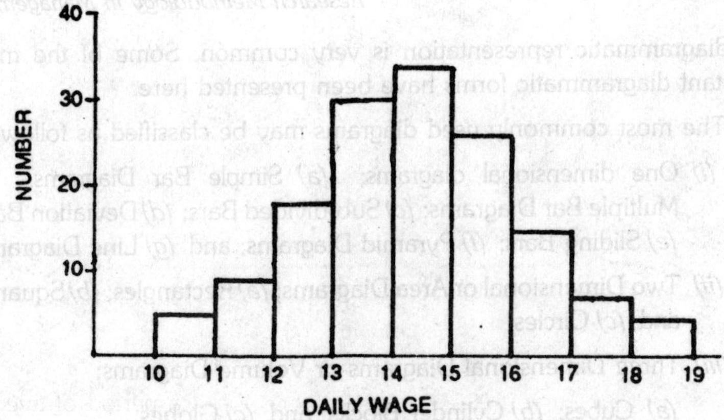

Fig. 5 Histogram

frequency polygon also shows the same data. While the histogram depicts each frequency groups separately, the frequency polygon indicates it collectively. If we mark the midpoints of the tops of all the rectangles of the histogram and join them with the help of straight lines, we shall have a curve with sharp corners at each joint. The two extremes are then connected with the base in such a way that the curve touches the base at half the distance outside the extreme rectangle. The curve thus drawn is a polygon. A polygon can also be drawn directly without drawing a histogram. A polygon has been shown in Fig. 6.

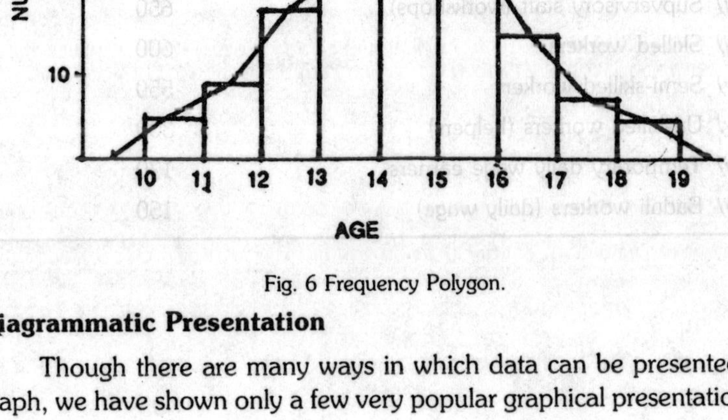

Fig. 6 Frequency Polygon.

Diagrammatic Presentation

Though there are many ways in which data can be presented in a graph, we have shown only a few very popular graphical presentations. In fact, diagrammatic representation is very common. Some of the most important diagrammatic forms have been presented here.

The most commonly used diagrams may be classified as follows:

(i) One dimensional diagrams; *(a)* Simple Bar Diagrams, *(b)* Multiple Bar Diagrams; *(c)* Sub-divided Bars; *(d)* Deviation Bars; *(e)* Sliding Bars; *(f)* Pyramid Diagrams; and *(g)* Line Diagrams.

(ii) Two Dimensional or Area Diagrams; *(a)* Rectangles; *(b)* Squares; and *(c)* Circles.

(iii) Three Dimensional Diagrams or Volume Diagrams;

(a) Cubes; *(b)* Cylinder Blocks; and *(c)* Globes.

(iv) Pictograms;

(v) Cartograms and Maps.

Only one dimension is taken into account in one-dimensional diagrams. For example, in a bar diagram, the height (length) alone represents the data. Its breadth colour contributes to its attractiveness. A simple bar diagram showing the average wage rate of the workers in a factory has been presented in Fig. 7.

There are six categories of workes in the factory. Their monthly average wage rates and the factory average monthly wage rates have been given in the following table, on the basis of which a simple bar diagram has been drawn. (Fig. 7).

Category	*Average Monthly Wage Rate of Workers (in Rs.)*
(i) Factory average	350
(ii) Supvervisory staff (workshops)	650
(iii) Skilled workers	600
(iv) Semi-skilled workers	550
(v) Unskilled workers (helpers)	300
(vi) Temporary daily wage earners	170
(vii) Badali workers (daily wage)	150

Average monthly wage rates of workers in X factory.

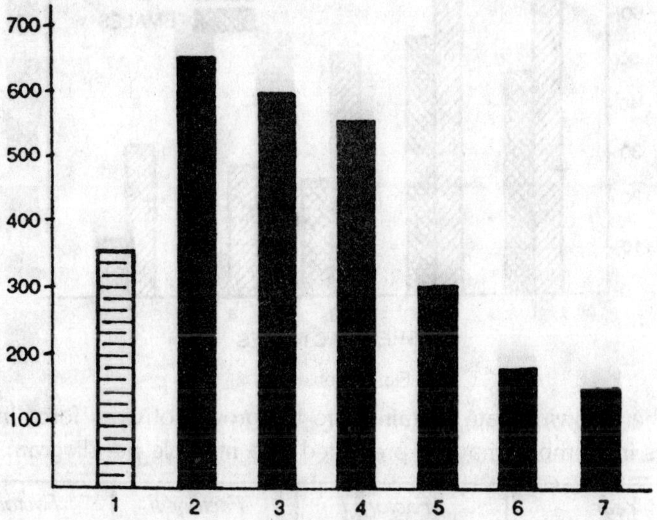

Fig. 7 Simple Bar Diagram

Multiple Bar Diagrams show more than one item on each bar. Double bar diagrams are very common, because they are as simple as simple bar diagrams.

The following data pertain to the educational level of cashew workers in five cashew factories in Quilon, Kerala;

Factories		No.	Males	Females
		Percentage of Workers having SSLC or above		
TKM	I	1	63.71	47.75
TKM	II	2	66.62	54.31
GDP	I	3	51.04	26.43
RP	I	4	28.74	8.45
AA	I	5	31.50	10.55

Percentage of Cahsew workers having SSLC qualification or above in Quilon.

Three or four bars can also be drawn together as multiple bar diagrams according to requirements. The following problem can be presented on a multiple bar diagram (3 bars).

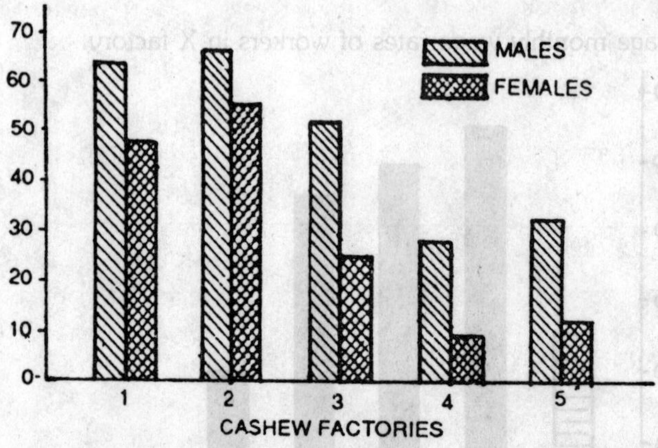

Fig. 8 Doble Bar

The following data pertaining to the growth of work force in three factories in Bombay may be presented in a multiple bar diagram.

Year	*Factory I*	*Factory II*	*Factory III*
1985	250	200	200
1987	400	220	270
1989	480	260	330

A multiple bar diagram shows more than one bar in the same diagram. Fig. 9 shows three bars together in each item, though any number of bars can be combined together. However, for the purpose of clarity and simplicity, it is better not to combine more than three of four bars.

Growth of work force in three factories in Bombay from 1985 to 1989.

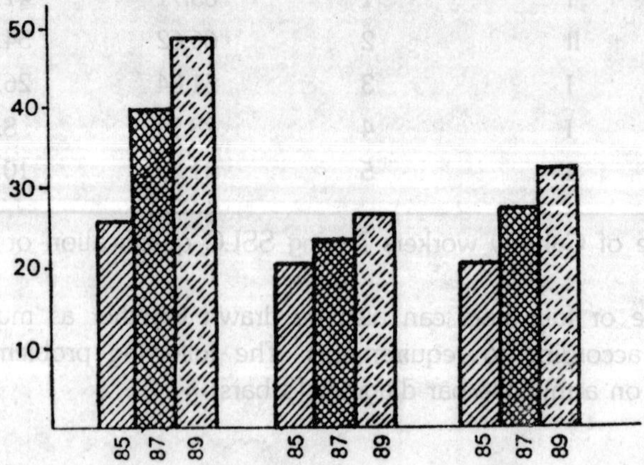

Fig. 9 Multiple bar Diagram (3 bars)

Sub-divided bar diagrams present many items on the same bar as shown in Fig. 10.

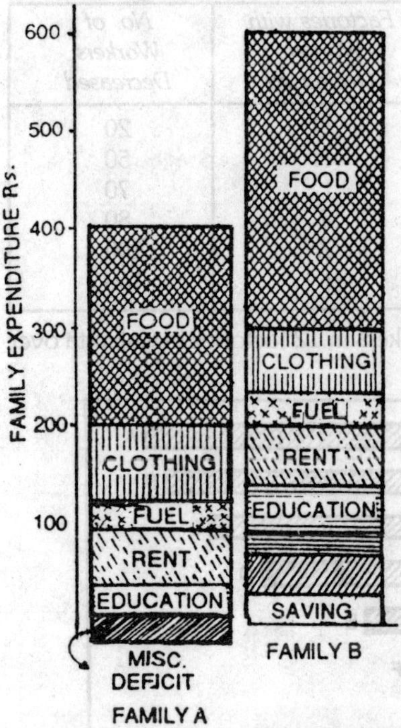

	Family A	*Family B*
	Rs.	*Rs.*
Income	400	600
Expenditure		
Food	220	300
Clothing	72	72
Fuel	20	30
Rent	48	60
Education	32	60
Misc.	28	48
Total	420	570

Fig. 10 Sub-divided Bar Diagram

The deviation bar diagram is another type of diagrammatic presentation of data, especially to show the deviations or differences from a given number. The deviation may be negative or positive. Negative deviations are generally shown on left side and positive deviations on the right side. Obviously, the base line is drawn at the centre and may be vertical for convenience sake (horizontal presentation is also permitted). In the diagram given below (Fig. 11), the negative values are given at the bottom left and the positive values at the top right side.

The following data show the changes in the employment of workers in 12 factories in Calcutta over a period of 5 years. In 6 of these, the number of workers employed went down and in 6 the employment went up.

Factories in which Workers Increased	*No. of Workers Increased*	*Factories with Workers Decreased*	*No. of Workers Decreased*
A	160	G	20
B	150	H	50
C	130	I	70
D	100	J	80
E	50	K	140
F	20	L	160

Change in the employment of workers in 12 factories in Calcutta over a period of five years from 1985.

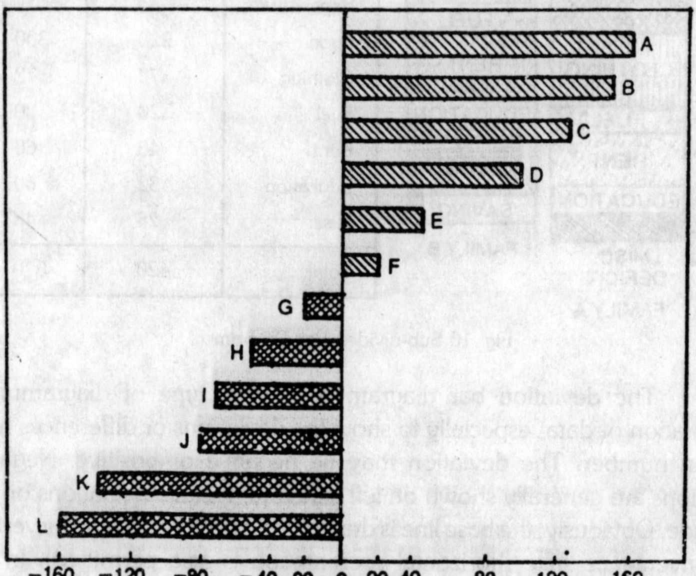

Fig. 11 Deviation Bars

A sliding bar diagram consists of horizontal bars, which represented the changes in the ratio of the component parts. A vertical base line is first drawn and the bars are fitted after dividing them among the component parts according to the ratio. Bars keep shifting in accordance with the changes in ratios. The length of the bars, however, remains the same.

The distribution of male and female workers in 7 factories (percentage to total) has been presented below in the form of a sliding bar diagram. (Fig. 12).

Factory	*Male Worker %*	*Female Workers % in Total*
A	76	24
B	64	36
C	60	40
D	55	45
E	44	56
F	40	50
G	35	65

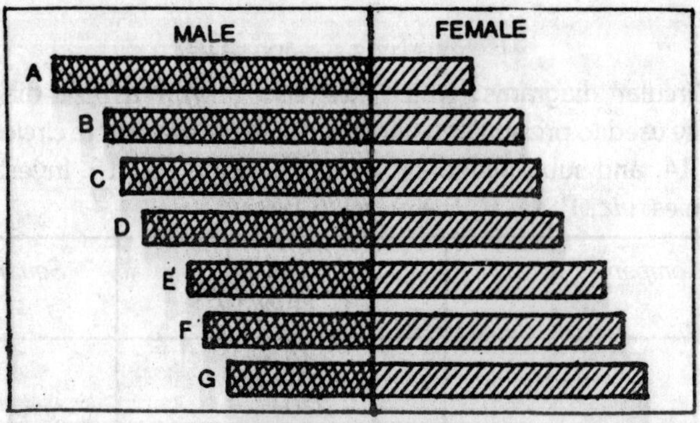

Fig. 12 Sliding Bar Diagram

Pyramid diagrams are useful in presenting large data, particularly population data, for many groups or strata. The distribution of people under various categories, males, females, age groups, educational groups etc., — may be presented in the diagram, which may be called the population pyramid, because the shape of the diagram is like that of a pyramid. As this is not very often used in business research, we do not present in this chapter.

Two-dimensional diagrams, such as rectangles, squares, and circles, are also increasingly in use. When only one aspect is to be compared, and the ratio between the highest and the lowest measurements is more than 10:1, the squares are employed. The square root of the values is first taken, and then the base of the squares is determined proportionately to draw the square. The population of four cities A, B, C, and D (4146, 2644, 948, and 643 in thousands) their respective square roots (64.4, 51.4, 30.8 and 25.2), and the bases of the squares worked out (2.6; 2.0; 1.2; 1.0) have been presented in the following square diagrams (Fig. 13). From the size of the square, the population of the cities A, B, C, and D may be determined.

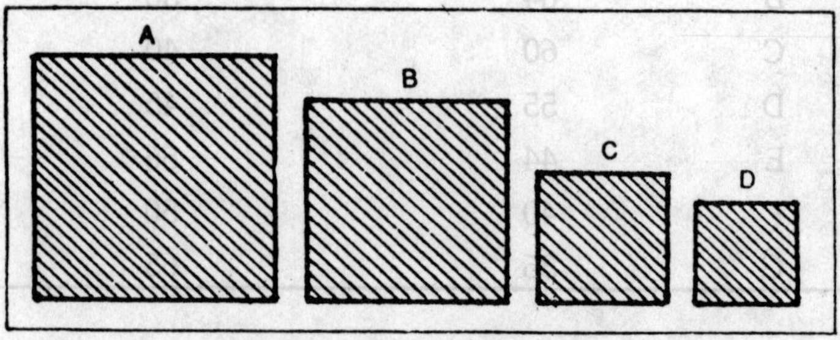

Fig. 13 Square Diagram

Circular diagrams, which are also known as pie diagrams, are generally used to present analytical data. These are simple circles, as shown in Fig. 14, and sub-divided circles as shown in Fig. 15. Investments of 4 companies *viz.*, P, Q, R, S are given below:

Companies	*Investment (Rs. in lakhs)*	*Square Root*
P	540.4	24.3
Q	330.5	17.9
R	190.5	13.6
S	81.3	9.0

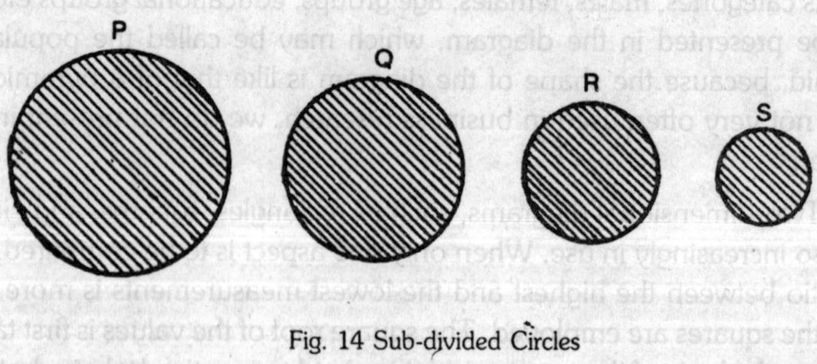

Fig. 14 Sub-divided Circles

First, the square roots have been worked out. The ratio of the circles are then found out on the basis of the square roots which have been mentioned above.

Sub-divided circles are also commonly used to show data pertaining to managerial analysis. For the purpose of sub-division, the angle value of each sub-part of the circle has to be worked out. The value of all the angles of a circles is 360°, from which the angle value of every division can be found out.

$$\text{Angle Value of Sub-group} = \frac{\text{Value of Sub - group}}{\text{Total Value}} \times 360^{\circ}$$

The total value of all the sub-angles is 360°. (However, some angles may be a little less or more, in which case slight adjustment can be made so that the total may come to 3600). Once the value of every sub-angle is found out, the circle may be sub-divided, as shown in Fig. 15.

Comparison of workers employed in X Factory in 1975 and 1990 (men, women and children).

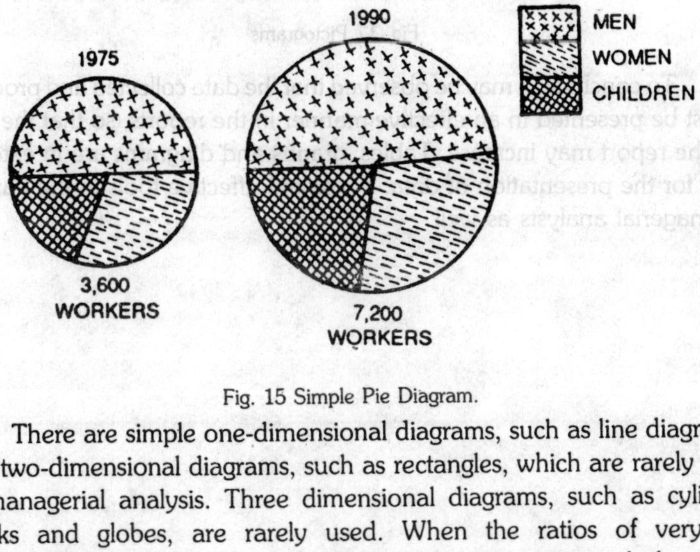

Fig. 15 Simple Pie Diagram.

There are simple one-dimensional diagrams, such as line diagrams, and two-dimensional diagrams, such as rectangles, which are rarely used in managerial analysis. Three dimensional diagrams, such as cylinder blocks and globes, are rarely used. When the ratios of very big measurements and a very small measurements are compared, the cubes are used. On the basis of the cube root of various measurements, the cubes are generally drawn. Some cubes have baned shown in Fig. 16.

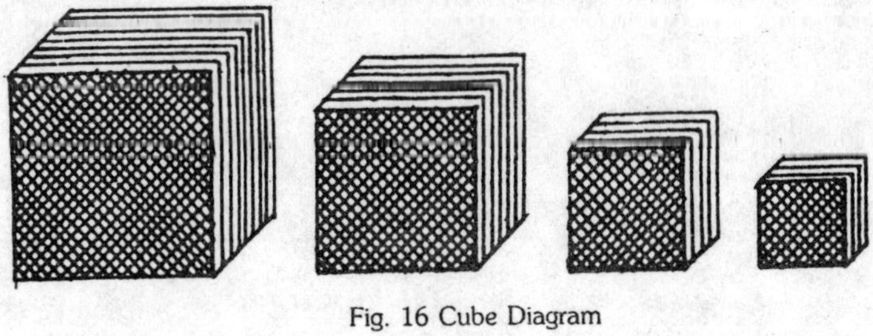

Fig. 16 Cube Diagram

Pictograms and cartograms are sometimes used when other methods are ineffective. Pictograms are the pictures of respective objects, while cartograms are the markings on the maps. Some pictograms have been shown in Fig. 17.

Fig. 17 Pictograms

To conclude, it may be observed that the data collected and processed must be presented in an effective manner in the reports, so that the utility of the report may increase. Tables, graphs and diagrams are in extensive use for the presentation of data. These are effective tools in the hands of managerial analysts as well.

Chapter 9

Scaling Techniques

We have examined how a research should be conducted and how to collect, classify, tabulate, and present data in the process of research; and how to identify variables and establish their relationships with the help of statistical data. Variables can be identified and measured in quantitative terms; and that is why they are known as quantitative series. But qualitative facts also exist in the universe, which are known as attributes. Of late researchers, particularly social researchers have started making attempts to turn "qualitative facts (attributes) into quantitative series (variables)." The scaling technique is an important contribution in this direction.

A scale is a measuring rod, or a numerical system of units measured successively and marked, at given distances on a line. It may be a device for the measurement of length, height, depth, width, etc., which are quantitative in nature. But attributes or qualitative facts can be measured by ordering items along a continuum, may be non-numerical in nature, and may be divided into various clearly distinguishable categories. For example the loyalty of workers in the machine shop of factory can be measured on a continuum as "deceitful-unloyal-tolerable-loyal-most loyal." The pendulum moves between the negative end "deceitful" to the positive and "most loyal" of the continuum. Then on the basis of frequency distribution, we can find out how many can be accepted.

A hypothetical table of this continuum in five departments of a factory is given below.

Scores of Loyalty of Workers in X Factory

Departments	Number of Workers					
	Deceitful	Unloyal	Tolerable	Loyal	Most Loyal	Total
D1	5	12	15	125	7	164
D2	9	21	52	130	5	217
D3	12	50	60	135	3	260
D4	10	48	10	20	1	89
D5	20	50	12	9	—	91
Total	56	181	149	419	16	821

The information in the table is eloquent about the composition of the work force in this factory. It follows a survey of the managers and supervisors of the factory. That is why the manager's approach to workers and the attitude of workers to the management, as the managers observe it, are very relevant. If we probe deeper, smaller classes and differences may emerge.

On the basis of this table, various types of comparisons can be made. Comparison between departments, various groups in the same department, various individuals within one department, or identical position in different departments, and so on. Many of the attributes are rigid, *ceteris paribus,* while variables are flexible because of the possibility of numerical treatment. In managerial analysis, especially in a study in the human side of the enterprise, attributes, *i.e.,* qualitative facts, are of great importance. Unless attributes are subjected to appropriate examination, managerial studies may not produce the desired results. Qualitative factors, therefore, deserve to be properly studied in managerial researches, where scaling techniques offer great advantages. Consumer behaviour studies, corporate image studies, motivation, worker-management relations studies and such other areas can make an extensive use of scaling techniques.

Basic Elements in Scaling

In this context, it is proper to throw some light on the basic aspects of scaling. As we have already observed, the most important aspect of scaling is the identification of an appropriate scale. It is here that the need for a continuum arises.

The Continuum

A continuum is a continuous, and not discrete, scale on which the various gradations of the same attribute can be continuously measured. In our hypothetical table given above, the attribute "loyalty" is presented in

5 grades, *viz.,* deceitful, unloyal, tolerable, loyal, and most loyal. When these gradations are given in the same order on a scale, there are two parts; negative end (consisting of deceitful and unloyal) and positive end (consisting of loyal and most loyal). In between, at the centre, there is a neutral grade "tolerable" which can be included in both, though it has greater attachment to the positive side of the continuum. If one moves from the neutral grade *tolerable* to the positive side of the continuum, one may become loyal and then most loyal. Similarly, one can move to the negative end of the continuum.

Of course, the nature of the continuum is to be inferred from the character of the selected items, as rightly observed by Goode and Hatt. "Scaling always hypothesizes the existence of a continuum of some kind. Its nature must be inferred from the character of the items selected to make up the scale. Logically unrelated items, therefore, cannot be included in the same scale without resulting in a confusion of continuum within one scale. Consequently, the first step in the scaling procedure, regardless of the technique employed, is a thorough knowledge of the subject."[1] The construction of a scale must be preceded by an in-depth study, evaluation, and observation.

In constructing, a scale, the researcher should have a thorough knowledge of the subject, and have to confirm the representative character of the selected items. Only then would be able to have a clear understanding of the nature of the population to be scaled, which is the prerequisite for the definition of the continuum. Though the scale is formulated after extensive studies, it should be treated as tentative when it is tested in a new universe.

As Goode and Hatt have observed: "The construction and application of a scale require a high degree of consciousness of the logical problems surrounding the twin assumptions of the existence of continuum, and the representativeness of that continuum, achieved by the particular scale in mind."[2] Tests of validity would be useful in studying the representative nature of the continuum, while the existence of the continuum can be tested with the help of value judgement, jury opinion, checking with the known groups, etc.

The researcher must ensure that the scale selected statisfies the conditions of reliability, validity, accuracy, equality of the units, and representativeness. If a scale produces the same result consistently when tested with the same sample consecutively, it may be considered to be

1. *Op. cit.,* 234
2. *Ibid.*

reliable. In order to determine the reliability of the continuum, tests and re-tests have to be conducted. In order to ensure greater validity, alternate scales may be tested and re-tested on the same sample successively, and the scale which produces the best result may be selected. The scale can also be divided into two halves, ensuring the random nature, and be tested which is known as split-half method. The split-half method can be effective when at least two conditions are met, *viz.,* the scale has been empirically tested; and each half scale has a sufficient number of items.

Validity is another important requirement for any scale. When a scale measures what is to be measured, it may be deemed to be a valid scale. The validity of the scale of the continuum depends much on the value judgement of the researcher. Logical validation, sometimes, seems to be a method of checking the validity of the scale. Jury opinion, checking with opinion leaders or known groups may also help in determining the validity. Independent criteria can also be adopted to check the validity of the continuum. Rational and logical value judgements of experienced researchers or practitioners may go a long way in the determination of the validity of the scale or continuum in the scaling technique. For increasing the validity of the scale the need for weighting the items cannot be ruled out.

The accuracy of scaling postulates the accuracy of the continuum. Of course, an absolute accuracy is a near impossibility. However, if proper care if exercised, the degree of reliability and accuracy can be considerably increased. As already mentioned, a quantitative treatment of the attributes is not possible, and hence quantitative accuracy cannot be demanded from scales. Accuracy in accordance with value judgement in ordering and ranking can be expected, particularly in developing the continuum. In this context, it may be pointed out that many limitations stand in the way of perfect scaling.

Limitations of Scaling

From the foregoing, discussion it is evident that perfect scaling is not possible. In fact, perfect scaling is not necessary. Logically suited factors, and attributes which are suitable for value judgement, can be brought under scaling. Equality of sampling would be necessary if scaling is to be used in various situations; but equality is not possible; and if equality is not possible, internal consistency and adequate identicalness would be enough if the scaling technique is used. As human behaviour changes over time and from situation to situation, scales developed may not always suit various situations. In fact, different scales suiting different situations would become more appropriate than ready-made scales, which need not be all pervasive. Hence, even if universality of scaling is not possible, this cannot be a very serious problem; especially when there are different techniques and approaches to scaling.

Scaling techniques are generally used in accordance with the universe we deal with and our own approach to the universe. Hence, there are different approaches to scaling techniques, *viz.,* social distance scaling sociometric measurement, rating scales, *etc.*

Social Distance Scaling

The social distance concept was propounded by Robert E. Park as early as 1902. The term *social distance* stands for a continuum specified as "the grades and degrees of understanding and intimacy which characterise pre-social and social relations."[3] The continuum suggested by Park ranges from close, warm, and intimate contact on the one hand, through indifference, to active dislike, hostility, and rejection on the other. Two points to be borne in mind in this context are:

(i) It is necessary to define the remainder of the continuum, that is, to define the measurement as social distance toward something a social group, a value or an individual; and

(ii) To measure the social distance which does exist.

Park's social distance scaling is very flexible; and that is why it would be useful on various occasions.

	(1)	*(2)*	*(3)*	*(4)*	*(5)*	*(6)*	*(7)*
Regarding ethnic minorities listed	*To Close kinship by marriage*	*To my club as personal chums*	*To my street as neighbours*	*To employment my occupation*	*To citizenship my country*	*As visitors only to my country*	*Would exclude from my country*
English	93.7	96.7	97.3	95.4	95.9	1.7	0.0
Swedes	45.3	62.1	75.6	78.0	86.3	5.4	1.0
Poles	11.0	11.6	28.3	44.3	58.3	19.7	4.7
Korean	1.1	6.8	13.0	21.4	23.7	47.1	19.1

* Adapted from Emery S. Bogardus, *Immigration and Race Attitude* (Boston : Heath, 1928). p. 25.

Though the concept of social distance has been initially formulated by Robert Park, it has been applied to various social groups by such sociologists as Emery S. Bogardus. They have tried this method to ethnic minorities, social classes, and occupational types, as well as to more abstract social values. In a study of 1,725 Americans regarding their social distance to four ethnic minorities in the USA, *viz.,* English, Swedes, Poles

3. Robert E. Park, 'The Concept of Social Distrance', *Journal of Applied Sociology,* Vol, VIII (1902), pp. 339-344

and Koreans, very interesting results were produced. The relations of these Americans have been presented in Table 1 on a social distance scale of seven points, as quoted by Goode and Hatt from Emery S. Bogardus.[4] Table 1.

Reactions of 1,725 Americans regarding their social distance to four ethnic minorities by percentage.

An examination of Table 1 shows the very interesting reactions of Americans regarding their social distance to the four ethnic groups in question (of course all the four groups are whites; if they had been blacks, the result would have been different). A very appreciable fact is that almost all Americans like to have the presence of other ethnic groups in their midst since only a little over 19 per cent expressed themselves in the negative (7th point in the table and that, too, against the Koreans. The social distance of Americans to the English is very narrow because most Americans (over 97 per cent) would like to accommodate English people to all the five positive points (see Table 1-points 1 to 5). In fact the social distance shows the social nearness as well. In respect of social nearness, the highest scores go to the English, then to the Swedes; the Poles come third in the gradation.

The social distance of Americans has been graphically expressed in Fig. 1 and Fig. 2 Though Americans (most of them) do not like to have kinship by marriage with Koreans and Poles, their social nearness to the English people is indicated almost as a straight line curve.

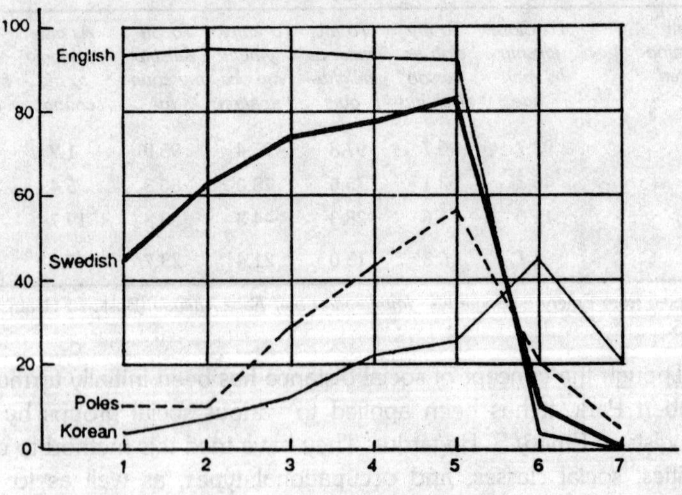

Fig.1 Graphic representation of social distance of Americans to four ethnic groups of immigrants

4. Emery S. Bogardus, *Immigration and Race Attidues,* Boston: Heath, 1928, p.25

The social distance of the Americans to the Koreans and the Poles is greater than to other two groups. The greater the social distance, the narrower the social proximity and attachment. When the curves are smoothened, the social distance of 1,725 Americans under study clearly expresses the steep trend in respect of both Swedes and Poles. While it is almost a straight horizontal line regarding English and is in the negative continuum for both the Koreans and the Poles.

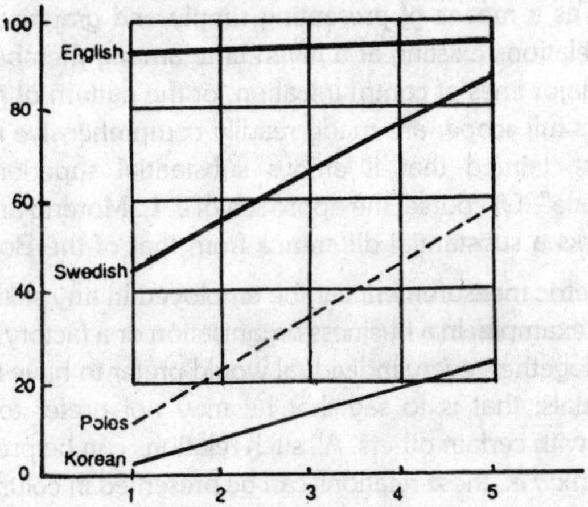

Fig.2 Graphic representation of the social distance of Americans, to four ethnic grouns of immigrants (smoothened curves).

The height of the line, their slopes and the angles which the lines make with the perpendicular show the actual social distance of the Americans to the respective groups. The steeper the slope, the more actue the angle, indicating a rapid drop from the proportion accepting the group at position 5 to the proportion accepting it at position 1. The English are in the most advantageous position over others; and this is shown by the intersection of their curve with the perpendicular at the highest level.

The social distance scaling technique may be use full in various areas of managerial analysis. To examine the consumer behaviour toward any product or a number of products (substitutes), corporate image, attitude studies of workers, etc., this technique can be employed. However, the use of this method is limited to pilot studies, because of its limitation *viz.,*

(a) The assumption of equidistance between the scale point;

(b) The assumption that each point is necessarily beyond the preceding one; and

(c) It can be tested for reliability only by the test re-test technique which can be considered as a trial-and error method.

This may perhaps be the reason why at least some social researchers emphasise the importance of sociometric measurement.

Sociometric Measurement

Helen Hall Jennings, is her *Sociometry in Group Relations* has highlighted "attractions, repulsions between individuals within a small group." Sociometry is defined in a direct manner. "Stated briefly, sociometry may be described as a means of presenting simply and graphically the entire structure of relations existing at a given time among members of a given group. The major lines of communication, or the pattern of attraction and rejection in its full scope, are made readily comprehensive at a glance"[5]. Jennings has claimed that it enjoys substantial superiority over the "Bogardus scale". Of course, the approach of J. L. Moreno and Helen Hall Jennings marks a substantial difference from that of the Bogardus scale.

Sociometric measurement can be employed in any setting of human relations. For example, in a business organisation or a factory, where many people work together, every individual would prefer to have relations with other individuals; that is to say that he may not prefer to have group cohesiveness with certain others. All such relations can be presented in the form of a matrix; *i.e.,* these relations can be presented in columns and rows of interdependence. According to Jennings, a sociometric test can have three characteristics.[6] These are:

(i) A specific number of choices is allowed, varying according to the size of the group tested;

(ii) A specific criterion for choice is used, varying with the functional activity of the group.

(iii) Different levels of preference are designated for each choice.

Jennings' *Sociometry in Group Relations* deals with the technique of studying school classes. Three choices were allowed to each child. The situation was defined as one in which the criterion for selecting other children in the class was "liking to work with them on a study committee." The levels of choice were designated by asking the children to make their first choice, second choice, and third choice of the child with whom they would like to be in the study committee. Then the reactions of the children were tabulated and presented in a matrix form. The same data can be presented graphically (call it a sociogram). Acceptability, scaling is possible in this study, on the basis of the frequency distribution of the choices made

5. Helen Hall Jennings, *Sociometry in Group Relations*. American Council on Education, Washington DC 1948, p. 11.
6. Jennings, *Leadership and Isolation,* Longmans New York, 1943, p. 19.

by the school children. The result may depend on such factors as definition of the continuum, reliability of the scale, and the validity of sociometric tests. There can be mutual choices, triangular or quadrangular choices, choice for a clique, star choice, or secondary star choices. The level of choice can be presented either on a matrix or a graph.

Rating Scales

Rating scales are common. Students are rated by their teachers, workers are rated by their supervisors, employees are rated by their employers and so on. Generally speaking, three elements are taken into account in designing the rating technique, *viz.,* the judges, the subjects, and the continuum. The judges who make the rating should be capable of making an impartial approach, while the continuum should accommodate the attributes realistically, and the subjects should be amenable to rating.

There can be one judge or many judges, and sometimes even a large group can do this job. The selection of judges depends on many factors — the ability of the person, expertise, acquaintance, status, etc. The elements or subjects to be judged also make a considerable impact on rating. The rating scale or the continuum must fit in with the framework of the rating need and nature. We have already referred to the continuum. Some major factors now be identified which would be common, and the rating grades can be assigned to each factor. But a rating, system, like any other evaluation system, should satisfy the conditions of reliability, validity, utility and objectivity.

Various other techniques such as ranking, checking internal consistency, scalogram scales, etc., also deserve some sort of attention in this context.

Ranking Scales

Ranking scales are identical to rating scales. A comparison of a series of stimuli is extensively done in the ranking scale. At first, a continuum is defined and stimuli presented for comparison, Guilford has described a method for rating a complex problem, which is more of academic use than of utility value.

Paired comparisons that deal with the comparison of two stimuli may be useful in some simple cases. By adding the number of preferences and considering the highest scores in favour of each item one would be able to rank every item. The method of equal appearing intervals is referred to as the "Thurstone technique of attitude measurement" because it was developed by L.L. Thurstone[7]. This is a psychophysical method. Goode

7. Thurstone L. L.,Chave E. J., *The Measurement of Attitude,* Chicago University Press 1929. pp. 57-58

and Hatt have quoted an example from experimental psychology to refer to this method. "If a large number of objects of the same size and appearance but of differing weights are given to a series of judges, it is possible to arrange them in order, from the lightest to the heaviest. Moreover, if the number of these objects is large and the total range of weight small, there will be a very slight difference between any two which are next to each other on the weight scale. Thus, if this number is increased to the point where the difference between any two neighbouring weights is just discernible" the difference between any neighbouring pair can be thought of as representing the same 'distance' on the scale; in other words, as constituting a scale unit.[8]

Even thought writers like Fechner have tried to run experiments, the applicability of these theories and techniques to primary sensory stimuli is limited, and hence attitude measurement with the help of such techniques is difficult, if not impossible. The most important problem in this context is the difficulty of finding out the just discernible differences. Of course, as in other methods, defining a proper continuum is difficult.

Thurstone himself later realised the difficulty about the application of this theory, and therefore has modified his technique and coinverted his "just discernible difference" to "equal-appearing intervals". It has been presumed that an attitude continuum, ranging from the strongest, possible appreciation to the weakest possible point of a value may be thought of theoretically as divisible into a number of equal intervals. Then such equal-appearing intervals may be assigned appropriate positions along the attitude continuum. This would enable the researcher to secure equal-appearing intervals on the attitude scale. For a satisfactory result, Thurstone and Chave gave specific instructions to the subjects, which we do not attempt to deal with here. However, the internal consistency scales developed by Thurstone deserve a mention here.

Internal Consistency Scales

Thurstone himself was aware of the fact that the equal-appearing intervals theory has confronted serious limitations for the scale values were seriously influenced by the nature, character, and number of judges. This may be the reason why a method of internal consistency scales has been suggested by him. Thurstone has not only suggested a general proposition to construct a scale from the responses, but also to devise a technique which was later known as method of internal consistency. Thurstone has called it "an objective criterion of irrelevance."

8. *Op. cit.* pp. 262-263

Many thinkers have made their contributions to the concept of internal consistency, among whom Murphy and Likert,[9] as well as Rundquist and Sletto,[10] deserve special mention. All subjects are expected to respond to all items under this method. The subjects are asked to endorse only those items which they agree under the Thurstone method. But under the Murphy method, a response representing disagreement must be included. In both the cases, each item becomes a scale in itself, and the total scale is actually a battery of scales. Then it is no longer necessary to begin with a large number of items, as under the Thurstone method. This is an advantage of the internal consistency method.

Scale construction, and item selection as a part of scale construction, is an integral part of the internal part of the internal consistency method. Scoring a scale is the next step, and then the continuum is developed. At this stage, values may be assigned to every item or even response in the item. "It can be seen that in the case of well-constructed scales, the simpler scoring technique, though not, as safe as the stigma-scoring method, will serve quite adequately to produce a useful instrument." Thus, the construction of scales and scoring techniques would go a long way in ensuring internal consistency. Item selection is followed by item analysis, which is an alternative to the method of internal consistency.

This technique is not well developed, though it offers possibilities for future development. Though there is feasibility, there is also the possibility of the inclusion of anything to be considered as a "smart crack". In the refinement which Seeman has suggested, the actual construction of a scale is not very important, but rather a demonstration of a rationale for scale development. In brief, the method of internal consistency is a very flexible and useful method of scale construction. Of course, proper care must be exercised at all stages of internal consistency.

Thurstone, under his equal-appearing intervals method, has selected as many as 130 statements (ranging from the most positive to the most antagonistic) on the people's attitudes to the church, and has made separate slips of each statement.

Many bundles of such statements were made and distributed to 300 judges, with instructions to choose on a preference basis. All these statements were then arranged in frequency and cumulative frequency

---

9. Murphy Gardner and Rensis Likert, *Public Opinion and the Individual*, Harper, New York, 1938.
10. Edward A. Rundquist and Raymond Sletto, *Personality in the Depression*, Minneapolis, University of Minnesota Press. 1936.

distribution, and then the scale values of selected statements were fixed. The total score of a person to whom the scale was administered was determined either by the mean or the median. This way a very tedious method — a fact which Thurstone himself realised later.

At the same time, internal consistency method has eliminated the need for judges in sorting out the statements. A large number of statements pertaining to a particular attitude were taken. Likert took about 99 statements from American-born Japanese and compared them on a five-point scale (definitely agree, agree, undecided, disagree, and definitely disagree). Every point was weighted. Every person was to select one of the statement, and 500 informants were used. The critical ratio was taken by using the equation. Sigma (c) method could also be used. Both the methods were identical, except for marginal differences. These methods do not find favour with many social scientists of today though they are of academic interest.

Scalogram Scales

The scalogram technique is another development in the area of scaling techniques. A scale constructed by the internal consistency method contains several dimensions, (not one), and therefore gives us only a crude measure; that is, the dimensions which are not really wanted become involved, thereby making a possibility of the most wanted aspects not to get the proper attention, while unimportant dimensions receive more attention. Though limit-dimensionality is not necessarily a fault in an attitude scale, in places where uni-dimensionality deserves attention, multi-dimensionality may pose a danger to accuracy. In search of a solution for this problem, the factor analysis has been identified. Guttman's scalogram technique has, perhaps, emerged from the idea of scalable uni-dimensional universe.

A scalogram is derived from the response patterns yielded by a set of data. Stouffer associates the technique with Guttman. "He (Guttman) considered an area scalable if responses to a set of items in that area arranged themselves in certain specified ways. In particular, it must be possible to order the items that, ideally, persons who answer a given question favourably all have higher ranks than persons who answer the same question favourably. From a respondent's rank or scale score, we know exactly which items he endorsed. Thus, we can say that the response to any item provides a definition of the respondent's attitude." This ability to reproduce the responses to each item on the basis of the total score is called reproducibility, which is one of the tests of items making a scale.

The following example would make the concept clear. The following 4 questions were put to 16 executives of a factory with the answers.

Scalogram of Responses of Executives on Educational Background

Rank order of Response	*Yes Response to Items* 1	2	3	4	*No Response to Items* 1	2	3	4
1	x					x	x	x
2		x			x		x	x
3			x		x		x	x
4				x	x		x	x

In fact, a "scale analysis" indicates that a scale constructed by the criterion of internal consistency may contain more than one variable. The latent structure analysis has recently gained ground over factor analysis, which has yet to achieve any practical importance. But attitude measurements are popular with managerial researchers.

Attitude Measurement

Generally speaking, attitude measurement is qualitative in nature. An attitude is an internal psychic or mental state of a person. According to Dr. Michael, an attitude is a basic predisposition or tendency to respond, positively or negatively, to a set of circumstances"[11]. It is generally inferred from the responses of the individual. Behaviour is influenced by attitude. In an attitude scale, an individual responds to a set of carefully phrased questions. On the basis of these responses, he may be placed at a point on an attitude continuum which numerically presents his position between the positive and the negative poles.

The basic elements of attitude are:

Predisposition, and the direction of that predisposition. Opinion, response, belief and attitude are interdependent factors. While an attitude influences opinion, the former is reinforced by the latter, according to which a response is made. An attitude is a learned or motivated orientation or disposition towards an object or situation or issue which reinforces an individual to form response or a reaction. It can be latent or inactive, except in particular circumstances, when the individual is reinforced by his attitude to react in a favourable, unfavourable or indifferent manner.

As attitude influences behaviour, and the behaviour results in related attitude studies attitudes are of great importance in managerial researches.

11. Dr. Michael, V. P. *Organisational Behaviour and Managerial Effectiveness.* S. Chand Ltd. New Delhi, 1989, p. 117.

Attitude surveys enable the top management to formulate personnel policies that will promote cordial relations, and motivate workers to make their best contribution to the attainment of corporate objectives and goals. These surveys are very popular with sales people for the purpose of determining consumer behaviour, brand loyalty, etc. They are effective tools in the hands of advertising people for they enable them to evaluate advertising effectiveness. In brief, attitude surveys can be in extensive use in managerial analysis if its limitations can be eliminated.

Limitations of Attitude Measurement

The intangible nature of attitudes results in the inaccuracy of results. Only when the informant makes up his mind to give unbiased information, does the information becomes dependable. But one is not able to check the reliability of the information. A lot of guessing becomes necessary in attitude surveys. Moreover, human attitudes are complex, and there are many factors which influence them. Attitude changes from time to time, place to place and situation to situation are common. The results of attitude surveys are, therefore, bound to vary. A proper scale for accurate measurement, is therefore a near impossible. Languages, expressions, actions, gestures, etc., play very important roles in attitude and communication. Unless the researcher is able to evaluate all these, the attitude of the informant may not be properly understood. Hence, mere scaling or grading may not be enough in the study of attitudes. A detailed attitude survey is, therefore, necessary.

Attitude Surveys

A favourable attitude of the customers to a company or its products generally precedes a decision to buy, even if this favourable predisposition is at a pre-conscious level. Sometimes a buyer picks up a product on impulse without consciously identifying the motivation to buy it. His attitude toward that product may be subconsciously favourable.

Attitude measurement may consist of a general assessment or be restricted to the various dimensions of a specific situation or an object. Unfortunately, it is difficult to construct a true measure of a person's attitudes though several techniques have often been employed in combination to facilitate cross-checking. A direct survey can be conducted, by putting direct question to the respondent. Check-list questions with rating scales can be asked; what is your general opinion about Godrej Refrigerator? And then the rating scale may be given: Excellent/good/just tolerable/indifferent/bad.

A structured interview or a partially structured interview may be employed, or the respondent may be requested to fill a check-list by indicating the most appropriate answer. An attitude related to usage is usually considered a significant measure of advertising effectiveness. Preference for a particular product can be treated as a favourable attitude. But a favourable or unfavourable attitude alone is not enough. What is actually needed is the degree of intensity. Of course, all respondents may not be in a position to express the exact measurement of intensity. Hence, there is the need for the use of some attitude scales on the part of the researcher.

Attitude Scales

Some of the attitude scales are: intensity scales, points scales, and ranking scales. The scaling techniques have been considered earlier in this chapter. The identification of the continuum, the setting of standards, the measurement of attitude in comparison with the continuum, etc., have also been examined. An attitude scale should satisfy the conditions of reliability, validity, equality, and accuracy. Social distance scale, equal-appearing intervals, sociometric methods, rating scales, ranking scales, etc., have been dealt with.

It can be noticed in this context that all the attitude scales are now of academic interest. Many scales are of doubtful validity. A computation of scales and a determination of scale values are really complicated processes and hence the validity of the scaling technique itself is questioned. The reliability of attitudes scales is doubtful. However, the facts which are involved in scaling technique and attitude surveys cannot be disqualified from theoretical treatment, since theory and fact are closely linked with each other.

Theory Building

Factors are the basic elements in scaling techniques in particular and in the body of research as a whole in general. An intricate relationship exists between theory and facts in science. Facts are definite, realistic, certain, and meaningful, which help in the formulation of theory, and facilitate its proof.

Theory and fact are inextricably intertwined. A fact is an empirically verifiable observation, while theory is given birth when a relation is established between facts. Theory is a part and a tool of science. "Theory is a tool of science in many ways" according to Goode and Hatt.[12]

(i) Theory defines the major orientation of a science, by defining the kinds of data which are to be abstracted.

12. *Op. cit.* p. 8,

(ii) It offers a conceptual scheme by which the relevant phenomena are systematised, classified, and interrelated.

(iii) Theory summarises facts into empirical generalisations and systems of generalisations.

(iv) It predicts facts.

(v) Theory points to gaps in our knowledge.

At the same time, facts help to initiate the formation of theory, and lead to the reformulation of an existing theory. Theories which fail to fit in within the framework of facts are rejected. On the other hand, facts change the focus and orientation of theory. They also clarify and redefine theory. One who formulates a theory has to obtain, analyse, and recognise facts. Interpretation of facts and establishing relationships between facts come under the formulation of theory.

Theory builder makes abstraction from reality and facts keeping the attention on phenomena. It means that there should be a proper orientation for theory building. Conceptualisation is the crux of theory building for which the developments of systems of classification, a structure of concepts. Thus, an increasingly precise set of definitions of terms are required. "Every science is also organised by a structure of concepts, which refer to the major processes and objects to be studied. It is the relationships between these concepts, which are stated in the facts of science. Such terms make up the specialised vocabulary that the scientist uses. They change as the science develops, for different phenomena came to be of major importance. A major task in any science is the development of systems of classification, a structure of concepts, and an increasingly precise set of definitions for these terms."[13]

Theory building properly summarises what is already known about the subject-matter of study. Generalisations include both empirical generalisations and relations between variables and propositions. Inductions and deductions can also be included in the theory. Some theorists have attempted even to integrate the major empirical generalisations of an era.

Theory predicts facts, which can be an extrapolation from the known to the unknown. "Nevertheless, it is clear that theory performs the task of stating what factors are to be expected." For the prediction of facts, the available facts should be systematised and organised during the course of which gaps are identified and pointed out. Substantial research is the most essential prerequisite for fact finding, analysis, and interpretation on one hand and for theory building on the other. Conceptualisation is also an

---

13 Goode and Hatt, *Op. cit.*, p. 9,

indispensable task of theory building. We, therefore, throw some light on conceptualisation here.

Conceptualisation

A theory must have a conceptual clarity. Science is a conceptual system and concept is an empirically verified statement about phenomena. Thus, science, theory, and concept are interlinked. Conceptualisation therefore deserves a special mention in this context.

Basically, a concept is an abstraction from evaluations, sense impressions, percepts, or even fairly complex experiences. It may include phenomena. conceptualisation should, therefore, take phenomenon into consideration, while concept should be backed by facts. Concept symbolises empirical relationships, and the facts state the phenomena. Evidently, conceptualisation incorporates empirical relationships supported by facts and phenomena. Both concepts and facts are meaningful within some frame or reference, since they are abstractions. They take their meaning from the thought framework within which they are placed. "The distinction between fact and concept is that concepts symbolise the empirical relationships and phenomena which are stated by the facts. Thus, as noted before, a fact is stated as a relationship between concept, for each term stands for the phenomena described by the fact. In this sense, then, a fact is a logical presentation of concepts. A concept, in turn, is abstracted from many sense impressions, or percepts".[14]

Concepts is a basic element in a science and scientific method; and it is the foundation not only of scientific communication but a basis of every communication. A scientific concept is expected to be communicated; and that is why it is closely linked with scientific communication. Moreover, communication is the most indispensable part of every day business of life. There cannot be any communication without information; and the concept is involved in information.

Communication generally presupposes a communicator, and the person or persons for whom it is meant. There is a mutual sharing of information and concept. This is the reason why the concept is considered to develop from a shared experience.

Another important aspect of a concept is that its ultimate empirical referents should be determinable; that is a concept with no empirical referents is not acceptable to science. When science develops, new concepts may emerge and old ones may be discarded. The relevant conceptual tools

14. *Ibid.*, p. 42

must be clear to all, and there should be an awareness of ambiguity, if any. Reconceptualisation takes place then, which is the process of clarification or re-specification of the concept. It should then be confirmed as to whether the concept is properly used. Re-specification of the concept results in the formulation of fresh hypotehsis.

All the conceptualisations, studies and investigations lead to report writing, and hence no research can be fruitful without a systematic report. Next chapter, therefore unveils report writing.

Chapter 10

Report Writing

A managerial research is generally conducted to probe into a management problem resulting in a research report. It means that a research report is the end product of a research. On the other hand a business report or a management report is a report prepared by the management to portray certain important aspects or problems in business. Thus, two important types of report in the realm of mangement are: (1) business report or management report, and (2) managerial research report.

Business Report or Management Report

Management's report to the share holders, report from a functional area to the general management, report of a subordinate executive to the top management etc., come under the category of management report or business report. Thus, a business report is a report on certain aspects of business prepared for information or action of the management, or management people. This can be called a management report for the sake of management.

The business report starts with report planning and designing. Once a report is planned and its structure is decided, data and information pertaining to the subject are collected in support of the views represented in the report. On the other hand a research report is a report based on a research study conducted for which research is first planned, data collected, and analysis and interpretation made leading to report writing. First we deal with business reporting here followed by an examination of research reporting. A report is generally a formal communication as Brown[1] puts it. Let us start with the methodology of business reporting.

Methodology of Business Writing

Business reporting starts with report planning, which includes a determination of the objectives of the report, identification of the target reader of the report, consideration of the real purpose of the report, planning for the collection of proper materials for the report, preparation of the scheme of report writing, planning for proper utilisation of time in report writing, and crystallisation of the actual lay out of the report.

Once the report is planned, *material collection* starts. Checking and rechecking of materials collected against the actual objectives and lay out of the report then become necessary. Arranging the contents of the report should also not be forgotten. When the collected materials, data, observation, documentation, information, opinion, clarification, etc., are arranged and fitted together to a carefully articulated form, the writer will come to know as to which materials to put together in the report, and what is to be dispensed with. It should, however, be ensured that enough material has been selected to carry out the purpose of the report. When the prospective reader is less familiar with the situations and specifications than the writer, the writer must ensure that all the necessary details are given in the report. But the information must be to the point and in accordance with the needs of the reader. Beating about the bush must be avoided.

A proper selection of materials helps the writer to present his thoughts and ideas clearly and effectively. However, it may not automatically guarantee an effective communication. All too often, some writers feel complacent about report writing and the presentation of the data. Unless the materials are put together properly in order to project the subject-matter thoroughly, the report may be ineffective. Some report writers begin to compose the materials before gathering, selecting, and analysing the proper data and information thus defeating the very purpose of the report.

As soon as proper data and information are collected, selected, and arranged, adequate thought must be given to the purpose of the report that is: what is to be communicated? To whom is to be communicated? When is to be communicated and for what purpose? The report writer should place himself in the shoes of his reader before he starts writing. Ask this question: how would he/they react if I gave a short slant to the arguments in this fashion? Think over it, try to rearrange your materials, and then start writing the report. This will enable you to determine what should find a plae in your report and where: and what must not be included in it. It is an appropriate first to determine what is not to be included in the report as what is to find a place in the report.

It is the report writer who will have to decide about what is to be included in the report to make it effective. The more one is experienced, the more will one form be effective on report writing. Generally speaking, the following may for the contents of a report:

(a) A title;

(b) Abstracts, table of contents, and terms of reference if any;

(c) A summary, if the report is fairly long;

(d) The body of the report which may include a statement of the problem area, analysis and interpretation and presentation of data (if necessary),

(e) Observations, recommendations, suggestions, induction, deductions, conclusions, and

(f) Appendices, if any.

Note: Some specialised reports may carry additional sections.

A report should be so constructed as to enable the readers to pick it up and get what they need from it without much effort. (Almost all the principles of written communication are applicable here.) A good report is primarily devoted to an examination of problem areas, and makes generalisation based on precise results. Though both general and abstract approaches are made in the report, the report writer must be careful not to be too general or too abstract. A good abstract is, however, very useful not only for the reader of the report but also for the librarians or custodians of the report.

In table of contents an outline of the report, which contains major headings and sub-headings, as well as the various sub-sections are presented. There should be a summary of the report, especially when the report runs into many pages. The summary provides a reasonably complete resume of the report. and it helps the reader to grasp what is important in the report. A summary should be brief and to the point: and as far as possible, all the important points should be briefly touched upon, including conclusions and recommendations.

The body of the report is its chief part. It includes everything from the statement of the problem to a detalied analysis of the data and information. Statistics, documentation, and information are presented for analytical purposes. Everything should be organised in an elegant manner. This should be followewd by conclusions, suggestions, recommendations, etc. The appendix, if any, especially illustrative materials like tables, charts, etc., should be given at the end of the report.

Should nots		*Should*
Convenience writing	**Business Reports**	Analytical reporting
Roundabout manner		Accurate study
Provocative style		Authenticity of data
Unnecessary data		Consistency
Unnecessary jargon		Communicativeness
Vague writing		Clarity and conciseness
		Direct approach
		Investigative method
		Simplicity
		Suggestiveness
		Systematic presentation

There are topic-oriented writings and performance-oriented writings. The performance-oriented writing tells us what to do and how to do it. Topic-oriented writing focuses on the generalisations and concepts which constitute a body of knowledge. It deals with a subject area or a functional area, which may be treated as a general refrerence text. The following presents the "should" and "should nots" of business reports.

Business Report

It is necessary for the report writer to ensure the above eleven "shoulds" and six "should nots" in his report, so that it may be effective. However, many a reporter never cares to ensure perfection, and many executives do not attach much importance to such report. (We give a few simple reports at the end of this chapter.) This may, perhaps, be the reason why some report writers adopt a journalistic style.

Journalistic Style

Journalism "is the events of the day distilled into a few words, sounds or pictures, processed by the mechanics of communication to satisfy the human curiosity of a world that is always eager to know what's new".[2]

2. Wainwright, *Journalism*, Heinemann, London, 1982. p.1.

Journalism stands for daily news presented in an appealing manner. To that extent, it is an entertainment and reassurance to satisfy the human frailty of a world that is always eager to be comforted with knowledge. Now the journalistic style is a style of reporting the day-to-day news in the most effective and appealing way. The journalistic reporting is capable to reach a number of people, a handful of them or the whole population of the world. Though space-bridge telecast programmes can be carried to the whole world within a couple of minutes. Journalists report the matter that is news worthy. Internet surfing has, of late, become a dynamic communication network.

The journalistic style transforms even complicated news item into simple and intelligible news. The defeat of Mrs. Indira Gandhi in 1977 general elections was first reported by BBC, even before the Election Commission had announced it, and the news of her assasination had reached all over the world, within minutes. Journalism has succeeded in a fast communication of news and messages to the most remotest parts of the world. A profound change in the human communication system has, perhaps, stemed from the success of journalism.

Detailed newspaper reporting of the past has now developed into efficient and scientific reporting. Photographs and film strips of high precision occupy a conspicuous place in TV programmes. The electronic media have almost captured the realm of reporting, advertising and publicity, resulting in the emergence of new trends in communication. The press media have now been revolutionised. Obviously, a new journalistic style has emerged. Newspapers, TV and the radio have already become part of everyday human life. Computer aided communication is the order of the day.

Quick reporting and adveturous reporting have become the characteristics of the journalistic style. Any even has to communicated to the news-seeking ears as quickly as possible while its heat and smoke still remain. Eighty year old Jessica Tandy was given the Oscar in 1990 as the best leading actress for her role as crotchety old woman in the back seat of a car in **Driving Miss Daisy.** The award was announced in Hollywood on 27th March, and *The Times of India* carried the news on 28th March (early at dawn.) This is quick reporting. The example of Mr. Farzad Bazoft, a journalist of Iranian origin who worked for a British newspaper in Iraq, is an example of adventurous reporting. He placed his life at risk while reporting an explosion at a military installation near Baghdad in September 1989. (He was executed on charges of spying for Israel and Britain.)

Investigative reporting is a part of the journalistic style. The report of **Mr. N. Ram** of *The Hindu* on the Bofors episode is an example. in fact, every journalist is an investigator. In a way, research and investigation cannot be isolated from journalism. Of course, investigation helps everyday reporting. It need not be professional research or a very formal type of research. But making every enquiry to facilitate reporting is the type of research which a journalist does.

Today's journalist is the one who moves in accordance with the demands of the time. Once upon a time, the journalist had to adopt a diffused and detailed style. But the executive of today has very little time for reading, and obviously he needs brief but all-inclusive, simple but thought-provoking, light but enlightening, and sweet but deep reading material for his evening or morning reading. It is here that journalistic skill becomes demanding. A new journalistic style is now emerging to satisfy this kind of need.

A few years ago, in well-to-do families vernacular newspapers satisfied the morning reading. Those with low means had depended on public reading rooms and others did not care for any serious reading in big cities. Only a small percentage of the population used to read English language newspapers. Consequent to this trend, journalistis had enjoyed a lot of homogeneity in their writing style. Now there is extensive heterogeneity in the readership, resulting in a need for a heterogeneous journalistic style.

From an armchair reading style, the executive of today has shifted to bedside transistor radio which switches itself on with an alarm exactly at news time. Mother has her transistor on the kitchen table and children do have their own transistor radios. They may watch the breakfast TV news, They may not have much time to ponder over every news item, but may just try to skip over news headlines to gain some grasp of the news and information as fast as possible. A journalist, to be successful in such a situation, has to tone up his writing style in accordance with the emerging pattern of the reading habits of the people. He must be able to capture the attention of the reader with eyecatching headlines and sub-headings, as well as simple and brief news.

A good journalist improves his efficiency by typing his own reports. His typewriter can now be replaced by a word processor, thus eliminating the tedious retyping chore. He can use an electronic data processing system and an information data bank to increase his efficiency.

House journals are of comparatively recent origin in India. They can play a very vital role in educating and motivating the workers of our industrial society. This is the reason why many industrial units have now shifted to the house journal philosophy. In a strainful and troubled industrial relations environment, a house journal (particularly an internal house journal) can do a good job if it is planned well. A house journal is a publication issued periodically by an industrial unit, a business house, or a public service for the information of their workers and not for profit. it provides adequate knowledge and information through attractive, simple, interesting, informative, and entertaining articles and materials; and this calls for a special type of journalistic style.

From the foregoing discussion, it is evident that journalists have a special style of their own.

Specialisation in Journalistic Style

The journalistic style is a special reporting style because it not only communicates but also satisfies people. Hence, it may be referred to as social reporting. It has a tremendous social impact, for it chiefly deals with social problems; what the journalist writes is for the society at large.

It seems relevant to quote. Nicholas Tomalin about the specialisation in style. "The only qualities essential for real success in journalism are rat-like cunning, a plausible manner, and a little literary ability".[3] Wainwright has rightly pointed out that the rat-like cunning approach is needed to ferret out and publish things that people don't want to be known, "which is—and always will be—the best definition of news." This cunning craftiness, represents the guts and skill to publish facts which people do not want to be known. It is the ability to probe, present, and publicise facts in their entirety. The way Mr. Ram has probed, presented, and publicised the Bofors episode is an exmaple. The rat-like cunning or craftiness is thus considered to be a positive quality of the specialised journalistic style. In the interests of the society at large, certain vested interests are to be exposed, which is the job of journalism. Unfortunately, however, on many occasions, we wonder whether present day journalism is moving in the opposite direction making a mess of everything for their political interests.

The plausible manner of writing is very useful. It is not only essential for survival, but also for success in a journalistic career.

Literary ability is another important characteristic of journalistic style. This ability is not the ability to put in black and white all that one comes to hear or know. It is the ability to present precisely and effectively what is to be presented at the exact place and time. This is perhaps lacking in many journalists of our time. Rather than weaving his own career, the journalist should discriminate in the interest of the whole society.

---

3. *Ibid.*, p.7.

The freedom of the press, demand reliability, truthfulness and clarity. At the same time, the familiarity factor should be taken care of. Wainwright's observation is relevant here. "The familiarity factor is important. It must not be despised. For to get through to his readers, his listeners, or his viewers, the journalist must lay down some guidelines to lead the public from what is familiar to what seems strange, dangerous and frightening. The journalist is an agent of change in a society. he must seek it and not stay too comfortably in the familiar present. For the society changes, media or no media: and the press that does not change wakes up to find that its readers have left it behind." [4]

The journalist must determine the news worthiness of an item of information. Reporting anything and everything at all times may land the journalist himself in trouble. One may not rule out the value of sensational news. But for the sake of sensation, one must not make indiscriminate or irresponsible use of information. The journalist or the chief sub-editor or chief editor of a newspaper, must be extremely cautious in choosing news items, especially in the selection of the lead story. This of course depends on the nature, image and standing of the newspaper.

When there is press censorship, the journalists must abide by it. The quality newspapers, which are otherwise called the "papers of record" always maintain their image and standing in all their news reporting. For example, *The Times of India* is very cautious in news selection. It can print stories which it is convinced of and are ought to be made known to the public even if they are dull and unlikely to appeal to many readers.

Then the question arises: How do journalists evaluate what is to be selected, emphasised, and published? Generally speaking, their intuitive rule-of-thumb judgement plays an important role in this respect. Their value judgements as to the type of news that be appreciated and preferred by readers may determine their selection of news. For what type of readers does the company produce the newspapers? This too is, a decisive factor in determining the journalistic style. In this context, it is always good for a journalist to follow specific procedures.

Writing Procedures

Various journalists follow various procedures for their journalistic reporting. Each adopts the procedure most convenient for him. For a long time in the past development journalism, was popular in western countries. After independence, particularly after the emergence of economic planning this journalistic style has been gaining ground in India also. *Yojana* the

4. *Ibid.*, pp. 6.7

house journal of the Planning Commission, is devoted to development journalism. Development reporting has now reached substantial proportions in India, since the Indian press is committed to development reporting on a large scale.

The Indian Institute of Mass Communication has put out a manual for news agency reporters. According to it, development reporting creates a sense of involvement and concern among the people for their own development. It is expected to describe the terms and concepts of development. The success stories of people who have adopted new techno-logy and methods, and have benefited are projected as a part of development reporting. The basic nature of development reporting is that it is devoid of the sensational element in reporting; and is considerably backed by research and analysis. Development is measured by the improvement in the lives of the people, and the reporting that takes care of this aspect is known as development reporting.

Writing for newspapers and writing for electronic media (TV and radio) are substantially different. The former permits recourse to style; lengthy sentences, detailed write-up, change of pace for paragraph construction, etc. Writing for newspapers is meant for reading, while writing for radio and TV is for being heard. Obviously, procedures can differ. Fairly lengthy sentences may stay in the minds of readers, while short sentences are conducive to better hearing. Hence, short sentences are appreciated in TV and radio news, while long sentences may not be bad in newspaper reporting. It is, however, better to have a succinct and simple writing for the press media. Commenting on radio journalistic style, M. V. Kamath appropriately remarks.[5] "In the case of a radio broadcast, the listener can easily be put off if the broadcaster rambles on and on. Inevitably, his sentences will have to be short and terse. He will have to come to the point and waste no word for embellishment."

Newspaper reporting starts with a brief heading, place, data, and the name of the news agency (if necessary). Then the report is given in short paragraphs. Some newspaper reports are given at the end of this chapter.

A radio newscast starts with the headlines. The broadcaster then reads out the more important news. The same technique is generally used in TV broadcasting, though some film clips are shown occasionally in TV telecasting.

Newspaper reporting uses headings, headlines etc., to make an impression in the reader, while the news broadcaster uses such tools as pauses,

5. Kamath M. V. *Journalist's Handbook*, Vikas Publishing, New Delhi, 1983. p. 217.

inflection of voice, etc. Kamath's observation is very relevant here. "The newspaperman relies very largely on headlines, cross-heads, italics, general display and layout to make his impression on the reader. The news broadcaster has none of these aids available to him. In the circumstances, he has to depend upon pauses and inflection of voice to mark his delivery."[6] To quote Kamath again.

"Delivery becomes all-important. The pause cannot be too long, lest the listener lose interest. A newspaper reader can glance back over anythng he has missed or failed to grasp or understand; but the radio listener cannot pull the announcer up and ask him to repeat what he has said. The announcer therefore has necessarily to speak smoothly, his words must flow uninterruptedly, all of which calls for the use of short words and unadorned sentences." There can be some differences when commentaries, reviews, interviews, etc., are used providing change and avoiding a dull uniformity.

In commentaries, reviews etc., a conversational style and an informal and free posture would look more natural, but in news, brevity is the soul of wit.

While a short conclusion of a couple of sentences may close a newspaper write-up, a brief summary—particularly main points—is given in the electronic media. As the average receptive capacity or digestive ability of the radio listeners, even TV viewers, is low, because of the extensive nature of this media, extreme care must be taken to use simple and short sentences without using big and difficult words and commercial jargon. Radio plays or TV serials must be enlightening, simple, interesting, and thought-provoking, while preparation of radio talks (each of which is generally 14 minutes duration) deserve extreme care. To put across a thought-provoking message, which is capable of reaching a wide spectrum of audience in about 1,300 words is not a very easy task. As far as possible, the talk should be conversational style meant to give certain basic information and not to present extensive data. It should not be a lecture or a research paper showing the great knowledge of the speaker. Some pauses may be meaningful if they are used properly.

Words can be used for sound effect, but statistical data (figures) should be avoided. Talks are generally heard and hence a language style that motivates the listeners should be used. Pleasing words and sounds, simple and meaningful words, a sweet expression etc., would make the talk more effective. On certain occasions, the use of euphoric words becomes necessary. A proper organisation of a journalistic work is of importance if efficiency in writing is to be achieved.

---

6. *Ibid.*, p. 223.

Organisation of Writing

Organising a journalistic work is the job of journalists and journalistic executives. In a newspaper at the top of the journalistic work is the editor, who is in over-all charge, though the associate editor is the one who actually does the job on behalf of the chief editor. The associate editor directly reports to the chief editor. In a big organisation, there can be more than one associate editor. Under the associate editor there are news editors for specific types of news editing; say, general news editors, economic news editors, sports news editors, etc. In small newspaper organisations only one news editor may look after all the jobs. The sub-editor, too , is an important journalist in the news reporting organisation. News reporters and correspondents functioning at various reporting centres are also a part of organised news writing.

Sub-Editing

It is the sub-editor who prepares copy for the printers. From a number of sources, *viz.,* reporters, telephone copy takers, paper's own correspondents aborad, news agency tapes etc, copies arrive. It is the sub-editor who processes this copy and makes a copy of the respective news items to be published. some stories arrive from a single source, which the sub-editor marks up for setting.

But very often the sub-editor has to cut down the stories to the required length (generally 4 inches or so) without detriment to their meaning and emphasis. This is always a difficult job for the sub-editor. He has to measure every piece of copy precisely to required length. By examining the basic text size, he has to gauge how much space can be assigned to every story which many reporters do not like. Hence, some sort of a battle between the subs and some reporters is always going on.

The subs claim that they represent the newspaper reader (very often, that is ture too) and hence it is their duty to tune up the copy according to the reader's tastes. As a result, a lot of deletions and additions become necessary. Of course, nobody can deny that the subs must be accurate. They must check the facts, trace out errors and check them out, and get any addition from the reporter if anything is missiing. Spelling mistakes, grammatical mistakes, wrong constructions, unwanted points, beating about the bush and unnecessary stretching ot matter have to be checked by the sub-editor. He should make the copy clear, legible and properly worded. Making proper headlines, caption writing, and taking the printer's problems into account etc.—these are the duties of the sub-editor. It is therefore he who does a conspicuous job in the organisation of writing.

Though the press and the organisation of news in India may be treated as free press, one cannot deny the fact that the government exercises some control over the press in India. It imposes some sort of restraints on the press, in the interest of the national security.

In organising news in India the Press Council, too, plays some role. It helps to maintain the standards of newspapers; and attempts to ensure the freedom of the press. The objectives of the Press Council have been outlined in the Press Council Act of 1978. As a detailed approach to this institution is beyond the scope of this book, we do not attempt to do that. We refer directly now to research report.

Research Report

It is most proper to examine the research report here since research is one of the main topics of discussion in this book. A research study culminates in report writing, which is a tool for communicating the various aspects of the study, *viz.*, the problem or topic investigated, the method employed to investigate, its objectives scope and limitation, etc. However, before writing the report, proper report planning is essential. Report planning should take into account such details as defining the problem, the purpose of the report, tracking the material collected, identifying the utility of the report, and so on. The ability to write effective reports is one of the most useful skills a researcher can acquire. In this connection, Brown observes: "We say it as simply as we possibly can, and that is, that a report is a communication from someone to another who wants to use that information. The report may be elaborately formal, it may be a letter, or in a great many organisations, it is simply a memorandum; but it is always planned for use."[7]

The usefulness of a report is the basic requisite of any research report. For example, a study that deals with market segmentation for a company should report on the exact distinction between customer groups and their needs for the purpose of sub-dividing its market into specific subsets of customers. Customers are likely to differ in various respects. A study of the market segmentation of toilet soaps of Hindustan Lever should specifically report the exact segment of customers for a transparent glycerine soap (Pears), for a luxury beauty soap (Supreme), for a lemon soap (Liril), for a low-priced toilet soap (Rexona) for an economic health soap (Lifebuoy). While the report is expected to convey all the aspects of the result of the study in all its details to the interested parties; it should highlight the actual utility areas as well.

7. Brown, C. A. referred to by Shurter in *Communication in Business*, McGraw-Hill, International Student Edition, p. 290.

The report identifies areas for further research, if any, and for fresh hypothesis. Analysis and inferences, suggestions and observations, foot-notes and appendices etc., should also find a place in the report which should include specific recommendations for the course of action to be adopted. All the necessary information materials should be presented in the most appropriate manner. It should be purposeful and should take into account the reader and his reading habits and interests.

In the normal course, the report writer has to consider such questions as: Who will read the report? In what way is the report going to be useful? What are the questions to be answered? How much information is needed? What is the best way of presenting the information? And so on. An effective report improves interpersonal relationships in an organisation, since it suggests solutions to problem areas. In this connection, Arthur D. Little observes: "In short, remember that the reader is a human being, not a corporation. He is not omniscient; if he were, he wouldn't have asked for your help. Remember also that he doesn't want to devote his whole career to deciphering what you have to say. The project you are reporting on is undoubtedly only one of the many that require his attention. Your report should provide answers, not create more problem."[8] For the purpose of a report to be effective, whatever kind it may be, it is to throw ligh on how to solve problems.

Types of Reports

For the sake of convenience, reports may be classified either on the basis of approach or on the basis of the nature of presentation.

On the basis of approach a report may be:

(i) Journalistic report:

(ii) Business report and memorandum:

(iii) Project reports

(iv) Dissertation:

(v) Enquiry reports (Commission Reports); and

(vi) Thesis.

On the basis of the nature of presentation, reports may be classified as:

(i) Inductive reports;

(ii) Deductive reports;

8. *Ibid.*, p. 319.

(iii) Step-by-step reports; and

(iv) Time-sequence reports.

Reports prepared by journalists for publication in the media may be journalistic reports. These reports have news and information values. A business report or memorandum may be defined as report for business communication from one departmental head to another, one functional area to another, or even from top to bottom in the organisational structure on any specific aspect of business activity. These are observational reports which facilitate business decisions.

A project report is the report on a project undertaken by an individual or a group of individuals relating to any functional area or any segment of a functional area or any aspect of business, industry or society. A dissertation, on the other hand, is a detailed discourse or report on the subject of study. Dissertations are generally used as documents to be submitted for the acquisitions of higher research degrees from a university or an academic institution. The thesis is an example in point.

An enquiry report or a commission of enquiry report is a detailed report prepared by a commission appointed for the specific purpose of conducting a detailed study of any matter of dispute or of a subject requiring greater insight. These reports facilitate action, since they contain expert opinions.

The inductive pattern of report writing is one of the oldest forms of presenting one's thoughts. In this connection Aristotle had pointed out long ago "A whole is that which has a beginning, a middle, and an end." This type of report goes from the specifics — facts, figures, materials of research — to general conclusions, summary recommendations, etc. These reports use the well-tested method of starting with introductory material and progressing through factual support to conclusions. The reader, who likes to examine all the evidences, wants to look at the whole situation carefully before he makes up his mind. Readers usually welcome reports of this kind. Generally speaking these reports arouse less antagonism than those which are 'unfounded' conclusions and recommendations. This is from specific to the general.

The deductive pattern of report writing is most accepted in the business world. It is variously known as the executive report, the management report, or the action-getting report. In this kind of report, the pattern of presentation is from the general to the specific, *i.e.,* from the more important to the less important. It tends to become detailed or more specialised in its concluding sections because it is designed for a reader whose fundamental question is: "What do I need to know to act or to decide?" The writer has a special obligation to think his way through to the central issue or the main point. It is almost like a newspaper report. One, who goes through the title or initial introduction, would get a general idea; and when one goes on reading, the specific areas are unveiled. The writer has to start on common ground with tthe reader in the deductive pattern of report writing.

A step-by-step presentation does not follow any hard and fast rule; it simply presents the material blow-by-blow. It is a way of presenting the events or steps in an operation frequently following one another in point of time. But the steps need not necessarily come to a conclusion or an end. A step-by-step pattern is well adapted to reports on manufacturing operations, where a step-by-step analysis is essential. PERT/CPM is well known, which systematically operates on a step-by-step basis. Sometimes, this pattern is well suited to progress reports which cover only a short period of time.

The time-sequence pattern of report writing is almost like that of the step-by-step presentation; but it lays greater emphasis on the time element. It is an easy way of writing a report by merely following the pattern the research material itself offers in a sequence of the time of events. They foster a notion that such a pattern is the best way of presenting all the background information to those who never like the report to be summarised or condensed.

In all types of reports, it is better to follow some systematic steps in preparation and writing. Even though a hard and fast rule cannot be insisted upon, some generalisations may be made on the steps to be followed in report writing.

Steps in Report Writing

Many researchers find it difficult to make their research reports meaningful though they toil and moil to complete the project successfully. Many a time they lose heart when they start writing their report, because they realise that their effort is not up to the mark. They have the desire, but not the necessary skill, nor have they the will to humble themselves and to pick up; they pose too much. They are like a school boy who starts writing his home work with great enthusiasm. Though he is ignorant of what he is doing, he poses as an expert; and hence he has difficulty in learning it from somebody. It ultimately motivates him to be a copy-master, and ruin himself. This is how many so-called researchers happen to be copy-masters and compilers. Some wish to have a bed of roses in research and report writing. They may be task-masters, but they fail to complete their task.

Some may be good researchers, who may be painstaking but easy-going. They may keep on waiting complacently until the eleventh hour in the process. Their over-confidence may prove to be fatal for the whole mission. At last they are forced to complete a hotchpotch report.

Taking into account all these realities, a few steps may be suggested, which would enable the researcher to complete his task of writing a report clearly and cogently. These step are:

(i) Plan the project well in advance, fix the target and the final date of completing the report.

(ii) The time for completing data collection and data processing should be well planned.

(iii) The time for report writing should be planned in advance, and the task of report writing should not be put-off till the last minute. At least one-third of the total project time should be earmarked for this purpose.

(iv) Make a layout of the structure of the report, arrange the data, documents, bibliography, etc. in groups in conformity with the structure of the report.

(v) Prepare an outline based on the structure, which should cover the main points and sub-points in detail.

(vi) Prepare a rough point-by-point skeleton for each chapter theme, and crystallise the report in a mental exercise. Do not hesitate to discuss the skeleton with somebody who is well-versed in research and who can be taken into confidence.

(vii) In the event of any doubt, get it cleared by reading, thinking, recollecting and discussing, before going further. Put everything in a logical sequence.

(viii) It is always good to get the benefit of the guidance of a good guide at all stages.

(xi) Avoid easy going and short-cut methods and don't hesitate to write an entire first draft. The whole report is to be prepared in black and white; then be aware that it is not at all perfect, and, therefore, calls for much improvement.

(x) Keep the completed rough draft away for several days until you can bring a fresh mind to bear upon it. The reasearcher is then in a position to view it afresh and make substantial changes. It is also appropriate to get the help of some experienced and knowledgeable person at the revision stage.

(xi) Revise the draft thoroughly before the report is typed. Do not hesitate to eliminate all irrelevant and inappropriate portions and to include anythng which is essential.

(xii) The draft may have to be read many times and corrected before it is finalised for typing.

Once the report undergoes a proper purging process, and appropriate format may be selected, which makes the report more attractive.

Format of the Report

The report-writer cannot be ignorant of the need for an attractive format for the report. The format may have the following broad outline.

(1) Introductory section: It should include a definition of the problem and the problem area, rationale of the study, objectives of the study, methodology of the study, sources of data, a brief outline of the report (synopsis), hypothesis to be tested, scope and limitations fo the study, etc.

(2) The main body of the report may consist of classification and tabulation of data, analysis and interpretation, identifying variables and establishing their relationships, detailed investigation, testing of the hypotheses, induction, deductions, etc., presented in a systematic way, including diagrammatic or graphic presentation of data. The body may run into many chapters. (Though there is no hard and fast rule to govern the chapter scheme, all the chapters should be interlinked, though every chapter should remain an inseparable part, of the whole subject-matter under study).

(3) The concluding section may include conclusions, suggestions, inductions, deductions, and observations, as well as identification of areas for further research. The conclusion should be like a good receptionist of a well managed office who has all-round knowledge and capacity to systematicaly present a comprehensive picture of the whole office and to represent it to one who approaches her.

(4) The final section of the report includes bibliography, extra statistical tables, charts and materials, appendices, etc., (essential statistical tables and charts can be presented in the body of the report itself).

Thus, the format of the report must be an all inclusive system and a framework of what is relevant and appropriate to be presented on the basis of the study. Its contents and style should be complementary to the format.

Contents and Style

The contents and style of the report should make it attractive and interest-generating. Its overall get-up, presentation of data, especially diagrammatic and graphic representation, simplicity of statistical tables, its approach, sentence construction, clarity, and even the words, phrases, and idioms used substantially contribute to the style of the report. Thus, the content, format and style are closely related. The report writer is expected to bestow his utmost attention and care on using even a word or a punctuation mark in the report. Continuity, clarity, simplicity, and brevity must adorn every chapter or every paragraph of the report.

Though the report begins with the introduction, sometimes the researcher may not be in a position to start with a meaningful introductionary chapter, or any specific description or analysis. In such a case, much time should not be wasted merely on pondering over something specific. One may start with any chapter which one feels confident of handling satisfactorily.

In general four aspects should be taken into account in making the content and style effective.

(i) The statement of what the report is all about must be clear and simple.

(ii) The writer's proposition must be relevant, realistic, understandable and theoretically sound.

(iii) The thesis, conclusions and suggestions must be based on an analysis of data and facts.

(iv) The whole presentation should generate interest in the people for whom the report is produced.

You may know many things. But the report is not an instrument for you to present all that you happen to know. The report is an instrument through which the most essential aspects of the study should be reported and communicated to the people concerned. Hence, the writer must satisfy at least these four aspects of the content of his report.

If the content is planned to satisfy at least the above four aspects, one can start writing anywhere one wants. Of course, the report should include inferences, analogies, assumptions, logical approaches etc. Paragraphing is an important feature of any report. A paragraph linked by logical relationships is a basic unit in the organisation of a report. It serves to break the text into readable units; it groups sentences around one of the central thoughts or subjects, and presents information in easily assimilated units because it clusters sentences around one central theme or idea.

Linking the paragraphs and various chapters is an essential technique for maintaining continuity and for creating interest among the readers. Many paragraphs and chapters maintain their mutual relationships by virtue of the topic discussed in them in the ordinary course. But the possibility, for some paragraphs or chapters being fallen in water tight compartments, cannot be ruled out. In such situations, the report writer should make a special effort to link these independent units with the other parts of the body of the text by using a transitional paragraph or a transitional sentence in between two paragaphs. The traditional paragraph makes a transition between the material preceding it and the material following it. It includes a brief summary of what has already been written, and is linked with what is going to be written.

Using headings and sub-headings is another way in which one makes a report attractive and readable. It breaks the text into readable units, which is a boon for business readers who are frequently interrupted in their reading by the exigencies of their jobs. However, there is a dangerous tendency among some writers of business reports; they seem to think that any writing, howsoever unorganised, becomes well-organised and highly imaginative when some headings are inserted here and there. Bear in mind that the heading is never a substitute for order in writing, nor a panacea for all the literary ills. If the organisation of material is bad, an inaccurate heading makes it worse, while on a good write-up an appropriate heading is an ornament.

The way in which thoughts and information are expressed and presented is referred to as the style. Simple, lucid expression in the third person is generally appreciated by readers. "Good style is slightly formal; impersonality is the rule. Instead of "we completed the experiment" the preferable form is "the experiment was completed."[9] All pronouns of the first and second person colloquialisms such as 'lot of'; and contractions like "don't" should be seldom used. Yet, despite the professional tone, a successful report reflects its writer's personality, as Shurter puts it. "According to the nature of the situation, the language and the style of expression should vary. To generalise, simple idiomatic English would be more attractive than complicated business jargon. As stated, though an impersonal style is apt in certain respects, there are occasions where the personal style would be far better, particularly when a situation needs to be emphasised. In any case, every word, even a punctuation mark, should count.

A "comma kills" is a very famous statement which is appropriate in this context. A person on the gallows was to be hanged to death. On a *habeas corpus* petition, a pardon was pronounced on him. That decision was taken on the last day. A message was sent: "Hang him not, release

9. Shurter, *Ibid.,* p. 223.

him." "The message reached its destination just in the nick of time. But a typographical error had crept in; *i.e.,* a comma changed its place and the message that reached its destination was: "Hang him, not release him." It is the bounden duty of the report writer to take care of every word that he writes, if his report is to be effective. Short and simple sentences are always better for this purpose.

The concluding chapter should contain in the sum and substance of all that has been written in the whole report; and the concluding paragraph should be a brief summary which ends up in a final conclusion.

"Everything has an end, except a sausage which has two." The conclusion should satisfy three basic points. First, it should give the reader a sense of completeness. Second, the things that deserves emphasis must be projected. Third, it should indicate what the reader must understand and what further action the reader can take. In brief, the report should end by indicating what the whole analytical framework stands for.

Some sample illustrative reports are given below:

1. Report of the Standardisation Commission on E. C. Standards

The Commission headed by Shri C. B. Chandorkar, Dy. Director of BIS, was appointed by the Bureau of Indian Standards to study the quality standards required for Indian exports.

The commission has gone into the various aspects of the problem, and its finding are reported below:

The Task of BIS

The Bureau of Indian Standards (BIS) has a monumental task ahead of it in laying down high quality standards for Indian exports. The task is particularly vital in respect of Indian export to the European market.

EEC Market

The EEC market (European Economic Community Market) accounts for about one-fifth of India's total exports and about one-third of its imports. Upgradation of the quality of goods exported to EEC becomes necessary by 1992, when India will have to compete with developed countries at the international level. Hence, a fresh look at the upgradation of quality is necessary. All the 12 member countries of the EEC lay emphasis on improvement in quality standards, and hence the task of BIS becomes very important.

India and the European Commission

India and the European Commission have been collaborating on programmes of industrial co-operation since 1987. BIS plays a very vital role in the programmes related to industrial standards quality assurance, conformance testing, information technology, electronics and telecommunication, and such other areas of pivotal importance. Important steps have been taken in this direction. A considerable exchange of information as well as experts exchanges in the field of standardisation and certification has already taken place on a mutual basis. Since we follow the international standardisation system, adopting European standards will not pose much of a problem. It is, however, useful to set up an Indo-EEC business forum to look into the standardisation process in mutual interest.

Though a stringent export standardisation process may not materially affect internal business, the standardisation and certification procedure may help to eliminate barriers to internal business. The concept of a single market is now gaining ground. Mr. John B. Farnell of the Commission of the European Communities (CEC) has recently said that the concept of a single market and a new approach to testing and certification will make the community market more transparent, coherent and accessible. Mr. Enrico Maritnotti, Vice-President, Deluge of Ente Nazionale, Italiono di Unification (UNI), the national standard body in Italy has, at the same time, observed that European standard will not be different from international standards.

At present, every country has its own standardisation system. This creates problems for exporters, who have to get through the certification tests of different countries, even if it is the same product. There is a possibility of the EEC using India as a value-added base for South Asian countries. Hence, a common standardisation seems to be better for India.

Special Training

Taking into account all the factors, 90 professionals from all over India were selected for special training in testing and certification techniques in Madras and Bombay in April 1990 under the guidance of experts from Europe. Mr. L. G. Banerjee, Director, of BIS, is of the opinion that India has still a long way to go in this direction, especially in respect of harmonisation of Indian standards.

Harmonisation of the Indian Standards

Harmonisation of the Indian standards with the European standards will give exporters here a new dimension and save them from the rigorous exercise of securing testing certificates from every country. This would help to expand trade. Though many Indian businessmen have reservations about it, people like Mr. Wolfgang Macke, Managing Director of TUV India, are optimistic about the harmonisation process.

Summary and Recommendations

In brief, the recommendations include:

(1) Laying down quality standards for Indian exports would become necessary, and hence appropriate measures should be taken.

(2) Upgradation of the quality of goods exported to EEC becomes necessary by 1992; and hence a fresh look at it is necessary.

(3) European standards may bé adopted in due course, which are almost identical to the international standards which we now follow.

(4) An Indo-EEC Business Forum to look into the standardisation process in mutual interest may be set up.

(5) Training programmes for professionals should continue.

(6) Harmonisation of Indian standards with European standards would be helpful in boosting trade.

Bombay Sd/-

March 27, 1990 Chairman

II. Annual Report

In accordance with Section 217 of the Companies' Act, the Board of Directiors has to submit a report on the working of the company to the shareholders annually. The report may either be signed by the Chairman or the Managing Director.

The report generally starts with an expression of satisfaction on the part of the Board of Directors in submitting their report. It may include:

(i) A brief survey of the economic situation in the country, and how it affects the company's prospects, priorities, and growth.

(ii) Internal consistency, and the problems faced by the company (competition, financial problem, labour problem, production and materials, problem, marketing problem, government policies, price control, imports, exports, taxation, etc.)

(iii) The company's present state of affairs, inlcuding any proposal for change, expansion, or diversification.

(iv) Recommendations for the dividend to be paid to the shareholders.

(v) Reserve amounts for further expansion programme, if any.

(vi) Replies, justifications, and explanations to counter any adverse marks passed by the auditors in their report.

(vii) Details of bonus or any other welfare activity meant for the workers of the company.

All the above aspects have been explained in detail in the report of the directors. The formal is almost identical to that of the above report. A title, the name of the company and of the chairman who presents the report, paragraph by paragraph presentation, sub-headings, summary, signature of the chairman, place, data, etc., come under the format.

III. A Journalistic Report — News appeared in The Times of India of March 28, 1990 (page 15, single column news)

US OFFERS AGRO EXPERTISE TO INDIA

III. New Delhi, March 27 (PTI) — Journalistic Report

The United States has offered its technology and expertise to Indian in the fields of seeds, livestock improvement, genetics, dairy, brackish water agriculture, post-harvest technology and the food-processing industries.

This emerged from the talks which the US agircultural trade development mission had with the deputy Prime Minister and agriculture minister, Mr. Devi Lal, when they called on him here on Tuesday.

Mr. Devi Lal informed the delegation that the government was committed to ensuring that 50 per cent of the investible resources were deployed for the development of the rural sector, and that this year itself the outlay would go up to 49 per cent.

Considering the emphasis on diversification of agriculture and development of agro-based processing industries which would create larger markets in India and aborad, Mr. Devi Lal said that India looked forward to co-operation from the US by way of increased trade relations in agriculture produce marketing and also in technology transter.

The delegation, representing a cross section of US agricultural interests with emphasis on foodgrain's, feed grains, diary sector, forestry and the cooperative sector, was accompanied by the US ambassador in India Mr. William Clarke.

The above news report covers all the specific aspects of journalistic reporting. A title, place, date and the name of the news service (PTI) are given at the top. The whole matter is divided into small paragraphs. Every paragraph deals with one aspect. The contents, style and format of the report indicate how a journalistic report should be written.

IV. Journalistic Style — (TV News Reporting)

Evening News at 9.30 pm on April 17, 1990

Good Evening; The headlines:

Cabinet expansion by the week end, announces the Prime Minister. Yesterday's major fire put out. The Janata Dal elects its interim president on the first of next month. An 11-member coalition government to be sworn in on Thursday in Nepal. Nationwide campaign against carrying inflammable materials in trains. West Indies wrap up the series against England.

The News in Detail

There will be a cabinet expansion by the week end. The cabinet will be a three-tier one. New ministers will be inducted. The Prime Minister said that he is satisfied with the performance of the council of ministers. Some of them are over loaded with work due to the small size of his cabinet. He said that the human development ministry will have a cabinet minister in the proposed ministry.

The major fire, which broke out yesterday in Vigyan Bhavan and in the congested locality of Sadar Bazar in Delhi, has been put out. Some of the fire fighters were requisitioned from the Army and Air Force, and also from the neighbouring states of U.P., Haryana and Rajasthan, and deployed at Vigyan Bhavan to extinguish the fire which destroyed the prestigious conference complex. The fire in the congested business locality of Sadar Bazar is also under control. Three hundred shops were gutted in the fire that began yesterday at 7 in the evening. No loss of life has been reported so far. The Home Minister, Mufti Mohammed Sayeed, said that there is no evidence of sabotage. He told the Lok Sabha that the high-power committee set up to enquire into the fire accident in Vigyan Bhavan will probe into the fire accident in the Sadar Bazar also.

The election of the interim president of the Janata Dal will be held on the first of next month. This was decided by the political affairs committee of the party which met in New Delhi last evening, the party spokesman, Reddy said here today. The meeting was presided over by the Prime Minister, Mr. Jaipal Reddy said here today. The meeting has appointed the finance minister and senior party leader, Mr. Madhu Dandavate, as the returning officer for the election.

The Prime Minister designate of Nepal, Mr, Krishna Prasad Bhattarai, said that a cabinet of 11 members will be sworn in on Thursday. Later, talking to the newsmen, Mr. Bhattarai said that their first priority will be to normalise relations with India, and conclude a treaty so that the shattered economy can be revived.

The Uttar Pradesh government has ordered a magisterial enquiry into the food poisoning incident yesterday. The details of the incident were reported. Reports say that 87 persons died of food poisoning and many others were hospitalised. An ex gratia of Rs. 10,000 was ordered to be paid to the next of kin of those who died.

Curfew was relaxed in Srinagar this morning. Meanwhile 17 more terrorists have been arrested. Prime Minister V.P. Singh said that India wants friendly relations with Pakistan. But if the situation demands, the Air Force will be ready to meet any eventuality.

The president of the Bharatiya Mazdoor Sangh Mr. Manharbhai Mehta died in Bombay this morning. He was run over by a local train. He was trying to cross the railway line. He was 60. Mr. Mehta was elected to the recently constituted National Integration Council.

The Indian Oil Corporation eastern region staff struck work for one day today on the issue of dearness allowance. The government has described the strike as irresponsible. An official spokesman said in New Delhi today that public sector employees get much more than government employees.

Cricket: The West Indies have won the fifth and final cricket test against England by an innings and 32 runs.

Then the score details Federation Cup football, sports, etc., were dealt with.

Management Report (Business Report) *Vis-a-vis* Research Report

We have examined business reports and research reports in detail in this chapter separately. Management reports 'and business reports are identical, if not one and the same. Management report is a report written for the use of management in relation with a management problem, *i.e.,* dealing with a management problem in effectively managing its business. Business report is a report on managing a business though it need not necessarily be written by management. Generally speaking both focus on a problem in managing a business. So much so, both serve the same purpose, and obviously, use identical methods in report writing.

In both business report writing and management report writing, the report is first planned on a specific management problem or a business problem. In accordance with the needs of the report, data and information are collected. It means that the need for writing a report on a specific problem or aspect of business arises first. Then the managerial analyst plans his report. In order to aid his report he collects, compiles, manipulates, presents and interprets the relevant or supporting data. In a research report, the method is the other way round. The researcher identifies the problem, makes his observation and makes a statement of the management problem as research problem. Then data and information are collected, classified, presented and interpreted. Research report is therefore, a report of findings, observations, inventions, discoveries, inductions, deductions, etc., of the study.

Thus, a research report is the report of what he observed in the study, while a management or business report is the report of a management problem or the matter connected with it. Hence, a management report can provide a research problem for a management researcher, while a research report may provide solution to a problem raised in a management report. It means that a business report can become a source of a managerial research problem, while a managerial research report may provide solution to the problems raised in a business report.

Evidently it means that a business report may differ from a managerial research report. However, one cannot rule out a situation where a managerial research report itself is converted to be a business report or a business report can provide adequate background for a research report. Except when a research report is used as management report, both cannot be one and the same. It means that on most of the occasions a research report differs from a management report, though both may use the same method for data collection and analysis. Though there are many contrasting points between a research report and a management report, in research of a number of areas, the two can be compared with each other.

Management Report and Research Report: A Contrast

A management or business report has organisational analysis as its primary element, which includes organisational objectives on the one hand and the roles and relationships between individual performers and the various sub-units in the organisation, on the other.

It helps in identifying the actual decision-maker, identifying the constraints, strengths and weaknesses under which he operates, and gaining proper perspective in which the organisation operates. Research report, on the other hand, takes into account the research objective and the research problem more than the organisational analysis.

As mentioned earlier, business report stems from the need for a report, while research report is the result of a research exercise. Hence, a business or management problem occupies the main position in a business report, while a research report mainly contains data collection, analysis, interpretation, presentation of the problem under study etc.

Hence, a management report, being an instrument for the presentation of the very problem, need not contain something like the statement of a hypothesis, statistical testing of a hypothesis, extensive use of statistical or mathematical tools, etc. On the contrary a research report is generally based on scientific method and hypothesis and and hence the use of various statistical and mathematical tools, etc. is common. Moreover, a managerial analyst or a practitioner may not consider very seriously about the statistical or mathematical tools since they are more interested in a direct approach to problem solving.

At the same time simulation is considered as an effective tool in managerial analysis, while it may not receive much importance in a research report. Research report always highlights in depth an analytical framework. Similarly, operations research techniques are commonly used in research analysis of late whereas it is not of much importance in a business report because many a manager of today feels that it provides the basis of intellectual gymnastics and serves not much managerial purpose.

Research reports extensively make use of economic analysis which includes normative analysis and positive analysis. Positive economic analysis attempts to rigorously examine economic phenomena which includes econometrics and mathematical economics. Normative economics attempts to use the descriptions and findings. The former uses statistical inferences extensively which is common in research reports. Managerial reports very seldom make use of such techniques.

As already mentioned, operations research is a common technique in research reports. Writers like West Churchman, Russell Ackoff, and Leonard Arnoff[10] had identified six phases of operations research *viz., (a)* formulating the problem, *(b)* constructing a mathematical model to represent the system. *(c)* deriving a solution from the model, *(d)* testing the model and solution, *(e)* establishing controls over the solution, and *(f)* implementing the solution. For theoretical purposes these steps are comfortable. Hence, research reports use operations research technique extensively. But it has not found much favour with many management reporters.

Extensive use of statistics, presentation, analysis and interpretation of data, etc., make the basis for research report. But managerial report or a business report, being time bound, cannot go in for such extensive data base. Insights, observations, past experiences, etc., provide substantial background materials for business report very often, particularly due to time

10. Chruchman, Ackoff and Arnoff, *Introduction to Operations,* John Wiley & Sons, Inc., New York, 1957.

limit. Thus, in many respects a business report or a management report substantially differs from a research report. But in many other respects they are quite identical.

Research Report and Management Report: A Comparison

Though management report and managerial research report may differ in certain respects, one may not be able to draw a total contrast between the two. As both deal with the same subject-matter, they are identical, if not one and the same. Both are aids for decision-making, problem solving and policy making, and hence both serve the same purpose.

Though a business report or a management report may not contain a hypothesis and its testing directly, various relevant factors and their relationships are generally presented in a business report. Hypothesis is formulated by factors, variables and their skeptical relationships, which form part of research reports. So much so both are making use of hypothesis in one way or the other.

Even though a business report or a management report may not go in for extensive data collection and analysis as in the case of research, since every management report is a time-bound instrument, some amount of data analysis (particularly readily available data) is indispensable even in the management report. It means that data and information essentially make part of both. The difference is, therefore, only in terms of quantity and not quality.

While a business report deals with a management problem or a business problem directly, the same is restated in the managerial research report which is only a formality. Actually speaking, a management problem is at the centre of both, and both aim at finding out solutions to the problem involved. Hence, both serve the same purpose. Brown's observation is very relevant here. "We say it as simply as we possibly can, and that is, that a report is a communication from someone to another who wants to use that information. The report may be elaborately formal, it may be a letter, or, in a great many organisations, it is simply a memorandum, but it is always planned for use." Irrespective of any distinction, a report is meant for use whether it is a big report or a small report, or whether it is a management report or a research report.

Both the reports identify areas for further research in management practice, while analysis and inferences, suggestions, observations, etc., are common in both. Both the reports must be worth reading and utility-oriented if they are expected to serve the purpose.

Methods like sensitivity analysis, cost-benefit analysis, etc., are useful in business reporting, which are popular with managerial researchers also.

Thus, on a close observation, it can be remarked that management report or business report and managerial research report are the two arms of the body of management practice. Both are essential organs. Though they are not one and the same; but they are complementary. They are not at all competitive. Very often one can serve the purpose of the other. While research report is based on research, business report makes use of research methods to a certain extent. Both are aids to effective management practice.

Chapter 11

Research: An Aid to Decision-Making

The process of research has been briefly surveyed in the preceding chapters, and it has been demonstrated that research is a systematic and planned investigation activity which makes a substantial contribution to the organised body of knowledge. It is an aid to managerial functions also. To be more specific, it is a valuable aid to decision-making.

Decision-Making

Management is chiefly concerned with, among other things, decision-making and decision implementation. Each decision has an implementation aspect, and each decision implementation consists of a number of subsidiary decisions. In fact, decision-making is associated with all the managerial functions. It is generally approved as the process of choosing between alternatives. The choice activity necessarily means that decision-making is closely linked with rationality; and research is an effective aid in rational thinking.

Taylor viewed his "scientific management" as an ideal approach to decision-making, while in importance of delegation and authority were emphasised by Urwick and Fayol. Chester Bernard, who has contributed a meaningful analysis of the decision-making process, deserves special appreciation. "The processes of decision are largely techniques for narrowing choice."[1]

The three major phases in the process of decision-making, put forward by Herbert A. Simon, are worth mentioning in this context.

They are:

(i) Intelligence activity (scanning the environment for the conditions necessitating the decision);

(ii) Designing activity (identifying, developing and analysing the alternative courses of action); and

(iii) Choice activity (choosing the best course of action from among the alternatives).[2]

Newman, Summer and Warren made the process a little elaborate, and suggested four phases. These are:

(i) Making a diagnosis;

(ii) Identifying alternative solutions;

(iii) Analysing and comparing alternatives; and

(iv) Selecting the plan to follow.[3]

McFarland's time framework approach seems to be simpler. The steps in the time framework approach are the past (need for decision), the present (alternatives are identified and the choice is made), and the future (decisions are carried out and evaluated).[4] Elbing's systems approach to decision-making has observed five stages, *viz.,* disequilibrium, diagnostic process, problem statement, solution strategy and implementation. There are occasions for a manager to have a feeling of disequilibrium, leading to problem situations. It is then natural that he makes assumptions and diagnosis in the problem situation. He then makes a clear picture of the problem and defines it. His response to the problem is bound to make a selection of the method and find a solution. The process includes implementation of his choice to solve the problem. Elbing's[5] approach seems to be a little complicated.

1. Bernard, Chester I., *The Functions of the Executive,* Harvard University Press, Cambridge, Massachusetts, 1938, p. 14.
2. Simon, Herbert A., *The New Science of Management Decision,* Harper & Row Publishers, Inc. New York, 1960, p. 2.
3. Newman, William H., Summer Charles E., and Warren Kirby E., *The Process of Management,* 3rd Edn., Prentice-Hall, Inc., Englewood, pp. 72, 247-8.
4. McFarland, Dalton, E., *Management Principles and Practices,* 4th Ed., The Macmillan Company, New York, 1974, p. 262.
5. Elbing, Alvar O., *Behavioural Decisions in Organisations,* Scott, Foresman and Company, Glenview, Illinois 1970, p. 13.

Choice

Irrespective of ideological distinctions, it is imperative that any effective executive takes a number of decisions and solves many problems, both small and big. Obviously, he has no choice but to scan the environment in detail, design alternative courses of action, evaluate the expected result of each of such alternatives, and select or choose the best from among them. This is the process of decision to solve a problem. Once the best choice is made, the most decisive task is to implement it. For the purpose of implementation, the executive has to plan his course of action, make policy and strategy, control resources and manpower, co-ordinate, motivate staff, and direct them. Many decisions are involved in all these managerial functions, until the work is finally got done in the most optimum way possible. Thus, every managerial or business problem leads to decision-making: and each such decision results in a number of associated decisions.

A case would illustrate this point, *Hind Wire Industries Ltd.,* suffered a setback in its working in the year ended September, 1983. Production was marginally down by 8 per cent compared to the previous year, while the sales turnover dropped substantially to Rs. 4.65 crores as against Rs. 9.30 crores in the previous year. This was so because the bulk of the production was on a conversion basis in the interest of economy. Trading profit declined to Rs. 29.46 lakhs; and profit after interest was very nominal. Evidently, the company suffered a loss after provision was made for depreciation, bonus, tax, etc. No dividend was declared, though it was 15 per cent in the previous year. Moreover, the wire capacity reached the saturation point.

A number of decisions were called for in the wake of these events. As the wire capacity had reached the saturation point, how could further investments be made? What would be the course of action to improve the performance of the company? What was the cause of the immediate decline in turnover and profit and how could this problem be solved? How could the sales in quantitative terms be increased? How could production figures be sustained? Would there be any need for change in the production methods? All these questions offered a number of alternatives, one of which would have to be chosen. For example, the first question: As the wire capacity has reached the saturation point, how can further investments be made? The decision maker is expected to search the environment as well as the internal and external forces that would affect his decision. Then the alternatives are to be identified. In the typical situation of declining production, a more than proportionately declining trend of sales, turnover and profit, the saturation of the product capacity and so on, the decision-maker has to make an extensive investigation of the prevailing situation, where research plays a very vital role. The alternatives before the chief executive are:

(i) Continue production at the same pace and build up inventory;

(ii) Promote sales to the maximum extent possible;

(iii) Reduce operations in the same line and diversify.

(iv) Implement a more aggressive promotion programme, control production according to demand, and diversify into new areas — chemicals, pharmaceuticals, steel and off-shore equipments; or

(v) Reduce production operations and retrench manpower in accordance with the demand, and be satisfied with it.

It is here the "choice" operates and the decision of the chief executive is crucial.

Executive decisions should necessarily be based on appropriate studies, evaluations and observations. In the Hind Wire case, systematic studies were necessary to scan the environment, evaluate the performance, and to examine the circumstances under which the company's performance had declined, to undertake market studies for the evaluation of market potentiality and motivation research to develop the existing customers and the prospects; to determine the inventory carrying cost and conduct EOQ studies, feasibility studies for diversification, marginal cost analysis for pricing, etc. These studies would sharpen the decision process of the chief executive. The role of research in this decision-making is vital for the success.

Limiting Factor

Koontz, O'Donnell and Weihrich have emphasised that any decision-maker has essentially to take into account the limiting factors before arriving at business decisions. This would narrow the search for alternatives. "Only when we recognize and solve those factors that stand critically in our way to our goal can we better select the best alternative course of action."[6] However, it is a difficult task to identify the limiting factors. Even though some factors are evident and identifiable, there are many others which are very often obscure. While many dependent variables can be identified, a

6. Koontz, Harold, O'Donnell, Cyril and Weihrich Heinz, *Essentials of Management,* TMH Edn., New Delhi, 1983. p. 114

number of independent variables cannot easily be observed. A systematic research alone can make possible the identification of the determinants. In the process of planning and control, a recognition of limiting factors is inescapable. Under certain conditions, some factors are critical but there are some which may not be relevant in a different environment, where the variables, quite unimportant in the former situation, would be very prominent.

Indicarb Ltd. has showed a better performance during the year ending Septemeber, 1983. Its turnover has revealed a substantial growth of 49 per cent — from Rs. 118.65 lakhs in 1982 to 170.71 lakhs in 1983. Depreciation during the year was of the order of Rs. 19.53 lakhs as against 16.02 lakhs in the previous year. Its net loss was about Rs. 28 lakhs in 1983, in spite of a considerable growth in turnover. Of course, the net loss in 1983 was less than 50 per cent of the loss in the previous year (Rs. 57.67 lakhs), a fact which cannot be ignored. It is, however, not a negligible fact that the company is still incurring a heavy loss. Its unsatisfactory performance is associated with some limiting factors — labour unrest, severe power cut in Tamil Nadu, etc. To be precise, the company has increased its captive power generation and is hopeful of a much higher output in 1984. It has also a tremendous growth potential. Moreover, its order book position is comfortable in spite of a servere recession in the industry.

Indicarb seems to be a healthy company, though it functions at a loss. The production and sales potentials are highly favourable. The order book position is comfortable. In spite of all these favourable factors, the decisions on supply, sales and marketing policies, distribution, production, wage policies, employment, profit planning, etc. are substantially influenced by such limiting factors as labour unrest and power cut, to mention only the identifiable variables. There can be a number of other limiting factors, such as government policies, political pressure, manpower behaviour, absenteeism, trade union behaviour, labour habits and social involvement, corporate financial policies, labour policies, and so on. All these variables, including the identifiable ones, are required to be probed into before any meaningful policy decisions can be taken to place the company into a comfortable position. A detailed research and investigation of the limiting factors should be considered decisive in connection with any corporate decision of Indicab. Many Indian companies face such situations, all of which underscore the importance of research. Limiting factors are expected to be taken into account in connection with choice determination also, emphasising the greater role played by research in choice activity.

Evaluation of Alternatives

As already seen, the determination of choice necessitates a prudent evaluation of alternatives; and both are inseparably interlinked with the decision-making process. For a meaningful and rational evaluation, the decision-maker ought to take care of internal and external factors, controllable and uncontrollable factors, quantitative and qualitative factors, as well as long-term and contingency factors. The internal factors may include resources, cash flow, manpower, technological development, trade unions, the political affiliation of the representative unions, the organisational commitment of the executives, internal consistency, organisationl philosophy, culture and climate, corporate policy, etc. The external factors may consist of, among others, governmental policies, political factors, legal framework, socio-economic factors, and geographical and cultural factors. The controllable factors are the factors which are amenable to control; these are resources, production process, etc. Many external factors, however, are uncontrollable factors. Quantitative factors consist of things that can be measured in numerical terms, such as resources, cost factors, time etc. Qualitative factors are intangible factors, which cannot be easily or quantitatively measured. For example, the organisational commitments of executives, the cohesiveness and sense of belonging of the workers, the risk of technological change — all these are qualitative factors. Long-term factors include the long-term plan, corporate planning, technological innovation, growth prospects, product life cycle, etc., while contingency factors are the temporary factors or factors of uncertainty. In order to identify all these factors, quantify them and determine their possible relation with corporate functioning, as well as their mutual relationships, research has a great role to play.

There are various methods and scales to evaluate the alternatives. Some of these tools are cost-benefit analysis, marginality analysis, statistical methods like probability and sampling; simulation, linear programming, queuing theory, PERT/CPM technique, dynamic programming, etc. In all these methods, systematic data collection, analysis, and interpretation form the backbone, which is nothing but research (these tools are examined in a separate chapter). One of the most comprehensive and systematic research and analysis approaches to decision-making is operations research, which is the application of the systems methodology of the physical sciences to management decision-making. It is 'the application of scientific method to the study of alternatives in a problem situation, with a view to obtaining a quantitative basis for arriving at the best solution'. The factors emphasised in OR are scientific method, use of quantitative data, goal setting, determination of the best means of reaching the goals, etc. It is the best use of common sense in quantitative terms. (Management too can be defined as the optimum application of common sense.) One cannot claim that operations research is the panacea for all management malignancies; nor does it provide any decision. On the contrary, it develops quantitative data presented and analysed in a systematic way to help managers gain a penetration into the existing situations and the variables related to such situations. It does not give a decision, though it helps one to make a proper decision. In the transportation problem or production planning, the results of OR are accurate and the solutions are positive with the help of research.

OR, as an aid to decision-making, is a source of model building, and a basis for conceptualisation. Its characteristics are:

(i) It enables one to identify the variables affecting each business situation, facilitating effective decision-making;

(ii) It emphasises model building, which facilitates problem-solving and decision-making;

(iii) It incorporates variables, both dependent and independent, in the decision models, englightening the decision-maker on the exact problem and its solution;

(iv) It emphasises goal-setting in the problem areas and identification of quantitative solution to the problems;

(v) It determines the potentiality of such solutions to achieve the goal;

(vi) It builds the model as well as its variables, constraints, and goals in mathematical terms, so that they may be clearly identified and readily utilized for calculation by the substitution of quantities for symbols;

(vii) It quantifies the variables, highlighting the actual magnitude of he problem, and facilitating appropriate decisions;

(viii) OR has mathematical and statistical devices to supplement the data, and works, within a small margin of error. It may be considered as useful tool for assisting in decision-making if the decision-maker has a good exposure to this technique.

Research backed by analysis is necessarily an effective aid to decision-making, since it helps in the selection of the best from the alternatives. Research involves a search for relationships among the critical variables, constraints and premises that influence the objectives and goals. Similarly, planning and decision-making are interlinked. Any planing problem should be broken into its component parts before its analysis, evaluation, and solutions. It is research that does this work. Experimentation is one of the prominent methods of research, which assists the decision-maker to decide among alternatives. In this context, it may be pointed out that many scientific decisions are impossible without adequate experimentation. Economists, physical scientists or natural scientists conduct experiments, before making recommendations on policy decisions. Test marketing research for any product facilitates product decisions; while market research enables one to evaluate the market, which facilitates marketing decisions. Decision-making is at the core of planning, while it is related to all the management functions. It requires collection of data, analysis and interpretation as well as selection of alternatives, *Satisficing,* which is a term sometimes used to portray the course of choosing an action that is satisfactory under the given circumstances, is directly linked with some sort of research. Even in the systems approach to decision-making, each decision area is a sub-system of the whole system of organisational decision-making, *i.e.,* all the decision areas are interlinked. Research and analysis are closely associated with decision-making in all the areas.

Decision-Making Under Uncertainty

Uncertainty is a common phenomenon in business, especially in the modern age of technological development and dynamic social change. In such a situation, decision-making is a great task, because each decision involves a lot of risk. Research and analysis can play a very vital role in uncertainties by providing those valuable details and meaningful forecasts which would reduce risk.

Uncertainty is a business situation where the outcome or effect of a certain action or decision (condition) is not known in advance. It is a situation where the result of any managerial decision is uncertain. When we toss a coin its outcome is uncertain. But this is not a real uncertainty because we know for certain that the result would either be "head" or "tail". If we see a bird flying, the result is uncertain because we do not know where the bird is going to alight. In the former case, it is not uncertainty, while in the latter it is. In the former, there is definiteness about the likelihood of "either head or tail". But in the latter, no likelihood can be predicted. We do not know whether the bird would choose to build its nest on 'X' tree or 'Y' tree; and hence this is a situation of uncertainty. Of course, there is some element of uncertainty in the former case too, which is common in all sorts of business except a monopoly. (This can exist even in some monopoly businesses.) The sun rises in the east is a certainty, while the sun would rise in the east tomorrow would be a probability. (Tomorrow can be a rainy or cloudy day, and there is a possibility that the sun may not be visible tomorrow morning.) If someone says that the sun is going to rise in the west tomorrow, the probability is "Zero", *i.e.,* it is certain that this can never happen. As far as a decision-maker is concerned, it is essential for him to determine the degree of effectiveness of his decision on the basis of probability or certainty.

The possibility of extreme values of zero and one is also not ruled out. If an executive's decision results in zero outcome, the probability is zero, and if the outcome is 100 per cent, the probability is one. Intermediate values, such as 0.3, 0.5, 0.7, etc., would then correspond to varying degrees of uncertainty as to whether the event would occur or not. if the decision-maker is provided with a set of probabilities to help him reach a rational decision on any event or set of events, he would be decisive in his decisions, even in situation of uncertainty. It is here that research becomes important. On the basis of research, evaluation and analysis, the researcher is in a position to enlighten the decision-maker of the set of probabilities concerning the events that would take place. A case would explain this aspect clearly.

Ennore Foundries had a success story in the past. They are optimistic about future prospects, also. The production in the first quarter of 1984 was 70 per cent higher than that in the same period last year — 5,581 tonnes as against 3,282 tonnes. The turnover during the same period was Rs. 5.83 crores and Rs. 3.9 crores respectively. The company expects to make a better show in future, *ceteris paribus.* The chairman, Mr. Mantosh Sondhi, is very optimistic that the public policy during the final year of the Sixth Five-Year Plan (1984-1989) would be conducive to a rise in the manufacture and sale of commercial vehicles, tractors and other allied products which the company markets. Obviously, he expects a better performance on the part of his company. These expectations are based on the real time planning. But the company has not been able to achieve adaptive planning. Their original strategy did not take into account the future uncertainty delineating the anticipated events, especially rapid technological change.

An unprecendented and dynamic change takes place in the automobile technology and design. With the advent of new designs of vehicles, many automobile and commercial vehicle manufacturers have made rapid strides in updating their machining facilities with the latest CNC *machining centre* and sophisticatd testing equipment with a view to improving the fuel efficiency of their vehicles. Emphasis is laid on weight and cost reduction. This has constrained the foundry industry to update itself to suit the emerging technological development. The company faces some sort of uncertainty now as a result of these developments. Of late, however, it has made the best efforts to modernise and update the process technology. But until the process of modernisation is completed and it starts functioning smoothly, uncertainty would persist. That is why the lack of adequate and timely research and analysis in the foundry industry has been underscored by the chairman of the company. It is obvious that the present uncertainty in the operations of the company arises mainly out of the lack of an adequate research, which would have enlightened the management of the future uncertainty delineating the anticipated technological development.

The courses of action which may be adopted to tackle uncertainties in business and the relevant decisions pertaining thereto have attracted the attention of many in recent times. This may be the reason why a number of techniques have been developed to deal with decision-making in conditions of uncertanties. Risk analysis, decision trees and preference theory are prominent among these. Risk analysis enables the decision-maker to determine the size and nature of the risk he has to undertake if he chooses a given course of action. Every decision is based on the interaction of a number of dependent and independent variables. The variables with a low degree of probability are redundant. The decisions determined by a majority of determinants with a fairly high degree of probability are preferred in conditions of uncertainty. "Risk analysis attempts to develop for every critical variable in a decision problem a probability distribution curve." This is possible only when the necessary research and analysis have been made, revealing the importance of research in uncertainties.

The decision tree method is another way of analysing a decision. It sketches the various decision points in the form of a tree. The chance events and the probabilities of various courses of action are also plotted. Let us consider a simple marketing problem. X consumer product has been newly introduced into the market. The marketing executive has two alternatives before him:

(i) Approach the market on a long-term basis, make a promotion expenditure of Rs. 2 lakhs, and operate in an extensive market.

(ii) Approach the market on a short-term basis, limit the promotion expenditure to a maximum of Rs. 10,000/-, and operate in an intensive market.

These alternatives can be sketched in a simple way in the form of a tree.

A Simple Decision Tree for a Marketing Problem

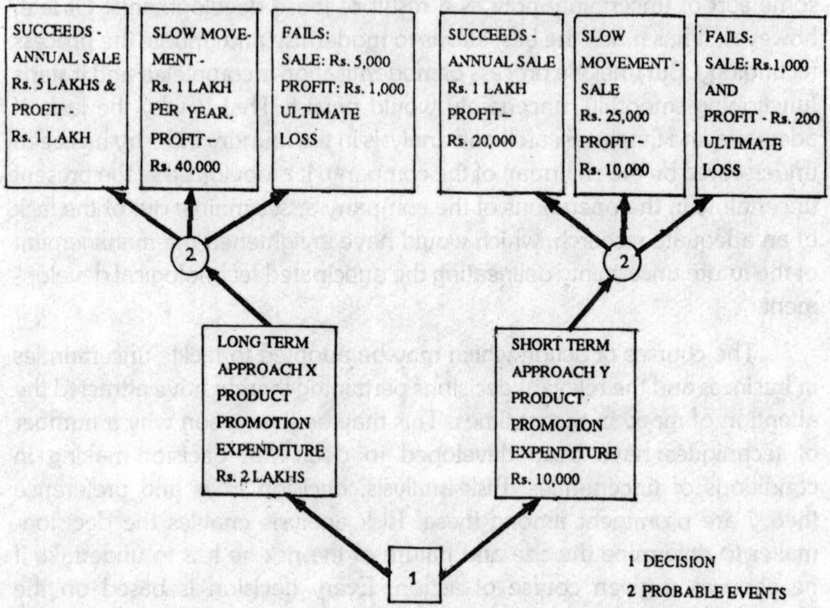

Fig. 1

A marketing manager, who has to take a decision on the distribution of two products, X and Y, considers three alternatives for each. Product X requires extensive marketing, for which an expenditure of Rs. 2 lakhs has to be made with a long-term marketing strategy. Product Y requires intensive marketing and short-term strategy, with a promotion expenditure of Rs. 10,000/-. Each of the products entails a set of possible future events. An assessment of the probability for each course of possible events is necessary, for which the decision tree is helpful. In respect of product X, the course of action which includes extensive marketing, with an annual sale of Rs. 5 lakhs and a profit of 20 per cent, seems to be the best decision. In regard to product Y, under the intensive marketing strategy, there will be a sales turnover of Rs. 1 lakh and a profit of Rs. 20,000. Now the decision depends on his investment capacity. If he is able and willing to invest Rs. 2 lakhs for the purpose of promotion, his decision would be in favour of the former; and if he prefers to invest only Rs. 10,000, his decision would be in favour of the latter. Again, it would depend on whether he would like to have an extensive marketing and long-term strategy or intensive marketing and short-term strategy. But for a decision tree to be drawn and the decision to be taken, the necessary data should be collected, and an analysis and interpretation made. The decision tree technique is closely linked with research.

The preference theory, which is otherwise known as the utility theory, assumes that individual attitudes to risk vary. Some love to take a great risk, for example smugglers, while certain people do not like to take any risk at all. Many managers' decisions are influenced by the probability of the less risk involved in them, far too many managers are risktes. Certain people are fond of pure statistical averages because they want to avoid risk. However, individual preference curves may be established, on the basis of which decisions may be arrived at. Rational individual preference is based on facts and figures, as well as probabilities, which are the result of some sort of analysis of the situation. Marginality analysis, for example, which can act as the basis for rational individual preferences, depends on a systematic analysis and interpretation.

Decision Criteria

Any decision-maker would be very particular that his decision should be the best in the interest of achieving his or her objective. For example, an executive, to take an "make or buy" decision, would analyse all the aspects of making as well as of buying. Only by comparing the advantages and disadvantages of "making and buying" would he take his final decision. And a number of considerations will have to be taken into account in the then prevailing situation. That is why a generalisation that is suitable in all situations may not be possible. However, a few general conditions may be listed here. They are, maximax, minimax, maximum likelihood, equal likelihood, etc.

Maximax refers to the act which "maximises the maximum" possible profit. Maximising profit would be the basic requirement of maximax. The possible losses will be ignored. "It would seem desirable systematically to incorporate into the decision the probabilities of success and failure. Minimax, at the same time, refers to the act which "minimises the maximum loss", or, alternatively, which "maximises the minimum profit," Maximum likelihood considers the consequences of the state of nature which is most likely to occur and chooses the best act for that state of nature. The possible consequences of each act are added amd divided by the number of possible events in the equal likelihood principle. Systematic studies are necessary to determine all these situations.

Decision-Making *vis-a-vis* Management Functions

Decision-making is closely associated with all the traditional management functions. Albers places planning, motivating and controlling under decision-making.[7] while Newman and others have equated the process of

7. Alber, Henry H., *Principles of Management,* 4th Edn. Jn. Vly. 1974, pp. 43-4.

decision-making with planning.[8] It would be interesting to note that Simon[9] equates decision-making with management itself. According to him, "in treating decision-making as synonymous with managing, I shall be referring not merely to the final act of choice among alternatives, but rather to the whole process of decision-making." In a nutshell, there is an element of decision-making in all functions of management, whatever be the functions of management. In a modern business, a manager is expected to be a problem-solver. "Problem-solving is any goal-directed activity that must overcome some type of barrier to accomplish the goal." Of course, problem-solving is not decision-making itself, though it involves prudent decision-making. As a matter of fact, all the management functions are based on a systematic analysis of the situation, and of the evaluation and interpretation of the data; while decision-making is a part of all these functions. Decision-making in all the management functions is, therefore, bound to be based on research. The following case makes this point clear.

Punjab Anand Batteries has suffered a setback in its working during the year-ended September, 1983. Sales during the year dropped to Rs. 12.77 crores from 19.23 crores in the previous 15 months. The gross profit declined steeply from Rs. 112.56 lakhs to Rs. 38.48 lakhs. Depreciation and investment allowance were Rs. 27.13 lakhs, 45 lakhs, and Rs. 19.91 lakhs respectively in 1982 and 1983. Surplus was reduced to Rs. 15.21 lakhs in 1983 from Rs. 40.43 lakhs in the previous year. Equity dividend, also, was slashed to 5 per cent from 20 per cent in 1982. The general reserve was limited to Rs. 9 lakhs as against Rs. 25 lakhs during the period in question. There have been steep increases in the cost of major raw materials, while the incidence of excise, customs duty and sales tax has been very high. The market has, at the same time, faced a sluggish demand and severe consumer resistance. A decline in purchasing power, as well as price escalations, have also affected the market. The production of dry cells during the period was 48.86 million pieces as against 86.64 million pieces in the previous 15 months. Large-scale smuggling of button cells into India has affected the company's market for button cells.

Government have withdrawn the excise duty on button cells for a period of two years, which would probably influence their prices. A collaboration agreement with N. V. Philips of Holland has been approved by Government for the setting-up of a new project for the manufacture of CLS lamps, fluorescent tubelights and glass shells. The company proposes to set up a new project in co-operation with PSIDC (Philips International).

8. Newman, et.al., *op.cit.,* p. 243.
9. Simon, *op.cit.,* p. 1.

In the last 15 months, the company's export figures have declined considerably, from Rs. 50.62 lakhs in the preceding 15-month period to Rs. 4.2 lakhs, showing that the company's performance has been less than satisfactory even on the export front, though there is an excellent export market potential.

In the circumstances, the company is expected to conduct extensive studies and market analysis with a view to formulating a fresh corporate strategy. Financial studies are undertaken to reinvigorate financial planning as well as profit planning. A comparative marketing analysis is necessary for formulating a new marketing strategy, competition strategy, price skimming, market segmentating, product positioning, etc. A co-ordination of various functional areas and sub-systems is also necessary under the revised planning. Extensive export market potentiality analysis is essential before a fresh export policy, especially on the basis of government policies, is embarked upon. Government policies should be studied in detail with a view to evolving a competitive pricing strategy. Production, inventory and distribution functions require a meaningful co-ordination, for which a comparative analysis is essential. The organisation of a new project calls for project planning, which should be based on a realistic analysis and an interpretation of the existing situation in all its aspects. On the basis of a substantial drop in market demand, studies such as those bearing on motivation and marketing, should be conducted prior to the introduction of a new marketing strategy, motivational strategy, staffing policies, etc. It is now evident that research is a part and parcel of a company's decision in relation to all the aspects of its functioning.

Types of Management Decisions

There are various types of management decisions to suit different situations. The most popular among them are:

(i) Basic and routine decisions; and

(ii) Personal and organisational decisions.

According to McFarland, "Basic decisions are those which are unique, one-time decisions involving long-range commitments of relative permanence or duration, large investments, and a degree of importance such that a mistake would seriously injure the organisation."[10] Policy decisions bearing on plant location, organisation structure, product line, labour policies, etc., are basic decisions. Routine decisions, on the contrary, are everyday operational decisions. Most of the decisions pertaining to day-to-

10. McFariand, *op.cit.,* p. 268.

day management are routine decisions. However, one should realise that there is no watertight compartment to specifically separate a routine decision from a basic decision. On many occasions, routine decisions are a part of basic decisions. Both the decisions are based on an adequate analysis of the situation. Research has, therefore, a role to play in both types of decisions. The more basic the nature of the decision is, the greater is its dependence on research.

Chester Bernard has made a clear-cut distinction between personal decisions and organisational decisions. "Personal decisions cannot ordinarily be delegated to others, whereas organisational decisions can often, if not always, be delegated."[11] Organisational decisions generally aim at organisational goals and personal decisions attempt to achieve personal goals. It is, however, not an easy task to distinguish between these two because they are interlinked in many ways. While organisational decisions are usually based on systematic analysis, personal decisions are backed by personal observation and investigation. In any case, research is the basis for decision-making, though the techniques may change or differ.

Decision Techniques

We have already examined the role of research in various methods—cost-benefit analysis, marginality analysis, statistical methods, etc. Decision-making can make use of various other techniques, such as creative techniques, brainstorming techniques, participative techniques, the Delphi technique, the nominal group technique, the heuristic technique, etc. Decisions which facilitate creativity and the creativity that facilitates rational business decisions fall under creative techniques. Thinkers like Newman, Summer and Warren have favoured creative techniques,[12] while Osborn[13] has advocated brainstorming as a method for triggering creative ideas in the field of advertising. It is the function of the brain to storm a creative problem. Brainstorming is now used for decision-making in all areas. Though brainstorming is not research, it can extensively make use of research findings and observations, *i.e.,* each stormer can audaciously attack in favour of his idea with the help of research findings.

In order to enable the manager to gain acceptance of his decision, one of the most effective methods he uses is the participative technique. It envisages intellectual, emotional and physical involvement of people concerned with the decision-making process. It may be formal or informal. There may be individual and group participation, as well as positive and

11. Bernard Chester I., *op. cit.,* p. 188.
12. Newman et al. *op. cit.,* pp. 274-280
13. Osborn Alen F., *Applied Imagination,* Charles Scribener's Sons, New York, 1953, p. 297.

negative participation. "The technique of involvement, to define is a process through which a permanent communication and involvement mechanism is developed between each worker and the management, through which an informal system is developed for the spontaneous involvement of each worker in the affairs of the enterprise."[14] Some sort of evaluation of the potentiality and temperament of the individuals concerned is a pre-requisite for a meaningful participative way of management and decision-making.

The *Delphi* technique was first developed by Dalkey and his associates in 1950 at the Rand Corporation's Think Tank. However, only very recently has it attained popularity in respect of risk-uncertainty decisions. This technique is named after the oracle at Delphi in ancient Greece, which works in the following way: "A panel of experts on the particular problem in hand is drawn from both inside and outside the organisation. Each expert is asked to make anonymous predictions. Each panelist then gets a composite feedback of the way the other experts answered the questions. Based upon the feedback, new estimates are made and the process is repeated several times." This itself is a way of collecting primary data from people who are exposed to a given situation; and working out its averages and moving averages with a view to arriving at the dependable forecast figures. Actually speaking, the Delphi technique is synonymous with research and forecasting.

The *nominal group technique* (NGT) is closely related to the Delphi technique. The NGT is a process of group decision-making. The nominal group is a simple paper group, its members do not indulge in any verbal exchange. NGT consists of the following steps; silent generation of ideas in writing, round-robin feedback from group members to record each idea in a terse phrase on a flip chart, discussion of each recorded idea for clarification and evaluation, and individual voting on priority ideas, with the group decision being mathematically derived by rank-ordering or rating. NGT members may be acquainted with one another, unlike in the Delphi technique. This may also be treated as a sort of investigation, analysis and forecasting.

The *heuristic* technique too is similar to the Delphi technique and nominal group technique. Though it has been in existence for a long time, it is only recently that it has come into the limelight as a decision-making technique. It may be considered as a controlled type of trial-and-error method. According to Hutchinson: "In other words, the heuristic technique allows the decision-maker to consider less-than-rational paths and thus

---

14. Michael, V.P., *Industrial Relations in India and Worker's Involvement in Management*, Himalaya Publishing House, Bombay, 1984, p. 259

preclude frustration when more preferable alternatives are somehow available."[15] However, its adaptability to computer programming has made it very popular now. Heuristic programming makes use of an exploratory method of solving a problem. Progress is continually evaluated, and through analysis of results, the next step is determined, each leading to the final solution. Value judgement has a considerable role to play in this method. This is almost like a chess game. The player uses sequence, judgement, memory, trial and error to plan the next move immediately after an attack. Observation, value judgement and sequence are essential elements in research as well, revealing the application of research in the heuristic method.

To conclude, it may be observed that decision-making plays a pivotal role in the system of management. It includes the actual choice activity preceded by gathering of information and identification of alternatives. In all areas of decision-making, some element of research is manifested, so much so, research cannot be isolated from executive decision-making.

The whole decision making process gets its support from analytical framework which is the crux of research. In fact research is an effective aid to all managerial functions.

15. Hutchinson, John G., *Management Strategy and Tactics*, Holt, Rhinehart and Winston Inc., New York, 1971, p. 126

Chapter 12

Research in Managerial Functions

Research is an essential aid to decision-making. It is equally helpful in such managerial functions as planning, organising, staffing, leading, and controlling.

Planning

Planning is closely linked with decision-making. It involves the determination of the course of action in advance, *i.e.,* deciding in advance what to do, how to do it, when to do it, and who is to do it. Planning also throws light on where we are; and where we want to go within the given future period. In determining the future course of action, a choice activity becomes necessary; *i.e.,* choosing the best course of action from among the alternatives, as in the case of decision-making.

Choice activity depends on the organisational objectives which can be achieved with the help of people involved in the accomplishment of the task. It involves selecting, from among the available alternatives, future courses of action, not only for the enterprise as a whole, but for all its functional departments. It underscores the importance of achieving the organisational objectives on the one hand and departmental goals on the other. "Planning is an intellectually demanding process; it requires that we consciously determine courses of action and base our decisions on purposes, knowledge, and considered estimates."

Generally speaking, research is a basic aid to decision-making, which is closely linked with planning; and therefore it is an important aid to planning as well. Moreover, one may not be in a position to decide in advance what to do, how to do it, when to do it, and who is to do it, without the necessary investigation, examination, and evaluation, which form a part of the research. Choice activity, formulation of objectives and goals, and identification of alternative courses of action; these are backed by relevant analysis and interpretation.

Planning is backed by forecasting; and forecasting is possible only through research, analysis, and interpretation. It is evident, that planning is redundant without adequate research connected with it. The major aspects of planning are its contribution to the purposes and objectives, its primacy among the manager's tasks, its pervasiveness, and the effectiveness of plans — all of which are closely linked with observation, induction, and deduction. Resultantly research is an important support for effective planning. There can, therefore, be no planning worth the name without research.

"Managerial functions of organising, staffing, leading, and controlling are designed to support the accomplishment of objectives; and hence planning logically precedes the execution of all other managerial functions." It is preceded by the formulation of objective, and is closely linked with forecasting. The setting of the objectives of the organisation should be based on its strengths, weaknesses, opportunities, and the potential threats it may have to face; and these can be determined by research and analysis. On the other hand, possible; and forecasting precedes planning. Obviously, research provides the basis for planning.

Planning is closely associated with control. "Control means keeping activities on course by correcting deviation from plans." Koontz and others have rightly pointed out: "Any attempt to control without plans is meaningless, since there is no way for people to tell whether they are going where they want to go (the result of the task of control) unless they first know where they want to go (part of the task of planning). Plans thus furnish the standards of control."[1] Fixing of standards necessitates investigation and analysis of opportunities, needs and aspirations, the performance and prospects of the enterprise, industry, and its competitors, and various environmental forces and determinants. Evidently, research is the basis for standards, while research itself facilitates a comparison of performance with pre-established standards. Thus, while planning and control are interlinked with each other, research and analysis are closely connected with both.

1. Koontz, O'Donnell, and Welhrich, *Essentials of Management*, TMH, 1983, p. 62.

The term *pervasiveness of planning* refers to the fact that planning is a universal managerial function, which is linked with policy. Every organisation has a policy, which is based on the relevant analytical frame-work (the basic ingredient of research) that pervades planning at all levels of the management from top to bottom. In fact, one of the most important factors that help every manager to achieve success in his ability to plan properly; and planning must be backed by appropriate data and information, which are obtained through research.

"Plans are efficient if they achieve their purpose at a reasonable cost, when cost is measured not only in terms of time or money or production, but also in the degree of individual and group satisfaction as well."[2] Research and analysis are help in evaluating the efficiency of plan in terms of not only cost, revenue, or time, but also in terms of the achievement of the company's objectives and the satisfaction of the hopes and aspirations of the people associated with it. This is the reason why it has been said that the "plan encompasses any course of future action." The courses of action generally contribute to the purposes and mission of the organisation. It is, however, the duty of an organisation to determine whether its purposes and mission are capable of maximising the want satisfaction of its customers, prospects, and the community at large. An in-depth study and analysis would lead to the determination of the fact whether the company's purpose and mission would contribute to want satisfaction.

In this context, a reference may be made to the social responsibility of business which ensures its contribution to social needs, which can be determined by relevant studies and investigation with the programme planning of the business enterprise. The president of a company gets the studies done not only to identify the areas where he can avoid losing money, ensure increasing profit, and build up high morale, sense of belonging, and organisational commitment of his people, but also to recognise the needs of the social environment in which the company exists and operates.

The success of a company depends on the success in the achievement of the objectives and goals. Planning is realistic when the achievement of objectives becomes its primary purpose which "are the ends toward which activity is aimed." Planning, therefore, aims at achieving the objectives. Other managerial functions, such as organising, staffing, co-ordinating, leading, controlling and motivating, also are meant for the achievement of objectives and goals. Obviously, detailed studies become necessary at all

2. *Ibid.*, p. 64.

levels and stages of organisational existence; and planning becomes part and parcel of every activity.

Planning guides the action which establishes a proper method for managing future activities. It indicates the exact manner in which a certain activity can be accomplished; and represents a "chronological sequences of required actions." Planning takes care of programmes which are "complexes of goals, policies, procedures, rules, task assignments, steps to be taken, resources to be employed, and other elements necessary to carry out a given course of action; they are ordinarily supported by necessary budgets."[3]

A proper method and manner for carrying out activities can be identified with the help of adequate analytical framework. The planning of programmes of a complex nature consisting of goals, policies, task assignments, etc., calls for evaluations and interpretations at all stages, thus underscoring the pivotal role of research in planning. A primary programme planned for execution may call for many supporting programmes, each of which would be backed by some element of research and analysis. A decision to instal a new machine may result in planning of various activities, such as raising funds, obtaining the right make of machine, preparing manpower, streamlining operation of the machine, machine-hour utilisation, capital outlay, revenue, etc. Every event is backed by relevant analysis and its appropriation. A planner is aware of the fact that every programme and its supporting programmes can seldom stand by themselves; they have to be backed by research.

All planned programmes are supported by the budget, which is a statement of expected results expressed in numerical terms arrived at on the basis of data collection, presentation, analysis, and interpretation. The budget is a fundamental planning instrument and a control device, which is backed by research and analysis to ensure and purposefulness.

Planning also helps to offset uncertainty and change, to make economical operation possible, to focus attention on objectives, and to ensure proper control, all of which are perfected by relevant research. At all the steps of planning — namely, awareness of opportunities, establishing objectives, developing premises, determining alternative courses, evaluating alternative courses, selecting the best course, formulating derivative plans, making plans for numerical budgeting, etc. — must be backed by an appropriate information system. Research is the basis for this information system, for light is thrown on all the supporting situational factors by research. As a matter of fact, planning enables the manager to make

3. *Ibid.*, p. 71.

a rational approach to the accomplishment of objectives, while a rational approach to planning is made possible only by research.

Fig. 1 shows the role of research at all stages of planning. First, the planner should be aware of the opportunity which is supported by research with the provision of details of strengths, weaknesses, opportunities and threats. Pre-planning research also provides forecast figures, which one is able to set objectives and goals for achievement through planned activities. Planning premises are considered at this stage. While research helps to identify objectives and goals, an analytical framework is possible only through research for considering the planning premises.

Awareness of opportunity provided by research helps in setting objectives and goals. It is better to consider planning premises at this stage, for which research provides an analytical framework. Awareness of opportunity enables us to identify alternatives and to compare alternatives in the light of goals sought. Research provides the basis for identifying alternatives. While objectives and goals facilitate a comparison of alternatives, choice of the best alternative depends on objectives and goals. Planning premises (environment) may also have a substantial role in the choice of the best alternatives and in the formulation supporting plans. The identification of alternatives is followed by a comparison of the alternatives and a choice of the best alternative course of action backed by the formulation of supporting plans. Preparation of numerical budgets for future operations is an inevitable part of the plan framework. Research plays a vital role at every step of planning. (See Fig. 1)

Though planning is a universal management function, many executives tend to fail this task because of its practical difficulties. Other factors, such as inaccurate premising, rapid changes and complexities, internal inflexibilities, external inflexibilities, etc., also limit the planning effort. Unambiguous collection of data and timely research and analysis go a long way in helping one to tide over these difficulties.

The practical difficulties of planning include: lack of commitment to planning; confusing planning studies; failures to develop and implement sound strategies; lack of meaningful objectives or goals; tendency to underestimate the importance of planning premises; failure to envisage the scope of plans; failure to see planning and decision-making as a rational process; excessive reliance on experience; inadequate research and investigation; failure to use the principle of limiting factors; lack of co-operation on the part of subordinates; lack of top management support; lack of clear delegation of authority; lack of adequate information; lack of adequate control mechanism; and resistance to change. Most of these problems can

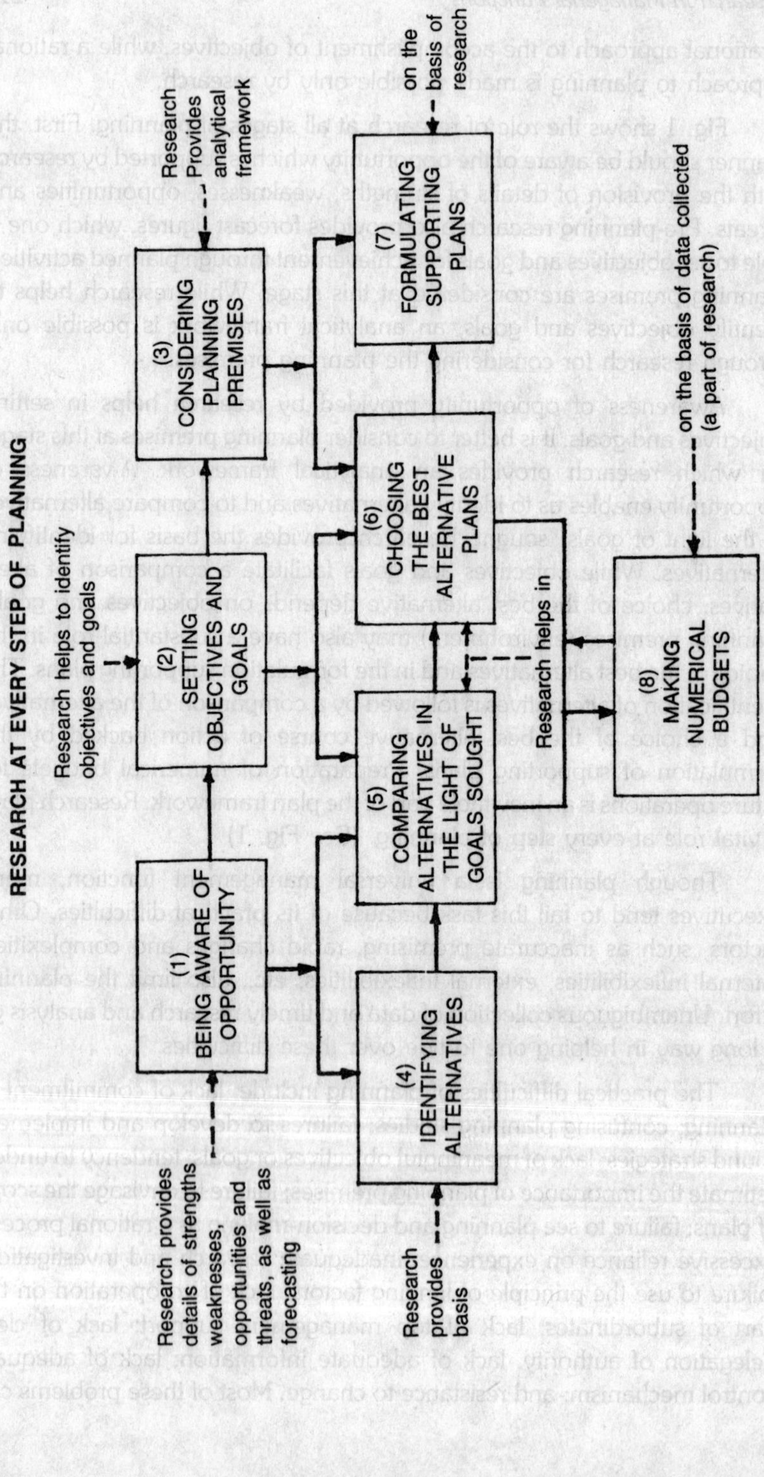
RESEARCH AT EVERY STEP OF PLANNING
Research provides details of strengths weaknesses, opportunities and threats, as well as forecasting
(1) BEING AWARE OF OPPORTUNITY
Research helps to identify objectives and goals
(2) SETTING OBJECTIVES AND GOALS
Research Provides analytical framework
(3) CONSIDERING PLANNING PREMISES
Research provides basis
(4) IDENTIFYING ALTERNATIVES
(5) COMPARING ALTERNATIVES IN THE LIGHT OF GOALS SOUGHT
(6) CHOOSING THE BEST ALTERNATIVE PLANS
(7) FORMULATING SUPPORTING PLANS
on the basis of research
Research helps in
(8) MAKING NUMERICAL BUDGETS
on the basis of data collected (a part of research)

Fig. 1

be effectively tackled with the help of pragmatic approaches based on appropriate investigation and research. It emphasises the crucial role played by research in making the plan effective.

Planning is closely associated with controlling. An examination of the controlling function, and the role of research in it, deserve to be considered here.

Controlling Function

According to Koontz and his associates,[4] "the managerial function of controlling is the measurement and correction of performance in order to make sure that enterprise objectives and the plans devised to attain them are being accomplished." Control as a function, involves three basic steps, *viz.*, establishing standards, measuring performance against predetermined standards, and correcting variations from standards and plans. Standards can be the criteria of performance, and are based on the objectives and goals on the one hand and the priorities on the other. They are generally set in quantitative terms, though the use of qualitative terms cannot be ruled out. Quantitative terms, such as sales volume, profit margin, sales turnover, labour productivity, quantities produced, etc., are generally used as standards. They are the selected points in an entire planning programme at which measure of performance are made so as to give managers signals as to how things are going without their having to watch every step in the execution of plans." It is always better to measure performance in comparison with standards, on a forward looking basis. This may help in determining deviations, if any, in advance.

The controlling function should be preceded by necessary studies for the purpose of setting realistic standards. The measurement and comparison of performance against predetermined standards calls for a detailed investigation, evaluation, and analysis of the relevant data on not only the environmental variables to determine the standards but also the factors associated with performance and prospects. A constant evaluation of performance calls for a continual process of research on the part of management with a view to knocking down unrealistic and inadequate standards and objectives, and updating policies and strategies. A constant analytical framework based on a proper communication network should be the basic characteristic of any forward-looking management as a part of their control process. Corrective actions are also expected to be based on studies.

4. *Ibid.*, p. 463.

William Newman and Kirby Warren[5] have identified three types of controls. They are:

(i) Steering Controls: Results are predicted and corrective action taken before the total operation is completed. This is almost lik flight control of the spacecraft. Trajectory measurements start immediately after take-off, and corrections are made much before the actual arrival.

(ii) Yes-no Controls: Work will proceed to the next step after it passes a screening test; *i.e.,* there should be an approval to continue the work. Quality checks or test flights of aircraft are examples of yes-no control.

(iii) Post-action Controls: Action is first completed, and then the results are measured and compared with the standard. School report cards, budgetary control, etc., are examples of this kind of controls.

The basic purpose of exercising control is to produce the best result. One who strives for the best result in accordance with predetermined objectives has to conceive good performance in terms of specified factors; that is, control should be ensured in terms of certain other factors. In depth investigation, analysis, induction, and deduction would be come necessary in order to identify the various controllable and uncontrollable variables. Evidently, research becomes an essential prerequisite for ensuring effective control, and for achieving the desired results.

The Morarjee Goculdas Spinning and Weaving Company achieved better working results during the first half of 1989-90 (July-December 1989) than in the same period in 1988. Sales totalled Rs. 54.80 crores against Rs. 54.30 crores. Exports amounted to Rs. 3.75 crores against Rs. 1.68 crores. There was a gross profit of Rs. 149.58 lakhs against Rs. 56.50 lakhs. Net profit was Rs. 14.68 lakhs (as against the net loss of Rs. 71.50 during the same period last year) after providing an amount of Rs. 135 lakhs for depreciation (Rs. 128 lakhs in the previous year). During the year ended June 1989, the company reported a gross profit of Rs. 1.03 crores against Rs. 60 lakhs in the previous year.

The company has been facing a difficult situation. However, the chairman Mr. Ajay G. Piramal, expects to perform better from 1990 onwards by exercising control variables. Various market segments have been reviewed in order to decrease the company's dependence on the traditional market; and increasing emphasis has been laid on exports on the one hand and exploring new market segment such as ready-made garments on the other. Cost controls are proposed to be exercised, while better utilisation of installed capacity and current assets is being ensured. Stringent conrol

5. Newman and Warren, *The Process of Management,* PHI, pp. 455-56.

on working capital has been proposed. While control on price and rejections must be exercised, high quality standards must be introduced to be competitive in the international market. Prospects for exporting ployester blended fabrics have been tapped. A modernisation programme is expected to be implemented.

Payment of interest must be controlled for the sake of which, sources of interest-free funds have been identified. In this context there is a proposal to sell the surplus land to meet capital needs for modernisation.

As a part of the forward-looking plan, the management has to control such factors as cost, price, quality, distribution, dependence on traditional markets, wastage of resources (especially installed capacity), working capital, loss, rejecton rate, interest payments etc. The company has, at the same time, to streamline such activities as sales, export marketing, exporing in new areas and segments for marketing, profitability, modernisation programme, capital formation, etc. In all these respects research, investigation, analysis and interpretation are necessary. "The energies devoted to research, experimentation, and exploration are fruitful ways of increasing in the size and scope of the business."[6]

Emerging business empires in India in the 20th century, especially in its latter half, reflect the personal inspiration and creative genius of their founders.These leaders around whom such businesses have been formed, are strong personalities, aggressive and energetic, guided by common sense and strong will power. Reliance, Thappar, Mahindra, Bajaj, all of them come under this category. They have had an array of effective managers. These leaders have provided strong direction and control. Whether it was "genius managements" or "Caesar management" (according to Earnest Dale.[7]), they provided strong direction to their organisations and took them to the pinnacle of success. Some may argue that these owner managers have been able to control, plan, direct, and strengthen their organisations without much research. In fact, if we probe deeper, we would realise that all of them have concentrated their attention on evaluation, analysis, and interpretation of every situation. They have been more calculative than the present day professional managers.

However, the challenges and complexities of modern business enterprises, and the growth achieved by most of these owner-manager run organisations have underscored the need for complex business decisions, and for a new approach to the concept and practice of management. The

6. MacFarland, Dalton E., 'Organisational Health and Company Efficiency in *Business Topics,* Vol. 13, No. 3 Summer, 1965, pp. 45-57.
7. Emest Dale, *The Great Organisers,* McGraw Hill, New York, 1960.

more complex the situations faced by organisations, and the greater the uncertainties faced by managers, the greater the need for research to support the process of planning, control and management.

The most important step in setting control stanards is to be clear about the results we desire. "What shall we accept as satisfactory performance?" Usually, we must answer this question in terms of:

(i) The outcome characteristics that are important in a particular situation, and

(ii) The level of achievement, or "par", for each characteristic. Research is the basic tool for the determination of these factors.

In the caes of Morarjee Goculdas Spinning and Weaving Co., the characteristics that would determine good performance are: improving sales, increasing profits and profitability establishing a good export market, diversifying to new areas like ready-made garments, strengthening the various market segments and reducing the dependence on traditional market, establishing a good costing system, economically utilising the working capital, improving quality, exporting polyester blended fabrics, achieving a better competitive ability in the international market etc. The top boss of the company should be able to conceive good performance in terms of these characteristics. Having identified the characteristics of good performance, the company must determine how high a level of achievement it should desire for each characteristic. So par is simply an ordinarily feasible achievement level. Variations beyond this level may be acceptable. Of course, there is a legitimate need, for the flexibility in control. Then control standards should be set up for the performance of each individual. Accountability for any deviation should be fixed, which may help to focus the search for causes and thereby sharpen corrective action of course, the establishment of standards for control purposes is largely dependent on the previous management decisions on plans and organisation, and specifically on predetermined objectives.

Evaluating the result with special reference to the contributio n of every person at all times may be a very difficult task; instead one hould be satisfied with the evaluation of aggregate result at various shor intervals, while individual performance may be evaluated after a given time period. Strategic points reflecting the total operation may be picked up and evaluated at every short interval. For exmple, the president of Morarjee Goculdas can keep his eye on such key areas as production, distribution, international, marketing, finance, and inventory by evaluating the data weekly or fortnightly; or he may keep an eye on the performance of key executives every month. However, steering controls can be used at various intervals, so that the top boss may move ahead before the final results come in by checking the points to serve as warning bells. At all levels and phases of evaluation, investigation and analysis are necessary. Research can play a very vital role in this area as well.

The evaluation of performance should take place after the standards are set. Thus, evaluation involves the measurement of the work or prediction of what will be done in accordance with the control standards; communication of deviations, if any; and then taking corrective action, which may not be possible without proper research and analysis. A study of deviations may throw light on the reasons for deviations.

Evaluation and analysis may take into account both quantitative and qualitative results, symptoms for control, predictions in control, personal observations and conclusions, control reports, etc. Sampling is a very useful method not only in evaluation, but in all the other forms of research. A comparison of performance with standards is an important aspect in this context. Standards include physical standards, cost standards, capital standards, revenue standards, programme standards, intangible standards, goals standards, etc., which are facilitated on the basis of available data. Feedback and feedforth communication may also be used as a means for control, which too, is based on available data. Data collection is undoubtedly a central part of research, which is closely linked with both planning and control. In short research cannot be isolated from the planning and control. In short research cannot be isolated from the planning and control function of management.

Research in Organising Function

Systematically organising activities on the one hand, and the people employed in the organisation on the other, come under the essential functions of mangement. "The organisation may be considered as a system of goals and activities, rationally coordinated and integrated with the help of appropriate communication for the sake of problem-solving, decision-making, operating, and result-making."[8] Organisations are, therefore, considered to be social systems established for effectively matching the business with the need of the society in which it exists.

Setting goals and objectives is the function of planning, while the control process leads to the achievement of goals and objectives.

8. Michael V.P., *Organisational Behaviour and Managerial Effectiveness,* S. Chand & Co., New Delhi, 1989, p. 38

The organising process, at the same time, determines the course of action to be taken for the achievement of such objectives and goals. Organisation is also concerned with deciding the various activities into segments appropriate enough to be handled by respective individuals; assigning the proper task to the proper person; delegating the necessary powers, and allotting adequate resources to carry out the task; and coordinating the various tasks, functions, individuals, and resources to ensure that no effort, nor resource are left impoverished, and no member of the organisation has the chance to get in another's way. Organisation is not an end in itself; it is a means to an end.

Each individual performs a specific job on the organisation, and each role is co-ordinated with the whole organisational structure. Larger organisational roles are also fulfilled through the various functions identified and co-ordinated. In this connection Edgar Scheir observes: "An organisation is the rational co-ordination of the activities of a number of people for the achievement of some common explicit purpose or goal, through division of labour and function, and, through an hierarchy or authority and responsibility."[9] Many activities are carried out by different people who have to work together in a co-ordinated fashion, though they have their own differences. It is here that the organisational framework comes into existence. Earnest Dale, therefore, observes: "Organisation will be considered a means of getting people to act together for a purpose, particularly for a business purpose."[10] An organisation "is a well planned social system, represented by a structure rationally co-ordinating various functions identifed with individual positions for the achievement of common predetermined objectives and goals through organisational hierarchy or delegation of authority and responsibility."[11] An organisation is basically concerned with the organising process, which should be based on proper studies and investigations of the environmental factors and social forces, the functions and people associated with them, the objectives and goals, and so on.

The organising function, like any other management function, is a rational activity, which is based on thinking, analysis, and investigation. Rationality is associated with reasoning, which is closely linked with research. One who emphasises rationality in the process of organising would be able to make human co-operation effective, because the task and mission of the organisation and the people who carry them out would be

---

9. Scheir, Edgar H., *Organisational Psychology,* (2nd edn.,) Prentice-Hall Inc., Englewood Cliffs, N.J. 1970, p. 9.
10. Ernest Dale, *Organisation,* American Mngt. Assn. Inc. 1967, p. 10.
11. Michael V.P., *Organisational Behaviour and Managerial Effectiveness,* op. cit., p. 39.

matched rationally. The reason for the different levels of organisation is evident in the limitations of the span of management. The organising process must take into account the levels of organisation on the one hand, and the span of management on the other. Obviously, the organising process ensures both delegation and co-ordination on the basis of rational investigation.

The following are some of the common characteristics associated with a rational organisation.

(i) Organisation is a social institution, which has a social role to play and a social objective to achieve, *i.e.,* a study of the social objectives may facilitate rationality in organising.

(ii) Organisation should be a deliberate and planned institution of people with common goals, which can be achieved through the achievement of individual goals and objectives. The matching of organisational goals and objectives with individual goals and objectives in organisational planning becomes necessary in this context, for which an analysis of necessary data and interpretation of the various factors would become necessary.

(iii) Organisational hierarchy and delegation of authority are well-defined in an organisation, for which a well-defined and established organisational framework becomes necessary. Without an in-depth study, this may not be possible.

(iv) There should be a well-established organisational structure and proper co-ordination and integration, which may be possible with the help of rersearch.

(v) Effective communication and interdependence cannot be isolated from an organisation. The effectiveness of communication depends on how the flow of material information, perception of message, and understanding between various parts and members of an organisation is achieved; and how information is effectively passed on.

Information is the most essential link between means and ends, which are of great concern for management. This fact should be studied, analysed, organised, stored for future reference, summarised, and displayed; and this process has a relationship with research.

There may be a mechanism for reviewing the performance of each individual, each functional area or profit centre in the organisation. The organisation should also substitute and recombine personnel within the organisation. No organisation can survive for long, if it does not prudently utilise its resources, including its people, among whom there should be inter-relationship. For all these purposes, research and communication are very helpful.

Organisational levels exist because of the limitations of managers in supervising number of people. When the organisational levels are few, there is a wide span of management, as against the narrow span of management when the levels of management are many. The number of subordinates a superior may manage determines his span of control in a given situation. The number of people a person can supervise depends on various factors, such as the nature of the subordinates, the ability of the supervisor, the nature of the situation, technical or technological expertise, other situational factors, etc., all of which can be evaluated with the help of research or analysis or both. Figs 2 and 3 show the organisational framework with narrow spans and wide spans.

Organisation with narrow spans

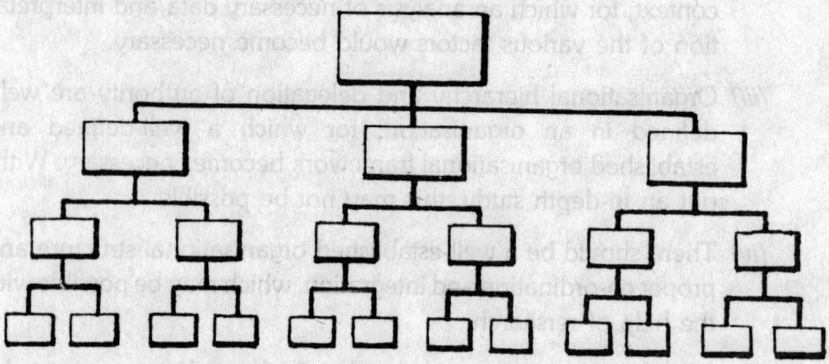

Fig. 2

Advantages	Disadvantages
• Close supervision	• Supervisors tend to get too involved in subordinates' work
• Close control	• Many levels of management
• Fast communication between subordinates and superiors	• High costs due to many levels lowest level and top level
• Excessive distance between organisation with wide spans	

Organisation with wide span

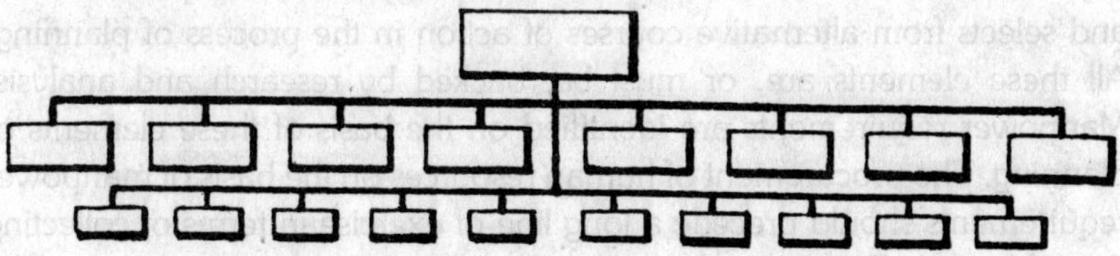

Advantages	Disadvantages
• Superiors are forced to delegate	• Tendency of overloaded superiors to become decision bottlenecks
• Clear policies must be made	• Danger of supervisor's loss of control
• Subordinates must be carefully selected	• Requires exceptional qualtiy of managers

Fig. 3

In an effective organisation, there should be clarity of delegation of authority, clarity of plans, use of objective standards adaptability to changes, good communication channels and techniques, facility for good personal contacts, proper balancing, adequate departmentalisation, appropriate levels of centralisation as well as decentralisation proper levels of organisation and spans of management and control, authority relationships, etc., all of which must necessarily be based on adequate analysis. Of course, "the best organisation arises when a manager hires good people who are allowed to do a job in their own way." Without appropriate evaluation of the credentials, it may not be possible for the manager to hire suitable persons. It is here that prudent staffing becomes an important job of the manager. Obviously, staffing is closely linked with organising.

Staffing

Staffing is the process of "filling positions in the organisation structure through identifying workforce requirements, inventorying the workforce, recruitment, selection, placement, promotion, appraisal, compensation and training people."[12] Staffing has a close relationhip with both interval and external environment. Internal factors, such as the organisational climate, organisational philosophy, personnel policies, reward and compensation systems, etc., and external factors, such as technical and technology demands, demand and supply of highly skilled manpower, tends in trade unionism, government regulations, and so on; all these affect the staffing pattern in any organisation.

12 Koontz and Others, *Essentials of Management*, TMH, 1983, p 307.

Staffing is a systematic, but complex, way of managing human resources. An organisation identifies opportunites for the enterprise, sets objectives based on forecasts, formulates strategy, and develops, evaluates, and selects from alternative courses of action in the process of planning. All these elements are, or must be, backed by research and analysis. Manpower requirements are identified on the basis of these elements of planning. The procurement of human resources on the basis of manpower requirements should precede a long line of exercise in terms of collecting data from applicants, evaluation, comparison, interpretation, etc. The training needs of selected people are also determined by a necessary evaluation of organisational needs on the one hand and of individual ability and potential on the other.

Induction and placement should be backed by relevant analysis, while compensation depends on the evaluation and investigation of the relative worth of employees and the contribution made by each individual to the achievement of organisational goals and objectives, for all of which job analysis, job evaluation, performance evaluation, etc., would be helpful. These evaluation schemes make extensive use of research methods, compensation, appraisal, etc., are also supported by data collection, analysis and interpretation.

As the organisation has certain given expectations of every person associated with it, so every individual in the organisation has his own aspirations. The more the orgnisation is able to help the individuals to meet their aspirations, the greater the involvement of the people in the achievement of organisational goals. This may be the reason why Maslow has highlighted the basic needs of the individual — physiological needs, safety needs, love needs, self-actualisation needs, esteem needs, etc. Research and analysis help the organisation to determine the aspirations of its people on the one hand and to examine whether the organisation and its programmes are capable of meeting the aspirations of the people on the other. This is necessary to achieve effectiveness in manpower management.

Industrial relations and labour welfare areas of today deserve a lot of studies and investigations. This is an age of persistent industrial disputes, strikes, and extensive trade unionism. Strikes, lockouts, closures, agitations, and concerted demands are very common. Every such case deserves to be investigated with a view to finding out the problem and its magnitude, causes, effects, alternatives, and solutions. Research and analysis become necessary in all such cases.

Management of inventory is essential in all organisations, especially in big organisations. For the maintenance of an inventory chart of manpower resources, appropriate studies are necessary, so that proper action may be taken in respect of every person in the organisation. Some have to be promoted, some to be promoted later, some to be retained in the same position, some to be retrenched, some deserve incentives, and to some more responsibilities may be assigned. For the determination of all these, evaluation and investigation are essential.

Motivation and morale boosting, leading and controlling, training and development, delegating and decentralising, innovation and resistance to change, and many other areas should be subject to proper analysis and investigation. It may be observed here that staffing should be backed by proper investigation so that the manpower in the organisation can be managed effectively, and leadership becomes meaningful.

Research in Leading Function

The managerial function of staffing is closely linked with leading, because a manager who has people under him is expected to be a leader rather than a boss. The philosophy of leading and the approach to leadership are very relevant in management functions. It is, therefore, proper to throw some light on how research facilitates the performance of the managerial function of leading employees or providing good leadership.

"Leading is the process of influencing people so that they will strive willingly and enthusiastically toward the achievement of organisational goals."[13] Robert Tannenbaum has defined leadership as "interpersonal influence exercised in a situation and directed, through the communication process, toward the attainment of a specialised goal or goals."[14] A leader is the one who is able to "influence others to follow him for the achievement of common goals, and to lead them by exercising authority and commanding adherence, who may possess leadership qualities. The leader should be able to develop responsibility and initiative among his followers."[15] Leader is a person who influences and persuades, while leadership is the ability and potential to persuade and influence others to follow him. Keith Davis, has, therefore, viewed leadership as the ultimate act that brings to success all the potential that is in an organisation and its people."[16]

Leading is the process by which the leader influences his followers to follow his instructions and implement his policies willingly and enthusia-

13. *Ibid.*, p. 381.
14. Referred to by Dr. Michael, *Organisational Behaviour and Managerial Effectiveness*, p. 127.
15. *Ibid.*
16. Keith Davis, *Human Behaviour at Work*, p. 107

stically, so that the goals and objectives of the organisation may be achieved. As Koontz observes, "leading must be based on an understanding of what motivates people and what brings them satisfaction as they contribute to organisational goals."[17] This understanding is a learning process, which is based on analysis, investigation, and interpretation (research) of the relevant factors and situations.

The manager's perceptual awareness of the behaviour of his people would go a long way in shaping an ability to lead them. Systematic studies apparently facilitate this perceptual awareness. Koontz has, therefore, remarked: "Because managing involves the creation and maintenance of an environment in which individuals, working together in groups, are led to accomplish objectives, a consideration of what motivates people is central to effective managing. A significant amount of theory and research has been undertaken in this area."[18] Leadership qualities become useful only when the leader is able to effectively lead his people for which a lot of evaluation is essential. All these managerial functions would accomplish very little if the manager does not understand the human factor in his operations. Research plays a very important role in this respect.

The leading process is closely associated with motivation. A motive is an inner state which stimulates activities or moves. It may be the cause of an inner drive. Such terms as wants, desires, wishes, aims, goals, needs, drives, motives, etc. are related to motivation; and the relationship between needs, drives, and goals is an integral part of motivation. Motivation implies a goal toward which the movement occurs, which may be the reason behind the action. Needs are synonymous with wants, and motives or impulses which result in activity; while a drive is a force that affects a situation by pushing one in a specific direction. To be precise, the term motivation may include any inner condition of the person, who initiates or directs his behaviour towards a particular goal. It is the inner drive of a person which energises his action for the achievement of certain goals, and for the statistician of the given wants or needs. As motivation is a key determnant of a person's behaviour, it is necessary on the part of any manager or leader to study the motives and motivations of his people.

In-depth studies are invitable for evaluating the various aspects of motivation, especially such factors as needs, drives, motives, and goals. These variables are the determinants of motivating and are, therefore, subject to close observation and evaluation as a part of the leading process. Motivational selectivity deserves to be analysed. The motives of people

17. *Op.cit.*
18. *Ibid.*, p. 382.

exercise a continuing influence over what they notice, how they see and think, and what they learn from it as well as what they perceive of it. Motives are therefore, to be evaluated with the help of research. Motrivational tools become effective when the influence process is effective. Crystallisation of each motivational element becomes necessary for this purpose, and research plays a very decisive role in this process.

Any motivational tool is expected to satisfy at least one of the needs, *viz.,* physiological needs, sociological needs, or psychological needs. It is research that helps us to determine whether the motivational tool is effective and in which area it is effective. When the individual finds that his needs are not satisfied, conflicts take place in his motives, and he becomes frustrated. These may be both environmental and personal barriers as well which result in frustration. The leader-manager must take into account all these factors so that he may effectively use the appropriate motivational tools, for which research plays a vital role.

A leader must develop high morale among his followers. The greater the motivation, the greater the job satisfaction , and the higher the morale. Morale and productivity have a positive correlation. Extensive research is necessary to determine this relationship.

Managerial function of leading, or influencing, managing, or not motivating people can be effective only when the leading process or policy is based on a detailed analysis of the nature of the individual concerned. Research is useful in this context.

It may, therefore, be concluded that research is a very useful aid to all the managerial functions. Managers are expected to make use of research and analysis extensively in connection with all the managerial functions of planning, controlling, organising, co-ordinating, staffing, motivating, leading and so on.

But it is doubtful whether managers of our time concentrate much on research. They are players of pure statistical averages, if at all they use it. In many cases, they do not pay much attention to research and analysis. Their decisions rest on their past experiences, intuitions, observations, and routine procedures. Very often, individual preferences are more valued than analytical exercises. Their planning is not generally based on research or proper forecasting. Some top bosses, though they engage consultants, never attach much importance to research reports. They develop their own preference curves, and their subordinates are expected to be "yes-men."

Many managers act as controllers. By hook or by crook, they prefer to keep their employees under control. Research or analysis does not matter much in their control process. Neither staffing nor leading is based on research so far as they are concerned. While the selection process is guided by personal principles, influence, and recommendations; co-ordination is ensured by the use of feudalistic methods. Traditional value judgement methods are widely used by such managers to lead and manage manpower. In many such cases, research is not believed to serve any useful purpose.

In the business organisations which are managed by families, research does not play any part in their day-to-day management. This, however, is not true in all such organisations. There are progressive, forward-looking organisations in India, which give due weightage for research. We may hope that research will play a very meaningful role in the management of Indian business houses in the years to come.

Mahindra and Mahindra have been market leaders in both utility vehicles and tractors. They have planned for a massive and comprehensive modernisation-cum-expansion programme with a capital outlay of Rs. 350 crores to Rs. 400 crores over the next four or five years. The installed capacity is planned to be substantially increased from 35,000 to 52,000 tractors, from 18,000 to 25,000 engines and from 25,000 to 52, 000 utility vehicles.

The company now plans to introduce a five-door station wagon, a new fuel efficient vehicle in collaboration with Automobiles Peugeot of France, a pick-up vehicle (Peugeot 504) and the development of a more powerful fuel efficient petrol engine. According to the company's chairman, Mr. Kayshab Mahindra, this will enable the company to tap newer export markets for its products, which will be its main strategy of growth in the 1990s. The company also plans to diversify into new areas of business and support investment in associated subsidiary companies.

The company has already received the consent of CCI (the Controller of Capital Issues) for the issue of 48.16 lakhs, 12.5 per cent fully convertible debentures of Rs. 110 each and/or zero interest fully convertible bonds of Rs. 90 each to the shareholders on a right basis in the ratio of one debenture/bond for every four shares held, as also for 2.41 lakh debentures/bonds to employees (including working directors). 8.64 lakh debentures/bonds to Mahindra companies and 8.64 lakh debentures/bonds to International Finance Corporation, Washington. It hopes to get CCI sanction for offering 8.64 lakh debentures/bonds to Automobile Peugeot of France and their associates. The rights issue was opened on January 18, 1990. The company proposes to retain excess subscriptions up to 15 per cent of the offer.

There are 3 options for the company, *viz.,* to apply for debentures; or for bonds; or partly for debentures and partly for bonds. The novel financial instrument is being introduced in the country by the company for the first time, the zero interest bonds, which carry nil interest rate but will be converted into two equity shares of Rs. 10 each in two stages (on April 1, 1991 and at the end of the 18 months from the allotment date), at a premium of Rs. 35 per share against the premium of Rs. 45 per share on conversion of each 12.5 per cent debentures. Thus, the shareholders will have some flexibility in their investment plans.

At the end of March 1989, the company's equity capital stood at Rs. 19.26 crores with reserves of Rs. 105.91 crores. The last bonus issue was made in 1984 in the ratio of two shares for three share held. For the 17-month period ended March 1989, the income was Rs. 992.79 crores. In the first eight months of the year 1989-90 (April-November, 1989), sales totalled Rs. 535.85 crores, with a net profit of Rs. 9.15 crores.

All the managerial functions and functional areas are involved in this case of expansion. In-depth research and analysis were required in every management function in all the functional areas related to this project. Every decision was based on research.

Chapter 13

Research in Functional Areas

Research is an analytical, observational and interpretative process which aids the manager to make decisions. Decision-making is an essential function not only of the top management, but also of the functional management or even lower levels of management. The variation may be only in terms of degree. As far as the area of management is concerned, the key problem today is getting research results effectively translated into operations or functions. For a manager, research is meaningful only if the idea generated can be put into practice. It is in this context that we emphasise the role of research in such functional areas as production, finance, HRM marketing, and so on.

Managerial research, as an aid to managerial decisions, should recognise organisational goals, relationships between the organisational goals and functional goals, relationship between variables (dependent and independent), and the need to generate ideas which assist in policy making and decision-making. It should assist in such prime managerial activities as:

(i) Setting organisational goals and objectives;

(ii) Developing plans to fulfil these objectives;

(iii) Combining human and physical resources so that the objectives are met;

(iv) Monitoring the results with a view to ensuring that the desired objectives are achieved; and

(v) Identifying the relative roles played by the functional areas for the achievement of organisational goals and objectives.

We make an attempt to unveil the utility of research and analysis in the functional areas in this chapter.

Functional Areas

Any managerial analysis should take into account both the external and internal systems, especially the internal system. A knowledge of internal system requires an understanding of the physical, human, financial and technological make-up of the organisation. It includes all the functional areas that operate as sub-systems of the organisational system. An analysis of the external system enables us to evaluate consumer behaviour, while a study of the internal system makes it possible for the firm to have greater discretion. The researcher should analyse the decision centres as well as the profit and information centres in the firm to identify the operating conditions of the functional areas. These functional areas are the sub-systems, or separate areas of operational activity of an organisational system. These are the production, marketing, finance, HRM, and the general administration functions, and such other areas as can effectively contribute to the achievement of organisational goals with the help of research and analysis.

Characteristics and Problems

A research to be utilised for operations and functions should ensure organisational analysis, identification of goals, resources and opportunities, reckoning with institutional versus operational constraints, interaction of resources and goals, identification of the problem areas, identification with organisational objectives and the establishment of their relationship with resources and opportunities as a means of developing a general understanding of both the organisation in general and its each functional area in particular. It should take into account not only the institutional framework, but also the operational existence of the various functional areas and their respective contribution to organisational goals. All organisations, be they profit-oriented organisations, charitable organisations or other kinds of organisation, exist to fulfil one or more purposes or objectives. The true value of any managerial research hinges on one's ability to identify the objectives of the organisation and to determine the best course of action that may be required at the functional area level to fulfil those objectives.

Every action taken by every functional area manager should contribute to the overall objective of the organisation. Hence the process of establishing organisational objectives and objectives for all its sub-units helps the organisation in its basic direction. Any action of any of the functional areas should be measured by comparing it with the organisational objectives. The formulation of a hierarchy of contributions emphasising the priorities would possibly facilitate a meaningful comparison. Any managerial research would be of interest, if it is able to aid in this process.

The objectives and activities of any organisation are identified while forming the organisation. The identification of any of the activities follows the formulation of objectives. For example, a business organisation identifies its objectives first; the kind of product or service to be produced and distributed comes next. In some cases, it is the other way round. However, it is only after the identification of the product that the way of distribution, the production process, personnel policies, etc., are evolved. The functional areas obviously derive their objectives and activities from the overall objectives and goals of the organisation, while the contributions of the various functional areas may be aggregated as the sum total of the organisational output. A managerial research should necessarily take into account this inter-relationship between objectives and functions.

In a profit oriented organisation, profitability studies are result-oriented. (A short-run profitability measurement is easier than a long-run profitability determination.) But there are many organisations where profits may not be the sole or even a partial goal. In such situations, the researcher finds it difficult to measure or identify the effect of certain fulfilling objectives, policies and procedures in quantitative terms. Similar is the position in the case of quality consciousness. Since quality is intangible, it cannot be directly measured. However, there are certain characteristics variables and determinants in the functional areas like statistical quality control and various quality control techniques which can be subjected to research. In spite of their limitations, many managerial studies in the functional areas like production, marketing and finance have become very common nowadays.

Production Function

Researches are not rare in the production area. Product development research, innovation research, cost reduction research, performance improvement research, work simplification research, profitability improvement research, inventory control research, product design analysis, process improvement studies, manufacturing process research — these are some of the prominent areas of research in the production function. In fact, there are numerous areas for research in production and materials, while research and development activities mainly concentrate on product development and the production process.

Manufacturing research identifies new and better ways of producing goods, invents new technologies, reduces costs and improves product quality. Capacitors for electrical circuits, for example, were once made by interleaving metal in alternate layers with paper or plastic. This process was costly because it used a great deal of metal. Now capacitors are made by evaporating thin films of metal on paper or plastic, which is then wound into a roll. This process, by which less metal is used and better capacitors are produced, is the result of manufacturing research. Electronics, micro-miniaturisation, solid state devices, computers and magnetic alloys, and the concomitant tying together of manufacturing research and product design are the result of constant research in production.

The sources of manufacturing research projects or topics may consist of:

(i) Suggestions from the top management;

(ii) Proposals from production engineers;

(iii) Suggestions from the research staff;

(iv) Hints from product research;

(v) Suggestions from the marketing department;

(vi) Interest generated by the general technolgical scene, etc.

The information from the production system may include details of raw material inventory, finished goods inventories, work-in-process inventories and component parts inventories. The data on maintenance and the characteristics of production equipment may be used for equipment replacement analysis. The data on the composition of the work force, the availability of work force skills, turnover, absenteeism, accidents, shifts, labour-turnover, etc. also are relevant to the studies in production management, while cost information is useful for cost control studies, cost-benefits analysis, and such other areas.

Selection of a Manufacturing Research Project

It is often a difficult task to select a worthwhile research project based on definite criteria. An adequate rate of return should be the basic characteristic of any production research. No organisation can afford to go in for a trial-and-error method. For example, in a cost reduction engineering project, the rate of return may be worked out by bearing in mind:

(i) The cost of the engineering effort required to carry out the project;

(ii) The investment to be made in the plant for the purpose of development and modernisation;

(iii) The contribution of the new project to savings over a period of years;

(iv) The average rate of return as a percentage and ROI;

(v) A comparison among the alternative technologies.

It is not easy to calculate the rate of return accurately. But the effort required and the potential benefits should be examined to make certain that the game is worth the candle. Long-term profitability is another important factor to be taken into account before a manufacturing project is selected. There should be reasonable probability for success if any manufacturing research should be undertaken. The time factor is another important aspect. One would not ordinarily engage in manufacturing research if the project is so long-range that the benefits of success will be in the far distant future, because further technological change may take place in the long run.

The outcome of the study should have a wide scope of application, which is one of the decisive criteria for the selection of research projects in production. However, certain projects of limited applicability would initially be acceptable, if there is a possibility of extending the results to several similar fields of activity. For example, in the research on the development of the powder metallurgy technique in making bearings, the porosity of the resulting product was a feature that made the process particularly desirable. Only when the result of the investigation is of utility value, and the organisation concerned intends to make use of it, does the project have viability. Manufacturing researchers, therefore, make it a point to select the projects which are backed by the need for satisfying factors, so that the pressure in favour of adoption may make their utilisation more likely. The probability of acquiring patents is another positive factor aiding the selection of a production research. However, in certain cases, there may not be scope for patents, though they are of great utility. For example, a research that leads to statistical quality control and quality assurance may not have any scope for patent development, though it is of a very high utility. A very prominent factor to be taken into account in the selection of a production research project is that it should be compatible with existing staff skills. If, however, certain people do not develop enthusiasm, another group may be entrusted with the responsibility, especially in a large organisation.

The scientific method is the basis of any research. However, in manufacturing research, the researcher is expected to undertake more result-oriented research projects than method-oriented theoretical studies.

Some people, who have the training, background and intellectual capacity to undertake research in manufacturing technology, have a strong bias toward pure or basic research. They avoid work which is justified by practical needs. One of the most important criteria in selecting a project is the extent to which it contributes to the knowledge and application of the company in current fields or a field which has utility value for the company. Manufacturing research should not only provide answers to definite problems but build up a stock of knowledge on how to make things. The production planner should be in a position to draw vital information from the fund of knowledge contributed by manufacturing research. Unfortnately, many researchers conveniently ignore this need. Such research studies then become intellectual gimmicks.

It is, however, unwise on the part of the researcher to select gigantic projects which tie up huge resources of the organisation even if all the other factors are favourable. The selection of a research project in manufacturing management should not be based on hit-or-miss estimates or cursory considerations. The choice of a research project should be a prudent action which takes in to account all the relevant aspects, including utility, outcome, time, money, manpower and, obviously the corporate objectives.

Scope of Research in Production

A considerable percentage of industrial development work is done in manufacturing, and engineering cost forms a substantial portion of the production cost. Research in production, therefore, is capable of bringing about cost reduction. The industrial and production processes have become increasingly complex nowadays, especially in the context of dynamic technological development, complex labour problems backed by politically motivated and militant trade unions, conspicuous socio-economic changes, changes in human values, tastes and preferences, and government policies. In such a dynamic business environment, the need for manufacturing research is vital for the purpose of establishing a manufacturing climate which is in harmony with environmental conditions.

Research in production aids innovation, product development, product differentiation and diversification, on the one hand, and industrial development, on the other. Research and development encourage the continuity of activity level in the manufacturing organisation, which creates a climate for the development and growth of production activity. Research in production not only reduces the cost of material and manpower, but lowers the inventory carrying cost as well. It leads to a reduction in the volume of unskilled labour. Moreover, it increases the efficiency and skill of the work force and shop floor supervisors, and enables the organisation to update itself. It reduces the possibility of obsolosence.

Research Results in Operation

Any research result in the area of production should have a practical application; and there should be an effective system for moving technology from research to operations. Technology is a knowledge of the physical and life sciences as applied to practical purposes. This knowledge is effectively developed by a number of technical activities, and in scientific ways as in fundamental research, applied research, etc. While fundamental research seeks to establish the principles and relations underlying this knowledge, applied research crystallises the true nature of the knowledge and demonstrates its potential utility by the employment of bench-scale apparatus. The development of the production process puts this knowledge to practical use in a workable prototype form, while engineering refines the knowledge for commercial exploitation, or other practical uses. In other words, this knowledge or technology is the result of research, which is put to use by the operational management. Many companies have faced the problems of moving research results effectively on the shop floor. It is mainly because no single solution is universally applicable that there cannot be a very acceptable procedure to reduce the research results to practice in all situations.

Quinn and Mueller have, however, suggested a general framework or a four-step programme which has been derived from the accumulated experience of over 200 operating and research managers of leading US companies.[1]

Step 1. Examine technological transfer points. Analyse the critical points across which technology must flow if it is to be successfully exploited. Recognise the potential resistances to the flow at each of these interfaces.

Step 2. Provide information to target research. Generate adequate information so that research can be targeted towards company goals and needs. Develop a comprehensive long-range planning programme to determine what technology is relevant to the company's future and to serve as a focal point for information flows. Establish special organisations, where needed, to seek specific new technological opportunities for the company, to provide commercial intelligence information about competitive activities, and to make careful economic evaluations of technologically-based new ventures.

Step 3. Foster a positive motivational environment. Establish a motivational environment which actively stimulates technological progress and its associated organisational change. Develop tough-minded top-

1. Quinn, James Br an and Mueller, James, A., "Transferring Research Results to Operations," *Harvard Business Review,* Vol. No.1, January 1963, pp. 49-66.

management attitudes, policies, and long-term controls which foster rather than hinder the production and use of new technologies.

Step 4. Plan and control exploitation of research and development results. Design special exploitation organisations and procedures to ensure:

(a) That competent groups have both the authority and the obligation to develop new technologies at each of their critical stages;

(b) That each major technological transfer is planned and monitored to control effort expenditures, cash flows and timing; and,

(c) That the entire transfer system implements the critical strategy, which determines success or failure, at each major technological transfer point.

Despite serious attempts, many companies have their own constraints to target R&D and to create a positive motivational environment for moving the research results to the actual operational field. When the technologies and products are totally new to the company, the magnitude of constraints widens, and the difficulties to reduce the research result to operational areas are serious. Then entirely new skills may be required at each technical stage, *i.e.,* scientific inquiry, reduction to practice, entrepreneuring a new enterprise and operating a full-scale facility. The synchoronization of these skills to successfully exploit a new technology calls for a strong co-ordinating authority which cuts across the usual formal lines of research, development, engineering, marketing, and manufacturing. In the absence of such a prudent co-ordination, each functional group may tend to look after its own interests, and thus jeopardise the common and organisational objectives. Then there is the possibility of unnecessary delays, dilution of effectiveness of the new technology and cost escalation; sometimes, even total abandonment. In order to avoid such an eventuality, the company should have an action plan consisting of:

(i) The creation of specific formal organisations of experts and competent people;

(ii) The establishment of thorough procedures for planning and monitoring of the effect; and

(iii) The integration of these organisations and procedures to implement the critical strategy that determines the success of each specific technological exploitation.

If a large company wants to diversify effectively through research or to make radical technical advances, the stimulus must come from the top corporate level. The top management must be willing to underwrite long-term fundamental and new product research, backed by corporate-level opportunity-seeking; and economic evaluation groups should help target research activities and refine the commercial potential of research results. The company should then develop a procedure which efficiently links together the series of sequential steps, leading from the initial technical inquiries to the eventual goal of exploitation. It must ensure that the programme is adequately planned — from research to exploitation. It must provide a basis for controlling the transfer of research throughout its cycle. The procedure must monitor the three factors related to technical progress, *viz.,* technical and commercial effort versus results, rupee costs and returns, and the time interval. For the purpose of planning and controlling such techniques as PERT/CPM, budget reviews, venture analyses, rational, decision models, etc., are widely used. As each major programme comes through the management is in a position to evaluate and incorporate changes, if any, from time to time.

Inventory studies and model building are a part of the research in the production and materials area. "Inventory is the physical stock of goods that a business keeps on hand in order to promote the smooth and efficient running of its affairs. It may be held before the production cycle, in the form of raw material inventory, at an intermediate stage in the production cycle, as in-process inventory; or as the end of the production cycle, as finished goods inventory." There may be a spare parts inventory, too, depending on the actual need for these parts. However, the finished goods inventory is considered to be the most prominent, though the procedure developed can be adapted with minor changes in other types of inventory as well. There can be inventory control in uncertainty without reordering, inventory control with ordering with a certain amount of demand, and inventory with reordering and uncertain demand.

A certain amount of inventory is essential for efficient functioning in any company. It, however, depends on the actual study of various factors, such as economic order quantity (EOQ), lead time, the magnitude of certainty, determinant forces, and so on. Control over inventory can be exercised by changing the timing of production runs, by changing the size of the runs and by changes in promotional effort or sales inducements. Inventory control becomes more effective when the marketing activity is constant, or demand is determined by various methods. It is in this context that the marketing and market researches assume significance. Inventory studies enable the manager to determine the exact size of the inventory to be maintaned. Of course there are advantages and disadvantages associated with increased inventory. The advantages include economies of production with large-run sizes; faster supply of orders to customers;

stabilise work loads; more than proportionate profits and windfalls from speculation in a market with inflationary tendencies.

The disadvantages of a large inventory are: greater inventory carrying cost (examples, warehouse rent, depreciation and deterioration, interest on additional cost, physical handling and accounting), blocking up of funds and increased uncertainty. In normal circumstances, increased inventory is desirable only when the marginal profits considerably exceeds the marginal inventory carrying cost. Systematic research has a great role to play in determining the economic inventory level (EIL).

To sum up, it may be asserted that research is inseparable from the functional area of production and materials management.

Research in Marketing Function

It has already been pointed out that market research and marketing research provide a major part of the marketing information which influences the inventory level. In fact, production and marketing are closely linked with each other. Here, the relation between porduction and marketing functions and the researches in them are imminent.

Marketing Research

Marketing research is the research activity which is undertaken to aid the marketing function. It makes a conspicuous contribution to the marketing information system in particular, and helps the marketing management to get the products more efficently into the hands of the consumer, in general. Marketing research stimulates the flow of marketing data from the environment to the marketing information system of the company. "The marketing information system, on the other hand, turns this data flow into a marketing information flow that goes to its executives. On the basis of this information, the executives develop plans and programmes, which enter a marketing communication flow that goes back to the environment." It may study the problems and opportunities; and may include market survey, product-preference test, sales forescasting studies, motivation research, advertising effectiveness evaluation, test marketing studies, etc, Full-line marketing research studies, speciality-line marketing researches, and syndicated information gathering may also come under marketing research. Advertising media research, packaging research, performance evaluation studies, potentiality analysis studies, market share and trends analysis, sales analysis, sales quota and territory setting analysis, distribution channel studies etc., may also be included in marketing research. It may be observed that research is closely associated with all the stages in the marketing function, from product planning and development to physical distribution and sales after service.

The steps involved in marketing research include:

(i) Problem definition;

(ii) Research design;

(iii) Field work;

(iv) Data analysis;

(v) Interpretation and observation; and

(vi) Report writing, presentation and implementation, which are quite identical to the research steps in any area of management.

To be precise it may be asserted that the executive decision bearing on all the Ps (product, price, promotion, place and physical distribution) have a fair amount of dependence on research findings. Though the research would highlight the particular problem area, it would make considerable impact on all decision areas. An example that Kotler has quoted from Mason Haire[2] is very relevant in this context. When instant coffee was first introduced, housewives complained that it did not taste like real coffee. Yet, in blindfold tests, many of the same housewives could not distinguish between a cup of instant coffee and real coffee. This indicated that much of their resistance was psychological. The researcher decided to design two almost identical shopping lists, the only difference being that regular coffee was on the one list and instant coffee, on the other. The regular coffee list was given to one group of housewives and the instant coffee list was given to a different, but comparable, group. Both groups were asked to guess the social and personal characteristics of the woman whose shopping list they saw. The comments were pretty much the same, with one significant difference. A higher proportion of housewives, whose list contained instant coffee, described the subjects as "lazy, a spendthrift, a poor wife and failing to plan well for her family." The researcher could very well reveal that it was nothing but their prejudice against the instant coffee that provoked them to make these critical comments. The marketing man is now in a position to foresee the type of resistance the housewife would put up. The marketing policies for instant coffee should, therefore, be formulated by taking in to account the decisions on the marketing of instant coffee are now influenced by those research findings.

Any marketing decision, like any managerial decisions, has to be backed by adequate and reliable facts and information that help to identify and solve the set of the marketing problems related to it. The more the decision-maker bases his decision on facts rather than on guesses, the less

2. Mason Haire, "Projective Technique in Marketing Research," *Journal of Marketing*, April, 1950, pp. 649-56, quoted by Kotler, *Marketing*, p. 617.

likelihood there is of his making a wrong decision. In other words, research helps to eliminate guesswork from decision-making. Marketing research attempts to provide the tools whereby the marketing executive may obtain accurate and adequate facts and information regrading "who, where, why, how and at what price" the customers would like to buy his product. Statistical techniques based on the probability theory have been widely used to select samples of consumers. Devices like group interviewing and projective tests have been borrowed from the social sciences to help in probing into the psychological meanings attached to certain brands and products. Questionnaires and personal interviews have been employed to investigate the problems and prospects of product positioning, as well as of the marketing forces in operation. Statistical techniques, OR methods, mathematical and econometric models, and analytical skills are widely used in the marketing area also nowadays.

It should, however, be realised that marketing research does not apply to any haphazard accumulation of facts; it implies a systematic approach to gathering facts which have a certain definite potential to be used to aid in the marketing decisions. The term marketing research is, therefore, applicable to a wide variety of techniques, tools and approaches. It embraces the kinds of research that are commonly implied in the terms "Sales Analysis," "Product Testing", "Estimating Market Potentials." "Advertising Research," "Analysis of Geographical Market," "Motivation Research," "Sales Forecasting", "Test Market Research," "Market Surveys," "Consumer Behaviour Studies," and so on. The use of inappropriate and biased data can, however, be as dangerous and misleading as the absence of facts. Similarly, misinterpretation of accurate facts results in dubious or fallacious findings which are worse than mere guesswork. Inappropriate and inaccurate decision, leading to precarious results, are the ultimate outcome of such researches. All these facts highlight the importance of research in the functional area of marketing.

Research in Industrial Marketing

The preparation of plans, their execution and control of operations to achieve the most profitable allocation of the company's resources to current and future market opportunities for the sake of effectively satisfying the customers, entertaining the prospects, and influencing the market at large — these should be the basic tasks of any marketing management. In the changing market situations, the marketing executive can be effective only if he is able to narrow the area of guesswork and make use of prudent and analytical value juidgements before arriving at effective decisions. The role of research is decisive in this context.

The modern industrial market is characterised by constant changes. Growing technological development results in flow of new products, new processes, and new materials, which make obsolete the existing products and methods. Conventional automobiles are giving way to automatic transmission technology. The semiconductor produced a new industry and ushered in significant improvements in a vast range of products. New plastic materials are replacing traditional fibres, metals and films. Mechanisation and automation have revolutionised industrial process. Changes in the living habits and tastes of the general public call for different types of consumer products, leading to revolutionary changes in the industrial market. The industrial goods marketer is now faced with multifarious marketing problems which were unknown to him in the past. Industrial marketing research has, therefore, become the order of the day. Many industrial goods manufacturers have already organised marketing research departments and have engaged marketing research executives.

Marketing research now functions as an intelligence service for the industrial marketer. It helps in short and long-range forecasting, studies of business trends, new product acceptance and potential, competitive products studies, development of market potentials, market share analysis, determination of market characteristics, sales analysis, and the establishment of quotas and territories. In certain organisation; in India, such departments as commercial development, corporate planning, R & D, and customer service, look after the job of industrial products research. In many cases, marketing research consultants are engaged to do this job.

The step in marketing research for industrial products are identical to those in the consumer goods marketing research or any other research. However, the research is effective if the investigators and researchers are technically capable and trained to acquire knowledge of industrial goods. This may be an essential prerequisite in any other areas of research. The design of samples for industrial market studies presents some important differences from the typical sample designs for consumer marketing research. These differences, however, are of degree rather than of kind. For consumer goods, the customer circle is extensive; and hence proper care should be taken to estimate the characterstics of the universe (total groups) prior to sampling. (A census survey is uneconomical and inconvenient). A proper and careful stratification is necessary, while the sample should accurately fit in with the characteristics of the universe. The sample, moreover, must be designed on the basis of probability concepts. It is possible to design such samples and to make use of them reasonably well in consumer research, even though a complete coverage of a probability sample is very difficult to achieve. As for industrial marketing research, several important factors affect the sample design. For example, vertical market industrial products have a much smaller number of buyers, while horizontal market products have extensive customer circles—various industrial sectors, centres, processes, technologies, industries, manufacturing units, and so on. Sampling is simple; even a census is possible, as far as the former types of goods are concerned, while both census and accurate sampling are impossible in the latter.

Another important difference, which relates more to interviewing than to the design of the samples, lies in the multiple purchasing characteristic of industrial buyers, and the consequent complexity of the purchasing process. Unless this is adequately recognised in the interviewing procedure, the result is bound to be biased. Moreover, in view of the heavy concerntration in many industrial markets, and the possibility of high variability in the buying motives, behaviour and practices, and attitudes among companies in each industry group, it has been customary to stratify an industrial sample according to the size of the firms, and to insist on a complete coverage of the largest concerns. In consumer goods, marketing samples are usually stratified on the basis market segmentation. Again, by virtue of the high variability among industry market, it is more difficult to plan a sample in detail and follow the plan exactly than it is in a consumer market.

The methods for the collection of data in industrial marketing research may include interview, telephone interview and mail questionnaire. The personal interview is the most popular among these. Specially trained market research executives, and the field sales force, including sales engineers may act as investigators in industrial research. Though a marketing research can be conducted in any convenient way and for any purpose, there are five basic types of this research in industrial goods. They are:

(i) Sales Forecasting;

(ii) Measuring the size of markets;

(iii) Analysing the sales results;

(iv) Analysing the customers' buying motives, practices, attitudes and behaviour; and

(v) Analysing the competitors' marketing strategy.

To sum up, it may be observed that marketing research is an effective tool in the industrial marketing process.

Market Research

Marketing research and market research are considered to be synonyms in many contexts, at least by some writers. A discussion of marketing research would not, therefore, be complete without some light on the term "market reseaarch." The marketing function consists of the various functional aspects in relation to the marketing mix elements — broadly speaking, the five Ps, *viz.,* product, price, place, promotion and physical distribution. Research in connection with the functional aspects of any of these elements or forces that affect them may be treated as marketing research. Marketing research, therefore, is a broad term which encompasses the total process of marketing.. At the same time, market is the framework in which the buyers or customers and sellers act in the process of transferring the ownership of products. Precisely speaking, it deals with the place elements and forces in the market, say, customers, prospects, wholesalers, retailers, stockists, geographical forces, and so on. Livingstone, therefore, calls it "the study of a market situation."[3]

Market research may include demand forecasting, study of the competitors, consumer behaviour studies, analysis of environmental or external forces, public policy studies, investigation of economic variables, and so on. It may, therefore, be asserted that market research may be included in marketing research. It facilitates marketing information on market segments, on present and potential market, the prospects for growth of the market, the potential markets, on buying habits and consumption pattern, on the size and location of the potential market, the prospects for growth of the market, the potential of the competitors, their comptitive position, channnels of distribution, media and the effectiveness of advertising, and various social, economic and political forces that operate in the market. In a nutshell, market research is another potential area of research activity in the functional area of marketing.

Mathematical Research

Motivational research is one of the most controversinal aspects of market research. It deals with the forces that affect behaviour. The quantitative method of data collection provides scope for quantifying the variables, but it does not definitely identify the exact reason why an individual behaves in a given way in a particular situation. Of course, statistical methods and econometric methods succeed in identifying the determinants. Motivational research makes use of qualitative technique. One may not be able to quantify why the customers of a soft drink behaved

---

3. Livingstone, James M. A. *Management Guide to Market Research, Studies in Marketing Management,* Macmillan, London, 1977, p. 1.

in a given pattern in the market. But motivational research identifies the motivational factors that determine consumer behaviour. The two methods of interviewing in motivational research are depth interview and projective techniques. With the help of the former, the researcher can go deep into the consumers' mind, using an unstructured questionnaire. Projective techniques stem largely from the area of clinical psychology and should be administered by a clinician as far as possible. The word association technique enables the respondent to complete a sentence by associating a word with a given stimulus word.

"In the motivational research, the practitioner is seeking a subconscious, possibly irrational, motive for a consumer's action which may cause him to act in a manner which does not necessarily correspond with the answers he can be expected to give at a straightforward question-and-answer interview." In many cases, there may not be such subconscious motivation for the respondent to act in an unpredictable manner. Here, there is an obvious danger of a negative or biased reporting on the part of the investigator. This may be the reason why motivation research has not been so popular in recent years. The negative report situation may create something of a dilemma. Moreover, any meaningful result can be arrived at in the motivation research only if it is conducted by experts and trained professionals, which is bound to be immensely expensive and time-consuming. This is, however, one of the prominent ways in which the research technique is used in the marketing function.

Forecasting

One of the most important functions that makes use of the research technique in the functional area of marketing is forecasting. Forecasting is a necessary pre-requisite for planning, which is the basic function of management. In other words, forecasting is the element of management, either in general management or in functional areas. As a matter of fact, marketing planning is directly based on forecasting. But the basic tool of forecasting is research. The measurement of market demand is the chief function of forecasting. "Market demand for a product is the total volume that would be bought by a defined customer group in a defined geographical area in a defined time period in a defined marketing environment under a defined marketing programme."[4]

A forecast is a prediction or estimation of a future situation. It shows the expected level of market demand for the expected level of industry marketing effort in the given environment. A firm likes to examine the sensitivity of its sales in relation to a number of its alternative policy

4. Kotler, Philip, *Marketing Management,* Prentice-Hall, Delhi, p. 214.

decisions. Certain people mistake the forecast as "the highest possible market demand." In fact, it is the "expected market demand." It is an estimate based on yesterday's plan and performance and tomorrow's expectations. There can be short-term, medium-term, and long-term forecasts which are identical to planning. A forecast can also estimate company potentials, total market potentials, and territorial potentials. Irrespective of the type of forecast, the fact remains that systematic analysis, interpretation and estimation are the basic elements of forecasting. Any marketing executive who plans his sales operations is expected to extensively make use of the research which leads to forecasting.*

Marketing Information System

A marketing problem has to be dealt with in asystematic manner, and the marketing decisions should be based on appropriate marketing information. This may be the reason why a company, operating under the marketing concept, relies largely on constant gathering of information. The marketing information system, which consists of an organised set of procedures, information-handling routines, reporting techniques, and recording procedures, has the basic task of providing marketing information to facilitate marketing decisions. An adequate MIS enables one to minimise the use of guesswork in decision-making. MIS may also exist if it is supported by a collection and processing of information, on the one hand, and timely information flow, on the other. The collection and processing of information fall within the scope of research.

The actual task of the marketing information system is to process large quantities of marketing data, and to present them to the management in the most understandable, identifiable and usable form. (The larger the volume of the data, the greater the need for computer software.) In fact, the processing, presentation and interpretation of data stem from the basic task of research. The identification of the required information outputs is one of the most critical characteristics of the MIS design. Tailoring information outputs to each executive's information need it is another decisive aspect of the MIS design. The former is the task of the research investigator, while the latter is that of a research analyst. The actual ingredient for any MIS design is the determination and discrimination of the exact type of information required by each executive in connection with each problem. This is more or less the task of a research designer. MIS also deals with customer information, product information, and sales force information, operating ratios, gross margin ratios, expense ratios, sales

* For a detailed reading, see, Michael, *Sales Management in India,* R. Chand & Co. New Delhi, 1979, Chapter 9.

returns and allowances ratios, net profit ratios, other analytical ratios, markdown percentages, stockt run over rates, and so on, which are directly related to data analysis and interpretation.

To sum up, it may be remarked that not only the marketing information system, but all the areas of the marketing function are closely linked with research; and the later cannot be isolated from the former.

Research in Finance Function

The growth and development of a business organisation is directly linked with the success of its finance function, which is concerned with determining long-term and short-term financial objectives, formulating and promulgating financial policies, and developing procedures that aid in the promulgation of the firm's policies. The finance function includes financial control, which consists of two steps, *viz.,*

(i) Developing standards of performance; and

(ii) Comparing activities with these standards.

Financial managers cannot evade the responsibility of replanning either. In the pursuit of managing finance, the firm's primary goals have to be converted into the immediate goals of the finance department. Usually, there are two approaches of financial goals. These are:

(i) Profit-Risk Approach to Financial Goals; and

(ii) Liquidity-Profitability Approach to Financial Goals.

This does not, however, signify that all other approaches are ruled out.

The *profit-risk* approach recognises that finance deals with creating a proper framework to maximise profits while minimising risk. For the achievement of this balance, controls over fund flows are ensured, and adequate flexibility to respond to changes in the operating environment is maintained. This approach generally takes care of four aspects — maximising profit, minimising risk, maintaining control, and ensuring flexibility. For profit maximisation, a high level of long-term corporate profit is planned by the financial management. This is possible only if the finance department is enriched with sufficient information inflow on the internal and external forces that influence corporate goals, decisions, and actions. The Management Information System (MIS) aids in this process, provided it is backed by adequate research and analysis. The finance executive anticipates the problem areas, and considers ways and means of tackling the difficulties in order to plan the steps that would enable him to minimise risk. Anticipating problem areas and alternative courses of action, as well as choosing the best course — these depend on a systematic analysis of the situation, which is the work of a research analyst. Maintaining control over flows of funds requires a financial reporting system which can provide a timely and accurate picture of the firm's activities. It enables one to locate and correct errors or weaknesses, if any, from time to time. That is why, the collection, compilation, presentation and interpretation of up-to-date data are the basic tools of any financial reporting system.

Uncertainty is a part of any business; and, therefore, sufficient provision is made for financial flexibility to tide over the uncertainty. Flexibility refers to an appropriate relationship between the finance function and other functional areas, which are interdependent. An adequate information flow between them is a prerequisite. And here, too, research plays an important role.

The *liquidity-profitability approach* emphasises the two variables of liquidity and profitability. Liquidity indicates that a firm has adequate cash on hand to meet its obligations at all times, including unforeseen situations. It calls for the maintenance of a cash reserve for emergencies as well. Profitability is the rate of profit on investment. The achievement of liquidity in the liquidity-profitability approach requires the minimisation of risk and an adequate control over the firm's activities. Thus, both the approaches are interlinked. Profitability analysis itself is a sort of research, while the maintenance of liquidity for emergencies and unforeseen situations is a result of the studies of the future (forecasting and adaptive planning). That is why, systematic studies occupy a central place in the liquidity-profitability analysis.

Functions of Financial Management

Liquidity and profitability are essential elements for financial management, though assets management and funds management are not unimportant. The financial manager's functions in relation to liquidity include forecasting cash flows, raising funds, and managing the flow of internal funds. The success of any funds flow management depends on the matching of cash inflows with cash outflows. Cash flow forecasting, based on an analysis and interpretation of the appropriate data, is the basis of the "matching" process. The financial manager is expected to identify the various sources of funds available for the company from time to time. It is his duty to analyse each source of funds in comparison with respective needs at the given point of time before choosing the best and the most economic source of funds. Any decision on raising funds should be based on an adequate analytical framework. For example, a company may have a number of alternative sources, *viz.,* new shares, debentures, market borrowing, bank loans, etc. The finance department has to analyse all the sources in comparison with the nature of the company's requirements, and the availability of funds, and to choose the best from among them. Even in managing the funds flows effectively, a constant vigil should be maintained on the various bank accounts and funds. All these postulate some sort of research and analysis.

The functions that lead to probability include cost control, pricing, forecasting future profits, and measuring the cost of capital, among other things. A detailed cost accounting system is a part of large-scale business operation, which requires a large quantity of processed data, and its systematic presentation and interpretation. Pricing decisions are joint decisions of the marketing and finance managers; and both cost and marketing data and analytical framework support them. In order to forecast future profits, an adequate analysis of current costs, likely cost escalations, likely changes in the ability of the firm to sell its products, market changes, internal and external forces — all these are essential. Both debts and equity make relative contributions to the capital requirement of the firm. Each source of capital involves the cost of capital. Short-term debt may be more expensive than long-term debt. Preferred or common stock yields different returns to the holders. All these factors have to be studied in detail with a view to measuring the cost of capital. The cost component of each source is investigated in detail prior to determining the profit margin that will pay for the borrowed funds and yield a satisfactory return on investment (ROI) as well as a share of the factors of production. Profitability analysis, therefore, is a sort of research conducted by the finance department.

In the management of assets, funds, and the overall finance function, there is an element of research, though it may not be identified as a formal research activity. Hampton has observed: "Financial tools should be applied in a logical, overall problem-solving process. It is the manager's job to find a systematic manner of developing valid information from available data."[5] The operation of financial tools can be explained in certain steps in sequence. These sequential steps are almost identified to the steps in research. These are:

(i) Gather the relevant data;

(ii) Process the data;

(iii) Examine the information;

(iv) Select the appropriate tools;

5. Hampton , John J., *Financial Decision-Making,* Prentice, Hall of India, New Delhi, p. 16.

(v) Apply the tools to decision-making;

(vi) Identify alternative courses of action; and

(vi) Select the best alternative.

As a matter of fact, research is the basic ingredient of financial decision-making. The tools of financial analysis, *viz.*, funds flow analysis, ratio analysis, cost-volume profit analysis (break-even analysis), an analysis of financial leverages, etc. extensively make use of research tools in the process of analysis. It may, therefore, be conducted that research tools are closely linked with the tools of financial management; and that the finance function largely depends on research tools, either directly or indirectly.

Human Resource Management

The personnel function is not an exception in the application of research as an aid to effective decision-making. It makes use of research more than any other functional area, because human behaviour is prone to constant changes; and the personnel management's task is to deal with human beings. Individual behaviour is different from collective behaviour human attitudes to work life differ substantially from those to social life. Individual approaches and motives are not identical; and heredity's influence and environment's impact on human behaviour affect organisational behaviour and productivity. Research in personnel management is, therefore, more vital than in any other functional area because of the greater importance of the human element in the enterprise.

An individual's motivation to work is associated with his needs and their satisfaction. These needs may be physical needs, security needs, social needs, egoistic needs, and so on. An effective personnel manager determines the respective needs of his work force, and formulates personnel policies to satisfy those needs, so that they can be motivated to contr bute their best to the attainment of organisational goals. A systematic research plays a great role in the determination of the individual needs of the work force. That is why personnel policies have to be guided by research.

Job satisfaction enables workmen to derive a sense of accomplishment which leads to creativity. It creates a sense of belonging in the minds of the people at work. Management approaches to the people make a great impact on their accomplishments. These approaches may be classified into:

(i) Traditional approach;

(ii) Human relations approach;

(iii) Collective bargaining approach;

(iv) Motivational approach;

(v) Redemptive approach;

(vi) Stick to rule approach; and

(vii) Neglecting approach.

Though the managerial approach to manpower is largely influenced by organisational philosophy, the individual and group behaviour of the workers towards the organisation plays no less an important role. In fact, organisational approach to the people is not an isolated event. Many factors are to be evaluated and taken into account by the personnel department prior to formulating the approach to their people. Any personnel policy or decision should be analysis-based and result-oriented.

The modern age is characterised by a low profile of worker logic and constantly declining trend in job satisfaction and work motivation. In order to counteract these trends, a number of techniques have been applied, which however, have proved to be futile. Goal setting, participative management, job redesign, carrot-and-stick motivational tools, etc. are prominent among them. While job rerdesign seeks to make the job more challenging, the goal setting approach ignores the job itself but makes it easier for workers to leave it. Nevertheless, the two approaches share a common interest in increasing workers' discretion and self-control. Participative management attempts to ensure workers' participation in the management of the enterprise, and the carrot-and-stick approach makes the use of both the negative and positive means of motivation. Each approach is the result of research. But, in course of time, human behaviour changes and fresh researches become necessary to tackle fresh problems. The factory system, technological development, large-scale operations, political changes, politically-motivated trade unionism, recent trends in managerial outlook, etc. — all these bring about substantial changes in the workers' behaviour. Obviously, personnel policies should be relevant to the changes and based on fresh empirical studies. There is, therefore, great scope for studies in personnel management.

Recent developments in the process of production necessitate job enrichment programmes, which consist of the following elements:

(i) Workers should be given full task;

(ii) New and more difficult tasks should be introduced;

(iii) The accountability of individual workers should be increased;

(iv) Elements of planning and co-ordination should be introduced;

(v) Workers should be given additional authority and freedom;

(vi) Workers should be empowered to deal directly with clients or suppliers.

All these elements are incorporated only after a well-defined analysis. One of the most advanced forms of job redesign is self-managing work teams (autonomous work groups), which meet periodicially to determine job assignments, scheduled work breaks, and lay down the rate of production.

In fact every decision or action of the work group is based on analysis and investigation.

In this context, it can be observed that research is a part and parcel of effective management of all the functional areas. Production function extensively makes use of research and development for new product development, product differentiation, diversification, innovation, technological advancement, etc., leave aside the other areas; while the marketing man makes use of marketing research, forecasting, market research, motivation research, evaluation research, promotion research and so on for formulating effective marketing strategies. The financial executive is able to guide the company to the path of success only with the help of research and analysis. Research and analysis play no less a role in the personal function also — say: selection, training and development, placement and induction, compensation, job evaluation, motivation, manpower planning, labour relations, labour welfare, industrial disputes and their settlements, collective bargaining—especially in the modern age of industrial disharmony and strife. Management information system, at the same time, is closely linked with research and analysis. To conclude, it can be observed that research is an essential aid not only to functional areas, but also to the general and top management. However, on a close observation, one would be able to realise that it would take many more years for the research to receive its due emphasis in the realm of Indian business.

Chapter 14

Statistical Methods in Managerial Analysis

Statistics is a quantitative approach of the scientific method which seeks to develop quantitative tools for managerial decisions. Its contribution to decision-making in an uncertainty is great. It enables us to develop techniques to make valid inferences or judgements by virtue of its conspicuous role in managerial analysis. While probability considerably influences managerial decision-making, it provides a basis for statistical analysis, since the probability theory lays the very foundation of the Law of Large Numbers or the Law of Statistical Regularity.

It is obvious, then, that the statistical method is considerably influenced by this theory. (This law states that what has to be regarded as a chance or random occurrence in one or a few individual cases may become a regularity when applied to a large group.) In fact, managerial decision is often based on statistical regularity, especially when the decision needs are not backed by full or comprehensive information. In such cases, efforts at collecting and organising the data relevant to the problem, distilling from these data certain key values, and deciding on the basis of the small amount of information available in the collected data, become meaningful. To be precise, statistics and statistical methods are of immense use in the solution of management problems and managerial analyses.

Statistics in Management of Business

A statistical method is very useful in three specific areas, *viz.,*

(i) It is useful in the planning of operations of special projects, or in the recurring activities of a firm over a specific period of time;

(ii) In facilitates the establishment of standards in relation to the volume of sales, quality standards for manufactured goods, standard rates of output per day, or standard operating or financial ratios, and forecasting;

(iii) It assists in control, which is effected by comparing achievements with plans or standards, and, when the former is too far out of line with the latter, taking appropriate action. It facilitates the discovery of what is wrong and then the correction of the disequilibrium or, in certain cases, the revision of the standards. "Planning, standard setting, and control are separate concepts, but they are interwoven in practice. Budgetary control includes planning and control, whereas quality control includes standard setting and control." Functional areas also employ statistical methods extensively.

The marketing function makes extensive use of the statistical method, especially in conducting a sales analysis, a market analysis, or a marketing analysis. The sales analysis is a study of sales records, properly classified. The results of sales campaigns may be evaluated with the aid of a sales analysis based on sales statistics. In the market analysis, which entails a study of market areas to estimate potential sales, and marketing methods, statistics plays an important part. Statistical quality control may be one of the most important areas in production which makes extensive use of statistics. With the help of statistics, standards, of the quality of the manufactured products are established to control the manufacturing process, so that the quality is maintained, and to ensure that the individual lots sold or purchased are of acceptable quality. Time and motion analysis, tests for new products planning of the replacement of physical equipment, etc. — these also constantly use statistical methods, which are also employed to devise and determine the validity and reliability of various aptitude and achievement tests for promotion purposes as well as for job evaluation. Nor is the use of statistics negligible in the various areas of personnel management and industrial relations.

Financing and accounting functions extensively make use of statistics and statistical methods. In the computation and comparison of various financial ratios, statistics plays a very vital role. Among the various other financial areas, forecasting, for the sake of borrowing needs and borrowings costs, is directly linked with statistical methods. In the evaluation of accounts receivable and various other accounting functions, statistics is an effective aid. Statistical techniques are useful in periodic inventory analysis, the calculation of reserves for depreciation, and in adjustment for the effects of price changes on depreciation and other reserves, as well as in the analysis of financial stability and the company's financial growth. Statistics provides the basis for investment management, insurance, speculation, and in the analysis of games of chance. In this context, a few statistical techniques, which are very often used in the managerial analysis, deserve consideration.

Statistical Techniques in Management

Many statistical methods, techniques and tools are often employed in the analysis and interpretation of data as an aid to management and managerial decisions, which cannot be explained exhaustively within the framework of this chapter. An attempt has, therefore, been made to discuss briefly a few of them here.

Graphical and Diagrammatic Representations

Graphical and diagrammatic representations are very common and effective in depicting the statistical data in the simplest and most intelligible way. They facilitate data analysis, presentation and interpretation; and help us to arrive at inferences. As an attractive way of representing the statistical data, any diagrammatic expression makes an impressive effect on the minds of the readers. Some of the commonly used expressions are histogram, frequency polygon, cumulative frequency graph, cumulative percentage frequency graph, or ogive; diagrammatic representations such as bar diagrams, pie charts, squares, circles, rectangles, pictorial representations, etc. These are elementary statistical techniques; but they are extensively used to represent large volumes of statistical data. (Any elementary statistical text would be sufficient for a detailed discussion.)

Measures of Central Tendency

A large quantity of data collected for any research or managerial analysis should be processed and interpreted. During the course of the presentation and analysis of the data, efforts are made to find some measure of the variable which would be the representative of a group of values as a whole, or a measure that holds a central position among them, or a measure that is most often encountered or used. Such values are called measures of central tendency or statistical averages. The most often used measures of central tendency are the arithmetic mean, the median and the mode. A layman's use of the term average means the arithmetical mean, while in statistical terminology, average includes all the above three measures, in addition to the geometric mean and the harmonic mean.

The arithmetic mean, which is very often called the mean of a number of measures is that score or measure, the sum of the deviations from which is zero. Suppose X stands for a score or measure and N for the total number of measures in the series, the mean M is $MN = \Sigma X$, which means that $M = \Sigma X/N$. In other words, $\Sigma X - NM = 0$. It means that the arithmetic mean of a number of measures is that measures which, when multiplied by the total number of measures, is equal to the sum of all measures. An average, to sum up, is a "single figure which sums up the characteristics of a whole group of figures." It gives us a clear and concise picture of a large number of numerical data, which facilitates comparison between different groups.

The arithmetic average or mean is a very useful device in the filed of management, especially in managerial analysis. It is, therefore, one of the most effective tools in the kit of the decision-maker. It is very useful in revenue and expenditure analysis, average output and productivity analysis, sales volume and sales performance evaluation, job evaluation of a work force, its relative contribution, market share analysis, time and motion study, average allocation of fixed expenses (department-wise), operation costs, compensation and incentives, machine-hour rates, recovering cost etc. The arithmetic means is nothing but the product of total frequency divided by total number; *e.g.*, $\overline{X}$ (arithmetic mean) = $\Sigma X/N$ (sum of the values or total frequency divided by the total number $\overline{X} = \Sigma X/N$). This is the usual way of finding out the average, which is easier in simple cases. However, in long and complicated cases, this method is a little tedious; and that is why the formula may be used to work out the arithmetic area. An example will make this clear.

$$\overline{X} = A + \frac{\Sigma fd}{N}$$

In a study on the wage and salary administration of the engineering industry in Pune, the wage rate of skilled workers was evaluated. The details have been collected from 457 sample skilled workers at random from 14 sample organisations; and the frequency distribution is given in Table 1.

Table 1

Organisations	*Wage Rate Monthly Rs. 100* X	*Number of workers (Frequency)* f
1.	4.5	1
2.	5.0	2
3.	5.5	4
4.	6.0	5
5.	6.5	15
6.	7.0	30
7.	7.5	60
8.	8.0	95
9.	8.5	82
10.	9.0	75
11.	9.5	44
12.	10.0	25
13.	10.5	15
14.	11.0	4
Total number of workers (N)		457

The formula used to work out the arithmetic mean is

$$\overline{X} = A + \frac{\Sigma fd}{N}$$

where,

f = frequency

A = assumed average (as far as possible, the mid-value of the X values may be selected. From Table 1, 8 is chosen as A.)

d = deviation from each X value (for example, deviation of assumed average '8' from first X value, *i.e.*, 4.5 – 8 = 3.5)

fd = frequency multiplied by the corresponding deviation

Σfd = sum of all the 'fd's

N = total frequency (457)

These columns have been worked out in Table 2.

Table 2

Monthly Wage Rate X	Frequency Average f	Deviation from Assumed Average d	Total Deviation fd
4.5	1	– 3.5	– 3.5
5	2	– 3	– 6
5.5	4	– 2.5	– 10
6	5	– 2	– 10
6.5	15	– 1.5	– 22.5
7	30	– 1	– 30
7.5	60	– 0.5	– 30
8	95	0	0
8.5	82	+ 0.5	+ 41
9	75	+ 1	+ 75
9.5	44	+ 1.5	+ 66
10	25	+ 2	+ 50
10.5	15	+ 2.5	+ 37.5
11	4	+ 3	+ 12
	N = 457 Σfd = 169.5		+ 281.5 - 112

$$\overline{X} = A + \frac{\Sigma fd}{N}$$

$$8 + \frac{(169.5)}{457} = 8 + 0.37$$

$$= 8.37$$

The average wage of skilled workers in engineering industry in Pune is Rs. 837/-, according to the arithmetic mean worked out. It faciliates the comparison of the average wage rate in other industries in Pune with the average wage rate of unskilled workers in Pune, with the wage rates in other places, and so on.

The median of a set of scores or measures is that score or measure which is such that there are as many scores or measures greater than it as there are scores or measures less than it. If, therefore the items are ranked, *i.e.,* arranged in the order of greater and greater or of less and less, the median would be the size of the mid-ranked item if there is an odd number of scores, or the score which would be midway between the two mid-ranked items if there is an even number of scores. The median (grouped scores) may be worked out with the help of the formula $\dfrac{1+\dfrac{(N-F)i}{2}}{f}$ from the lower limit

where,

I is the exact lower limit of the median interval

N is the number of scores

F is the cumulative frequency associated with the exact lower limits of the median interval

f is the frequency (number of scores) belonging to the median interval

i is the length of the class-interval.

Computing from the other end, the following formula may be used:

$$L-\frac{\frac{(N-F)i}{2}}{f}$$

where,

L = exact upper limit of the median interval

N stands for the total number of scores,

F stands for the cumulative frequency associated with the exact upper limit of the median interval.

The median enables the business executive to compare the performance of various periods, say months or seasons of a year, and to determine the medianal period of performance in planning and strategy formulation.

A mode may be considered as the value in a series that occurs most frequently. It may be worked out with the help of the equation, *viz.*, Mean-mode = 3 (mean-median).

It enables us to determine the value that appears the largest number of times, which is useful in demand analysis. The median enjoys certain advantages, *viz.*, it is representative; it is simple to understand; and its value is not being affected by extreme items. It may be obtained even when the values of all the items are not known, and be used to measure the qualities and factors to which mathematical measurement cannot be given. Its disadvantages are: if the items are few, it is not likely to be representative; and if the distribution is irregular, the location of the median may be indefinite. The arrangement of the data in the necessary array is often tedious. And it cannot be used to determine the total value for all the examples of the items.

The advantages of the mode are:

It is easy to understand-extreme items do not affect its value; with a knowledge of the middle item, the mode can be worked out.

Its disadvantages are:

It is often not clearly defined; Its exact location is often uncertain; and the arrangement of the data is tedious.

Geometric and harmonic means also come under the measures of the central tendency. The geometric mean is always less than the arithmetic mean. Here, it may be pointed out that the geometric mean of the numbers is also the geometric mean of the arithmetic mean and the harmonic mean; but the geometric mean is greater than the harmonic mean.

The moving average is a much more accurate method of getting the trend line, and is an effective tool for trend analysis. When a time-series of the values of a variable, say, Y are given during successive intervals of time, the averages of the Y measures over sets of equal numbers of consecutive intervals of time, each set of intervals making up a period, are called moving or running averages. The curve thus obtained from the time series is the smoothed curve of the general trend. First, the histogram of the data may be drawn with a view to observing the regular fluctuations in a given period. Then, the moving averages are worked out.

Let a, b, c, d, e, f, g,... be the successive magnitudes in the time series. Then, the average of the first six is worked out first; *i.e.,* a + b + c + d + f/6. The next running average is b + c + d + e + f + g + /6, which is the same as the first one, plus (g - a)/6. Each subsequent moving average is worked out in the same way.

Coefficient of Correlation

Among the various other methods such as standard deviation, index numbers, dispersion, skewness and correlation — the coefficient of correlation is one of the most frequently used statistical techniques in business analysis. It identifies the relationships between two or more variables. If two quantities vary in such a way that movements in one are accompanied by movements in the other, these quantities are correlated. If, for example, an increase in the advertising expenditure is accompanied by a corresponding increase in the sales revenue, the two variables are correlated. If the movement of the two variables takes place in the same direction, the correlation may be treated as positive, and if the movements are in the opposite direction, they reveal a negative correlation. The coefficient of correlation is the measurement of the degree of correlation between the variables, and will vary between + 1 and - 1. If there is perfect correlation, the coefficient will be + 1 in a positive correlation and - 1 in a negative correlation.

The liner correlation can be worked out with the help of the formula:

$$r = \frac{\Sigma xy}{\sqrt{(\Sigma x^2 \Sigma y}}$$

where,

r is coefficient of correlation

x is the deviation from the mean of one of the variables

y is the deviation from the mean of the corresponding variable.

The formula

$$r = \frac{\Sigma\ dxdy - \frac{(\Sigma dx \times \Sigma dy)}{N}}{\sqrt{\Sigma dx^2 - \frac{(\Sigma dx)^2}{N}} \times \sqrt{\Sigma dy^2 - \frac{(\Sigma dy)^2}{N}}}$$

can also be used to work out the coefficient of correlation. If the coefficient of correlation is 0.5 or above, the relation between the variables is conspicuous.

However, a sample coefficient of correlation cannot always be taken at its face value. It is always better to know something about the data, and to plot them as a scatter diagram. In this connection, it may be mentioned that there are certain aspects which must be taken into account. Are the data homogeneous? Are the data subject to large errors of measurement? Are the data individual measures, or are they averages? Have some of the data been eliminated? Have important variables been neglected? It is the type of estimating equation appropriate? Are the data unbiased? A systematic approach to the correlation coefficient enables us to arrive at regression models and establish conspicuous relationships between variables and their changes over time.

Probability Distribution

A proper presentation and analysis of data are the prerequisites of a correlation analysis. In this context, probability has considerable importance, especially in connection with business decisions. Generally speaking, statistics is concerned with decision-making by the application of the theory of probability to observed numerical data. The probability may be the ratio of the number of ways an event can occur to the total number of possible outcomes, when each possible outcome is equality likely. Many philosophers and mathematicians have offered the view of probabilities as long-run relative frequencies. It may be considered then, that probability is the limit of the relative frequency of success in an infinite sequence of trials. But this suffers from two basic practical difficulties, They are:

(i) Since an infinite sequence of trials is required to determine the probability of an event with exactitude, such a determination is almost impossible in practice;

(ii) Businessmen very often deal with the events that never occurred earlier, and decision-making becomes necessary in uncertainties, where probability has a lot of limitations. This may be the reason why there are both subjective and objective approaches to probability; and each one is applicable in particular situations.

Certain axioms are necessary for the development of the probability theory. Each elementary event, or combination of elementary events, must have associated with it a probability greater than, or equal to, zero, but less than, or equal to, one. This means that if 'A' is an event within a sample space, 0 < Prob A < 1. Similarly, the probability of an entire sample space is one. Thus, if S presents an entire sample space, Prob S = 1. Another necessary axiom is that when one or the other or both of the two mutually exclusive events occur, probability is equal to the sum of the individual probabilities of these events. Hence,

$$\text{Prob } (A \cup B) = \text{Prob } A + \text{Prob } B$$

These are usually the properties of discrete probability distributions, which are associated with experiments whose outcomes are of the discrete nature. Normal probability distribution need not always be characterised by these properties. (The term *normal* is a generic term applied to a well-defined continuous probability distribution, which is otherwise known as the Gaussian or Laplacean distribution.)

Simulation

A proper use of probability distribution, especially the normal distribution, is based on certain assumptions concerning the characteristics of the data and the processes which generate them. The situations in which such assumptions are applicable relate to probability distribution. In other situations, however, simulation has a considerable bearing. In a situation where the complexity of problems does not readily lend themselves to generalised assumptions concerning the probability distribution governing the situations, as well as the problems involving uncertainty, the Monte Carlo method of simulation is a boon. The essence of the Monte Carlo technique is a game which models the real-life problem situation, and results in an outcome which is determined by the values of the relevant variables affecting the situation. In turn, the random selection process determines the values taken by these vairables. The probability distributions of the relevant variables may be selected from the body of distributions whose characteristics are largely known. They are bound to reflect the empirical evidence available in the form of a distribution of relative frequencies.

An analytical solution follows from the logic of the rules of probability, which represents the expectation of the process in the sense of probability. It analyses all the relevant aspects of the situation and makes estimates on the basis of a sample taken from the output of a process. Though the basic idea is the same in the simulation, too, the sample is artificially generated by successive trials of an experiment. If the market for colour TV is influenced by the income level of the prospects and customers, the price of the black and white TVs, and the percentage of colour telecasts, we in order to simulate the process of the marketing of the colour TV, will have to evaluate the effect of each factor in our experiments. Each of the determinations must be made in a random manner, and in such a way as to be subject to the underlying probabilities associated with each circumstance. Then the best probability can be chosen. Having chosen an assumed state of the market situation arising from each trial, we must then randomly select a value for the simulated market situation arising from each trial. The simulation procedure, then, proceeds in three stages, *viz.*,

(i) Simulation of the process state (mean);

(ii) Simulation of a random normal variate with values of the mean and standard deviation equal to those of the process state determined in the first stage (the term 'variate' refers to a particular value taken by a random variable); and

(iii) Combining the results of these two stages for a series of trials, to arrive at an estimate of the defective rate.

The selection of the process state, which is to be accomplished in a random manner, is a critical element in the simulation procedure.

Randomness is achieved by the use of random numbers. Random numbers are distributed according to a uniform probability distribution. This means that the probability of any one digit, 0 through 9, appearing in the random sequence of numbers is equal to that of any other digit. For any one digit, the probability would be one-tenth. The same property would hold for all possible two-digit numbers (one hundredth), three-digit numbers (one thousandth), and so on.

The simulation demands the conversion of a uniformly distributed set of random numbers into another random variable with a different distribution. In this case, the second random variable should have a normal distribution. This can be easily accomplished with the aid of a table for the standardised normal distribution, such as Table 3 (according to Monte Carlo method).

Table 3

First Row of the Table

z	.00	.01	.02	.03	.04	.05	.06	.07	.08	.09
0.0	.0000	.0040	.0080	.0120	.0160	.0199	.0239	.0279	.0319	.0359

We note that the values appearing in the body of Table 3 are four-digit numbers. The first row of the table is reproduced here, from which it is evident that the four-dgit numbers of the row range from .0000 to .0359. Thus, in the interva lof z from 0.00 to 0.09, there are 359 possible four-digit numbers (0359-0000 = 359)

Sixth Row of the Table

z	.00	.01	.02	.03	.04	.05	.06	.07	.08	.09
1.6	.4452	.4463	.4474	.4484	.4495	.4505	.4515	.4525	.4535	.4545

There are 93 possible four-digit numbers (4545-4452) corresponding to the interval of z from 1.60 to 1.69. The 16th row of the table indicates a density of four-digit numbers which is only about one-fourth of the first row (93/359 = 1/4), even though both the rows represent the same width of interval for z. This means that the probability that a four-digit random number will fall in the interval of the 16th row is only about one-fourth of the probability associated with the first row. A similar relationship can exist between any other pair of rows. If the random four-digit number selected is 0199, the value of z would be set at 0.05. From the 16th row, and so on. In short, the simulation method is extensively used for business analysis.

Time Series Analysis

Another prominent statistical method for business analysis is the time series analysis. A time series is a set of observations arranged chronologically, usually at equal intervals of time. The actual problem in the process of time series analysis is to convert the data into meaningful components of the series. For example, the sales data for the past 20 or 25 years can be presented in a time series. It may consist of secular trend (T), cycles (C), seasonal movements (S), and irregular fluctuations, if any (I). The actual process of the time series is the decomposition of the data (time series) into these four components. Hence the time series (Y) may be a product of T, C, S, and I. Then the time series analysis is

$$Y = TCSI$$

It may aid in business planning, because it yields the trend of the past on the basis of which forecasting and planning for the future may be made. Once the past trend is identified on the basis of the time series, a projection may be made for a further given period. The time series analysis that portrays the trends enables the analyst to evaluate other movements, such as trade cycles. It facilitates economic generalisations in the business or industry in particular and generally in the economy as a whole. It helps in a comparison of the various trends at various times and in various industries. The time series analysis, moreover, enables the business planner to establish a secular trend. (A graph that portrays the actual trend joining the various points plotted may be a time series curve, while a straight line from the first point to the last point may show a secular trend).

While the time series analysis and the moving average portray the trends of business, various other methods, which have been examined in this chapter, facilitate managerial analysis. Thus, statistics and statistical methods pave the way for research, which is an essential ingredient of any managerial analysis.

Chapter 15

Quantitative Techniques in Management

It has been pointed out in the last chapter that statistical methods play a vital role in managerial analysis and decision-making. We now propose to throw some light on the fact that quantitative techniques play no less important role in managerial analysis and problem solving.

The Manager and His Task

Management can justify their existence basically by their economic performance, as Peter Drucker observes, for which they are expected to get acquainted with a plurality of economic factors that influence the conditions under which they must act. Any business, today, operates in an environment that changes; and, therefore, the socio-economic factors that affect the economic performance of any company should be subjected to a detailed evaluation from time to time. Up-to-date information is required for the current understanding of the facts that indicate the problems which call for solutions. Business, organisational, and managerial problems tend to be enormously complex; and, therefore, the facts are literally uncountable in number in any empirical situation.

Managers pursue different approaches when analysing and interpreting facts, and solving business problems. The complexity of the problem itself indicates to the manager the most appropriate way of analysing it and arriving at a proper solution. Every potential course of action demands the establishment of a chain of cause-effect relationships and interaction, which are innumerable. It may not be possible to analyse and take into account all the endless aspects of a problem. The decision-maker must abstract from the empirical situation those variables which he considers to be the most relevant to the problem he has to tackle. For this objective, various methods have usually been applied. Observational approach, scientific approach and model building are the most prominent among these.

Observational Approach

The manager observes and learns from the actions of other managers in similar situations; he copies, sometimes with slight modifications, the solutions that have already been adopted. Though it helps in the decision-making process, its contribution to the management technique is marginal. Managerial situations and environments differ, one from the other, and hence there cannot be a ready-made solution of each management problem. The observational approach is, therefore, of limited utility.

Scientific Approach

The scientific method refers to the formulation of an hypothesis and its testing by research, controlled experiments and trials, so that the decision-maker may be guided in the selection of a solution. Taylor's scientific management theory, which was principally meant for the production function, may be applied to any kind of business problem. It has promoted procedures and methods, and has built, in the meantime, schemes and suggestions of controls based on defined standards. Nevertheless, the scientific method is not a tailor-made system for all the management problems. Each problem should be evaluated on the basis of its own merits and demerits; and the solutions identified. Substantial facts and information should be collected for this purpose. The analysis that follows must be based on a logical sequential approach.

Observations of, and statements about, the situation must be accurately prepared in a written form in such a way that the problem assumes a precise and irrefutable aspect by reason of a concise description. Casual effects and constant influences must be investigated. Information is gathered by breaking down the work into common units; meanwhile, marginal or additional data related to the problems are considered. Statistical procedures are extensively used with the aim of obtaining summarised tables, prospects, trends, and diagrams, all of which describe the behaviour of each component event with respect to time or other variables. This enables the manager to gain a clear understanding of the problem.

Once the manager has a clear understanding of the problem and can evaluate it by measuring actions, reactions, and consequences, he can attempt to draw up a hypothesis or a tentative solution to the problem. At this point, managerial experience and actual exposure to the identical situations are of great advantage; and the observational approach helps in the solution. The selection of a proposed solution, or an alternative one, which best fits the situation, is then made by the executive. When several problems cannot be separated from each other, their individual solutions must be mutually related. It is up to the manager to investigate these relationships. The managerial task of making a thorough and detailed analysis of all components in relation to the whole situation can be considered a step in itself. To discharge this responsibility the manager has to break up the aggregated hypothesis into its component parts, and scan each part accurately and separately. In using the scientific method in a search for new knowledge or an addition to the existing knowledge, all the variables which affect the final result are kept constant, except the one which is left untouched in order to detect its behaviour.

Inductive and deductive reasoning may be adopted to obtain a tentative solution to the entire problem. When a tentative solution has been selected, it must be tested, The answer to the problem as a remedy to the situation may or may not be obtained as a result of the first analysis. A trial, when it is possible, given the manager the best yardstick for measuring the efficacy of the proposal. Alterations in the tentative solution may be made in the light of the results of the trial. Experimentation and adjustments may be alternately repeated as many times as necessary, until a satisfactory solution is reached. Obviously, the application of this trial-and-error method takes time. It is also costly. However, when the complex problem is solved, the time and money required for the research have been well spent, though it is often very costly, time-consuming, and inaccurate. It is here that the quantitative techniques seem to be of greater importance.

When the behaviour of a business event is investigated, the manager starts by collecting the data on the phenomenon under consideration, and then tries to systematise them. The data collected are numerous in most cases; and therefore, it becomes necessary to plot them in a diagram in order to study, in a systematic form, the behaviour of the event. Such data may be presented in a chronological order. The resulting diagram represents a broken line wavering up and down without any apparent design or pattern; it is necessary, therefore, to separate the main variables from the occasional ones to eliminate the external composite forces from the time series of values. By following a scientific approach, the secular, cyclical, and seasonal movements can be determined and eliminated, enabling the analyst to apply his investigation only to the essential variables.

In order to establish policies for future decision-making, it should be determined whether the event shows a tendency to growth or decline. The possibility of substantiating the intensity of growth or decline over a long term may be determined by the application of statistical methods; even if the measurement of the trends is on the level of estimation. Such an investigation is applicable only for a long time span, since the growth factor cannot be determined in the short run. The prediction of future trends is called forecasting, and the process of extending a known trend into the future is called extrapolation.

When decisions are based on extrapolated values, the data employed for this purpose should represent the essential behaviour of the variables. This calls for the elimination of the deviating forces from the original data. In this context, the application of appropriate statistical methods is necessary. Curve-fitting is the usually employed method for this purpose. It is partitioned into groups of rules and processes known as univariate bivariate, and multivariate analyses, according to the number of related variables considered in the phenomenon. Moreover, a distinction is made as to whether the variables behave under certainty or under some law of probability distribution. The least squares methods is commonly used in univariate analysis. However, the cumulative method (Marchesi's method), which is of a comparatively recent origin, is more accurate.

The Least Squares Method

This method, which was introduced in 1809 by the French mathematician, Adrien Marie Legendre, is applicable to the study of the basic behaviour of curvilinear as well as straight-line trends. The basic assumption here is that it shows the manner of fitting a straight line among and through points of an irregular curve. This line represents the tendency of the phenomenon. The line of the best fit, obtained by the least squares method, minimises the error in substituting a line for an original curve. Any straight line is indicated by the function $Y = a + bx$, where a represents the intercept and b the slope in a system of Cartesian co-ordinates in which the independent variables (x's) are indicated on the abscissa (X-axis) and the dependent variables (y's) on the ordinate. The least squares line is defined with the intercept a and the slope b. There are several methods for determining the line of the best fit which is to be used as a substitute for the irregular line formed by plotting in a graph the raw data of a given phenomenon. All of these methods, including the Tchebycheff-Pareto method, require a substantial number of preliminary operations, such as making summations and calculating products and powers, in order to solve systems of equations with several unknowns. When the line of the best fit is no longer represented by straight line, but by parabolas of the 2nd,

3rd....... or *n*th order. These methods are so complex that very often computational errors may occur. It is in these conditions that the advantages of the cumulative method may be considered.

The Cumulative Method

The use of this method reduces the possibility of mistakes, for an extremely simple computational procedure is involved in preparing the set of new data that substitute for the raw data expressing the problem. By means of the cumulative process, straight lines or curves which best fit are easily found by the use of pre-calculated tables. By using these tables of fixed values, we can reduce the computing work to a few simple operations that are performed according to a scheduled uniform routine, regardless of the number of raw data and the order of the curve that may be found. The use of this generalised method has the limitation that values of the independent variable must be ordered in an arithmetic progression. This however, is the most common case encountered in economic, statistical and business problems. One half of the sequence of the values is located in the positive field and one half is located in the negative field. If we let n be the number of pairs of data, the two extreme values of the new variables will be:

$$\frac{n-1}{2} \text{ and } \frac{n-1}{2}$$

When n is odd, the central value is zero, and when it is even, the two central values are -0.5 and $+0.5$.

The only preliminary operations required by this method, are the construction, next to the array of the n observed data (yi), of a new list of values obtained by computing the cumulative values of yi. The last value in this new array (which equals the $\Sigma\ yi$ of the original data) is indicated by K_1. The summation of this new list of values, which is labelled K_2, is defined as the cumulated sum of the second order, *i.e.*

$$K2 = \Sigma^{11}\ yi$$

The value of K_2 may be checked by multplying each value of yi by the weighting coefficient, $zi = n + 1 - i$, and by summing up the results. In other words, each original datum is multiplied by the position value in the reverse order. The sum of these products in K_2.

In computing a curve having three parameters, another column of cumulative values is required in Table 1, *i.e.*, E^{11} column, which is obtained by adding all the preceding cumulated values taken from the preceding column. (In the following exmple, E^{11} would have these values: 46, 140,

281, etc.) For the sum of the E^{11} column K_3 is used a symbol; for E^{111}, K_4; and so on. However, in the example, only Σ and Σ^{11} are required, since a straight line is considered the best fit, and their value are $K_1 = 1{,}084$ and $K_2 = 11{,}820$. The two parametric constants, *a* and *b* of the interpolatory line $yi = a + bxi$, are obtained by linearly combining the value of K_1 K_2 with the appropirate parametric multipliers. In this example, since 21 pairs of data constitute the set which describes the phenomenon, the parametric multipliers to be used are found in Table 1 in correspondence with the entry N = 21 (in the example given below.) The basic formulas for securing the values of the two parameters of a straight line are:

(i) $a = K_1A_1 + K_2A_2$
(ii) $b = K_1B_1 + K_2B_2$

Table 1

Sales of X Company for 21 years

Original Data for Application of the Cumulative Method

ti Year	*i*	*yi* Sales (Thousands of items)		E^1 (Cumulated Sums)
t_1	1	46		46
t_2	2	48	(46 + 48 =)	94
t_3	3	47	(94 + 47 =)	141
t_4	4	49	(141 + 49 =)	190
t_5	5	52		242
t_6	6	54		296
t_7	7	54		350
t_8	8	56		406
t_9	9	53		459
t_{10}	10	50		509
t_{11}	11	49		558
t_{12}	12	52		610
t_{13}	13	54		664
t_{14}	14	55		719
t_{15}	15	58		777
t_{16}	16	56		833
t_{17}	17	53		886
t_{18}	18	51		937
t_{19}	19	48		985
t_{20}	20	49		1,034
t_{21}	21	50		1,084
	$\sum_{i=i}^{21} Y_i = K_i = 1.084$		$\sum_{i=1}^{31} Y_i = K_1 = 11{,}820$	

Determinants

In 1693, Leibnitz, a German mathematician, was the first to employ a new symbolism and procedure in simplifying expressions arising in the elimination of the unknown quantity. He did not, however, fully realise the significance of his discovery. Leibnitz's method was deeply analysed by Gabriel Cramer after almost fifty years. Cramer, a Swiss mathematician, rediscovered determinants while he was working on the analysis of curves. He was studying the way of passing a curve of rth order through any

$\frac{r^2}{2}+\frac{3^r}{2}$ given points. He defined the general rule for the solution of *n*

simultaneous linear equations (non-homogeneous) containing *n* unknown quantities. This was inferred without proof from the form of values of the unknown quantities obtained in solving sets of two and three equations. A French mathematician, Augustin L. Cauchy, gave this technique of *resultants,* Gauss' name determinants; and this name was adopted later by everybody. In 1841, Karl G. Jacobi, a German mathematician and physicist, published *De Formatione de Proprietatibus Determinantiun,* which is considered to be the primary scientific approach to the establishment of foundations for a treatise on the theory of determinants.

The concept has gained prominence over the years. At the end of 19th century, Arthur Cayley and James J. Sylvester, English mathematicians, studied special forms of the functions applied in the determinant technique, showing its wonderful power and usefulness as an instrument of mathematical investigation. A determinant is a square configuration. When it contains only one row and one column, it also contains only one element; and it is said to be of the first order. When an array of elements (or grid) is a determinant, it has two vertical lines as a symbol, one on each side of the array. A capital script D indicates a determinant (D), which is also symbolised by a capital delta (Δ). A subject indicates the order of the determinant. The elements are called *a, b, c, ... n.* The notation, which makes use of alphabetic characters, is quite impractical, especially because of the limitations of the alphabet itself. A better notation, which has been generally adopted and is also used in matrix algebra, is to give two subscripts to a common element (say, *a*). The first digit indicates the row and the second digit the column wherein that value is located. The three determinants (say D_1, D_2 and D_3) may then be depicted in the following manner:

$$\begin{vmatrix} a \end{vmatrix} \; ; \; \begin{vmatrix} a_{11} & a_{12} \\ a_{21} & a_{22} \end{vmatrix} \; ; \; \begin{vmatrix} a_{11} & a_{12} & a_{13} \\ a_{22} & a_{22} & a_{23} \\ a_{31} & a_{32} & a_{33} \end{vmatrix}$$

A *restricted notation* is generally in use in addition to the 'double subscript'. A determinant may be individualised by this short method, since it is a square array:

$$| \; a_{11} \quad a_{22} \quad a_{33} \quad a_{44} \; |$$

The notation may be further shortened, indicating a determinant of *n* order by:

$$| \; a_{1,\, n} \; |.$$

The umbral notation is not another way of indicating a D, which is expressed as:

$$|a^{i}_{1} \; a^{ii}_{2} \; a^{iii}_{3} \; a^{(n)}_{n} \; | \; 1^{(n)}_{n}$$

In an abridged form, it may be expressed as:

$$a^{(n)}_{i}$$

The most general expression of a determinant n^{th}_{i} order is as follows, where *j* is the generic column and i the generic row:

$$\begin{vmatrix} a_{11} & a_{12} & a_{13} & \cdots & a_{1n} \\ a_{21} & a_{22} & a_{23} & \cdots & a_{2n} \\ a_{31} & a_{32} & a_{33} & \cdots & a_{2n} \\ \cdots & \cdots & \cdots & \cdots & \cdots \\ a_{i1} & a_{i2} & a_{i3} & \cdots & a_{in} \\ \cdots & \cdots & \cdots & \cdots & \cdots \\ a_{n1} & a_{n2} & a_{n3} & \cdots & a_{nn} \end{vmatrix}$$

When a number of events of a management problem are related to each other, and if we can define the appropriate coefficient of each unknown in all the equations, it is possible to determine the values of the unknowns. A manager can find the values when he simultaneously solves the linear equations previously determined. But conventional methods of solving a system of equations may not be adequate for handling the problems described by the systems of equations in several unknowns. When the number of unknowns equals the number of equations, the system of equations may be solved by the use of determinants. Since a considerable amount of tedious work is involved in simultaneously solving systems with large numbers of equations, electronic computers may be put to use. In this context, it should be emphasised that each determinant has only one value, while every element preserves its own arithmetic sign in the array. For the solution of the determinants of the second or third order, the Sarrus rule is applicable, while for the determinants of a higher than third order, the Cofactor rule may be appropriate. On many occasions, the Leibnitz-Cramer Rule has been useful in the solution of managerial problems. Managers must often find the solution to several equations, when each one contains a certain number of unknowns that refer to real business or production problem. Among the many analytical methods of solving systems of simultaneous linear equations, the use of determinants appears to be the simplest and the most common. This process is known as the Leibnitz-Cramer method.

Matrix

In the simultaneous solution of many equations, a determinant model is of great use. The matrix analysis applicable to models for obtaining analytical solutions to a particular series of problems. It is extensively used in various fields of applications — in geometry, mathematics (especially differential equations), analytical dynamics, managerial statistics, and quite recently, in business through linear programming techniques. When the elements are displayed in rows and columns, the obtained grid, array, or table is called a matrix. It may be pointed out that the matrices and determinants are differentiated from one another by the fact that the matrix table is closed either by vertical brackets or by curved parcenthesis, even if a strict relationship exists among them.

$$\begin{bmatrix} a_{11} & a_{12} & a_{13} \\ a_{21} & a_{22} & a_{23} \\ a_{31} & a_{32} & a_{33} \end{bmatrix} \quad \begin{bmatrix} a_{11} & a_{12} & a_{13} \\ a_{21} & a_{22} & a_{23} \\ a_{31} & a_{32} & a_{33} \end{bmatrix}$$

A matrix consists of a rectangular or square array of values. Usually, m is the number of rows, and n the number of columns. The row symbol preceeds the column symbol. A matrix m-n consists of m vectors, each of nth order, and the matrix is said to be of order (m, n). When $m = n$, the matrix is square (matrix of order n).

A rectangular matrix does not correspond to a determinant but a square matrix may generate a determinant which assumes a scalar value. The notation of a matrix may be shortened as that of a determinant; say, (aij) m, n, where m represents the number of rows; n the columns, and aij is the generic element within the matrix. Two matrices are equal only when all the corresponding values of the two arrays are equal.

There are four basic properties of the equality of matrices. They are: symmetric property, determinative property, reflexive property, and transitive property. If one matrix is equal to another, the latter is equal to the former (A = B; hence B = A), indicating the symmetric property. Any two matrices, when compared, are either equal or not equal, *i.e.*, A = B or A = B, expressing the quality of the determinative property. For example, the concept of similarity, which is used in plain geometry to indicate relationships between triangles (Δ ABC = Δ DEF), has no meaning in matrix analysis. In fact, no approximation properties can be used when considering matrices. The term *reflexive property* refers to any matrix which is equal to itself (A = A; B = B; etc.). The *transitive property* states that if a matrix is equal to another one, this last is equal to third one, and this last is equal to the first matrix (A = B, and B = C; hence C = A or A = C). Matrix analysis is an effective technique, and represents not only the determinants, but business analysis as well; while the set theory is complementary for the sake of interpretation. In this context, we shall now consider the *set theory.*

Set Theory

The set theory forms the foundation of a correct interpretation of matrix algebra and vector analysis. A set may be considered as a "group of things having at least one characteristic in common." The definition of a set necessitates an appropriate definition of the characteristic that enables the elements to be considered members of the same family of elements. For instance, a set of real numbers is composed of elements, each of which has the characteristic of being a real number. If S is a set of positive even integers less than 20, each member of the set is "positive, even, an integer."

In the example here, for instance, S = (2, 4, 6, 8, 10, 12, 14, 16, 18). The male workers within the age group 20 to 30, appointed for a particular work, represent a set, in which each worker has the characteristic of getting himself involved in the work. Other attributes, such as qualifications, experience, intellectual level, etc., which facilitate the grouping of the workers in different sets, can also be taken into account to make specific groups. A set is usually represented by a capital letter, while a lower-case letter indicates an element of the set. For example, A is an association and *m* stands for members (an element). The symbol used for denoting that an element belongs to a specific set is Σ. The symbol ∈ is read as is *an element of* or *is a member of.* The above symbol may, therefore, be read as *m is an element of A.* When an element does not have the characteristic required by a set, it does not belong to the set and is represented by the ∉ (the above symbol crossed by a stroke).

There are subsets, null sets, and universal sets. A set may be sub-divided into two or more subsets when their characteristics are separated. For example, the set of a class of students is composed of two subsets when the characteristic "sex" is considered. The symbol denoting a proper subset is C, and it is read as "is a subset of." The *null set,* represented by ϕ, is a set which contains no elements and, for that reason, is called a void set or an empty set. A set may have several subsets, and hence A = $(a_1 a_2 a_3 \ldots a_n) = \phi$. The universal set (U) is the one which generates all the possible subsets. The two subsets are considered equal if, and only if, both contain exactly the same elements. In other words, when a set is defined by a series of characteristics, and then the same set is described by another series of characteristics, the two differently stated sets are equal.

Chapter 16

Quantitative Techniques: Linear Programming

An attempt has been made in Chapter 11 to throw some light on some of the quantitative techniques in management, with a view to providing an elementary knowledge to the business executives and students of management. We shall now consider linear programming as a quantitative technique, which has extensive use for managerial problem solving.

Linear programming is a mathematical technique, which has a considerable practical application in managerial analysis and problem solving, especially in the allocation of scarce resources. Credit goes to Dr. George B. Dantzig, an American mathematician, who introduced some basic mathematical formulae in 1947, paving the way for the development of the linear programming technique. In 1941, Hitchcock first interpreted a transportation problem. Koopmans studied the same topic in 1947, while a diet problem was evaluated by Stigler in 1945. However, it wads Dantzig who developed a systematic procedure for solving a great portion of linear programming problems by what has come to be known as the Simplex Method. Dantzig's search for a technique capable of solving military planning problems for the United States Air Force led him to develop linear programming. In his own words; "The objective was to secure an inexpensive edition as quickly as possible in order to serve a variety of persons who made their interest in the matter known to us; practising and academic economists, engineers, practising statisticians, mathematicians, and persons associated with business and industrial enterprises."[1]

The linear programming technique serves as a tool for decision-making when the manager faces a business problem that cannot be solved by using managerial experience or subjectivity. Linear programming models are now considered to be a part of the scientific method of solving problems for which an optimum solution is sought from among the many possible alternatives which are shaped by the observation of certain conditions. Linear programming is a method for allocating a group of limited resources in a manner which satisfies a certain group of competing demands under known and fixed limitations. Mathematically speaking, it is a process of solving specific problems in which an objective function must be maximised or minimised considering a set of definite restrictions and limited resources. The word programming stands for *computing or calculating some* unknowns of a set of equations (and/or inequalities) under the specific conditions expressed in terms of mathematics.

Linear programming, which is often known as mathematical programming should satisfy five basic requirements, *viz.*,

(i) Proper definition of objective;

(ii) Quantitative measurement of problem elements;

(iii) Alternative choices;

(iv) Linearity; and

(v) Mathematical formulation.

The identification of the solutions to problems necessitates a clear definition of objective. Linear programming is meant for problem solving; and therefore the definition of the objective is the basic requirement of any linear programming model. In other words, an objective function must be clearly defined in order to meet, by applying the technique, the desired ultimate goal expressed by this function.

This is the first aspect of the linear programming method. The second linear programming approach is a quantitative approach; and obviously a quantitative measurement of problem elements is essential. For the application of a mathematical model too, a quantitative measurement is essential. Numerical data must depict the problem in terms of the relationships involved among the elements that are considered, while physical and real measurement must be the media for stating the problem; that is, the problem elements should be computed in terms of accurate quantitative

1. Charmes A. Cooper, W.W., and Henderson, A. *An Introduction to Linear Programming,* New York, John Wiley, 1961, p. vii.

means of measurement, such as rupees, kilograms, degrees, and so on.

It is possible to make selection of the six M's (men, materials, machinery, money, methods, and markets) with a view to attaining a solution which satisfies the objective functions. Decision-making involves a rational selection of the best course of action from among the alternatives. Linear programming is an aid to decision-making; and therefore, a choice from among the alternatives is obvious in the linear programming process. Linearity is the basic characteristic of this technique. Equations and inequalities must describe the problem in a linear form, for which only linear equations are suitable. Non-linear or curvilinear programming covers problems in which the behaviour of the elementary events is involved in the phenomenon under consideration. Linearity is a precise mathematical term which applies to the processing of the computation of simultaneous equations with the aim of satisfying the objective functions and restrictions.

An example would make the linearity principle clear. A production manager is expected to know the number of units of products that he should produce in order to maximise the profit (or minimnise the cost), determining the expected profit (cost) per unit of products X and Y (assuming the products are X and Y). We also assume that there are two machines, and that the time available is limited for the production operations; *i.e.*, 40 hours of use of the first machine and 90 hours of use of the second machine (assumed). The quantities of the products X and Y to be manufactured are indicated by x and y, which are the two unknowns of the system. The coefficients 3 and 5 the hours required by the first machine for producing one unit of X and Y respectively. For the second machine, the required hours are 5 and 9. A linear function takes place in the production function. It means that Machine 1 takes 3 hours to produce 1 unit of X, 6 hours for 2 units, 9 hours for 3 units, and so on. If this behaviour is plotted in a diagram, the joining of the plotted points would make a straight line. This linear relationship, together with its restrictions (constraints), may be depicted in the following equations:

$$3x + 5y \leqslant 40$$

$$5x + 9y \leqslant 90$$

Linearity is a technical condition, under the assumption that a phenomenon varies in a linear trend, which is an approximation of reality. The degree of approximation determines its acceptance in replacing the real behaviour of the event by another and a more sophisticated one, *i.e.*, the one in which the ratio of change is constant. A special case of the general relationship is represented by linearity. Such a relationship, say, $y = f(x)$, may be defined as linear only if all the possible values of x determine a given value of *y* located on a straight line when it is plotted on a graph.

Advantages of Linear Programming

Linear programming is undoubtedly an efficient medium of obtaining objective solutions of complicated queries and it offers a number of substantial advantages. The most prominent among these are:

(i) The possibility of optimum use of the productive factors;

(ii) Higher quality of decision;

(iii) The making of efficient managers; and

(iv) Mathematical and linear programming solutions are amenable to modification.

An improvement in the conditions under which business is handled is possible with the aid of linear programming methods, which indicate how a manager may most effectively employ his productive factors by using the existing and usable facilities, and by more efficiently selecting and distributing these elements. A more efficient use of productive factors thus becomes possible. Second, the quality of the manager's decisions substan-tially improves. This is especially so because the manager, who makes use of linear programming techniques, must analyse business problems in their real and essential appearance, and must collect and select only the pertinent data useful for mathematical formulation according to the requirements of the process that he is about to apply. This investigation causes the manager to study and consider problems in their realistic and true setting, disregarding components that do not affect the essential structure of these problems. Having a clear picture of the happenings within the basic restrictions and possibilities of the compound behaviour of the elements involved in the problem, the manager better understands both the problems and their solutions. By comparing the impersonal solution with the personal interpretation of a possible solution, a manager gets experience, and can form his decisions under better conditions when he must appoint productive factors in a schedule of operations.

Moreover, it helps to make efficient managers; *i.e.,* the linear programming techniques offer a substantial means for improving the knowledge and skill of executives. It calls for an analysis and evaluation of business problems in detail, enabling the executive to gain wider dimensions in exposure; which would sharpen his analysing and decision-making capacity. The rule-of-thumb will no longer be the chief method of decision. In order to arrive at mathematical solutions, the problems are subjected to mathematical scannng, simultating accuracy.

The fourth advantage of linear programming is that the mathematical solutions have sufficient scope for modifications. Solutions to managerial problems differ from situation to situation and organisation to organisation. Mathematical solutions always provide scope for such modifications.

Limitations of Linear Programming

The linear programming technique has its own limitations. It requires large data to be electronically processed. But electronic computer or tabulating equipment may not be easily available. Similarly, from the practical point of view, it may not be possible to formulate accurately or aptly state the business problems in terms of mathematical models, limiting the accuracy of mathematical solutions. Another limitation lies in the initial approximation made by using in the computation a straight line in lieu of the real non-linear behaviour of the components. This is also subjected to lack of accurate approximation and certainty. For example, a perfect replacement of the real conduct of an event by a mathematically expressed curve (or a line, which is a special case of a curve) occurs very rarely. The reliability of the result is, therefore, limited. Higher monetary and time costs of electronic processing and mathematical analysis also affect its extensive use. Constant change is the most prevailing situation in the business environment. Consequently, the basic data which have been collected may no longer be up-to-date.

Another limitation is of a technical nature; and this is the difficulty, or even the impossibility, of combining two or more objective functions into one optimum solution. A business decision is expected to find solutions to problems in which the maximum expected return is combined with the minimum cost of performance, not as an implicit consequence but rather as a result of computation throughout an appropriate model which considers both simultaneously. Linear programming is a systematic technique; it is a process capable of optimising a system as a whole according to one objective function rather than optimising any one or more parts of the whole. Since most business problems involve many variables and many cross-relationships, some of which are clearly evident and some hidden, it is difficult for a decision-maker to cope, intuitively, with the complexity of these problems. In this connection, one should realise that linear programming techniques and other mathematical models do not substitute for the manager in the task of deciding the most appropriate solution to a business problem. It is only a tool, an analytical process, that offers, by the presentation of an optimum solution, tremendous advantages.

However, the management is faced with two kinds of difficulties in using linear programming models, *viz.*

(i) Difficulties arising out of the preparation of the description of the problems by a mathematical formulation; and

(ii) Difficulties arising out of the interpretation and proper use of the objectively obtained solution or of the technically so-called optimum solution.

In response to the first difficulty, the managerial analyst should ensure a thorough analysis of the problem, representing, with quantitative measurements, all the data and facts directly influencing the behaviour of the event. The more rigidly the data adhere to the reality of the situation considered and analysed, the more trustworthy the solution would be. The second difficulty that many concern the manager arises when the so-called optimum solution is presented to him by the programmer. The appropriate interpretation on the part of the manager for an objective solution and its modification from time to time, if necessary, is pivotal for the success.

Simplex Method

The Simplex Method is an algebraic iterative procedure for the solution of any linear programming problem in a finite number of steps. It takes one of the corner points lying on the feasible production area and then tests whether an improvement in profit can be made by moving to an adjacent corner point on the feasible production area. If an improvement can be made, a new corner point is tested to see if further improvement is possible. When this leads to a situation where no further improvement is possible by moving to an adjacent point, it may be said that the optimal solution has been reached. The Simplex Method is considered one of the basic models from which many linear programming techniques are directly or indirectly derived. The step-by-step process involved in the Simplex Method ultimately reaches the objective function of maximisation or minimisation.

The number of iterations to be applied is not fixed and cannot be predicted with a high degree of accuracy. However, it may be observed that the most frequent number of iterations is not less than the number of inequalities in a given set. Even though it is a trial-and-error method, it has the following systematic features:

(i) There is a mechanical rule to determine the next step based on the completed trial, after each step;

(ii) The procedure ensures that each trial will give values which are closer to the answer than the last one;

(iii) In a majority of the types of problems, the procedure guarantees that the optimal solution is reached in a finite number of steps.

Its utility is widespread, especially with the help of electronic computers or punched card equipment. When each ineration is completed, the results are automatically checked, and if the required objective has not yet been attained, another completed cycle is repeated by computing the data obtained from the previous iteration. One cannot ignore the fact that it is a tremendously tedious task, especially when the number of products is large. This method selects in a planned way only those arrangements which are suitable for consideration with the aim of determining step by step, the sought optimum solution. The most important advantage is that it avoids guess work.

It has already been pointed out, the maximisation and minimisation objectives are very prominent in the Simplex Method. The objective function can be satisfied by maximising certain function, such as profit, margin, returns, utilisation, capacities, occupancy, time; or by minimising such functions as cost, distance, weight, rejection rate, scrap, time, etc. A mathematical notation should be used to present the problems; and all the restrictions or constraints, which confine the solution into a well-bounded area, must be presented in the form of inequalities. The problem to be solved should be presented in a proper form in such a way that restrictions, contraints, confines, and all other possible conditions limiting the problem are not overlooked.

The basic requirements of the linear programming models should be observed in the simplex method as well. These requirements are:

(i) A well-defined objective must be clearly stated and expressed by a function;

(ii) All the data entered in the description of the problems must be expressed in a quantitative form;

(iii) An alternative choice among factors must be feasible, say, for example, the possibility of choosing between machine work or manual work;

(iv) Only linear functions, expressing constraints and restrictions, should be used. For example, the direct proportional change in sales revenue, as a result of a variation of advertising expenditure, may be verified. If such a direct relationship does not exist, an approximation to a straight line should be made in such a way that only the data behaving in a linear form are acceptable;

(v) In terms of mathematical notations, the problem must be completely described. As a matter of fact, the analyst should bear in mind that no computation, more complex than the four elementary operations (addition, substraction, multiplication and division), is used in the simplex method.

A simple example would explain this method clearly. A factory has two machines. One machine has 12 hours and the other has 8 hours of available capacity. The factory manufactures products A and B. Each unit of product A requires two hours of time on both machines. Each unit of product B requires three hours of time on the first machine and one hour on the second machine. The incremental profit is Rs. 6 per unit of A and Rs. 7 per unit of B, and the factory can sell as many units of either product it can manufacture. Assuming that the objective is to maximise profit, how many units of Product A and Product B should be produced? For solving the problem, let us consider the following proposition:

Machine $P = 6X_1 + 7X_2$

Subject $2X_1 + 3X_2 \leqslant 12$

$2X_1 + X_2 \leqslant 8$

$X_1 > 0$

$X_2 > 0$

where

X_1 = Number of units of Product A

X_2 = number of units of Product B

6 = incremental profit per unit of Product A

7 = incremental profit per unit of Product B

The conversion of the inequality expressions in the problem into equalities is the first step in the application of the Simplex Method: and this is possible by adding two new variables, X_3 and X_4, called the slack variables. The slack variables represent the unused capacity in the first and second constraint respectively. The inequalities may be converted into equalities because there must be some amount — the unused capacity X_3 — which would be qual to 12 when added $(2X_1 + 3X_2)$, while X_3 can be equal to or greater than zero. The constraints of the problem may be rewritten as follows:

$$2X_1 + 3X_2 + X_3 = 12$$

$$2X_1 + X_2 + X_4 = 8$$

All the variables are represented in each equation. We add the slack variables with zero coefficients to the equations which are lacking some variables. For example, OX_4 is added to the first equation, and OX_3 is added to the second.

$$2X_1 + 3X_2 + OX_3 + OX_4 = 12$$

$$2X_1 + X_2 + OX_3 + X_4 = 8$$

And this may be summed up to the profit equation as follows:

$$P = 6X_1 + 7X_2 + OX_3 + OX_4$$

The coefficients in the profit equation turn out to b zero, *i.e.,* no profit is introduced by the slack variables.

For the solution of the unique values for X's by using algebraic methods, the same number of equations would be required as the unknown. However, it is possible to solve the two (the two equations in two unknowns) variables, when two of the variables equal zero. For example, if it is assumed that $X_1 = X_2 = 0$, then $X_3 = 12$, and $X_4 = 8$ in this problem. All these solutions are given in Table 1

Table 1

Solution to Variables Assuming Zero Value for Two Variables

Variables of Zero Value	*Solution*		*Profit*	*Label in the Diagram*
X_1 and X_2	$X_3 = 12$	$X_4 = 8$	0	A
X_1 and X_3	$X_2 = 4$	$X_4 = 8$	28	E
X_1 and X_4	$X_2 = 8$	$X_3 = -12$	Infeasible	F
X_2 and X_3	$X_1 = 6$	$X_4 = -4$	Infeasible	B
X_2 and X_4	$X_1 = 4$	$X_3 = 4$	24	C
X_3 and X_4	$X_1 = 3$	$X_2 = 2$	32	D

Each of the above solutions represents the point of intersection of pairs of lines in the following diagram (Fig. 1), which is the graph of constraints. The feasible region is shaded. The corner points of the feasible region are A, C, E, and D in Fig.1. Points B and F are not feasible, mainly because the solutions to these points are of negative values, as shown in Table 1. The infeasible solutions, *i.e.,* negative values for any of the X's may be avoided first. The optimum solution may be identified by enumerating all the feasible corner points, calculating the profit for each and selecting the best from Table 1. It should be noted that the corner points are limited in this problem, since it is a very simple problem. In fact, many business problems have hundreds of corner points, That is why the forgoing procedure is not easy.

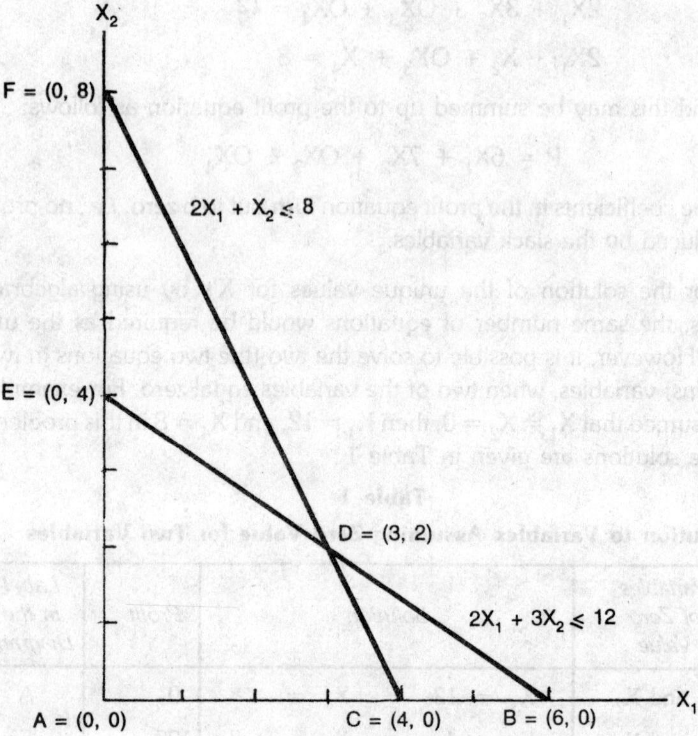

Fig. 1

An initial solution (a corner point), arrived at by setting selected variables equal to zero, is located first under the Simplex Method. The subsequent solutions are worked out step by step in a systematic way. Each solution is a corner point. The procedure ensures that:

(i) The profit increases at each new solution; and

(ii) The solution is feasible. The simplex procedure may be represented by a table for easy calculation of the solutions. This may be called the Simplex Table.

There are three kinds of spaces involved in a linear programming problem solved by the Simplex Method. The initial one is *n* space, the requirement is m space, and the solution is $n + m$ space. A feasible solution to a linear programming problem lies in an $n + m$ space and is a set of $n + m$ values. A feasible solution does not necessarily have to meet the requirements of the objective function. The word *solution* stands for a feasible solution. A non-degenerate basic feasible solution is a basic solution with exactly *m* positive *x*. A maximal solution requires that:

(i) All the values are positive;

(ii) The system of equations is completely fulfilled; and

(iii) The objective function has reached a maximum value.

In this context, however, it should be understood that the maximum of the negative objective function equals the minimum of the positive objective function

The Simplex Method may be applied by anyone who knows the routine, even without knowing the theory and the reasons for the steps in the process. In fact, it is a strategy to search for an optimum solution by modifying some basic solutions. The manager is involved in selecting the optimum solution from among the alternatives. It is here that the Simplex Method comes to use.

Simplex Method: Solving a Maximising Problem in Three Unknowns

For the purpose of solving a maximising problem in three unknowns, let us work out an example of three unknowns. Suppose a production manager wants to manufacture three commodities P, Q and R; and the quantities to be made are *p, q,* and *r,* which represent the number of items the machines must produce within the stipulated time. Each machine performs a single step in the production of each one of the items; *i.e.,* the same number of items will be handled by each machine. The chart showing the required time for production is presented in Table 2.

This problem, described by mathematical notations, appears as a set of three inequalities with three unknowns:

$$6p + 4q + 9r \leqslant 120$$
$$6p + 7.5q + 11r \leqslant 135$$
$$3.75p + 10q + 21r \leqslant 150$$

in which $p \geqslant 0$, $q \geqslant 0$, and $r \geqslant 0$.

Table 2

The Required Time for Production

	To produce One Item of			Available Monthly Time
	P	*Q*	*R*	
Machine I	6 hours	4 hours	2 hours	120 hours
Machine II	6 hours	7.50 hours	11 hours	135 hours
Machine III	3.75 hours	10 hours	21 hours	150 hours

Profit per unit: Rs. 116.60; Rs. 118.10; Rs. 121.3

The manager knows that from each item of Product R, he may expect a profit of Rs. 121.30. In this problem also the objective function must be maximised. By mathematical notation it is:

$$(\text{Rs. } 116.60)\ (p) + (\text{Rs.}118.10)\ (q) + (\text{Rs.}121.30)\ (r) = Z'$$

For the quantities the manager must schedule the production, and the problem can be expressed by mathematical notation through a system of three inequalities as given above. Here, $p > 0, q > 0, r > 0$. In addition to the restrictions on the hours, the problem requires that all the three products must be produced. The manager is eager to schedule the machine time in a manner which will maximise profits. Fractional lots of production are permissible because the available time is expressed on a monthly basis in such a way that every production cycle can be completed in the working period of the following month. The manager knows that a profit of Rs. 116.60 is obtained from each item of P, Rs. 118.10 from each item of Q, and Rs.121.30 from each item of R. The objective function to be maximised represented by the equation, which has already been given (Z').

The problem may be represented by a three-dimensional representation. It may be solved by an empirical process by considering three equalities instead of three inequalities. It is assumed that the limits for the use of the total available time, *viz.*, 120, 135, and 150 hours, will be strictly imposed. Linear programming techniques may be used either to maximise or minimise and objective function by considering a system of inequalities which depicts the set of restrictions. The Simplex Method is the most appropriate technique for the solution of this problem. The following steps have to be taken to solve the problem.

The machine-load problem fulfils the basic requirements for solution by linear programming techniques:

(i) The objective function is clearly stated;

(ii) The data and restrictions are expressed by quantitative measurement;

(iii) An alternative choice among the assignments of available time is possible; and

(iv) All the functions are linear.

First the system of inequalities must be transformed into a set of equations by inserting the appropriate slack variables as follows:

$$6p + 4q + 9r + w_1 = 120$$

$$6p + 7.5q + 11r + w_2 = 135$$

$$3.75 + 10q + 21r + w_3 = 150$$

Then the matrix shall be drawn according to the standard layout as shown in Table 3.

Table 3

Incomplete Matrix of the Machine Load Problem

	1	2	3	4	5	6	7	8	9	10
1			116.60	118.110	121.130	0	0	0		
2				p	q	r	w_1	w_2	w_3	Check
3	0	w_1	120	6	4	9	1	0	0	140.00
4	0	w_2	135	6	7.50	11	0	1	0	160.50
5	0	w_3	150	3.75	10	21	0	0	1	185.75
6										

First Iteration

The index row is first computed by multiplying each value of the objective column times the corresponding values (by rows) of the constant column and of the columns in the body and identity. These results are added by column. From the sums obtained, the values of the objective row are substracted in correspondence to each column. These results are the values to be inserted in the cells of the index row. By making this computation and inserting the values in the grid, the first tableau appears as follows:

Table 4

First Tableau of the Machine Load Problem

	1	2	3	4	5	6	7	8	9	10
1			116.60	118.10	121.30	0	0	0		
2				p	q	r	w_1	w_2	w_3	Check
3	0	w_1	120	6	4	9	1	0	0	140.00
4	0	w_2	135	6	7.50	11	0	1	0	160.50
5	0	w_3	150	3.75	10	21	0	0	1	185.75
6			0	–115.60	–118.10	–121.30	0	0	0	–356.00

In the first tableau, no profit is expected to be shown because the first simplex step is always one of zero production; therefore, one of zero total profit. In the cell of the first tableau, a zero is marked and the objective column is also filled by zeros. The computation shows that there **would be** no profit if there is no production and if no use has been attempted of the available hours. In fact:

$$(0)\ (120) + (0)\ (135) + (0)\ (150) = 0$$

The key column is the sixth column from the left because it has the largest negative number in the index row (-121.30).

The key row is the fifth row from the top because it has the smallest positive ratio of the constant column values over the key column values.

The key number 21.

The main row is obtained by dividing each value of the key row by the key number at the constant, body, identity, and check columns. The main row is 7.143, 0.179, 0.476, 1, 0, 0, 0.048, 8.846.

The replacement rule indicates that 121.30 and *r* have to be placed as stubs in the fifth row.

Second Iteration

The second tableau can now be set up. Table 5 indicates the computation at this stage.

Table 5

Second Tableau of the Machine Load Problem

	1	2	3	4	5	6	7	8	9	10
1				116.60	118.10		0	0	0	
2				p	q		w_1	w_2	w_3	Check
3	0	w_1	55.174	4.392	–0.285	0	1	0	–0.429	60.392
4	0	w_2	56.429	4.035	2.262	0	0	1	–0.524	63.202
5	121.30	r	7.143	0.179	0.476	1	0	0	0.048	8.846
6			866.446	–94.939	–60.338	0	0	0	5.776	–716.45

The solution shown in the second tableau indicates a production of 7.143 items of product R. The computation of the total profit obtainable by that programme is:

(0) (55.714) + (0) (56.429) + (121.30) (7.143) = Rs. 866.45. The second tableau shows Rs. 866.446 as the total expected profit.

The positive values in the index row below the body indicate the 'opportunity profit' of the system. Two negative figures are still present in the index row, hence, the process must be reiterated.

The key column is the fourth column.

The key row is the third row.

The key number is 4.392.

The main row is: 12.685, 1, –0.066, 0, –0.097, 13.750.

The replacement indicates that 116.60 and *p* are placed as stubs in the third row.

Third Iteration

Table 6 shows the solution at this stage of computation. In the tableau, two variables (*p* and *r*) are listed in the variable column. This means that a production of only two types of items has so far been considered. The total profit obtainable with this programme is:

(116.60) (12.685) + (0) (5.244) + (121.30) (4.872) = Rs. 2,070.04.

Table 6

Third Tableau of the Machine Load Problem

	1	2	3	4	5	6	7	8	9	10
1					118.110		0	0	0	
2					q		w_1	w_2	w_3	
3	116.60	p	12.685	1	–0.066	0	0.228	0	–0.097	13.750
4	0	w_2	5.244	0	2.524	0	–0.918	1	–0.130	7.720
5	121.30	r	4.872	0	0.488	1	–0.041	0	0.065	6.384
6			2069.923	0	–66.499	0	21.616	0	–3.497	2021.543

In the index row, negative figures are still present (where – 66.499) is the largest negative number); hence, the process must be iterated because the optimal solution has not yet been reached.

The key column is the fifth column.

The key row is the fourth row.

The main row is: 2.0780, 2.0, –3.363, 0.396, –0.052 and 3,059.

The replacement indicates that 118.10 and *q* becomes stubs in the fourth row.

These values are entered in a grid which becomes the fourth tableau.

Fourth Iteration

Table 7 shows the situation at this stage of the computation.

In this tableau, all the variable are entered in the variable column. The constant column contains the values representing the quantity to be produced, and the objective column shows the amount of rupees expected as unit profit by the manager.

The total profit is:

(116.60) (12.822) + (118.10) (2.078) + (121.30) (3.858) = Rs. 2,208.43.

Table 7 shows a profit Rs. 2,208.329.

Table 7

Fourth Tableau of the Machine Load Problem

	1	2	3	4	5	6	7	8	9	10
1							0	0	0	
2							w_1	w_2	w_3	
3	116.60	p	12.822	1	0	0	0.204	0.026	–0.100	13.952
4	118.10	q	2.078	0	1	0	–0.363	0.396	–0.052	3.059
5	121.30	r	3.858	0	0	1	0.137	–0.193	0.090	4.892
6			2208.923	0	0	0	–2.570	26.347	–6.922	2225.184

Two negative figures are still present in the index row. According to the Simplex Method, the process should be iterated by selecting the key column, the key row, the key number, and by developing a new matrix. Before applying the rules of this method, a few considerations at this stage of the computation may be taken into account. In the index row, there are only zeros under the body, while two negative values are present in the column of the slack variables. If the process is reiterated, the captions in the ninth column (w_3 and 0) will be moved to the fifth row, displacing the value "121.30" from the objective column and *r* from the variable column. The presence of the three values in the objective column, instead of in the objective row, as they are in the first tableau, indicates that it is possible to compute the total profit shown in solution. (This computation can be made at any stage, *i.e.,* by using data from any tableau).

Fifth Iteration: Profit Maximising Vs. Other Managerial Objectives

The last tableau (fourth tableau) obtained by the Simplex Method indicates the presence of two negative figures in the index row, namely, –2.570 and –6.922. When positive values exist in the index row under the body, these values show how much the profit will decrease if one more unit of the given product is produced. When zone are entered in cells they indicate that the solution carried by the tableau may be interpreted as a basic feasible solution. This particular managerial problem states that all the three products must be manufactured, and that three positive results are expected, *i.e.,*

$$p > 0, q > 0, \text{ and } r > 0,$$

since p = 0, q = 0 and, r = 0 are not acceptable.

The computation of this problem must be stopped here in spite of the presence of two negative numbers in the index row below the identity. In fact, if a new iteration is performed, a slack variable would appear in the variable column, thus limiting the production to two objects, But the Simplex Method searches for an optimisation of the profit. A comparison of the fourth and fifth tableaus shows, from a technical point of view, that an increase in total profit can be obtained by manufacturing only two items, *p* and *q* (Rs.2,208.33 versus Rs. 2,503.68). To find the two quantities to be produced, a new table must be computed. Starting from the fourth tableau, the calculations are as follows:

The key column is the ninth column (where –6.922 lies).

They key row is the fifth row because only in that row can a positive relationship be obtained (constant column values over key column values).

The key number is 0.090.

The main row is: 42.866, 0, 0, 11.111, 1.522, –2.144, 1 and 54.355.

The replacement indicates that 0 and w_3 become stubs of the fifth row.

The further iterated tableau appears as follows (see Table 8).

Table 8

Further Iterated Tableau of the Machine Load Problem

	1	2	3	4	5	6	7	8	9	10
1						121.30	0	0		
2						r	w_1	w_2		
3	116.60	p	17.109	1	0	1.111	0.356	-0.188	0	19.388
4	118.10	q	4.308	0	1	0.578	–0.284	0.284	0	5.886
5	0	w_3	42.866	0	0	11.111	1.522	–2.144	1	56.355
6			2503.684	0	0	76.911	7.967	11.504	0	2600.066

In this matrix, no negative numbers are present in the index row. Under the Simplex Method, the optimum solution has been reached.

The total expected profit shown is greater than the corresponding value entered in the preceding tableau (fourth tableau), i.e., Rs. 295.35 have been gained by the improved solution. But this solution is not acceptable because the manager has to produce all the items, as stated by the problem, where $r > 0$ and $r = 0$ as shown in Table 8.

(6) (17.109) + (4) (4.308) + 0 = 119.886 > 120 hours

(6) (17.109) + (7.50) (4.308) + 0 = 134.964 > 135 hours

(3.75) (17,109) + (10) (4.308) + 0 = 107.239 > 150 hours

The available time has not been completely used by performing the programme of the proceeding matrix (fourth tableau) in which, as required, all the three products have been manufactured. This again shows that the optimal solution obtained by the process does not always suit managerial requirements, and that an interpretation of the optimal is absolutely necessary. This interpretation and selection of the best programme is an executive duty and responsibility.

Since this managerial problem is concerned with the production of three products, P, Q, and R, the maximum return in this instance is shown by the fourth tableau, which indicates the optimum solution according to the requirements of the problem. Even if the maximum profits were obtained by producing only two types of commodities (i.e., P and Q as shown in the Table 8), the solution to be accepted by the decision-maker is to manufacture.as indicated in the table (fourth tableau).

12.822 items of P;

2.078 items of Q;

3.858 items of R,

Sensitivity Analysis

Once a problem is solved by the Simplex Method, *sensitivity analysis*, or *parametric linear programming*, may be used to determine whether or not a solution should be modified when one or more coefficients vary. Managers should aware of all the changes in the conditions under which they operate. By considering the event in which the original data have to be altered, compared with data used in the solution of the managerial problem, decision-makers keep themselves informed of the extent to which the optimum solution can be modified without affecting the validity of the objective function. This is more appropriate in the area of transportation problems. Usually, the data pertaining to costs, the quantity produced by one or more factories, the quantity required by one or more receiving points, etc., are frequently open to changes. The sesnsititvity analysis is usually employed to detect the effects of such variations in the business environment. This may be called parametric linear programming when applied in conjunction with linear programming techniques.

The word *sensitivity* stands for the possibility of altering the solution to a transportation problem when one or more variations in the original data are sensed. Sensitivity analysis has, as its goal, the determination of the ranges in which these variations do not affect the optimal solution. When the data vary to such an extent that the existing optimal solution cannot be used, even if it is alternated, another problem has to be considered. New data should be obtained for the new approach, and apparently a different solution will emerge.

The revised Simplex Method is also in use. It does not carry, in the layout of its tableaus, the matrix of the coefficients of the variables. Its layout is composed of the constant column, identity, two new columns added to the right hand side of the identity, and a column which carries the values of the variable to be eliminated from the solution. Even if it is not strictly necessary to carry these two new columns in each tableau, since the elements of these two vectors never change, it is customary to extend the identity by two added columns.

Linear programming is not only useful in general business problems, but in various other problems, such as transportation problems, caterer-type problems, etc. That is why it is extensively applicable to the analysis of the business problems with a view to obtaining the necessary solutions.

Chapter 17

Dynamic Programming

Dynamic programming is a numerical technique employed in the solution of optimisation problems involving a multi-stage decision process. It is of comparatively recent origin. This technique owes much of its development to Richard Bellman and his associates at the R and Corporation. It was in his book Dynamic Programming (1957) that the technique was first introduced. An attempt has been made here to represent briefly the concept and use of dynamic programming.

While the Simplex Method provides an iterative procedure of solving a managerial problem step by step, dynamic programming arrives at the optimum solution by breaking up a problem into a number of sub-problems. It is based on the mathematical notion of recursion. The dynamic programming approach is an optimal policy of maximisation of at least one variable in each sub-problem. The three basic concepts involved in this technique are:

(i) The total problem is divided into a number of sub-problems;

(ii) By working backward from the natural end of the problem, each sub-problem is solved to maximise at least one variable; and

(iii) After each sub-problem is solved, the answer is recorded, and the payoff (profit, cost, etc.) from that stage on to the end of the problem is also recorded.

An example would make the concept clear. A marketing manager is considering the problem of distributing his eight salesmen in the best way possible between the three zones of the company's market. The profit from each of the marketing zones vis-a-vis the number of salesmen employed is given in Table 1.

If the number of salesmen employed in each zone is beyond a certain number, the profit declines. This is due to the fact that the sales may not increase merely by employing more salesmen, though the expenses are bound to grow. What would be the optimum allocation of salesmen to each of the zones in order to maximise the total profit in this situation?

Table 1

No. of Salesmen	*Profit (Rs. in '000 for marketing zones)*		
	A	*B*	*C*
0	75	80	100
1	81	85	120
2	95	105	135
3	115	122	160
4	130	130	170
5	145	150	160
6	165	140	140
7	150	125	115
8	130	110	90

As already mentioned, the whole problem should be divided into sub-problems; and the maximum of at least one variable, say profit, in each sub-problem should be determined. In the first instance, consider only zones A and B. There are 9 possible combinations of allocating salesmen to A and B, viz., no salesmen to A and 8 salesmen to B, and so on. The profit realised under each of the 9 alternatives can easily be computed, and the combinations which yield the maximum profit can also be determined for different numbers of salesmen allocated to Zones A and B. This has been shown in Table 2.

Table 2

Number of Salesmen in Zone A

	No of salesmen in zone A		0	1	2	3	4	5	6	7	8
	PROFIT		75	81	95	115	130	145	165	150	190
No. of Salesmen in Zone C	0	80	**155**	**161**	175	195	**210**	**225**	**245**	230	210
	1	85	160	166	180	200	215	230	250	235	
	2	105	**180**	186	200	220	235	250	270		
	3	122	**197**	203	217	237	**252**	**267**			
	4	130	205	211	225	245	260				
	5	150	225	231	245	265					
	6	140	215	221	235						
	7	125	200	206							
	8	110	185								

(Profit in Rs. '000)

For different numbers of the total salesmen engaged, the bold type figures indicate the maximum (along each diagonal). If it is decided to assign only 7 out of 8 salesmen available among the marketing zones A and B, the best possible combination for profit maximisation is to engage 4 in zone A, and 3 in zone B, which yields a profit of Rs. 252,000/-. Similarly, the next step is to evaluate the marketing Zone C.

If a decision is taken to assign 4 salesmen to Zones A and B, and the remaining four to Zone C (then 4 persons are placed to zone A, 4 persons to Zone C and 0 persons to zone B), the maximum profit would be Rs. 380/- (Rs. 210 + 170). The question that would arise at this stage is: What is the basis of assigning exactly 4 salesmen to Zones A and B? It is only in terms of the marginality principle *i.e.,* the highest addition to the total benefit as a result of the addition of each salesman separately. For each of these allocations the best possible allocation between Zones A and B only will be relevant (*i.e.,* the underlined numbers in Table 2). Treating A and B together as Zone 1, the best possible allocation between A, B, and C can be found exactly in the same manner as it was found for Zones A and B. The method is illustrated in Table 3.

Table 3

Combined Number of Salesmen in Zones A and B

			0	1	2	3	4	5	6	7	8
	PROFIT		155	161	180	197	210	225	245	252	267
No. of Salesmen in Zone C	0	100	255	261	280	297	310	325	345	352	376
	1	120	275	281	300	317	330	345	365	372	
	2	135	290	296	315	332	345	360	380		
	3	160	315	321	340	357	370	385			
	4	170	325	331	350	367	380				
	5	160	315	321	340	357					
	6	140	295	301	320						
	7	115	270	276							
	8	90	245								

(Profit in thousand Rs.)

It is evident from Table 3 that the maximum profit is derived (385) when five salesmen are allocated to Zone A and B and 3 salesmen to Zone C. Let us refer back to Table 2 for Zones A and B; the best possible allocation between A and B for 5 salesmen is that of 5 salesmen to Zone A and none to Zone B (profit Rs. 225). Now we arrive at the combined allocation of salesmen to Zones A, B, and C; i.e., 5, 0, and 3 salesmen respectively. The total profit is as follows:

Zone	Profit Rs.
A	1,45,000
B	80,000
C	1,60,000
Total profit:	3,85,000

Dynamic programming may be extended to any number of salesmen and zones. The first step is to obtain the solution when there are only two zones; then more tables are prepared step by step. Finally, the solutions are obtained stage by stage. Similarly, it may be applied to any functional area — to production scheduling and allocation problems, inventory control, cargo-loading, investment analysis of multi-component devices, equipment replacement, etc.

This technique is formalised by referring to stages, state variable, optimal decision rules, and optimal policies. Each stage of the process refers to a particular decision. A state variable is a variable defining the current situation at any stage. An optimal decision rule specifies which decision should be made, as a function of the state variable and the stage number, while an optimal policy is a set of optimal decision rules which guide one's decisions through all the stages of the entire problem. The principle of optimality is the guiding principle in the dynamic programming technique. "An optimal policy has the property that whatever the initial state and the initial decision are, the remaining decisions must constitute an optimal policy with regard to the state resulting from the first decision."[1] According to the optimality principle, you divide the total problem and solve the last decision stage, then work backward and solve the second-to-last decision, etc., until the first decision is "solved."

Any managerial decision problem should be divided into a number of sub-problems in order that it may be formulated as a dynamic programming problem. It is necessary to be able to describe the state of the system by a state variable. Finally, one must be able to write the general recurrence relation between the maximum return at one stage and the maximum return at the next stage. The stage often refers to a time period, though this is not essential. Usually, a computer is used to work out a dynamic programming solution. Sometimes, the particular structure of a problem will allow the maximisation or minimisation in the recurrence relation to be performed by calculus, as in our example. Dynamic programming is possible in problems under uncertainty, also, and hence it is a very useful technique in effective business decisions.

1. Bellman, R.E. *Dynamic Programming,* Princeton Univenrsity Press, Princeton, 1957, p. 83.

Chapter 18

Quantitative Techniques: Some Additional Highlights

After having discussed the various aspects of quantitative techniques employed in business analysis, it would be relevant here to throw some light on some additional techniques — the game theory, the queueing theory, simulation, and PERT — because these techniques, too, are in use in business analysis and decision-making.

Game Theory

Credit goes to Von Neumann and Morgenstern for having contributed the Theory of Games and Economic Behaviour (1944).[1] The game theory is not very popular with management practitioners, though it has been accepted for theoretical purposes. A game is usually a presentation of conflict situations in business, and the motives of the participants are dichotomised in it. As the success of one party may be at the expenses of the others, the latter are bound to be in conflict with the former. However, both the parties would be interested in arriving at some sort of settlement in the game and therefore they participate in it. The game represents instances of business conflict situations, which create interest in the analysts.

1. Von Newmann and Morgenstem *Theory of Games and Economic Behaviour,* Princeton University Press, 1994.

Two-person zero-sum games are prominent in the game theory. In such a game, the interests of the two opponents are opposed in such a way that the sum of their utilities add to zero for every outcome of the game. For example, two individuals, who match some money, would have an equal utility. The sum of money won by one is the sum of money lost by the other. Both of them are aware of the payoff matrix in the game. It means that there is a minimax solution of the two-persons zero-sum game. Though minimax is likely to be a desirable procedure, it may not lead to the best possible outcome, if the opponent does not use a minimax solution. The minimax solution attempts to maximise a security level for the players, *i.e.* to minimise the maximum possible loss, or maximise the minimum gain. The strategies adopted by both of them in the example have been presented in Table 1, which shows both the minimum and the maximum.

TABLE 1

Payoffs in the Two-person Zero-Sum Game

I *II*	*Strategy I*	*Strategy II*	*Minimum of Row*
Strategy I	15	20	15
Strategy II	10	16	10
Maximum of Column	15	20	

For each strategy of player I, there is the maximum gain of player II, and *vice versa*. Similarly, the maximum gain of one is the maximum loss of the other, and *vice versa*. Player I chooses the largest of the row minimums (in this case, strategy I), and player II chooses the smallest of the column maximums (strategy I). Since the maximum equals the minimum (both have values of 15), there is an equilibrium. The values are known as the equilibrium pair. If one of the parties tried to move from this equilibrium while the other maintained his position, the mover would not improve his position. A pure strategy, a choice of only one strategy by each player, leads to a strictly determined game when the maximum of the minimum values of a row is equal to the minimum of the maximum values of the column. The value 15 is known as the *saddle point*. The margins of Table 1 offers a guaranteed minmum profit for player I or the guaranteed maximum costs for Player II.

Let us apply this technique to the settlement of an industrial dispute, and the negotiations between the management and the trade union. The company chooses the following feasible strategies in its negotiations:

S_1 = a hard aggressive bargaining approach

S_2 = a carry them with us approach

S_3 = a legalistic strategy

S_4 = a conciliatory approach.

The management wants to choose the best from among the feasible strategies which, however, depends on the strategy adopted by the union. It is assumed that the union would consider the following feasible strategies:

T_1 = a hard aggressive bargaining strategy

T_2 = a carry them with us approach

T_3 = a legalistic strategy

T_4 = a conciliatory approach.

The consequences of each of the approaches of the management in relation to each of the strategies of the union should now be considered. Accordingly, Table 2 has been constructed.

Table 2

Gains of the Trade Union in Relation to the Strategies and Costs of the Management

Union Strategies	*Company strategies*				*Row Minimums*
	S_1	S_2	S_3	S_4	*(in Rupees)*
T_1	20	12	12	35	12
T_2	25	15	8	10	8
T_3	40	2	10	5	2
T_4	–5	4	11	0	–5
Column Maximus	40	15	12	35	

If startegy S_1 is opted by the company and if the union adopts T_1, the final contract will involve a 20-rupee per week increase in wages. If the trade union adopts the T_2 strategy in response to the S_1 strategy of the management, the workers would gain an increase of Rs. 25 per week. The trade union's T_3 strategy against the management's S_1 is better from the point of view of the workers (gain of Rs. 40/-). However, if the union adopts T_4 against the S_1 strategy of the management, the workers will face a wage cut of Rs. 5/-, All the other combinations of strategies would have a corresponding effect, as shown in Table 2. Assume that both the management and the trade union have a conciliatory approach (T_4) as against the aggressive bargaining of the management (S_1), resulting in a wage decline of Rs. 5/- per week. However, if the management follows the S_1 approach, the union would prefer to have the T_3 approach, leading to a wage increase of Rs. 40/-. The second best solution from the company's point of view would be S_4 T_4, resulting in no increase in wages. But the union would then choose to opt for T_1, (say, S_4, T_1) — which would result in an increase of Rs.35/-. The parties may adopt a minimax strategy; *i.e.,* the company may adopt the strategy which minimises the maximum wage increase it should grant, regardless of the action of the union. If the union adopts this rule, it would choose that strategy which maximises the minimum wage increase. The minimax strategy for the company is S_3, with a minimum wage increase of Rs. 12; the minimax strategy for the union is T_1, with a minmum wage increase of Rs. 12/-. As is evident from Table 2, Rs. 12 is both the maximum of its S_3 column and the minimum of its T_1 row, it is the equilibrium solution of this situation. Thus, T_1 S_3 is the equilibrium situation of this game. In certain games, a minimax equilibrium may not be attainable; in that case by changing one of the critical figures an acceptable situation may be arrived at. It is also possible to arrive at graphical solutions, algebraic solutions and linear programming solutions in the games.

Queueing Theory (Waiting Line Theory)

Decision situations frequently arise in which the units arriving for service must wait before they can be serviced. Such queues are very common, not only in business situations, but in everyday life. If we know the principles governing the arrivals, the servicing times, and the order in which arriving units are taken up for service, then the nature of the waiting situation can be studied and evaluated mathematically; and this is known as the *queueing theory*, or the *waiting line theory*. It is primarily concerned with the processes which have the characteristics of having random arrivals, and the servicing of the customer at random.

Arriving units may form one line and be serviced by only one station, as in a doctor's office; or they may form one line and be serviced by several stations, as in a barber shop; or they may form several lines and be served by many stations, as at the checkout counters of a supermarket. If we assume that costs are associated with waiting in the line, and if there are costs of adding more channels, we would like to minimise the sum of the costs of waiting and the costs of providing service facilities. The computations will enables us to measure the expected number of people in a line or the expected waiting time of arrivals. Cost computations can then be made.

In general, arrivals take place at random, and service times are also random variables; that is, these variables may not be function dependent on time. Thus, we shall be concerned with estimating only the average length of the line at any time. When confronted with a problem involving waiting lines and the costs arising from them, the decision-maker uses his knowledge of the average characteristics of the queue in attempting to reduce costs, maximise output, or whatever. Some of the changes he might recommend are: changing the number of servicing stations; changing the average service time in one or more stations; spliting a single queue or amalgamating several queues; and so on. Such changes are evaluated by first considering their effect on the average characteristics of the waiting line, and then translating these changes in average characteristics into changes in the chosen measure of effectiveness. There are many waiting line situations in business, *viz.,* repairmen servicing machines, landing strips for aircraft, waiting at various types of service centres, manpower at the spare part counter, docks for ships, etc.

Queueing decisions can be made on the basis of past experience or on the basis of facts in the current situation. The management of a grocery chain knows approximately how many check-out counters should be installed in a new store by looking at the experience of comparable stores. It cannot be gainsaid that a number of problems encountered by an executive can be reasonably solved by the use of intuition or past experience. However, there may be a number of complex situations which cannot be solved by experience or intuition alone. Simulation or mathematical model procedure can solve the problems in such situations. The queueing problem also can be solved by mathematical models, when the following, when the following situations are considered:

(i) Arrivals and service occurring following a given time schedule;

(ii) Arrivals coming randomly from an infinite universe when there is only one service facility (there may be multiple service facilities; too);

(iiii) Arrivals come from a finite population.

In the first case, facilities should be exactly scheduled to meet the arrivals. A mass production assembly line may be an example of arrivals with a given time schedule. Though the assumptions are fairly restrictive, the results apply to some situations met with in practice.

Let us consider a single-service facility with arrivals from an infinite population, *i.e.,* there is one channel or service facillity. Service is rendered on a 'first come, first served' basis. It obviously means that a queue or a waiting line is expected. Individual arrivals take place from the infinite universe; and the process of arrivals and service is poisson. (The probability of the occurrence of an event is constant, and the occurrence of an event is independent of what has happened immediately preceding the present observation, according to the poisson distribution. We may be interested in what happens over a continuous interval, which may be a measure of distance). The assumptions in this context are:

(i) Arrivals are independent of each other. Services are also independent. What has happened in the past has nothing to do with the future.

(ii) In relation to time, both arrivals and services are homogeneous; that is, the average arrival and service rates do not change over time.

The elements of uncertainty are:

(i) The form of the theoretical probability distribution may not be known;

(ii) The parameters of the process may not be known, even If the probability is known; and

(iii) The actual outcome is unknown, even if the above two items are known.

A great deal of uncertainty, therefore, prevails as far as the solution is concerned. In connection with model building, let us identify the following variables:

A = Average number of customers arriving in one unit of time.

S = Average number of customers the facility services in one unit of time, assuming that there is shortage of customers.

n = Number of units being serviced or waiting in the system.

nq = Number in the queue (which does not include the unit that is serviced).

pn = Probability of having *n* units in the system.

w = Time an arrival must wait in the queue.

Some of the relationships of these variables may be very prominent in the queueing theory. They are:

(i) Po = 1 — A/S

(ii) pn = $(A/S)^n$po

(iii) pn = (A/S)pn — 1

(iv) $E(n) = \dfrac{A}{(S-A)}$ (The expected number in the waiting line or those that are serviced.)

(v) $E(n_a) = \dfrac{A^2}{S(S-A)}$ (The expected number in the queue.)

(vi) $E(w) = \dfrac{E(nq)}{A}$ (The average waiting time (in the queue of an arrival.)

(vii) $P(n > k) = (A/S)^{k+1}$ (Probability that the number in the queue and of those that are serviced is greater than k.)

Equations 1 to 7 are aplicable provided that:

$$\frac{A}{S} < 1.$$

If the arrival rate (A) is greater than the service rate, the queue will increase without end.

An example would make it clear. Cars arrive at random in a poisson process at an automobile service centre at an average rate of four cars an hour (one at a time). The service process is also poisson. The centre operates round the clock, and services at the rate of five cars an hour which is also poisson.

$$S = 5 \text{ and } A =$$

The relationship between these variables under a condition

$$\frac{A}{S} < 1 \text{ is:}$$

$$E(n) = \frac{A}{(S-A)} = \frac{4}{(5-4)} = 4$$

(An average of four cars are in line or being serviced.)

Vehicles in the queue can be worked out with the help of the equation

$$E(n_q) = \frac{A^2}{S(S-A)} = \frac{4 \times 4}{5(5-4)} = \frac{16}{5} = 3.2$$

It shows that there would be an average of 3.2 cars in the waiting line. The average waiting time of a vehicle may be worked out as 0.8 of an hour, with the help of the following equation:

$$E(w) = \frac{E(n_q)}{A} = \frac{16/5}{5} = \frac{4}{5} = 0.8$$

The average number of vehicles in the line has been worked out at 3.2 and the average waiting time of a vehicle may be worked out as 0.8 of an hour, with the help of the following equation:

For multiple service facilities, the following equations can be used. Let us assume that there are C channels and that there is one waiting line if all the service facilities are busy. Each channel has the same service rate (S). The variable *n* represents the sum of the customers being served. Then the equation are:

$$\text{(viii) } Po = \left[\frac{(A/S)^c}{C!\left(1 - \frac{A/S}{C}\right)} + 1 + \frac{(A/S)^1}{1!} + \frac{(A/S)^2}{2!} \right.$$

$$\left. = + \ldots + \frac{(A/S)^{c-1}}{(C-1)!} \right] - 1$$

$$\text{(ix) } Pn = Po \frac{(A/S)^n}{n!} \text{ if } n \leqslant C$$

$$\text{(x) } Pn = Po \frac{(A/S)^n}{C!^{\,n-c}} \text{ if } n > C$$

We can use the above equations if

$$\frac{A}{CS} < 1, \text{ If } \frac{A}{CS} > 1.$$

Then the waiting line grows larger and larger; *i.e.*, *n* becomes infinite if the process runs long enough.

When C = 1 (there is one service facility), equations *(ix)* and *(x)* are reduced to equation *(ii)*. From equation *(ix)*, we have:

$$Pn = Po\frac{(A/S)^n}{n!} \text{ if } n \leqslant C$$

But n can only take on values of zero or one if $< C = 1$

Thus: $Pn = Po\ (A/S)^n$

If C = 1, equation (i) is also reduced to equation *(ii).*

With C service facilities, the average number of customers in the queue is:

$$\text{(xi)}\quad E(n_q) = \frac{(A/S)^{c+1}}{C.C!\left(1-\frac{A/S}{C}\right)^2}Po$$

and, as before, the expected waiting time for an arrival is:

$$\text{(xii)}\qquad E(w) = \frac{E(n_q)}{A}$$

Simulations

Simulation is a numerical method which helps us to gain a better understanding of certain kinds of business situations in advance. It is very effective in an analysis of certain queueing problems; but when many queueing problems are beyond the effective reach of mathematics, simulation becomes successful. Simulation is useful in the solution of business problems, when all the values of the variables are not known or partly known, an there is no quick and easy way of finding these values.

Simulation may be defined as the process of conducting an experiment on a model or system instead of a direct experiment with the system itself or a direct analytical solution of some problems associated with the system. It is a process of trying out alternative policies, while the actual system is retained. It enables one to determine how to balance the costs of waiting against the costs of service in the queueing problems. It deals with the problems of allocation of resources among competitive uses. The economic order quantity pattern of inventory can be effectively determined with the help of simulation; and it is a useful technique in sequencing, especially in the arrangement of tasks in minimum time. In routing and replacement problems, too, it makes a considerable impact. The most prominent methods of simulation are the Monte Carlo Method, the System Simulation Method, and the Operational Gaining Method.

Generally speaking, the process of simulation may be made in four stages. These are decision stage, construction stage, prediction stages, and testing stage. The decision on the relevant variables, both dependent and independent; the decision on the controllable independent variables; the decision on the action to be taken when the model is built — these come under relationship by sets of equations and inequalities. It always excludes variables which have no significance. A model is a written description of presentation of certain events. Prediction is concerned with the behaviour of the system in obedience to the performance of the model, while testing requires successive refinements of the model.

Simulation models consist of a detailed set of procedures, which usually take the form of a flow chart of a computer programme. The large digital computers make simulation models easy. The key element in a simulation model is the close relationship between the logical sequence of events in real life and events within the computer. One should first decide what would be done with the model when it is built; and what question will it help to answer. When one question is answered, a new question comes to light. The main variables are identified next, and their relationship established, so that new relationships may come to light. A simulation model is built "to twist the cube of reality to view another face." It is necessary to start with the concept of how a model might be made; and then draw flow diagrams to define its action, There is considerable scope for imagination. The analyst should think of the events that occur in real life situations. When he throws light on each event, another one is unveiled. By carefully delineating the various ramifications and logical decisions that govern the various chains of events, a model can be developed. Then the flow charts can be drawn, defining the rules and procedures that govern the changes from one state to another. Successive refinements of the model enable us to bring it closer to the process of simulation.

When the model becomes accurate enough, it may be tested in segments; and as a whole, by working through the various procedures. Errors, if any, are invariably revealed at this juncture, and they should be removed if the model is to be made ready for computer programming. When the computer programme has been made, after being tested and "de-bugged", the simulation model is ready for experiments.

The simulation method suffers from three apparent limitations:

(i) It requires a long time for the construction and testing of a simulation method.

(ii) Its expenses are usually very high, and therefore, in ordinary circumstances, it is not employed by many managers.

(iii) It is not easy to make simulation models of many managerial problems, especially when the human element of decision-making is involved in it.

Because of these limitations, simulation does not find favour with many practising managers. It is, obviously, more of theoretical value than of practical utility. However, there has been an increasing application of the situation method in recent times.

Example of Simulation

At the XYZ refinery, there are five berths for ocean going vessels; but in 1983, only one of them, No. 5, was capable of handling vessels of 80,000 deadweight tons or more. It was expected that there would be 118 arrivals of these tankers in 1984 — on an average, about one every three days. It was clear that, as ships could not be scheduled to arrive with perfect regularity, there would be occasions when a large tanker would arrive before the previous one had left, and would have to wait at an extra cost of something like Rs. 100 an hour. It is possible to uprate the adjacent berth No. 4, to take these big ships by dredging and modifying the hose handling equipment. The cost was estimated at Rs. 70,000. The question was, what savings in ship waiting time would result from this expenditure?

The arrivals are irregular, and the nature of irregularities prevented the solution of the problem by analytical methods. The model represents the arrival and berthing only at No. 5 Berth, or at No. 4 or No. 5 and remaining alongside for various times. The model should first determine how many hours a year ships would be kept waiting if only Berth No. 5 is available for them, and then what the delays would be if both the berths were available. The difference, when valued at Rs. 100/- an hour, would be the incentive to spend Rs. 70,000 on Berth 4. The only problems in establishing the model were how to represent the arrival pattern and which "alongside" times to use.

The arrivals of tankers carrying crude oil can be adequately represented by a series of random advance or delays superimposed on a perfectly regular schedule. In order to generate a realistic arrival pattern, one starts with arrivals at regular intervals and then applies to each arrival time an advance or delay drawn at random from a selection of typical advancements and delays. The study was not concerned with delays waiting on tide or daylight, but only with delays arising out of awaiting a berth. In order to obtain the arrivals pattern, it was necessary to draw a sample from a distribution of typical advances and delays, and to apply the resulting figures to a regular three-day pattern, as shown in the first three columns of Table 3. A vessel effectively ties up a berth for two tidal days. In the model, therefore, a constant "alongside" time of two days was a valid representation. This eliminated the need for sampling from a distribution for "alongside" time.

Simulation

The simulation was simple enough to be carried out by hand. Having generated the arrival pattern, it was an elementary matter to berth the ships on paper, either at No. 5 only, or at No. 5 or No. 4 and record the waiting time for getting a berth, as shown in Table 3. After simulation for a suitable period, it was estimated that if Berth No. 4 was not uprated, delays would be 68 ship-days a year, while if the berth was uprated, these would be reduced to six — a saving of 62 ship-days.

The simulation should take care of a long period to ensure that a representative number of both slack and busy periods was encountered. Typical advancements and delays in berthng schedules, showing the arrival pattern, have been worked out in Table 3. Savings by uprating Berth No. 4 are 23 – 2 = 21 ship days. This is related to 40 ships.

The savings per year are, therefore, 21 × 118 ÷ 40 = 62 ship-days. The arrival pattern for the complementary simulation was obtained from the original merely by changing advances into delays and delays into advances. The savings estimated from this second simulation were 59 ship-days a year. The agreement with the first figure of 62 was sufficient to confirm that the simulation had been carried out for a long enough period. The average of the two was thus about 60, worth nearly Rs. 150,000 a year.

Two minor effects of uprating Berth 4 on shipping delays had then to be allowed for: One was that the use of Berth 4 by an 80,000 tanker prevented its use by a smaller ship. The other was that Berth No. 3 had to be free while a large vessel was being manoeuvred into position at Berth No. 4. Since these effects were small in comparison with the main credits of avoiding substantial delays to very large ships, a rought estimate of debit to the tune of Rs. 15,000 a year was made without recourse to simulation.

In the circumstances, two minor effects of uprating berth 4 had to be allowed for.

Such simulation problems can be solved very easily because of three reasons. First, the investigated effect was very substantial (almost double the existing facilities). Second, the resulting savings well justified the capital expenditure (if they had been just marginal, a more detailed consideration of the minor effects would have been necessary). Third, it happened that the quantities which were to be dealt with could be represented by small integers and the "alongside" time could be taken as constant. But many simulation problems would not be so easy of solution. Electronic devices then become necessary for processing and evaluation.

Table 3

Advancements and Delays in Berthing Schedules Showing Arrival Pattern

Planned	*Delay ( ) or advance (-)*	*Actual Arrival Date*	*No. 5 Berth Date of Berthing*	*Only Delay (Days)*	*No. 5 & No. 4 Berths Date of Berthing*	*Delay (Days)*
(1)	*(2)*	*(3)*	*(4)*	*(5)*	*(6)*	*(7)*
3	0	3	3		3	
6	1	7	7		7	
9	5	14	14		14	
12	0	12	12		12	
15	5	20	21	1	20	
18	1	19	19		19	
21	0	21	25	4	22	1
24	-4	20	23	3	21	1
27	1	28	28		28	
30	-2	28	30	2	28	
33	0	33	33		33	
36	3	39	39		39	
39	0	39	41	2	39	
42	1	43	45	2	43	
45	-4	41	43	2	41	
48	5	53	53		53	
51	5	56	56		56	
54	5	59	60	1	59	
57	1	58	58		58	
60	5	65	65		65	
63	-1	62	62		62	
66	2	68	68		68	
69	3	72	72		72	
72	1	73	74	1	73	
75	2	77	77		77	
78	3	81	81		81	
81	-2	79	79		79	
84	-2	82	83	1	82	
87	2	89	89		89	
90	2	92	92		92	
93	0	93	94	1	93	
96	5	101	101		101	
99	-4	95	96	1	95	
102	5	107	108	1	107	
105	1	106	106		106	
108	1	109	110	1	109	
111	3	114	114		114	
114	-2	112	112		112	
117	1	118	118		118	
120	1	121	121		121	
	Total delays			23		

Simulation of Random Variables

A source of random delays and advances was required to produce a realistic tanker arrivals pattern in the foregoing example. It becomes necessary to simulate random events in many simulation problems. For this purpose, it is essential to establish the distribution of these random variables first; and then to draw a sample from the distribution. This may be done directly by selecting at random from a set of numbers with the specified distribution, or by selecting a number from a uniform distribution and then making an appropriate transformation to obtain one with the required distribution. (The methods of doing this are described in any standard text book on Operations Research. Tables of uniformly distributed random numbers are common. Useful tables of normally distributed numbers are also available).

Pseudo-random numbers substitute the random numbers in a simulation that is carried out by a computer. These numbers are produced by a determinate process; but they do pass tests of randomness. If enough pseudo-random numbers are generated, this sequence of numbers will become cyclic, *i.e.,* the numbers first generated will be generated again, and in the same order.

There is a possibility that sampling errors would creep in. It is appropriate, therefore, to make use of some methods to reduce the sampling error. The *antithetic variate* method is one of the most commonly used techniques for this purpose, which involves running two simulation so that the random variables in one are negatively correlated with those in the others for the averaging of the results. This has been used in the example given in this chapter. In order to minimise the error, the samlpe samples have been used in each simulation for the purpose of comparing different things. The *importance sampling* in another method of reducing error. In a simulation, the frequency of a comparatively rate event is measured. The delay to a ship is used in the above example. In importance sampling, the frequency of rare events has been increased in the model by a known factor. "Spliting" can also be considered useful. Uprating Berth 4 can only reduce delays when ship are delayed if only Berth No. 5 is available. Therefore, we first simulate with only Berth No. 5 and restrict the simulation with both the berths in operation to the times when delays occur in the first. This is 'spiliting' the first simulation into two, one in which there are delays. The *Russian Roulette* simulation involves the carrying out of several subsidiary simulations; each time a busy period occurs, while the results are weighted appropriately.

Expressed values, systematic sampling and stratified sampling can also be used to reduce errors. If the proportion by which the delays for ships can be anticipated following the uprating of Berth 4, then it would be necessary to simulate to find the delays that would occur when only Berth 5 is available. A systematic simulation of the two berths can be carried out, first for one-hour delays with one berth only, and then for two-hour delays, and so on, weighting the results according to the known frequency distribution. Simulation becomes more useful if it is made error-free.

Though it is not very popular in many situations of managerial problem-solving, the simulation technique is a very useful addition to the tool-kit of managerial analysis. Moreover, with the development of electronic data processing devices, many of its limitations can be avoided.

Programme Evaluation and Review Technique (PERT)

Planning is one of the basic functions of management. Various tools and techniques have been developed over the years for effective planning. PERT is one of the latest management tools employed for planning, co-ordinating, scheduling, controlling, project execution, and so on. It was in the latter half of the 1950s that this technique emerged as an effective management tool. The US Navy and Du Pont Company have been jointly responsible for the birth of this technique concurrently.

The *programme evaluation and review technique* is considered to be an effective management tool in the planning, scheduling and controlling of a project. It allows a manager to calculate the expected total amount of time the entire project would take to complete. Two types of information are required for each activity in the project. On the one hand, the sequencing requirements for an activity, *i.e.,* the set of activities which must be completed prior to the beginning of each specific activity, and, on the other, an estimate of the time each activity would take. Both are required for programme evaluation.

The network diagram is an essential part of PERT. When a'l the activities are displayed on the Gantt Chart showing the starting time and the scheduled completion time, we have a network diagram. As the jobs progress, the horizontal bar, representing the schedule, is developed. At any point of time, it can be seen from the chart whether a particu ar activity is ahead or behind the schedule.

The Gantt Chart is simple to use but suffers from some limitations. It cannot show interdependencies of activities. It cannot indicate the possible delay in the entire project because of delays in certain activities. It cannot reflect the uncertainties inherent in time estimates. PERT overcomes these limitations. Each milestone in the Gantt Chart denotes the completion of a definite portion of activity in the network, and the arrows stand for the interdependencies of the various activities.

It may be asserted here that the network diagram is a graphical representation of the entire project. Each activity in the project is represented by a circle, and sequencing requirements are indicated by arrows. An example would make this clear.

A work consists of 6 activities which require a specific time for their completion, as shown in Table 4. The relationship between each activity has also been shown.

Table 4

Activity Events	*Immediate Predecessors*	*Estimated Time (months)*
P - - - -		2
Q - - - -	P	3
R - - - -	P	4
S - - - -	Q. R	6
T - - - -	....	2
U - - - -	T	8

Activity Q immediately follows activity P, which means that activity P should be completed before activity Q begins. The arrows in the network diagram stand for the sequencing requirements of the problem. The arrow from circle P to circle Q indicates that activity P must be completed before activity Q begins. Similarly, activities Q and R must both be completed before activity S begins. The representation of each activity in Fig. 1 (the network diagram) contains the estimated time for each activity.

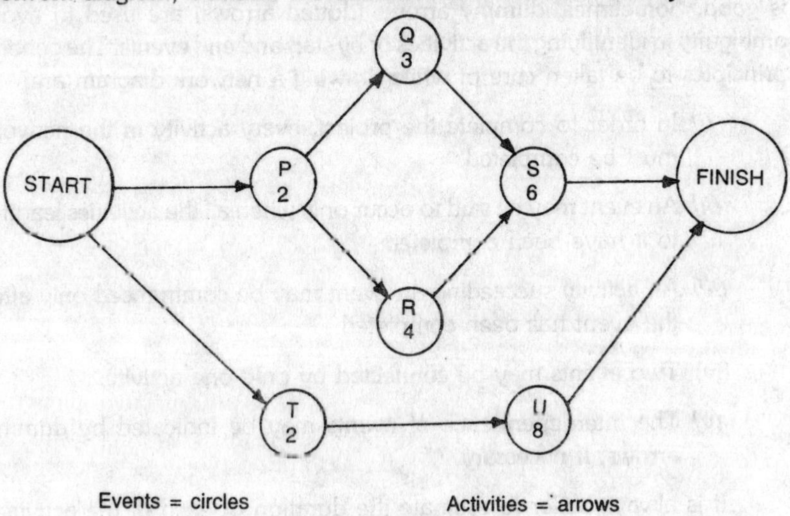

Fig. 1 Network Diagram

Activities	*Events*
Prepare Project Report	Project report preparation completed (P)
Obtain Finances	Finance obtained (Q)
Acquire Land	Land acquired (R)
Make enquiries for machinery	Enquiries for machinery completed (T)
Instal machinery	Machinery installed (U)
Construct buildings	Construction completed (S)

Finish: The project completed and production started.

Figures in circles indicate the time required for each event.

A project consists of a number of activities which should be listed before a new work is prepared. The logical sequence of the activities should then be established, determining the place of each activity in the network. The interdependence of the activities may be indicated with arrows. Once the various events are interlinked by arrows, the logic of the network is established. The events are numbered from left to right. The tail of events is the start and the head of events represents the end. The length of the arrow and its orientation need to be proportional to the duration of the activity, unlike in the case of a Gantt Chart, though some proportionality is good. Sometimes, dummy arrows (dotted arrows) are used to avoid ambiguity in identifying the activities or by start and end events. The general principles to be taken care of while drawing a network diagram are:

(i) In order to complete the project, every activity in the network must be completed.

(ii) An event may be said to occur only when all the activities leading to it have been completed.

(iii) An activity succeeding an event may be commenced only after the event has been completed.

(iv) Two events may be connected by only one activity.

(v) The interdependence of events may be indicated by dummy arrows, if necessary.

It is always better to estimate the duration of each of the activities independently without reference to the other activities.

Critical Path

A path may be defined as a sequence of connected activities in the project. The possible paths in the diagram (Fig. 1) are PQS, PRS, and TU. The first takes 11 months, the second 12 months and the third 10 months. The critical path is the path which has the largest amount of time associated with it. PRS, which has a period of 12 months, has the maximum period of time. The length of the critical path determines the minimum time in which the entire project may be completed. The activities on the critical path are the bottleneck activities in the project. There are usually two reasons for importance of the critical path:

(i) The completion time for the project cannot be reduced unless one or more activities on the critical path are completed in less time than the initial time estimated for them. The activitles which must be performed more rapdily if the total project completion time is to be reduced should be highlighted by the critical path.

(ii) Any delays in the activities which are on the critical path will result in delays in the completion of the project, whereas delays in non-critical activities may not actually delay the completion of the project.

LOP and EPO

It is the possible to obtain the critical path in a small network by tracing the various paths through it. But it is not an easy taks to trace it in a large network involving hundreds of activities and events without the aid of a systematic procedure. The Earliest Possible Occurrence (EPO) and the Latest Possible Occurrence (LPO) are the commonly used methods to trace the critical path. The former may be called the Algorithm ES_i (Earliest Start Time for Activity i), and the latter Algorithm EF_i (Earliest Finish Time for Activity i). The earliest start time for an activity is the earliest possible time that the activity can begin, assuming that all its predecessors, started at the earliest possible times. The earliest finsih time for an activity is the sum of the earliest start time and the estimated time to perform the activity. The earliest finish time represents the shortest possible time in which an activity can be finished, assuming that all its predecessors started at their earliest times. The fact that some of the activities in a project can be delayed, without affecting the project completion date, leads to the concept of *float.* Float indicates the flexibility available to the management in scheduling a project. There are various types of floats, *viz.,* free float, interfering float, independent float, etc.

The planner is expected to specify in detail the set of activities which will be undertaken under the project, and to estimate the times of their completion and state their sequencing requirements. If the critical path is longer than desired, the project may be replanned, and longer resources committed to critical activities. Though this technique helps much in managerial decision-making in many respects, it does not consider the resources required at variious stages of the project. However, for planning scheduling and controlling the activities. PERT is an effective technique.

Chapter 19

Computers in Management

During the course of discussion on the role of quantitative techniques in management, it has been felt that computers play a very vital role in managerial analysis. This chapter is, therefore, designed to provide the business manager and students of management with an elementary background of what the computers do in management and in managerial analysis. But before we discuss the role of computer, we shall acquaint the reader with the computer itself.

Computers

There are two major types of electronic computers, *viz.,* digital and analogue computers. The former records, computes and reports in terms of absolute digits, while the latter indicates only approximate figures. The functions that a digital computer performs are:

(i) It can accept information (numbers, letters, or character) and store them internally;

(ii) It can move this information from one place in internal memory to another;

(iii) It can perform arithmetical operations on the numerical data stored in the memory bank;

(iv) It compares two pieces of information in the memory bank and tells us whether they are equal or not (logic operation);

(v) It can write or print out the information that is stored in the memory bank.

The following three characteristics make a digital computer very useful:

(i) Its ability to store large quantities of information and to retrieve information very rapidly;

(ii) Its ability to perform arithmetic and logical operations at tremendous speeds;

(iii) Its capacity to function for various jobs with almost total accuracy;

(iv) Its contribution to the management information systems is not negligible.

The preparation of a set of step-by-step computer instructions is called programming, and the set of instructions is called a programme.

Computers make both managerial contribution and non-managerial contribution. The computer system may, therefore, be classified under two broad categories, *viz.,* technical information systems and business information systems. The technical uses of computers include solution of mathematical problems by numerical analysis, design of transformers, numerical control of machine tools, and real-time process control. Computers are in extensive use in applications (the design of transformers), in applications involving physical systems (simulation of a chemical plant), and real-time control systems (computer-controlled machinery). The tremendous capacity of the computer for calculations and for working out equations and coefficients has almost made it essential for structured technical operations. It has made the technical systems so predictable that no trial-and-error method is necessary regarding any technique. Innovations become easier with the help of computers. However, the distinction between technical (scientific) and business uses of a computer is almost obscure, because both are generally not distinguishable one from the other.

The modern high-speed digital computers play a very conspicuous role in the business information systems — a fact which has been highlighted elsewhere in this chapter. They are specifically used in sales analysis, production scheduling, inventory control, payroll, customer billing, cost accounting, accounts payable, general ledger accounting, etc., where managerial participation is considerable. Computerized business information systems are characterised by centralised processing, a high rate of change, internal programming, a high cost of modern data processing equipment, lack of accessibility of information, and so on. Most of the information in a modern data processing system is on floppy discs, CDs, etc.

Analogue computers have become unpopular these days, except in engineering applications. In such computers, the various quantities in the problem to be solved are represented by corresponding physical quantities. For example, in the slide rule (a simplest type of an analogue computer), each of the numbers in the problem is represented by a length which is proportional to the logarithm of the number. Similarly, a number may be represented by the amount of rotation that a shaft has undergone from an initial position in a mechanical analogue computer, which represents the information in a continuous form.

There are two factors which limit the accuracy of an analogue computer. They are:

(i) Limitations of the accuracy of the measuring mechanisms; and

(ii) The quality of the components which determine the accuracy by which the movements of the machine parts can be controlled.

However, the basic cost of an analogue computer is low compared to that of the digital computers. While operations are parallel in an analogue computer, sequential processing of information is associated with a digital computer. The output is in the form of a graphical trace on a plotting boaad in the analogue computer.

The preference for a computer, however, may be determined mainly in two ways, *viz.,* hardware options and software options. Hardware options take care of the computer as a mechanical device, in which the various aspects, such as cost, internal memory or primary storage, the speed of the computer in handling the data, and accurate arithmetic ability are taken into consideration. The hardware potential of a computer includes random access storage (very often disk files), channels that handle input and output operations (in a seven-channel computer, there is a possibility of seven input and seven output operations simultaneously), and buffers (an external memory unit that receives information at core speeds, and transmits it to an output unit at a relatively slow output speed). Software options relate to the programming features of the unit as well as data transmission facilities. These programming features chiefly consist of a number of instructions, index registers, floating point arithmetic, assemblers and compilers. Data transmission refers mainly to the capacity of the computer for high-speed transmission of the data between distant locations. This is a facility that will allow information to be transferred from a distant point to the computer direct. It includes dial-up services, such as data phone service, teletypewriter exchange service (TWX), wide area telephone service (WATS), and private-line service. Dial-up service and private-line service are generally called telephone and telegraph transmissions. Data transmission includes radio transmission. Modem through internet, E-commerce, internet surfing, website, etc. are recent development programming.

The programming function is, perhaps, the most important and costly element in the computer information system. The programme is a set of instructions step by step, given to the computer to perform various functions. The computer will continue to execute further instructions in sequence until the final instruction *halt* is sensed. It shows that the programme has been executed, enabling the programmer to feed another programme into the computer. The programmer is concerned with the instruction format, memory locations, and commands. An instruction consists of an operation code that instructs the computer to perform some operation (add, substract, move, etc.), and an operand which designates the address of a device to which the operation applies. The memory of a computer consists of a given number of words or characters, each having an address, while *command* is the instruction code for operation. The operation code A may be used for the instruction *add,* the code S for the instruction *substract* and so on. For the command, *erase storage,* operation code E can be used, and operand. A would contain the address of the information to be erased.

Anyone who is familiar with the decimal system of arithmetic can programme a computer. All machine instructions and data are translated by the machine from decimal into binary or binary coded decimals. The output is retranslated to decimal. The term *binary* refers to the system of representation of numbers (binary means two). The numerical system is used to represent quantities by symbols. A digital computer performs additions and substractions in the form of binary numbers (Adding and substtracting binary numbers – 0 + 0 = 0; 0 + 1= 1; 1 + 1 = 0 and 1 is carried forward; 1 – 0 = 1; 1 – 1 = 0; 0 – 1 = 1 and is borrowed from the column to the left. As in decimal arithmetic, binary operations begin at the right and work towards the left).

Examples of Binary Nos.

Adding		*+ Substracting*
001+	011 +	10010 –
001	011	0011
010	110	1111

Octal is also a number system in computer programming. It uses the number 8 instead of the number 10 as a base. A binary coded decimal is a usual system for representing letters as well as numbers. While 6 bits are used to represent letters and decimal numbers in the binary coded decimal,

2 bits are in use in the binary system. The present-day computers are the results of tremendous and revolutionary change. A computer has the capacity to carry out the respective commands.

Huge volumes of data can be processed in a computer with the help of respective commands. Any computer programmer is expected to prepare a block diagram before programming, which is a part of the documentation of the programme. Any symbol can be used for a block diagram — a rectangle, a diamond, circle, a square, etc. It is a graphic representation of how the computer will process the data.

Symbolic programming is another prominent activity in computer programming. Debugging (correcting errors) of a computer programme is an expensive affair. Therefore, in order to mitigate the need for debugging, symbolic programming has been developed by almost all the computer companies. Writing a programme is time-consuming, and there is a considerable likelihood of errors. That is why there is a need for a symbolic programme. The term refers to the method by which names or closely related symbols are used in writing a programme. The data to be processed are given a designation or a name. Operation codes are used in an easily remembered form rather than in the numerical language of the machine. Symbolic programming, moreover, assists in the avoidance of errors, and corrects clerical errors very quickly (transposition makes a machine language programme very difficult to debug).

With the help of symbolic programming, the programme is able to use labels instead of numerical addresses for the location of data in the memory of the computer. The advantages of such a replacement are:

(i) It reduces the possibility of clerical errors;

(ii) The programmer can remember the label better than a numerical address;

(iiii) Extra memory space is not required; and

(iv) Diagnostic routines help to correct the programme.

That is why every machine language instruction has a symbolic instruction. The programmer becomes more productive, and the cost of programming is reduced considerably.

Library routines have been developed by computer companies in order to avoid a repetition of the programme steps. The languages that employ these library routines are commonly known as *higher level languages.* An instruction in this language can lead to more than one machine language instruction.

Libraries of sub-routines include many operations which are common to many types of programmes. These are: input instructions, file maintenance, and error deduction. These sub-routines are in the form of either a *block of instructions* which may be incorporated directly into a programme, or *macro instructions* to use the library routine to specify particular requirements. Making use of *expander language* is identical to a symbolic language programme. A prescribed format is used to write the programme. The computer generates an appropriate machine language programme when the respective command is given. The programme is which such a conversion takes place is called a *compiler* or *assembler.* Such expander language is now very common (IBM 1401) autcoder).

The programmer is in a position these days to write his source programmes either in the English language or in mathematical language. Such computer languages are called *compilers;* that is, a programme that converts any source language programme into a machine language programmer is a compiler. Some are inclined to refer to all higher level languages as compilers, while for others, those computer language that use a natural language are compilers. Compared to *expanders,* compilers do enjoy two advantages. They are easier to learn and use because of the machine, *i.e.,* a programme written for one type of computer can be used on a different computer as well. The most prominent compiler languages are FORTRAN, COBOL.and PL 1. It would, therefore, be appropriate to throw some light on these computer languages.

FORTRAN

FORTRAN represents *formula translation.* A number of large installations can prepare almost all their programmes in FORTRAN. This language was first developed by J.W. Bachus and his associates for use on IBM 704. It is an algebraic language that finds primary use in mathematical and scientific work. The problems that contain large sets of formulae and many variables find that FORTRAN is very useful. Library sub-routines can be easily fitted into its structure, which is a very desirable feature. It enables the programmer to specify a numerical procedure, by using a concise language like that of mathematics; and he automatically obtains a programme to carry out the procedure. Compilers are already available to extend the use of FORTRAN to almost all commercial computers. It is one of the oldest compiler languages, which was introduced in 1957.

COBOL

The capitals stand for Common Business Oriented Language, which was initiated in 1959. The first version of COBOL was produced in 1960, and a sophisicated version in 1961. It has been widely accepted, and almost all business computers have COBOL compilers. Each COBOL programme consists of four parts:

(i) Identification, which provides the programme and programmer identification;

(ii) Specification of the equipment being used, which includes descriptions of the computer to be used, both for compiling the source of programme and running the object programme, memory size, number of tape units, hardware switches and printers;

(iii) Data division, which portrays the files of data to be manipulated and created by the programme, as well as the individual logical records which comprise these files;

(iv) Procedure division, which contains a list of those operations which are required to solve a given problem.

Some of the COBOL programme are very efficient. However, some of them show a comparatively poor performance — a fact which considerably affects its credibility and acceptance.

PL 1

This is an addition to the programming language, and enjoys the best qualities of both FORTRAN and COBOL. It did not become popular in India. As FORTRAN and COBOL programmes are already in extensive use, not much enthusiasm was shown for PL1.

An attempt has been made in this chapter to make modest evaluation of the computer in the context of business management. Neither the technicalities of the computer nor of the programming receives a detailed evaluation in this chapter, though a modest attempt has been made to introduce these aspects to the reader. A computer consists of four functional components, *viz.*, Input, Central Processing Unit (CPU), Storage, and Output. The *input device* is the mechanism for feeding information into the computer. Key board, mouse, MICR, OCR, Scanner, Barcode Reader, etc. are the input devices. The CPU is the control centre of the entire data processing system which can be divided into three sections, *viz.*, the arithmetic and the logical unit, memory unit and the control section. Storage consists of both primary storage and secondary storage. It is not possible to process any information without having had it placed in storage. The *primary storage* is the memory and the *secondary storage* is not directly available to the CPU. Output devices include monitor and printer. The chief contribution of the computer unit to business in its ability to aid in the management information systems (MIS). Some analysis of the role of the computer in management information system would therefore not to out place here. These languages have given way to other languages like SQL Server, Oracle, V.B., C ++, D2K, etc.

Management Information Systems

The success of any managerial activity largely depends on its information system It assists in management control and strategic planning, and in the formulation and implementation of organisational objectives and corporate policies. The computer is one of the most conspicuous aids in an information system and in the processing of the data related to it. It sometimes replaces some staff functions; but its greatest impact is in the logistics area. There are major and minor information systems in an organisation. A major communication system is one that affects the entire structure of an organisation, while the minor system is confined to a single functional area. The logistics information systems and financial information systems are major systems, while marketing information and executive observations come under the head of *minor systems.* But irrespective of the classification of the communication systems, a large quantity of information is expected to be processed, stored, memorised and interpreted in connection with any business activity. For this purpose, computerisation has been a boon, for the computer can be extensively used to improve the effectiveness of information systems.

The computer has the capacity to perform arithmetical and logical operations at tremendous speed. That is why many complicated managerial problems, with a number of interacting variables, can now be solved with the help of a computer. Before its development, much of the information could not be used for management tasks because huge data could not be processed with the required speed and precision. This problem has now been solved by the computer; and accuracy has substantially improved. Repetitive operations become necessary in many decision-making situations. Repetitive operations, especially when a large quantity of data is to be processed. In this connection, it may be pointed out that the logistics systems of a manufacturing company are generally the most adaptable to automation of management information systems.

One of the best examples of a logistics sub-system is production scheduling and control in a manufacturing plant. Many managerial decisions require instantaneous information, which can be supplied only by a computer. Similarly, all the areas of the information systems, say, the financial information system, the personnel information system, etc., can be effective only if they are backed by adequate data, which are now supplied by the computer. If the data processing function is to be reasonably effective in integrating the data requirements of the various systems using the same main reservoir of information, it is necessary for it co-ordinate carefully with the people responsible for systems specification, as Dearden has pointed out. It is, therefore, obvious that a careful integration of the data bank and manpower resources is the need of the hour, which can be safely entrusted to the computer.

Dearden has rightly pointed out: "The most important thing is to have an effective and efficient management information system. Any organisation that can accomplish this goal is satisfactory, regardless of how much it differs from the ideal organisation."

The computer plays a pivotal role in the maitenance of an efficient management information system.

There can be routine data processing systems derived from each of the major information systems. Routine data processing systems may not contribute much to the management's decision-making process; and such data processing may not, therefore, have any ideal specification. Customer billing, payroll, routine accounting data, etc., come under this category. Compared to all the computer applications, routine data processing systems are the easiest to develop; and the output is specified and precise. Because of its convenience, many automated data processing systems are of this kind (example: payrolls). What is done in such cases is to substitute equipment costs for salary costs; and the former is always greater than the latter. However, in such operations as banking and insurance, where the salary costs usually exceed the equipment costs, it is beneficial to automate routine data processing procedures. Payoff is bound to be substantially greater in the automation of the major information systems, especially because major information systems assist in major business decisions. Most major information systems or logistics information systems are complex in nature. Such processes are not amenable to manual methods of data processing. Specifications of such processing are expected to be provided by the functioning executive; full automation may not be possible.

The characteristics of major information systems are:

(i) The system is difficult to develop;

(ii) Administrative problems are important and difficult to solve;

(iii) The payoff is likely to be significant; and

(iv) Operating management is responsible for specifications.

Once the computerisation of the data processing system has been established, it is the duty of the management to evaluate its effectiveness, which is not often an easy task. Because of the absence of a technical background and experience, many a manager cannot evaluate the actual contribution of the computer, and consequently control becomes a problem for them. However, certain factors, such as payoff, computer time utilisation, meeting of time and cost commitments, customer satisfaction or the satisfaction of the operating executives, accuracy, etc. — all these can be taken into account for evaluating the performance of the computer and computer staff. The effectiveness of the computer system depends on the degree of competence of the computer personnel.

As we have already observed, the computer is of great utility in the management information systems, financial information systems, personnel information systems, logistics, and production. Quantitative, mathematical and statistical techniques, which have acquired great prominence these days, utilise the services of the computer in a big way in such areas as managerial analysis, problem-solving, and decision-making.

The financial system of any organisation depends on large amounts of historical recurring data. Automation, therefore, is essential, for it reduces the cost of data processing. However, one cannot expect great improvement in the quality of the information system, because the computer may not solve any of the critical problems that come up under the financial information system. In many financial areas, such as budgetary control, speed is not very crucial, as it is in the logistics system. Computerisation may not, therefore, contribute to efficiency. However, it would be economical to use a computer in budget reporting. In certain cases of reporting, speed has some advantage, though in many areas of the financial information system there may not be any need for a large number of interacting variables, nor for a precise determination of performance levels. As a matter of fact, the effect of computerisation may be marginal in a financial information system.

The personnel information system is also not much different where the effect of automation are concerned. An efficient storing and retrieval of personnel information is very often a problem. Obviously, the adaptability to automation is directly linked with the amount of information that is maintained on each person, the number of persons about whom information is maintained, and the speed with which any information is required. Personnel information is generally subject to change; and in this matter of changes, the computer has limited utility. Expect in the payroll, there is not much scope for mechanisation; and whatever is adaptable to automation, it is only of a routine nature. Personnel information systems are the least adaptable to computerisation The payoff, therefore, is bound to be negligible.

The area which is most adaptable to automation is the logistics information system. Automation results in efficiency, and consequently in economisation of the cost of data handling and greater pay-off (for example, optimum inventories). It has already been pointed out that automation is possible in the financial area only because of the large amount of data available for maintenance. Hence possibly by way of cost reduction, a marginal gain may be achieved. An increase in efficiency would also be marginal. Routine data processing systems tend to be subsystems of larger management information systems, which seldom provide any specific management information. They are usually adaptable to automation, while in terms of cost savings of the handling data, some amount of financial gains may be forthcoming. However, its contribution to managerial problem-solving and decision-making is quite marginal.

In many organisations in India, computerisation has become a fashion. Some are under the false impression that some sort of prestige is associated with mechanisation. In fact, a considerable percentage of computer time and computer manpower at present can be treated as idle resources. All management information cannot be improved by mere computerisation. Nor does all information generated by a computer qualify as management information. The most essential duty on the part of the management, therefore, is to determine the extent to which it would be used, failing which it is bound to be a white elephant. For a researcher, however, the computer is of great utility in the processing of the huge volume of data he has to analyze.

To conclude, computer applications may pay off where the level of activity is high. If the activity is low, do without the computer.

Chapter 20

Conclusion

The practice of management is an economic task, which should be result-oriented. The actual task before an executive has three dimensions. They are:

(i) To make the existing business most effective;

(ii) To identify and exploit the potential; and

(iii) To shape the business to fit in with the business environment.

In this context, a manager is expected to exploit the opportunities, tackle the threats, mitigate the uncertainties, and solve the problems, which require appropriate analysis and investigation of the relevant situation. This is, perhaps, the reason why managers now increasingly rely on managerial analysis and research.

The chapter scheme of this book is designed to explain the relevant areas of managerial research in a simple and lucid manner. The first chapter deals with the introductory areas of research in management; the definition, nature, scope and objectives of managerial research. Various types of research have been briefly dealt with and a detailed discussion of the role of case studies in managerial analysis has been made in Chapter 2. A researcher is expected to complete a line of action systematically if his research is to become meaningful, effective, and result-oriented. All such activities as carried out in connection with managerial research have been discussed under the title, "Process of Research," in Chapter 4.

Every manager is decision-maker, which each of his decisions is bound to be based on appropriate analysis and investigation of the various factors and alternatives open to him. The determinant variables also have to be identified before decisions are arrived at. Research, therefore, plays a very decisive role in the decision-making process. It is, as a matter of fact, closely associated with decision-making which has been highlighted in Chapter 8.

Corporate planning and policy making are closely linked with the top and general management functions, which are aided by research and analysis. But the scope of research never limits itself to general management functions alone. In fact, the functional areas in the operational side of any organisation considerably depend on investigation and analysis for their strategy implementation. This aspect has been examined in the Chapter 9.

The chapter entitled "Scientific Method and Hypothesis" examines the utility of the scientific method in managerial research. It is not only the basic ingredient of fundamental or social research, but fits in with the framework of managerial research. Managerial analysis, therefore, cannot dispense with the scientific method.

Research is a systematic course of investigation. The steps, methods, and techniques are crystallised at the stage of research design. It plans in advance the systematic course of action; and this has been examined in Chapter 3 entitled, "Research Design: Some Issues." Unlike a social research problem, a management research problem tends to be a management problem; and, obviously, a management research is a restatement of the management problem itself.

No research is possible without adequate data, their analysis and interpretation. Data collection, analysis, and interpretation, therefore, form a major part of any research. This is true of managerial research, too. Chapter 5 has, therefore, concentrated on the evaluation of the system of data collection and analysis. As sampling is a universal method of data collection, it has received due attention in this chapter.

As in social research so also in managerial research, the statistical method is extensively employed. Chapter 10, therefore, concentrates on the value and use of this method. Some of the commonly used statistical techniques, also have been dealt with to acquaint the readers with a preliminary understanding of these techniques. This would enable them, especially those who have no background of statistics, to generate an interest and acquire a basic knowledge of the subject.

Recent trends in managerial analysis reveal that there is a growing appreciation among professional researchers of the value of quantitative techniques in managerial research and managerial analysis. Unfortunately, however, a large number of professional executives and management practitioners lack any substantial knowledge of quantitative techniques, while some altogether ignore, the need for quantitative expression. Chapters 10 to 12, therefore, make an introductory approach to these techniques, though care has been taken to avoid entering into the advanced areas of these techniques. Conceptual clarity, however, has been maintained, and almost all the important techniques have been dealt with in the simplest possible language. Mathematical notations and complicated expressions have been totally dispensed with, and the whole area has been uncovered in a layman's language.

During the course of the discussion of the quantitative techniques, it has been observed that the computer, as the chief electronic data processing device, has a great applicability, in these techniques. Moreover, computerisation has now become the order of the day in business administration. Chapter 19, therefore, evaluates the utility of the computer in management.

The process of managerial analysis and its relevant areas have been clearly unveiled for the benefit of readers, be they students or professionals.

Bibliography

1. Croxton, Cowden and Bolch, *Practical Business Statistics,* Prentice Hall, New Delhi, 1974.
2. Hampton, John J., *Financial Decision Making,* Prentice Hall, 1977.
3. Roccaferrera, *Introduction to Linear Programming Progress,* South Western Publishing Co., Ohio, 1967.
4. O'Brien, James J., *Management Information Systems,* V Nostrand Reinhold Company, New York, 1970.
5. Johnson, Rossall J., *Executive Decisions,* South Western P sh- ing Co., Ohio, 1963.
6. Sasieni, Yaspan and Friedman, *Operations Research,* Wiley & Sons, Inc., London, 1959.
7. Odiorne, George S., *Management by Obje s,* Pitman Publishing, New York, 1965.
8. Wagner Harvey M., *Principles of Operation arch,* Prentice Hall of India, New Delhi, 1980.
9. Drucker Peter F., *Managing for R* Allied Publishers, Mumbai, 1964.
10. Schellenberger, Robert E., *Manag alysis,* Richard D. Irwin, Inc., 1960.
11. Goode & Hatt, *Methods of ial Research,* McGraw-Hill, Kogakusha.
12. Charnes, A., Cooper, W lenderson A., *An Introduction to Linear Programming,* ork, John Wiley, 1962.
13. Newmen, William mer, Charles E., and Warren Kirby, *The Process of M ment,* Prentice Hall, Inc., Englewood, 1972.
14. Rummel, Fra and Ballaine, Wesley C., *Research Methodology in B* Harper & Row.
15. Anderso than, Dorston & Poole, Millicent, *Thesis and Assign Writng,* Willey, Eastern, Ltd.

16. Bierman, Bonini and Hausman, *Quantitative Analysis for Business Decisions,* Richard D. Irwin Inc., Homewood, Illinois, 1973.

17. Sasaki, K., *Statistics for Modern Business Decision-Making,* Wadsworth Publishing Co., Belmount, California, 1968.

18. Raiffa H. and Schlaifer R., *Applied Statistical Decision Theory,* Boston, Harvard University, 1961.

19. Strum, J.E., *Introduction to Linear Programming,* San Francisco, Holden Day, Inc. 1972.

20. Shubik. M. (ed.), *Game Theory and Related Approaches to Social Behaviour,* New York, John Wiley & Sons, Inc., 1964.

'1, Naylor, T.H., *Computer Simulation Experiments with Models of Economic Systems,* New York, John Wiley & Sons Inc., 1971.

2.. Dearden, John, *Computers in Business Management,* Dow Jones
in, Inc., 1966.

23. Co G. Vanness, *Principles of Data Processing with*
ters, A Harper International Edition, 1966.

24. Schl
McGra , *Analysis of Decisions Under Uncertainty,* New York,
Book Co., 1969.

25. White, D.
Inc., 1969. *mic Programming,* San Francisco, Holden-Day

26. Samuelson, P.
University Press, *undations of Economic Analysis,* Harvard
ridge, 1967.

27. Spurr, William A.,
Business Decisions, nini, Charles P., *Statistical Analysis for*
1967. ood, Illinois, Richard D. Irwin Inc.,

28. Michael V.P., *Communic*
Himalaya Publishing Hous *nd Research for Management,*

29. Michael V.P., *Perspecti*
Publishing House, 1994. *anagement,* Himalaya

30. Michael V.P., *Organisational Beh*
tiveness, S. Chand, New Delhi, 198 *nd Managerial Effec-*